W9-AFE-811

Environmental Politics in Japan, Germany, and the United States

A decade of climate change negotiations almost ended in failure because of the different policy approaches of the industrialized states. Japan, Germany, and the United States exemplify the deep divisions that exist among states in their approaches to environmental protection. Germany is following what could be called the green social welfare state approach to environmental protection, which is increasingly guided by what is known as the precautionary principle. In contrast, the US is increasingly leaning away from the use of environmental regulations, towards the use of market-based mechanisms to control pollution and cost-benefit analysis to determine when environmental protection should take precedence over economic activities. Internal political divisions mean that Japan sits uneasily between these two approaches. Miranda A. Schreurs uses a variety of case studies to explore why these different policy approaches emerged and what their implications are, examining the differing ideas, actors, and institutions in each state.

MIRANDA A. SCHREURS is Associate Professor in the Department of Government and Politics of the University of Maryland, College Park. She is the editor of *The Internationalization of Environmental Protection* (with Elizabeth Economy, Cambridge, 1997) and *Ecological Security in Northeast Asia* (with Dennis Pirages, 1998).

Environmental Politics in Japan, Germany, and the United States

Miranda A. Schreurs

University of Maryland, College Park

CAMBRIDGE
UNIVERSITY PRESS

F.W. Olin College Library

PUBLISHED BY THE PRESS SYNDICATE OF THE UNIVERSITY OF CAMBRIDGE
The Pitt Building, Trumpington Street, Cambridge CB2 1RP, United Kingdom

CAMBRIDGE UNIVERSITY PRESS
The Edinburgh Building, Cambridge, CB2 2RU, UK
40 West 20th Street, New York, NY 10011-4211, USA
477 Williamstown Road, Port Melbourne, VIC 3207, Australia
Ruiz de Alarcón 13, 28014 Madrid, Spain
Dock House, The Waterfront, Cape Town 8001, South Africa

http://www.cambridge.org

First published 2002

Printed in the United Kingdom at the University Press, Cambridge

Typeface Plantin 10/12 pt   *System* LᴬTEX 2$_\varepsilon$ [TB]

A catalogue record for this book is available from the British Library

Library of Congress cataloguing in publication data

Schreurs, Miranda A. (Miranda Alice), 1963–
Environmental politics in Japan, Germany, and the United States / Miranda A.
   Schreurs.
     p.   cm.
Includes bibliographical references and index.
ISBN 0 521 81912 1 (hardback) – ISBN 0 521 52537 3 (paperback)
1. Environmental policy – Japan – Case studies.   2. Environmental
policy – Germany – Case studies.   3. Environmental policy – United States –
Case studies.   I. Title.
GE190.J3 S37   2002
363.7′056′0952 – dc21   2002067372

ISBN 0 521 81912 1 hardback
ISBN 0 521 52537 3 paperback

Contents

Figures

Tables

Acknowledgments

Many individuals, far more than I could possibly list, deserve thanks for the help they have given me. There are literally hundreds of people living in many different countries who shared their time with me for interviews, to discuss ideas, to share documents, to tour me through energy facilities or polluted areas, to read drafts of this manuscript, or comment on presentations of my research. It is impossible to thank all of these people individually, but I do thank each and everyone. Many are colleagues and good friends.

There are, however, a number of people who I would like to give special thanks to; these are the people who I consider my mentors and without whose encouragement, prodding, advice, letters of recommendation, and constructive criticism this project would never have been realized. First and foremost I wish to thank John C. Campbell, William C. Clark, and Harold (Jake) Jacobson who provided me with tremendous support and encouragement over the many years I worked on this book. I am saddened that Jake did not live to see the book published; he was a true inspiration as a pioneer in the field of environmental politics. I am also immensely grateful to my many mentors and sponsors overseas. These include Ikei Masaru, Tsuneyuki Morita, Akio Igarashi, Martin Jänicke, and Josée van Eijndhoven. Several others also provided substantial support of various kinds. These include Hiroshi Ohta, Yasuko Kameyama (formerly, Kawashima), Thomas Princen, John Kingdon, Susan Pharr, Lutz Mez, Alexander Carius, Helge Joergens, Kirsten Joergensen, and Kirsten Dellar.

The assistance provided by Katsura Fujiike with assembling a bibliography and editing the manuscript was indispensable. Sulan Chen helped put together the tables and graphs in this book. Anna Brettell did the painstaking work of putting together the index. My special appreciation goes to Linda Randall, who is certainly one of the world's speediest and efficient copy-editors, and John Haslam, who is a terrific editor.

My thinking as a comparative environmental politics scholar was strongly affected through my work with the Social Learning Project (led

ix

by William C. Clark, Josée van Eijndhoven, and Jill Jäger). This project involved about forty international and interdisciplinary scholars who spent the first half of the 1990s working together to research global environmental policy making in the areas of acid rain, stratospheric ozone depletion, and global climate change in nine countries, the European Union, and in international organizations from 1957 to 1992. My choice of cases for this book and my understanding of environmental policy making was in no small way influenced by this project. I wish to thank all of the project members, but in particular Nancy M. Dickson, Jeaninne Cavender Bares, Jill Jäger, and Angela Liberatore for helping my understanding of these issues and the art of comparison to mature.

Researching and writing this book would not have been possible without the generous support provided by a number of organizations. Academic research related to this project was conducted based at the following institutions: the Law Department of Keio University, Japan; the Environmental Research Institute of the Free University of Berlin; the National Institute for Environmental Studies, Japan; the University of Utrecht; the Political Science Department at the University of Michigan; the Center for Science and International Affairs, the John F. Kennedy School of Government, Harvard University; and the Department of Government and Politics at the University of Maryland at College Park.

I wish also to acknowledge the generous financial support provided by the Fulbright Foundation for supporting a year of research in Japan (1991) as well as a summer German Studies Program on Energy and the Environment (1998); the SSRC-MacArthur Foundation Program on International Peace and Security Affairs for providing two years of support for training and research in Germany, the Netherlands, and Cambridge, MA (1992–3); the National Science Foundation and the Japan Science and Technology Agency for providing short-term fellowship support (1997); and the Pacific Basin Research Center for providing a year of fellowship support for research while at Harvard University (1993–4).

Finally, I wish to take this opportunity to thank my host family, the Hoshinos, in Japan for providing me with a home away from home, and my parents, Jan and Martha Schreurs for their unwavering support and encouragement.

List of abbreviations

AGBM	Ad Hoc Group to the Berlin Mandate
AIJ	Activities Implemented Jointly
AOSIS	Association of Small Island States
API	American Petroleum Institute
BBU	Bundesverband Bürgerinitiativen Umwelt
BDI	Bund der Deutsche Industrie
BTU	British Thermal Unit
BUND	Bund für Naturschutz Deutschland
CAN	Climate Action Network
CASA	Citizens' Alliance for Saving the Atmosphere and the Earth
CCX	Chicago Climate Exchange
CDU	Christian Democratic Union
CFCs	chlorofluorocarbons
CMA	Chemical Manufacturers' Association
CNIC	Center for Nuclear Information
CO_2	carbon dioxide
COP	Conference of the Parties
CSU	Christian Socialist Union
DM	Deutsche Mark
DNR	Deutscher Naturschutzring
DSP	Democratic Socialist Party
EC	European Community
EDF	Environmental Defense Fund (Environmental Defense)
EMAS	Environmental Management and Audit System
EPA	Environmental Protection Agency
EU	European Union
FCCC	Framework Convention on Climate Change
FDP	Free Democratic Party
FOE	Friends of the Earth
FRG	Federal Republic of Germany
GAO	General Accounting Office

GCC	Global Climate Coalition
GDR	German Democratic Republic
GDP	Gross Domestic Product
GLOBE	Global Legislators Organization for a Balanced Environment
GNP	Gross National Product
HCFCs	hydrochlorofluorocarbons
ICLEI	International Council for Local Environmental Initiatives
INC	Intergovernmental Negotiating Committee
IPCC	Intergovernmental Panel on Climate Change
ISO	International Standards Organization
JANIC	Japanese NGO Center for International Cooperation
JATAN	Japan Tropical Action Network
JFGA	Japan Flon Gas Association
JSP	Japan Socialist Party
JUSCANSZ	Japan, United States, Canada, Switzerland
kg	kilograms
km	kilometer
kWh	kilowatt hours
LDP	Liberal Democratic Party
LRTAP	Long Range Transboundary Air Pollution
MAFF	Ministry of Agriculture, Forests, and Fisheries (Japan)
METI	Ministry of Economy, Trade, and Industry (Japan)
MITI	Ministry of International Trade and Industry (Japan)
MoC	Ministry of Construction (Japan)
MoFA	Ministry of Foreign Affairs (Japan)
MoHW	Ministry of Health and Welfare (Japan)
MoT	Ministry of Transportation (Japan)
Mt C	million tons carbon
MW	Megawatts
NASA	National Aeronautics and Space Administration
NCS	Nature Conservation Society
NEPA	National Environmental Policy Act
NGOs	non-governmental organizations
NIMBY	Not-In-My-Back-Yard
NO_x	nitrogen oxide
NPO	Non-Profit Organization
NRDC	Natural Resources Defense Council
NWF	National Wildlife Federation
ODA	official development assistance

OECD	Organization for Economic Cooperation and Development
OMB	Office of Management and Budget
OPEC	Organization of the Petroleum Exporting Countries
ppm	parts per million
RITE	Research Institute of Innovative Technologies for the Earth
SEA	Single European Act
SO_x	sulfur oxide
SO_2	sulfur dioxide
SPD	Social Democratic Party
SST	supersonic transport
TNC	The Nature Conservancy
UK	United Kingdom
UN	United Nations
UNCED	United Nations Conference on Environment and Development
UNEP	United Nations Environment Programme
US	United States
USD	United States dollars
WCED	World Commission on Environment and Development
WMO	World Meteorological Organization
WRI	World Resources Institute
WWF	World Wildlife Fund; Worldwide Fund for Nature

1   Introduction

As regional leaders and the world's largest economies, the US, Japan, and Germany[1] are particularly important players influencing the global environment and the direction of international environmental protection efforts. Yet, they are pursuing environmental protection with different levels of enthusiasm and with different policy tools. This book asks why differences in approaches to environmental management emerged in Germany, Japan, and the US and finds at least a partial answer in the development of quite different environmental communities and policy-making rules and procedures (both formal and informal) in the three countries.

At the turn of the twenty-first century, these three countries alone accounted for roughly half (49.63 percent) of the global Gross National Product (GNP).[2] As a result, these nations will both directly and indirectly affect the future sustainability of the planet in powerful ways.

Because of their wealth and the relatively large size of their populations, the US, Japan, and Germany are major consumers of natural resources and producers of waste (see Table 1.1). There are 80 cars in the US, 54 in Germany, and 56 in Japan for every 100 inhabitants. The yearly municipal waste produced per person is huge: 720 kg (15,840 pounds) in the US, 460 kg (10,120 pounds) in Germany, and 400 kg (880 pounds) in Japan. Decades of development have taken their toll on wildlife species, especially in Germany where close to 68 percent of all known species of fish and 37 percent of all known species of mammals are threatened with extinction. In the US over 10 percent of mammal species are threatened with extinction and in Japan close to 8 percent. These countries also have an enormous impact on the larger global environment. Combined they take in close to 12 percent of global fish catches (primarily Japan and the US)

---

[1] This book deals primarily with the Federal Republic of Germany (FRG) and Germany post-reunification. The former German Democratic Republic (GDR) is only dealt with in passing. For purposes of simplification, the term Germany is used throughout except when specific reference to the GDR is made.

[2] Total world GNP for 1999 was US $29.2 trillion. The US share of this was 28.57 percent, Japan 13.95 percent, and Germany 7.11 percent. World Development Indicators Database, World Bank 8/2/2000.

Table 1.1 *Japan, Germany, the US: area, population, population density, and economy*

	Germany	Japan	United States
Total area (km^2)	357,000	378,000	9,364,000
Population 1999	82.2 million	126.7 million	271.3 million
Pop. density 1999 (inhabitants/km^2)	230.2	335.4	29.0
1999 Gross Domestic Product (GDP) (billions of $US at 1995 purchasing power parity)	1,842	3,005	8,681

Source: OECD, *Environmental Performance Review: Achievements in OECD Countries* (Paris: OECD, 2001), pp. 72–5.

Table 1.2 *Select environmental quality indicators*

	Germany	Japan	United States
Public waste water treatment (% pop. served)	89	55	71
Major protected areas (% total area)	26.9	6.8	21.2
% forested area	30.1	66.8	32.6
Threatened mammals %	36.7	7.7	10.5
Threatened birds %	29.2	8.3	7.2
Threatened fish (% known species)	68.2	11.1	2.4
Industrial waste kg/1,000 US$ GDP	38	49	—
Municipal waste kg/cap.	460	400	720
1998 per capital distance traveled by vehicle (km/cap.)	7.3	6.1	15.7
1998 road vehicle stock	44,270,000	70,820,000	214,430,000
Vehicles/100 inhabitants	54	56	80
Tropical wood imports (USD/cap.)	2.0	18.4	1.6
Fish catches (% world)	0.3	6.3	5.4

Source: OECD, *Environmental Performance Review: Achievements in OECD Countries* (Paris: OECD, 2001), pp. 72–5.

and are major importers of tropical woods (primarily Japan) (see Table 1.2). The ecological footprint of these societies is large. If inhabitants in developing countries were all to live as well as individuals in these societies do, then it is highly questionable that the planet could survive the stress placed on its resources and the environmental damage it would cause.

At the same time, these countries are environmental leaders on several fronts. Japan, the US, and Germany are among the world's largest funders of overseas environmental protection efforts. They are respectively the first, second, and fourth largest providers of official development

Table 1.3 *Expenditures on environmental protection*

	Germany	Japan	United States
Domestic pollution control abatement (% GDP)	1.5	1.6	1.6
1999 bilateral foreign aid budget; % spent on environment	$5.515 billion; $1.65 billion (30%)	$15.323 billion; $3.83 billion (25%)	$9.145 billion; $0.96 billion (10.5%)

Source: OECD, *Environmental Performance Review: Achievements in OECD Countries* (Paris: OECD, 2001), pp. 72–5; OECD, www.oecd.org/dac/htm/dacstats.htm#Dactables; Japanese Ministry of Foreign Affairs; World Wildlife Fund.

assistance (ODA) in the world (France is the third). Between 10 and 30 percent of this amount is targeted at environmental initiatives (Table 1.3). Japan, Germany, and the US also dominate in the purchase and production of environmental technologies and services. They accounted for 74 percent of an estimated $185 billion world market of environmental technologies and services at the beginning of the 1990s (US, $80 billion; Japan, $30 billion; Germany, $27 billion). They similarly were among the largest markets for environmental equipment and services with the US accounting for 40 percent, Germany 9 percent, and Japan 12 percent of world sales of $200 billion.[3] Because of their extensive environmental regulations, research capacities, and technological know-how, they are often looked to by other states for technical and financial assistance, programatic ideas, and policy examples.

Germany accounts for close to one third of the European Union (EU)'s economy, meaning that it has considerable influence on EU environmental decisions as well as the decisions of possible accession states in central and eastern Europe. Japan too affects environmental conditions more widely, but especially in Asia, where its trade and investment activities are heavily concentrated. The US impact is the most widespread globally because of its unique role as an economic and military super power.

Another way these three states influence the environment that has not been given sufficient attention in the environmental policy-making literature is through the way environmental policies are incorporated into the socio-economic models they present to the world. Many developing

[3] Organization for Economic Cooperation and Development (OECD), "The OECD Environment Industry: Situation, Prospects and Government Policy," Paris: OECD 1992. OCDE/GD (92) 1.

countries model aspects of their own economies on the Japanese, German, and US models. Thus, the extent to which their own socio-economic models are "greened" could influence environmental outcomes elsewhere in the world as well.

A neo-liberal economic paradigm motivates US trade policy and is increasingly starting to influence US environmental policy. Not only must US environmental groups work in a system where they are in competition with other interest groups lobbying politicians and trying to sway public opinion, they also operate in a country where a deregulation fervor has begun to penetrate many different policy areas, including the environment. The shift is not complete nor is it embraced by all, but it is clearly happening.

In contrast, social market economics (some would say social welfare economics) influences unemployment, health, and environmental policy choices in Germany. The precautionary principle has become increasingly institutionalized. Germany has not embraced deregulation in the way the US has. Instead, taxes remain high and government regulations to tame market forces to promote social equality and environmental protection are generally accepted even though the cost of doing this is straining the government's budget and raising some concerns about international competitiveness.

In Japan, too, the state is actively engaged in the market. There has been considerable deregulation in Japan following the US example. Yet, government continues to play (or try to play) an important role in many economic areas negotiating with industry over how to address various policy concerns. This is true in the environmental realm as well. The environment is being linked to the country's concerns with energy security and foreign policy. The biggest struggle for Japan's environmental community is that it has historically been on the outside of the decision-making center. This contrasts with Germany, where there is considerable discussion between non-governmental organizations (NGOs), government, and business about policy decisions. The experiences of severe pollution in Japan in the 1960s, however, limit the ability of industry to be blatantly opposed to environmental regulations as some US industries have done with their strong opposition to the Kyoto Protocol.

Environmental movements

Three main sets of questions are addressed in this book. The first has to do with why environmental movements became institutionalized in such very different ways in Japan, Germany, and the US, and why the movements' goals and strategies have changed over time.[4] The differences among the three countries in how their environmental movements developed are striking. Germany has a Green Party, which, at the time of writing, is in a coalition government. The US has a large community of environmental NGOs that lobby out of Washington, DC. Japan, in contrast, has only a very small and weak community of environmental groups.

As is discussed in much more detail throughout this book, in Japan, environmental citizens' movements were critical to pushing environmental matters on to the governmental agenda in the 1960s and early 1970s. There was only a small handful of officials in the bureaucracy with a knowledge of, or interest in, environmental matters. Over time, however, the influence of environmental citizens' movements waned and environmental policy making became increasingly centered within the bureaucracy.[5] For several decades now, the bureaucracy has been at the center of environmental decision making.[6] Historically, jurisdictional divisions have been sharp among the ministries.

There are some signs of change. Prior to the governmental reform of 2001, which in a process of consolidation reduced the number of Japanese ministries and agencies from twenty-two to thirteen, the Environment Agency, the Ministry of International Trade and Industry (MITI), the Ministry of Finance, the Ministry of Foreign Affairs (MoFA), the Ministry of Agriculture, Forests, and Fisheries (MAFF), the Ministry of Transportation (MoT), and the Ministry of Construction (MoC) were the main ministries and agencies dealing with environmental regulation. For the period covered by this book, these bureaucratic entities were still in place and thus will be referred to throughout most of the text. It is important to note that with Japan's government restructuring, there was only one new ministry created: the Environment Ministry. This is just one indication that the environment is becoming a more important policy area in Japan.

---

[4] For the European and US contexts see Dieter Rucht, "The Impact of National Contexts on Social Movement Structures: A Cross-Movement and Cross-National Comparison," and Hanspeter Kriesi, "The Organizational Structure of New Social Movements in a Political Context," in Doug McAdam, John D. McCarthy, and Mayer N. Zald (eds.), *Comparative Perspectives on Social Movements: Political Opportunities, Mobilizing Structures, and Cultural Frames* (Cambridge: Cambridge University Press, 1986), pp. 152–84 and 185–204.

[5] For this line of argument see Michio Muramatsu and Ellis Krauss, "The Conservative Policy Line and the Development of Patterned Pluralism," in Kozo Yamamura and Yasukichi Yasuba (eds.), *The Political Economy of Japan, Vol. 1: The Domestic Transformation* (Stanford, CA: Stanford University Press, 1987), pp. 516–54; and John C. Campbell, "Bureaucratic Primacy: Japanese Policy Communities in American Perspective," *Governance: An International Journal of Policy and Administration* 2 (1989), 5–22.

[6] See Campbell, "Bureaucratic Primacy."

Japan's politicians have not been known as champions of green issues although this started to change in the 1990s. There are now numerous "green" politicians in the Diet across the many political parties. There is no one political party, however, that is seen as the champion of environmental issues, although the New Kômeitô may be closest in its policy orientation. Instead, politicians with an interest in environmental matters tend to become members of the environmental *zoku* (literally, a family or tribe; the term refers to a community of politicians in the Diet who share an interest in a particular issue area regardless of political party affiliation).[7]

In contrast with the situation in the US and in Germany, there are no well-known environmental think tanks, although new ones like the Institute for Global Environmental Strategies have been set up. There has also been a substantial growth in the number of environmental NGOs although the community remains small. Japanese courts are traditionally weak, but in the early 1970s played a very important role in stimulating legislative action on environmental matters.

Germany has attracted much attention because of its Green Party. The existence of the Green Party means that environmental interests have a direct voice in parliament. It also guarantees that politicians in other parties remain sensitive to environmental concerns. All the political parties in Germany portray themselves as champions of environmental interests, but they do so from different positions with the Christian Democratic Union (CDU) being more conservatively oriented than the Social Democratic Party (SPD). There is even some question as to whether or not Germany's Green Party will survive in parliament as other political parties increasingly take up its issues.

There also are strong local, federal, and international environmental groups, such as Greenpeace, the Bund für Naturschutz Deutschland (BUND), and the Bundesverband Bürgerinitiativen Umwelt (BBU), all of which boast large memberships. Several academic centers and think tanks like the Wuppertal Institute for Climate Research, Öko Institut, and the Max Plank Institutes also play critical roles in influencing environmental debates. The Federal Ministry for Environment, Nature Protection, and Reactor Safety (henceforth, Ministry for Environment) by no means dominates the German bureaucracy, but it is strong compared with its Japanese counterpart, as suggested by the fact that it was elevated to ministerial status already in 1986. The federal Environment Agency (Umwelt Bundesamt), first set up in 1974, was not dissolved when the

---

[7] Takashi Inoguchi and Tomoaki Iwai, *"Zoku giin" no Kenkyû* (Tokyo: Nihon Keizai Shimbunsha, 1987).

new ministry was created. Instead, it continues to play an important role in environmental research and in providing scientific and technical input into legislation. Other important environmental actors within the administration include the Federal Ministry of Consumer Protection, Food, and Agriculture; the Federal Ministry of Economics and Technology (henceforth Ministry of Economics) the Federal Ministry of Finance; the Federal Ministry of Transport, Construction, and Housing (henceforth Ministry of Transport); the Federal Ministry of Education and Research; and the Federal Ministry of the Interior.

In comparison with the situation in Japan, where the central government is quite strong in relation to prefectural and local governments, in Germany, the Länder governments also have much say over the shape of environmental policies. Also, in comparison with the bureaucracy-centered environmental policy community in Japan, in Germany, the environmental policy community is more pluralistic and political parties play a more prominent role in the agenda-setting process. German courts are very strong and have had a strong influence over the direction of German environmental legislation.

In taking Germany as a case, it is essential also to recognize the influence of the EU in environmental policy making. In response to efforts to harmonize environmental laws and standards across the EU, increasingly it is in Brussels where environmental policy making occurs. The 1986 Single European Act (SEA) explicitly included the environment as an area of EU competence and changed the rules for introducing EU laws from an absolute to a qualified majority system, essentially easing the process of introducing EU laws. While states still have the possibility to opt out of environmental directives that conflict with existing more stringent national laws, this requires that a member state be proactive and that it prove that existing legislation is not there as a trade barrier. Within the EU, Germany is typically, although by no means always, among the more proactive states on environmental matters, and often seeks to have its stricter environmental programs and philosophies adopted by the community as a whole. A benefit that can come from being proactive in domestic policy design is that a state can set the base line for international standards that may follow. This may be a reason for Germany's proactive role within the EU.[8]

Early chapters of this book deal almost exclusively with decision-making processes within Germany. As the importance of the European Community (EC) and subsequently the EU expands with time, the book

[8] Adrienne Héritier, Christoph Knill, Susanne Mingers, and Martina Beckka, *Die Veränderung von Staatlichkeit in Europa* (Opladen: Leske and Budrich, 1994).

includes more discussion of the EC and EU, exploring how Germany has worked to influence EC environmental directives and regulations and also has been restricted by the need to negotiate with other EU member states.

The US environmental community is highly pluralistic with many points of entry into the decision-making process. The White House and the executive branch, Congress, the states, large environmental groups, think tanks, and the scientific communities are all actively involved in influencing environmental policy outcome. Neither the Democratic nor the Republican Party portrays itself as the party of environmental interests, but of the two, the Democratic Party is typically more supportive of environmental regulations. Of the three countries, the US environmental policy community is the largest and most pluralistic, but divided government and the power of economic interest groups at times has made it difficult for the environmental policy community to gain political support for its agenda.

Survey results reveal some interesting information regarding the influence of various actors on the climate change debate in the US during the latter part of the Clinton administration. Congress and the White House were considered to be, on average, very influential. The US Environmental Protection Agency (EPA), the EPA administrator, and the EPA offices of Policy, Planning, and Evaluation, Air and Radiation, and Atmospheric Programs were all ranked as very important. The Department of Energy, the State Department, and in particular, the State Department's Office of Global Affairs, also were perceived as being highly influential policy actors. Outside of government, the Intergovernmental Panel on Climate Change (IPCC) was seen as an important player as were the print and electronic media. Also, several environmental organizations and economic interest groups were viewed as being very important. The environmental NGOs to receive the highest rankings were Environmental Defense (EDF), the Natural Resources Defense Council (NRDC), and the World Resources Institute (WRI). The Global Climate Coalition (GCC) was considered a particularly important representative of industrial interests. The survey results suggest the existence of a diverse community attempting to influence the direction of US climate change policy.[9]

---

[9] The survey is part of a larger international survey research project called the Global Environmental Policy Network Survey that was conducted in the US, Japan, Germany, and Korea under the leadership of Yutaka Tsujinaka. Fumiaki Kubo conducted the content analysis of climate change articles appearing in the *Washington Post*, the *New York Times*, *Inside EPA*, *Outlook*, and *Inside Congress* for 1997. Tsujinaka and Kubo then had the entire list of 292 actors identified by this content analysis reviewed by eight individuals identified as experts in the field. This expert review committee scored actors on their influence level. The 180 highest scoring actors were then targeted for interviews; 60 were

What explains these very divergent developments in the environmental movements of these countries? Do the differences have to do with the severity of pollution problems, public perceptions, cultural factors, or institutional differences?

A common assumption in much of the writing in environmental politics and on social movements in general is that the stronger the environmental movement in a country, the stronger environmental regulations are likely to be. Thus, we often hear that the reason that Germany is so environmentally oriented is because of its Green Party and why Japan continues to engage in whaling and tropical deforestation is because of the weakness of its environmental movement. Yet, we know that having a strong environmental community does not always equate to strong environmental programs. Despite Japan's relatively weak environmental movement, Japan has accepted the Kyoto Protocol addressing climate change. In contrast, the relatively strong environmental movement in the US was not able to persuade the George W. Bush administration to support the Kyoto Protocol.

In comparing environmental policy making in Japan, Germany, and the US across several environmental issues, I seek to bring a more nuanced understanding to how environmental communities influence the policy process. I also try to shed light on how changes in the relationships among environmental, business, and governmental actors over time can alter how environmental problems are understood and how policy making is approached.

Environmental policy approaches

The second set of questions addressed in this book asks in what ways differences in the make-up of environmental communities and their relationship to actors in the larger political and economic systems matters for environmental policy change and environmental management styles in Japan, Germany, and the US in relation to both domestic and international environmental problems.[10]

One of the best examples of differences in policy approaches among the three countries can be found in their response to climate change. The rocky international negotiations trying to work out a framework for the

interviewed by Anja Kurki, Tadashi Okimura, and myself. Results of the survey appear in Anja Kurki, Miranda Schreurs, Yutaka Tsujinaka, and Fumiaki Kubo, "Beikoku ni okeru Kikô Hendô Seisaku: Beikoku Oyobi Nikkan no Chikyû Kankyô Seisaku Netto Waaku Chôsa kara no Dôsatsu," *Leviathan* 27 (2000), 49–72.

10 A similar type of question is asked by David Vogel, *National Styles of Regulation: Environmental Policy in Great Britain and the United States* (Ithaca, NY: Cornell University Press, 1986).

Kyoto Protocol, an international agreement requiring the advanced industrialized states to reduce their greenhouse gas emissions, bogged down repeatedly because of policy differences among the industrialized states. Particularly the differences between the US, on the one hand, and the EU, on the other, made formulating an agreement difficult. Germany, both independently and as a member of the EU, has been an active advocate of immediate international action on climate change by the advanced industrialized states. Germany, the largest greenhouse gas emitter within the EU responsible for about one third of EU emissions, pushed hard within the EU and internationally for an international agreement that would require the developed world to take action domestically to reduce their own sources of greenhouse gases and set an ambitious target for its own emissions reductions. Japan similarly went into the negotiations with a domestic reduction target although it expressed concerns about whether in the short term large reduction goals could really be achieved. They were also concerned about the US position. While the US under the William Clinton administration agreed at the negotiations to a substantial emissions reduction target, there was strong opposition in the US Senate to the agreement on the grounds that it was unfair to the US economy.

Differences between the US and the EU/Japan widened with the shift in administration in the US. Shortly after assuming office, in March 2001, the George W. Bush administration announced that it was "unequivocally" opposed to the Kyoto Protocol. Japan, Germany, and the EU reacted with strong words and diplomatic efforts to convince the Bush administration to reconsider. When their efforts failed, the EU and Japan came to an agreement in June 2001 to move forward with the Kyoto Protocol's ratification even without the US.

The differences voiced in the climate change negotiations speak to larger differences that have developed among these countries in terms of the roles they feel that government and markets should play in environmental protection and where responsibility for taking action lies. They further reflect differences in the relationships that have emerged among governments, business, and environmental NGOs in the policy-making process. Finally, we see a different level of interest in working at the multilateral level for environmental protection emerging across the three countries.

The US was among the first countries in the world to introduce pollution control regulations in the 1960s and 1970s. Initially, there was a heavy reliance upon regulatory measures to control pollution. Regulations included emissions standards controlling point sources, ambient standards, and technology standards. Since the early 1980s, however, along with the broader effort to reduce the role of the government in the private sector, there has been a shift in the US away from the heavy use of regulation. Far more than is true in Germany or Japan, proponents of cost-benefit analysis, voluntary action by industries, and market-based mechanisms (e.g. emissions trading, joint implementation, and the clean development mechanism) for environmental protection are gaining ground. Both Japan and Germany have shown some interest in the use of market mechanisms to address environmental problems, but both continue to believe that government through the establishment of regulations must play a stronger role.

In Germany, where there is a social market economy, citizens expect government to play an interventionist role and to redistribute wealth. They also believe that the government must regulate to protect the environment. Of course, this is also true in the US, but there is a difference in emphasis. The German political parties are all far more supportive of regulatory measures to address climate change than appears to be the case in the US. Like in the US, industry is eager to avoid regulation, but it works more closely with government in finding solutions to environmental problems in a form of consultative decision making. German industry has also been the most willing of the three to accept taxes on polluters (also a market mechanism) to reduce pollution levels although not to the same degree as is true in some of Germany's smaller neighbors to the north.

One might argue that, of the three countries, Germany is the one that has gone farthest towards embracing not only environmental protection policies, but policies that seek to shift economic development in directions that are environmentally more sustainable.[11] The Red-Green government that has been in power in Germany since 1998 has experimented with introducing environmental taxes in an effort to shift the German economy in the direction that will reduce the size of the German ecological footprint, making the entire structure of the economy more sustainable. This is not to argue that Germany has really embraced the kinds of deep structural changes to the economy necessary to produce a socio-economic system that could be considered truly sustainable. Still, it has taken some ambitious initial steps in this direction.

In Japan, there is a tradition of close governmental consultation with, and some would argue, administrative guidance of industry (*gyôsei shidô*), but a weaker social market tradition than is found in Germany. Japan's powerful ministries are not eager to give up their regulatory power. They

---

[11] OECD, *Environmental Performance Review: Germany* (Paris: OECD, 2001).

continue to use administrative guidance in their efforts to alter industrial behavior. They have not embraced market-based approaches with the same enthusiasm as has been seen in the US (although this appears to be changing) and do not accept pollution taxes as readily as the Germans. Japan continues to rely heavily on regulations, but of a Japanese form. In Japan regulations are often initially quite vague in terms of specifics; they can be thought of as guidelines established to alter industrial behavior. Voluntary agreements are also commonplace. Once behavioral change has been achieved to at least some degree, then more stringent regulations are adopted. Japan falls in between the US and Germany in its approach to environmental protection. It has traditionally looked to the US for environmental policy ideas. Increasingly, it is looking now towards Germany and is arguing that the US could learn from Japan's successes in energy efficiency improvements.

Nuclear energy provides another interesting and important example of the different orientations that have emerged in the environmental and energy policies of Japan, Germany, and the US. All three countries are dependent on nuclear energy for producing between one fifth to one third of their electricity. Yet, the future of nuclear energy looks quite different in the three states. After the SPD and the Green Party formed a coalition in 1998, Germany announced its plans to phase out nuclear energy. In June 2000, the government and the nuclear industry agreed to phase out all existing plants over their operating life times, with the last plants being decommissioned in 2032.[12]

The US continues with its nuclear energy program although after the Three Mile Island nuclear accident, new construction of plants was brought to a halt. In contrast with Germany, however, in the US, there have been efforts in recent years to relicense existing plants, such as the Calvert Cliffs Nuclear Power Plant in Maryland. After the energy crisis in California in the summer of 2001 caused concerns about energy supply, there were some calls for a new look at nuclear energy. The energy policy plan announced by Vice President Richard Cheney in May 2001 called for increased development of fossil fuel supplies and a renewed look at nuclear energy. While the report engendered considerable critique, it indicates a strong interest in nuclear energy. Several Democratic Senators, including New Mexico Senator Jeffrey Binghaman, Chair of the Senate Energy Committee, have announced their support for nuclear energy development. Whether or not this is realized, especially after the September 11, 2001 terrorist attacks on New York and Washington, DC, remains

---

[12] Annette Piening, "Nuclear Energy in Germany," in Manfred Binder, Martin Jänicke, and Ulrich Petschow (eds.), *Green Industrial Restructuring: International Case Studies and Theoretical Considerations* (Berlin: Springer Verlag, 2001), 403–34.

highly uncertain. Still, there is no call to phase out nuclear energy, as is the case in Germany.

Of the three, Japan has most actively promoted nuclear energy primarily because it is the most energy poor. The Japanese Ministry of International Trade and Industry (MITI), which became the Ministry of Economy, Trade, and Industry (METI) in January 2001, has been promoting the expansion of nuclear energy production to help meet growing energy demands, to reduce dependence on imported energy, and to address climate change. While this policy is being reconsidered by METI as a result of the fatal Tôkaimura uranium reprocessing plant accident of 1999, Japan is far from phasing out nuclear energy as an option. In February 2001, Tokyo Electric Power Company announced that it was canceling all new plant construction because of a smaller growth in energy demand than had been expected. Only plans for the building of four nuclear power plants were to be maintained.[13]

Differences among these countries are also evident in how they addressed acid rain. In the US, acid rain was dealt with through reliance on emissions trading among polluting utilities. Regulatory measures had been demanded by environmental groups for close to a decade beginning in the early 1980s, but due to opposition from utility plants, no policy action was possible. It took the development of a new policy approach based on market mechanisms to get the government to act to address acid rain. The George H. W. Bush administration employed an emissions trading system for sulfur oxides in the 1990 amendments to the US Clean Air Act. In Germany, in contrast, regulation has been the dominant approach used to control acid rain producing particulates. Industrial opposition to regulations melted under strong public opinion and the rise of a Green Party. In Japan, a mix of regulation, tax incentives, and voluntary compliance have dominated in the control of domestic air pollutants. For Japan, acid rain is far more of an international problem stemming from China. Thus, there has also been a strong effort to aid China in dealing with acid rain.

While none of the three countries can boast to the rest of the world that they are models of sustainable development, since the 1990s, Germany has taken the boldest steps of the three in this direction with its eco taxes, the use of legislation to reduce waste at its source, mandatory recycling by manufacturers, its ambitious greenhouse gas emissions reduction target, and its active introduction of renewable energy sources. Germany also played a pivotal role in the EU's decision to ratify the Kyoto Protocol. It is important to note, however, that there are exceptions and Germany is

[13] *Daily Yomiuri*, February 10, 2001, p. 12.

criticized both by its own environmental community and sometimes by external actors for not doing enough. Germany, for example, has on a number of instances been found at fault by the European Community for agricultural and land use policies that are environmentally destructive or threaten migratory birds. Germany also blocked EU efforts to introduce regulations regarding the recycling of automobiles.

Japan has been most successful of the three in the areas of energy efficiency improvements and in some kinds of air pollution control (a noticeable exception is dioxins). It is also making strides in promoting recycling and has become a major international funder of environmental protection initiatives in the developing world, especially in Asia. Japan's international environmental image, however, remains somewhat clouded because of the role it has played in tropical deforestation, ocean fishing, and whaling.

In the US, there is much discussion about the importance of nature conservation and wildlife preservation. The US also has been a leader in the control of toxic chemicals and pioneered many of the air and water pollution regulations now found widely throughout the industrialized countries. Nevertheless, US environmental policy is arguably less influenced by sustainable development concerns than is the case in Germany or Japan.[14] In contrast with Japan and Germany, there has been only very limited interest in the US in promoting public transportation, reducing the level of consumption, or in introducing domestic political measures to reduce energy consumption.

Given that the US heavily influenced the early environmental laws and regulations of both Japan and Germany, why at the turn of the twenty-first century do their approaches to environmental protection vary as much as they do?

International environmental protection and domestic institutional change

Finally, a third question addressed in this book is how changing perceptions of what is meant by environmental protection and participation in international environmental policy-making processes has contributed to changes in the strategies and goals of domestic political actors and even altered policy-making institutions. This question looks at the impact of new more international or global ways of thinking about an issue that in

---

[14] Gary C. Bryner, "The United States – 'Sorry – Not Our Problem,'" in William M. Lafferty and James Meadowcroft (eds.), *Implementing Sustainable Development: Strategies and Initiatives in High Consumption Societies* (Oxford: Oxford University Press, 2000), pp. 273–302.

the past was primarily viewed as a national matter on domestic actors and institutions.

It also examines how actors within a system may look to the outside to try to find support for their ideas and possibilities for strengthening their position within the domestic political context. This is in line with the increasing attention being given in the field of political science to the ways in which international and domestic politics are linked.[15]

The comparison in this book has both a longitudinal and a horizontal component to it. Comparisons across countries are often done focusing on specific periods in time. The problem with this approach is that it treats the social, political, and economic contexts of a nation as being static. There has been much change within Japan, Germany, and the US in the relationships among state, industry, and society in the environmental realm, especially as environmental degradation and resource consumption is increasingly recognized to be a matter of global concern. Changes in actors and institutions are altering how environmental policy is being made and this has important implications for the future direction of environmental protection initiatives in these three countries.

Comparing environmental politics in Japan, Germany, and the US

This book is not the first to focus attention on these three countries' environmental policies. Others have been intrigued by the comparison as well. David Vogel, for example, compared Japanese and German environmental policy in an effort to understand why Japan and Germany switched positions in terms of the intensity of their environmental movements between the 1970s and the 1980s. Vogel argues that, because of shifts in public opinion, the movement was more intense in Japan than Germany in the 1970s and in Germany than Japan in the 1980s.[16] Helmut Weidner has written extensively on both Japanese and German environmental

---

[15] See Robert Putnam, "Diplomacy and Domestic Politics: The Logic of Two-Level Games," *International Organization* 42 (1988) 427–60; Peter Evans, Harold Jacobson, and Robert Putnam (eds.), *Double Edged Diplomacy: International Bargaining and Domestic Politics* (Berkeley: University of California Press, 1993); Thomas Risse-Kappan (ed.), *Bringing Transnational Relations Back In: Non-State Actors, Domestic Structures, and International Institutions* (New York: Cambridge University Press, 1995); Miranda A. Schreurs and Elizabeth Economy (eds.), *The Internationalization of Environmental Protection* (Cambridge: Cambridge University Press, 1997); Robert Keohane and Helen V. Milner, *Internationalization and Domestic Politics* (Cambridge: Cambridge University Press, 1996).

[16] David Vogel, "Environmental Policy in Japan and West Germany," paper prepared for presentation at the annual meeting of the Western Political Science Association, Newport Beach, CA, March 1990.

policy. His work focuses on air pollution policy formation in the 1970s and 1980s and is concerned with differences in the substance and implementation of air pollution laws. He argues that Japan out-performed Germany in air pollution control during this period because the Japanese government established an elaborate air pollution monitoring system that helped to keep citizens informed and provided incentives for industry to invest in pollution control. In Germany, in contrast, he argues there was an "implementation deficit," that is, that policy objectives were not obtained because of difficulties with implementation. He suggests, however, that the election of the Green Party to the German parliament in 1983 led to changes in Germany that pressured the government and industry to take pollution control more seriously.[17] Gesine Foljanty-Jost also has brought attention to the different ecological strategies of Germany and Japan in an edited volume examining the role of the state and industry in environmental protection.[18] Alan Miller and Curtis Moore have compared government and industry initiatives in environmental technology research and development in Japan, Germany, and the US. They argue that the US is falling behind Japan and Germany, which have both used strict environmental regulations to spur technological innovation.[19]

These works focus primarily on the domestic environmental politics of these countries. In contrast, this book examines how environmental policy making has developed over time in Japan, Germany, and the US, as the countries have gone from addressing domestic to regional and global environmental issues. It examines the dynamic relationships that exist in these countries among actors, interests, institutions, and ideas, exploring why the environmental policy approaches of these states diverged in such a way that the three could not come to agreement over how to address climate change, one of the world's most important environmental problems.[20]

---

[17] His many writings on Japanese and German environmental politics include *Air Pollution Control Strategies and Policies in the Federal Republic of Germany: Laws, Regulations, Implementation, and Shortcomings* (Berlin: Edition Sigma Bohn, 1986); *Basiselemente einer erfolgreichen Umweltpolitik: Eine Analyse und Evaluation der Instrumente der japanischen Umweltpolitik* (Berlin: Edition Sigma, 1996); "Globale Umweltherausforderungen," in Hanns W. Maull (ed.), *Japan und Europa: Getrennte Welten?* (Frankfurt: Campus Verlag, 1993), pp. 436–58.

[18] Gesine Foljanty-Jost (ed.), *Ökologische Strategien Deutschland/Japan: Umweltverträgliches Wirtschaften im Vergleich* (Opladen: Leske und Budrich, 1996), and Gesine Foljanty-Jost, "Kankyô Seisaku no Seikô Jôken," *Leviathan* 27 (2000), 35–48.

[19] Alan Miller and Curtis Moore, *Green Gold: Japan, Germany, the United States, and the Race for Environmental Technology* (Boston: Beacon Press, 1994).

[20] See also Miranda A. Schreurs, "Domestic Institutions and International Environmental Agendas in Japan and Germany," in Schreurs and Economy (eds.), *The Internationalization of Environmental Protection*, pp. 134–61.

Environmental policy approaches

Forces of convergence and divergence

While there are powerful domestic political and economic factors that have led Japan, Germany, and the US to develop different approaches to environmental protection, it is important to realize that there are also some powerful forces of convergence. These convergence factors help explain the similarity in the timing of some environmental policy changes and institutional developments in the three countries as well as their cooperation on some international environmental agreements.

Modern telecommunications and active international exchange and cooperation have helped rapidly to spread news about pollution problems, resource concerns, and destruction of natural areas among them. Environmental crises and scientific discoveries have helped to raise public consciousness across their political boundaries. Scientific confirmation in the mid-1980s that there was large-scale depletion of stratospheric ozone, for example, propelled forward the establishment of the Montreal Protocol on Substances that Deplete the Ozone Layer.

Cross-societal learning also influences environmental policy change.[21] Policy makers, industries, and NGOs in these three countries have looked to each other for policy ideas.[22] Both Japan and Germany looked to the US in the 1970s in formulating their own environmental laws. In the 1990s, Japan continued to look towards the US, but also increasingly towards Germany for environmental policy ideas. An example of this were the efforts in 2000 by an umbrella group of activists, researchers, and energy specialists called Green Energy Law Network in Japan who worked together with an alliance of over 240 politicians to try to pass a renewable

---

[21] See Peter Hall, "Policy Paradigms, Social Learning and the State: The Case of Economic Policymaking in Britain," *Comparative Politics* 25 (1993), 275–96; Paul A. Sabatier, "Policy Change Over a Decade or More," in Paul A. Sabatier and H. C. Jenkins-Smith, *Policy Change and Learning: An Advocacy Coalition Approach* (Boulder: Westview Press, 1993), pp. 13–40; William C. Clark, Jill Jäger, Josee van Eijndhoven, and Nancy M. Dickson (eds.), Social Learning Group, *Learning to Manage Global Environmental Risks*, vol. I: *A Comparative History of Social Responses to Climate Change, Ozone Depletion, and Acid Rain*, and vol. II: *A Functional Analysis of Social Responses to Climate Change, Ozone Depletion, and Acid Rain* (Cambridge, MA: MIT Press, 2001); and Martin Jänicke and Helmut Weidner (eds.), *National Environmental Policies: A Comparative Study of Capacity-Building* (Berlin: Springer Verlag, 1997); Ronnie Lipschutz, *Global Civil Society and Global Environmental Governance: The Politics of Nature from Place to Planet* (Albany: SUNY Press, 1996).
[22] Jack L. Walker, "The Diffusion of Innovations among the American States," *American Political Science Review* 63 (1979), 880–99; and Jack L. Walker, "Setting the Agenda in the U.S. Senate: A Theory of Problem Selection," *British Journal of Political Science* 7 (1977), 423–45.

energy promotion law that was modeled on a German law.[23] In the 1980s, Germany was trying to learn from Japanese successes in dealing with sulfur oxide (SO_x) emissions.

The US tends to be somewhat more reluctant than Japan or Germany to "learn" from other countries' examples. Yet, in the US case as well, we see adoption of some ideas coming from Japan and Germany, such as the use of voluntary environmental agreements with industry to address climate change. There have been active efforts among these three countries to share information about mutual policy priorities and environmental concerns.

At times, domestic policy actors also have actively tried to transmit foreign experiences to their own policy leaders in an effort to influence policy change domestically.[24] A good example of this have been the efforts by Japan's NGOs to push for the introduction of legislation allowing contributions to non-profit organizations to be deducted from taxable income as is done in the US. There also have been times that actors in one state or at the international level actively have tried to intervene in another state's domestic policy-making processes. For example, US manufacturers of ozone depleting chlorofluorocarbons (CFCs), working together with environmentalists, pushed US politicians to pressure other countries, including Japan and Germany, to join the US in establishing regulations on CFCs so that there would be a level playing field.[25]

Furthermore, over time, there has been a growth in the number of political actors that operate across these countries.[26] The Climate Action Network, a network of environmental groups working on climate change, helps groups exchange information and coordinate strategies to influence the international climate change negotiations. International NGOs may also establish boycotts of certain products in an effort to influence the policy behavior of multinational corporations or states. Nor are efforts to influence policy at the international level through transnational activism

---

[23] Discussion with Tetsunari Iida, Chairman of Green Energy Network, February 3, 2001.

[24] Hugh Heclo, *Modern Social Politics in Britain and Sweden* (New Haven: Yale University Press, 1974), pp. 10–11.

[25] See Elizabeth DeSombre, *Domestic Sources of International Environmental Policy* (Cambridge: MIT Press, 2000); and Joanne Kauffman, "Domestic and International Linkages in Global Environmental Politics: A Case-Study of the Montreal Protocol," in Schreurs and Economy (eds.), *The Internationalization of Environmental Protection*, pp. 74–96.

[26] See James N. Rosenau, *Turbulence in World Politics* (Princeton: Princeton University Press, 1990); Thomas Princen and Matthias Finger, *Environmental NGOs in World Politics: Linking the Local and the Global* (New York: Routledge, 1994); Lipschutz, *Global Civil Society and Global Environmental Governance*; Paul Wapner, *Environmental Activism and World Civic Politics* (Albany: SUNY Press, 1996); Ken Conca and Ronnie Lipschutz (eds.), *The State and Social Power in Global Environmental Politics* (New York: Columbia University Press, 1993); and Margaret Keck and Kathryn Sikkink, *Activists Beyond Borders* (Ithaca: Cornell University Press, 1998).

limited to the environmental activists. Multinational corporations have pushed for the introduction of similar standards across the industrialized countries to reduce their costs of doing business.[27] There is also a network of parliamentarians known as Global Legislators Organization for a Balanced Environment (GLOBE) International that works internationally to promote environmental awareness among parliamentarians in Japan, the EU, and the US.

Very important to policy developments in Japan, Germany, and the US have been the activities of international scientific and expert communities, or what are often called "epistemic communities," that not only work to improve basic scientific understanding of issues, but also to get national governments to pay attention to their research concerns.[28] International epistemic communities frequently try to influence the policy positions of policy makers on international environmental matters.[29] The IPCC, for example, has played a critical role in winning broad international recognition of the threat posed by a warming of the earth's atmosphere as a result of the burning of fossil fuels, deforestation, and other human activities.[30]

International trading regimes also push states to establish similar environmental standards. Within the EU, this has led to a ceding of sovereignty in many environmental areas to the larger community. Internationally, the World Trade Organization is increasingly pushing states towards common trade policies, some would argue at the cost of environmental protection.

There are certainly many different avenues by which new ideas about policy problems and policy solutions have been introduced into national political debates in Japan, Germany, and the US. The forces pushing states in similar directions in terms of their policy choices are often very strong and appear to be becoming increasingly so. Indeed, there are many similarities in their laws, institutional structures, and environmental policy successes and failures.

Given the many pressures pushing countries of the same economic level in the direction of common environmental policy change, however, it is

[27] See for example, Jonathan A. Fox and L. David Brown (eds.), *The Struggle for Accountability: The World Bank, NGOs, and Grassroots Movements* (Cambridge: MIT Press, 1998).
[28] Lynton K. Caldwell, *Between Two Worlds: Science, the Environmental Movement and Policy Choice* (Cambridge: Cambridge University Press, 1990).
[29] Peter Haas, *Saving the Mediterranean: The Politics of International Environmental Cooperation* (New York: Columbia University Press, 1990); and Peter Haas (ed.), *Knowledge, Power and International Coordination*, special edition *International Organization* 46 (1992).
[30] Peter Haas and David McCabe, "Amplifiers or Dampers: International Institutions in the Management of Global Environmental Risks," in Clark et al. (eds.), *Learning to Manage Global Environmental Risks*, I, pp. 323–48.

quite striking how many important differences still remain among them in their approaches to environmental management. This book examines both instances of convergence and divergence across the three countries but is particularly interested in the reasons for the differences in their environmental policy approaches.

Environmental movements and environmental policy communities

Before continuing a few definitions are in order. This book refers to both environmental movements and environmental policy communities (alternatively, environmental policy networks). The study of environmental movements draws upon theoretical insights from the social movement literature. Sidney Tarrow's much used definition of social movements defines them as "*collective challenges, based on common purposes and social solidarities, in sustained interaction with elites, opponents, and authorities.*"[31] In the environmental realm, the focus of attention is on collectivities of individuals or groups that are organized by common purpose and attempt to alter the policies or programs of industries, governments, or society that are believed to be harming human health or the environment through their actions or non-actions.

Typically, social movement organizations are treated as distinct from interest groups and political parties.[32] Yet, as Dieter Rucht suggests, it is often difficult to distinguish social movement organizations from interest groups, and in the case of the new social movements of Europe, even from political parties. The strategies or action repertoires of groups differ significantly depending on the political context in which they find themselves. Rucht proposes three different models of social movement organizations. Social movements may be primarily organized at the grass roots level, in sub-national or national organizations that resemble traditional interest groups, or in the form of parties.[33] These different forms of organization are found respectively in Japan, the US, and Germany in their environmental movements. In Japan, most environmental groups are still working at the grass roots level although there are some national groups as well. In the US, there are both many grass roots and many national environmental groups. In Germany, there are local and national groups and a Green Party.

---

[31] Sidney Tarrow, *Power in Movement: Social Movements, Collective Action and Mass Politics in the Modern State* (Cambridge: Cambridge University Press, 1994), p. 4.
[32] Tarrow, *Power in Movement*, p. 5.
[33] Rucht, "The Impact of National Contexts on Social Movement Structures," pp. 188–9.

In the first part of this book, I frequently use the term environmental citizens' movements. These are collectivities of individuals working primarily at the grass roots level for a common cause but that are bound together only by that cause. In later parts of the book, I continue to refer to environmental movements but I also frequently refer to environmental NGOs and environmental policy communities or policy networks.[34] Environmental NGOs can be thought of as formal organizations (that may or may not be recognized by the state) with a name and one or more causes they represent. Policy communities and policy networks are terms that are used to refer to the expert actors and organizations, which, united by a common or overlapping set of interests, work to influence the policy agenda. Policy communities are typically more structured than are more fluid policy networks although usage in the literature is often ambiguous. In Europe, the term policy networks may be somewhat more commonly used than in the US or Japan.[35]

Over time, as the environment as an issue area became a larger area of governmental activity and became more accepted in these societies, environmental policy communities or networks began to form. Environmental expertise has become a part of an increasingly broad spectrum of society cutting across environmental organizations, bureaucracies, legislatures, scientific communities, and industry. The environmental issues to gain political attention in recent decades, like biodiversity loss, sustainable development, and climate change, are also far more complex than the pollution problems that were being dealt with in the 1960s and 1970s.

Environmental politics has shifted considerably from the predominantly contentious politics of the 1960s and 1970s to a far more complex process that involves both contentious activities and more cooperative decision making. Environmental decision making today often entails highly scientific and technical policy advising by a wide array of actors. Whereas environmental movements tended to oppose elites in the 1960s and 1970s, by the 1990s, they were often integral members of environmental policy communities that included many of the actors they used openly to oppose. This is especially true in Germany, which has moved increasingly towards more cooperative decision-making structures. Thus,

[34] Anthony Downs, "Up and Down with Ecology: The Issue Attention Cycle," *Public Interest* 28 (1972), 38–50.

[35] See for example, Hugh Heclo, "Issue Networks and the Executive Establishment," in Anthony King (ed.), *The New American Political System* (Washington, DC: American Enterprise Institute, 1978), pp. 87–124; John Kingdon, *Agendas, Alternatives, and Public Policies* (Boston: Little, Brown, and Company, 1984); Stephen Brooks and Alain-G. Gagnon, *The Political Influence of Ideas: Policy Communities and the Social Sciences* (New York: Praeger, 1994); and David Marsh and R. A. W. Rhodes, *Policy Networks in British Government* (Oxford: Oxford University Press, 1992).

even though environmental groups often still openly oppose elites, at other times, they may work together in a cooperative fashion with them. The degree to which such cooperation among environmental movements, business leaders, and government officials can be found, however, differs substantially in Japan, Germany, and the US. Indeed, it is important to recognize that the membership of a policy community usually differs across environmental issues and political systems.[36]

Once an issue does have some political momentum behind it, other actors beyond the experts in the policy community may become interested in events as well. These may be industries that feel they will be adversely affected by regulatory developments, NGOs that come to see new ways to link their organizational goals to the issue at hand, or philanthropists who want to put their stamp on the way an issue is framed.

Institutions as political opportunity structures

How can the differences in the shape, goals, and activities of the environmental policy communities in Japan, Germany, and the US be explained? One hypothesis is that differences in the movements are a reflection of cultural differences among the countries. Certainly, anyone who has lived in all three countries would agree that there are important cultural differences among them. It would be difficult to say that cultural factors – e.g. the Germans' love of forests, the Americans' love of the open wilderness, or the Japanese love of rock gardens – or religious factors – such as the dominant Christian orientation of Germany and the US or the Shintoist, Buddhist, and Confucian traditions of Japan – have played no role in the development of their environmental policy communities, yet if culture were a dominant explanation, we would expect considerable continuity over time in the shape and activities of the movements within each country. This has not been the case. There have been major shifts over time in their environmental movements and in the priorities of those movements. Thus, while I do not completely dismiss cultural arguments, I find them rather limited in their explanatory power.

Another is that the differences have to do with levels of pollution, geographical conditions, and natural resource endowments. There is also a fairly strong argument to be made that one reason Americans appear to be less concerned with the concept of environmental sustainability than Japan or Germany is simply because Americans have a lot more space to

---

[36] John C. Campbell with Mark A. Baskin, Frank R. Baumgartner, and Nina P. Halpern, "Afterward on Policy Communities: A Framework for Comparative Research," *Governance: An International Journal of Policy and Administration*, 2 (1989), 86–94.

live in.[37] The high population density of Japan and Germany must make their inhabitants more conscious of pollution and environmental degradation. Also, Japanese and Germans are more dependent on energy imports than are Americans. Experiences with pollution and resource scarcity (a relative term) have most certainly influenced the timing and nature of environmental movement activities.

Yet, this argument also only takes us so far. It cannot really help explain why at several points in history, the US was the lead state in promoting stringent environmental regulations in a range of policy areas, ranging from national park formation, to the control of air, water, and soil pollutants, to the control of carcinogens. Nor, in the case of Japan, does it help explain why environmental movements are not stronger given the obvious destruction to nature that has occurred as a result of Japan's urban expansion and its many public works projects. Pollution, environmental degradation, and general geographical and population circumstances are important to understanding the growth and decline of environmental movements as well as the nature of campaigns, but other factors matter as well.

A third hypothesis and the one that is explored most fully in this book is that differences in the environmental policy communities' strength and effectiveness have a lot to do with institutional structures and the opportunities and barriers they present to environmental actors. Peter Hall defined institutions as "formal rules, compliance procedures, and standard operating practices that structure the relationship between individuals in various units of the polity and economy."[38] Institutions can be thought of as intervening variables that mediate power relations among actors and establish certain political incentives and constraints. A large literature points to the ways in which institutions can structure the relationships among actors and thus indirectly influence policy outcomes. Institutions are important because they establish the channels through which groups can obtain influence in the policy-making process.[39]

Institutions include both formal and informal rules and procedures. At one level, there are formal political structures that are legally established

[37] Lafferty and Meadowcroft (eds.), *Implementing Sustainable Development*.

[38] Peter Hall, *Governing the Economy: The Politics of State Intervention in Britain and France* (New York: Oxford University Press, 1986), p. 19.

[39] See also John Ikenberry, *Reasons of State: Oil Politics and the Capacities of American Government* (Ithaca: Cornell University Press, 1988); Karol Soltan, Eric M. Uslaner, and Virginia Haufler (eds.), *Institutions and Social Order* (Ann Arbor: Michigan University Press, 1998); Kathleen Thelen and Sven Steinmo, "Historical Institutionalism in Comparative Politics," in Sven Steinmo, Kathleen Thelen, and Frank Longstreth (eds.), *Structuring Politics: Historical Institutionalism in Comparative Politics* (New York: Cambridge University Press, 1992), pp. 1–32.

and relatively enduring (although as the collapse of the German Democratic Republic suggests this is not always the case). This includes constitutionally defined governmental structures that define the relationship between executive, legislative, and judicial branches of government and between national and prefectural or state governments. There are important differences, for example, in the power of US states, Japanese prefectures, and German Länder in their ability to introduce and implement environmental legislation. There are also institutions that legally define the relationship among actors and rules and procedures regarding behavior.[40]

At another level, there are informal rules and practices. They are a part of what helps to shape political culture. One example is the practice of consultative decision making that brings together actors with different interests to find compromise positions on issues as is a common practice in the Netherlands and is increasingly being done in Germany. Another is the administrative guidance that is often used by the Japanese government in its dealings with industry. Rather than applying rigid rules, government and industry in Japan often form flexible pacts of understanding regarding industrial behavior.

Both formal and informal institutional arrangements can create incentives or barriers for different groups trying to influence policy outcome. They can also influence the forms that protest and lobbying activities will take. Institutions include the laws and rules that determine how actors relate to the governmental system. There are rules in most states, for example, determining how groups obtain non-profit status and others determining rights of standing in courts. Differences in institutional arrangements and funding structures mean that there are major differences in the resources that are available to different societal groups and in their access to decision-making centers.

Institutional structures may provide more or less open political opportunity structures for groups trying to get issues on to the political agenda. A nation's political opportunity structure, "comprised of specific configurations of resources, institutional arrangements and historical precedents for social mobilization," helps or hinders social movement formation and institutionalization.[41] The rise of issue-based parties in Germany certainly has been facilitated by the federalist system and an electoral system

---

[40] R. Kent Weaver and Bert A. Rockman (eds.), *Do Institutions Matter? Government Capabilities in the United States and Abroad* (Washington, DC: Brookings Institution, 1993).
[41] Herbert S. Kitschelt, "Political Opportunity Structures and Political Protest: Anti-Nuclear Movements in Four Democracies," *British Journal of Political Science* 16 (1986), 57–85, quotation on 76. See also McAdam, McCarthy, and Zald (eds.), *Comparative Perspectives on Social Movements.*

that includes proportional representation. This contrasts with the US federalist system, which is presidential and employs a first-past-the-post electoral system that tends to maintain a two-party dominant system. Until the early 1990s, the electoral system in Japan was based on a complicated multimember constituency system that employed a single non-transferable vote. This first-past-the-post system pitted candidates from different parties as well as from the same party against each other. The system favored candidates with high levels of recognition and did not do much to foster ideological debate among parties. Into the early 1990s, most new parties formed when a group of candidates bolted from one of the major parties. New parties did not form in response to ideological concerns in society. Although there is now a new electoral system in Japan that employs both proportional representation and a plurality vote system, to date no environmental party has won representation in the Diet. As will be discussed more in later chapters, the electoral system in Germany was certainly quite important in the rise of the Green Party, but the differences in the electoral systems alone cannot explain the differences in the strength of the environmental movements in the three countries.

Very important for groups are the access they have to finances, technical and scientific information, qualified staff, and other benefits such as special mailing privileges that facilitate their efforts to organize and mobilize.[42] Also important are what rights of standing groups have in the judicial system. There are many differences among Japan, Germany, and the US in terms of the resources environmental groups have at their hands and the legal standing they are accorded by government and the courts. In Japan, environmental groups struggle to obtain legal recognition as non-profit organizations and access to government documents and scientific and technical information. In the US, environmental groups and think tanks receive funds from membership dues, financial institutions, and/or government contracts, and can easily obtain non-profit status along with all of its many benefits. In Germany, environmental groups and think tanks may not be rich, but they can obtain substantial funding from the government and some from membership dues. They are rich enough to hire full-time staff and have access to considerably more information than their Japanese counterparts.

The different tactics of these groups to influence policy also reflects the institutional structures in which they must operate. In Japan,

---

[42] John D. McCarthy and Mayer N. Zald, "Resource Mobilization and Social Movements: A Partial Theory," *American Journal of Sociology* 82 (1977), 1212–41; Ronald G. Shaiko, *Voices and Echoes for the Environment: Public Interest Representation in the 1990s and Beyond* (New York: Columbia University Press, 2000); and Kriesi, "The Organizational Structure of New Social Movements in a Political Context."

environmental groups have traditionally been kept out of decision-making processes. They have also suffered from limited funding. As a result, many of their activities remain locally focused and deal with visible forms of pollution or particular societal behavior that contributes to pollution problems (such as the pouring of used cooking oil down kitchen drains or recycling of household waste). Only recently have a small number of national environmental groups become involved in preparation of policy proposals and in advising their government in international negotiations. This shift reflects some important institutional and value changes that are occurring in Japan. In Germany, environmental groups have been able to both campaign throughout the country and bring their concerns directly into the parliament through the Green Party. The biggest problem for the environmental community in Germany today may be its own success. After the Green Party became a coalition member, it had to make many policy compromises, not all of which were well received by its members. The future of the party remains uncertain. In the US, the environmental community is divided in organizational form between local grass roots and national groups, and strategies between more radical "deep ecologists" and more moderate and pragmatically oriented groups. As a whole the US environmental community is strong, sophisticated, and adept at lobbying and campaigning. Yet, they face other groups that can employ the same tactics that they do and often have far more money than they have. Thus, the US environmental community can not always achieve the kinds of victories that are won by the German Greens.

Dynamic interactions: institutions, ideas, actors, and interests

Most environmental policy making is incremental in nature, such as when budgets are slightly modified from one year to the next.[43] Less frequently, larger policy changes occur as was the case in the 1970s when new environmental legislation was adopted to deal with the increasingly severe pollution problems affecting most of the advanced industrialized countries or when an Environment Ministry was created in Germany in 1986 and in Japan in 2001. Even less common are policy shifts that are so large that they result not only in changes to laws but also in major changes to underlying institutions.

This kind of dramatic change to policy institutions and fundamental normative beliefs is in fact being called for by proponents of the

---

[43] Charles Lindblom, "The Science of Muddling Through," *Public Administration Review* 19 (1959), 79–88. See also John C. Campbell, *How Policies Change: The Japanese Government and the Aging Society* (Princeton: Princeton University Press, 1992).

development of more ecologically sustainable socio-economic structures. Development of an environmentally sustainable, yet modern society will require major changes to socio-economic structures and decision-making institutions. It will require a shift to a new socio-economic paradigm that incorporates environmental concerns in a far more integral way than is currently the case in the US, Japan, or Germany. While it can be argued that none of the three countries considered in this study has undergone the kind of sweeping institutional change called for by proponents of ecological modernization, certainly important shifts have occurred in policy direction. There are differences, however, in the extent to which these countries have moved towards making the kinds of major institutional changes that are necessary to become more environmentally sustainable.

There is considerable theoretical work that addresses issues of policy and institutional change. Peter Hall suggests a useful typology of first-, second-, and third-order policy change. He classifies first-order policy change as routine, incremental changes to existing policies or programs. Bureaucratic actors, he suggests, are usually responsible for incremental decisions. Second-order policy change, in contrast, does not follow some kind of routine. Rather it occurs as a result of social learning about the inadequacies of past policies – typically on the part of bureaucrats, rather than politicians and without much pressure or participation from outside actors. There are also less common third-order policy changes. Third-order policy change not only substantially alters policies but also the hierarchy of goals and set of instruments used to guide policy. Hall gives as example the changes associated with the movement from a Keynesian mode of policy making to one based on monetarist economic theory. He suggests that politicians typically are behind third-order policy changes.[44]

Stephen Krasner has suggested that major policy change of a third-order nature can occur in times of crisis when institutions that have been relatively stable for a long period of time are suddenly forced to change and there is a "punctuation" of the system because of extreme circumstances and the involvement of new policy actors in the decision-making process.[45]

Others have similarly focused attention to the causes of major policy and institutional change, but they take a more incrementalist approach pointing to the importance of ideas as a force in policy change. While many ideas simply deal with our basic understanding of observable events and causal relationships (such as the effect of a chemical on the environment), others go deeper and may touch our fundamental belief structures.

[44] Hall, "Policy Paradigms."
[45] Stephen Krasner, "Approaches to the State: Alternative Conceptions and Historical Dynamics," *Comparative Politics* 16 (1984), 223–46.

Widely accepted and powerful ideas are at the basis of our socio-economic and political institutions.[46] They help us structure how we view the world and guide our behavior. Some social scientists have likened these powerful ideas to the kinds of "paradigms" that shape scientific traditions.[47]

Frank Baumgartner and Brian Jones argue that major change to policies and institutions (of a second- or third-order nature) may occur not only as a result of crisis, but also because of a more gradual change in ideas that over time can come to challenge underlying belief structures. They take the case of nuclear energy in the US as an example. They show how in the US, popular attitudes towards nuclear energy went from being highly positive in the 1950s and 1960s when nuclear energy was widely viewed as a solution to energy problems, to increasingly negative in the 1970s as the public began to perceive problems with nuclear safety and radioactive waste disposal. This kind of gradual, but major shift in how an issue is viewed does not happen very often, they argue, but when it does, one set of propositions can displace another that for a substantial time provided individuals with a guiding framework for formulating policy. Furthermore, they show that when a shift of this nature occurs, it is usually accompanied by changes in the power relationships among relevant actors and the opening up of new channels (venues) for influencing decision makers.[48]

What Baumgartner and Jones do not do is consider how similar shifts in knowledge and understanding may lead to different kinds of institutional and policy change in different national settings. That is, in essence, what this book tries to do. It shows that there have been both gradual, and at times more shocking environmental challenges to the economic growth and development paradigm that has been at the foundation of most socio-economic decision making in Japan, Germany, and the US. New knowledge and perceptions have resulted in the development of environmental laws and organizations. The changes have not been so dramatic as to put any of the three societies considered in this study on a new trajectory, yet the changes are also not insubstantial. They are, however, quite different across Japan, Germany, and the US in terms of their depth and direction.

This book argues that, in order to understand the differences that have emerged in Japanese, German, and US approaches to environmental

[46] Judith Goldstein and Robert O. Keohane, "Ideas and Foreign Policy: An Analytic Framework," in Judith Goldstein and Robert O. Keohane (eds.), *Ideas and Foreign Policy: Beliefs, Institutions, and Political Change* (Ithaca: Cornell University Press), pp. 3–30.
[47] Thomas S. Kuhn, *The Structure of Scientific Revolutions* (Chicago: University of Chicago Press, 1962).
[48] Frank R. Baumgartner and Brian D. Jones, *Agendas and Instability in American Politics* (Chicago: University of Chicago Press, 1993).

protection, it is necessary to understand the dynamic and unique relationships that exist in each country among institutions, actors, and their
interests and ideas. The different relations among environmental groups,
businesses, and government that have emerged over time in these three
states have influenced the goals and strategies of actors and the environmental paradigms that are taking root.

Research design and methodology

The book follows a comparative case study methodology. Field work
in Japan and Germany included hundreds of formal and less formal
interviews and discussions with politicians, bureaucrats, environmental
activists, reporters, and academics in these countries as well as internationally. Many of these discussions were confidential and off the record. I
conducted field work in Japan based at Keio University during the calen-
dar year of 1991. I returned to Japan for follow-up interviews and related
conferences every year for the remainder of the decade, sometimes two
or three times a year, except in 1995. I spent several summers in Japan
as well as spending a month at the National Institute for Environmental
Studies in January 1997. My research in Germany covers a somewhat
shorter period than my time in Japan. I conducted eight months of research at the Free University of Berlin in 1993. I returned to Germany for
research and conferences every year from 1996 on through and including
2000. The material on the US in this book is based on a combination of
secondary literature and interviews and many informal discussions with
environmental groups, bureaucrats, academics, and some Congressional
staff regarding US environmental policy making.

In addition to in-country research, in the latter half of the 1990s, I organized several environmental conferences focusing on Japanese, German
and US environmental and energy policies bringing together academics,
bureaucrats, and NGO representatives from these countries. I have also
been invited to participate in numerous environmental conferences in all
of these countries and to consult governments. I also spent many hours
reading Japanese, German, and some US newspaper clippings, movement letters, government documents, and other archival materials. Many
of these materials could only be obtained through such field work. This
is especially true for Japan where there was almost no published material
available in Japanese or English on global environmental policy making
when I first began this work. Interviews and collection of unpublished
"gray" material were critical to building the case studies. This material
could often only be obtained in interviews with sympathetic bureaucrats,
politicians, and movement activists.

The environmental cases examined in greatest detail in this book focus on air and atmospheric pollution issues. The cases receiving the most attention are traditional air pollution, acid rain, stratospheric ozone depletion, and global climate change. There is also some discussion of nuclear energy in the final chapters of the book. All the cases examined have some relationship to atmospheric pollution; this makes comparison across the issues easier. Rather different communities of actors are involved with wildlife issues, for example, than are involved with atmospheric pollution matters. Thus, comparison would have been more difficult across very different kinds of problems. Case selection was also heavily influenced by my participation in a major international research effort that focused attention on acid rain, stratospheric ozone depletion, and global climate change.[49] There were also practical issues involved, such as the need to become sufficiently versed in the science behind these issues to be able to ask reasonably informed questions in interviews being conducted in multiple languages and to be able to read documents. Thus, my research does not include many other environmental issues that could also be interesting cases for comparison. The level of attention given to each country varies somewhat depending on the point being made in the chapter.

The outline of this book

The next chapter describes the emergence of environmental movements and the creation of new administrative institutions and routines for dealing with environmental problems in Japan, Germany, and the US. Specific attention is given to the formation of air pollution control programs in each country. Chapter 3 deals with the divergent fate of environmental citizens' movements in Japan, Germany, and the US during the 1970s. Chapters 4, 5, 6, and 7 examine how the institutionalization of different kinds of environmental policy communities in Japan, Germany, and the US – a bureaucracy-centered community in Japan; a more pluralistic movement centered around the parliament and the Green Party in Germany; and the highly pluralistic US environmental policy community that includes large environmental NGOs – influenced the nature of their responses to the emergence of new kinds of regional and global environmental problems in the 1980s and early 1990s. In particular, Chapter 4 deals with acid rain and the divergent environmental policy approaches that became increasingly evident at this time in the three countries. Chapter 5 deals with the successful completion of the Montreal Protocol. Chapters 6 and 7 deal with the highly contentious debates regarding the

---

[49] Clark et al. (eds.), *Learning to Manage Global Environmental Risks*, vols. I and II.

future of the Kyoto Protocol. Chapter 8 then compares how the Japanese, German, and US environmental communities have responded to their changing circumstances. Chapter 9 concludes the volume with comparisons among the three countries and discusses some general patterns that can be drawn from this study for use in future comparative research of this kind.

2 The birth of environmental movements and programs

This chapter provides a historical overview of the emergence of environmental programs in Japan, Germany, and the US. The beginnings of the
modern environmental movements can be associated with the establishment of environmental administrations and the introduction of national
pollution control legislation in the 1960s and 1970s. Until the 1960s,
pollution control was perceived primarily as a local matter. Yet, the authority and capacity of local governments to act on their own to deal with
pollution or to prevent environmental degradation was not well established. Development tended to take precedence over environmental protection at all levels of government. This slowly began to change as new
environmental ideas challenged the status quo.

The rise of the modern environmental movement: the influence of the US

In the US, one of the most profound changes in modern times was
the transformation of societal attitudes regarding pollution and environmental preservation that began in the 1960s. There were many voices
that came together to alter the country's understanding of the relationship between humans and the natural world. Rachel Carson warned of
the damage that agricultural chemicals were having on wildlife.[1] Barry
Commoner played an instrumental role in altering views regarding above
ground testing of nuclear devices and the threat that some technologies
posed to the earth's biological systems.[2] Paul Ehrlich drew attention to
the pressures of a growing population in his 1968 best seller, *The Population Bomb*.[3] The Club of Rome, a group of businessmen and scientists,
issued an influential report in 1972 warning that the world was running
out of natural resources.[4] Conservation groups challenged development

[1] Rachel Carson, *Silent Spring* (New York: Fawcett Crest, 1964).
[2] Barry Commoner, *The Closing Circle* (New York: Alfred A. Knopf, 1971).
[3] Paul R. Ehrlich, *The Population Bomb* (New York: Ballantine Books, 1968).
[4] Donnella H. Meadows, Dennis L. Meadows, Jorgen Randers, and William W. Behrens,
III, *The Limits to Growth* (New York: Universe Books, 1972).

projects that threatened the country's national parks. Journalists began reporting more and more on environmental matters.

This new environmental awareness led to the birth of many of the environmental groups that are today recognized as among the most influential in the country, including the NRDC (formed in 1970), EDF (1967), Friends of the Earth (FoE, 1969), and Greenpeace (1971). Several of the conservation groups of an earlier decade, such as the Sierra Club, also revamped and broadened the scope of their campaigns. The new groups helped to redefine thinking about environmental problems and to pressure the government and industry to alter their policies. They were varied in style and purpose, but came to play a crucial role in environmental policy making from this time forward.[5]

In the prewar and immediate postwar years, with the exception of the national park movement, environmental matters were largely treated as local affairs in the US. At the time a 1955 air pollution act was being debated in Congress, for example, an internal Bureau of the Budget memorandum stated that "unlike water pollution, air pollution . . . is essentially a local problem," implying that national measures to address air quality were unnecessary.[6] Slowly over the course of the 1950s and 1960s, these attitudes changed and the government adopted measures to push the states to do more to control pollution. It was not until the end of the 1960s, however, when these efforts proved insufficient, that the federal government stepped in and created a role for itself in environmental management. The development of national air pollution standards provides an example of the changes that occurred in US environmental practices. In Los Angeles, where air pollution had become quite severe, scientists began to study the effects of pollution on human health in the 1940s. In 1948, dozens of people died in Donora, Pennsylvania, as a result of smog. A few years later, in December 1952, there was a "Killer Smog" in London that killed several thousands of people, causing great concern not only in the UK, but in other industrialized countries as well.

The health problems that appeared to be associated with pollution triggered some limited Congressional action. In July 1955, Congress passed its first air pollution act, authorizing $5 million annually for five years for research and assistance to states in carrying out air pollution research and control. The act was extended for an additional four years in 1959. It was not until the early 1960s, several years after Great Britain enacted a Clean Air Act in 1956, however, that a consensus began to emerge in the US behind federal air pollution control legislation.

---

[5] Shaiko, *Voices and Echoes for the Environment.*
[6] Quoted in J. Clarence Davies III and Barbara S. Davies, *The Politics of Pollution* (Indianapolis: Pegasus, 1977), p. 45.

In 1962, Oregon became the first state in the country to establish a comprehensive air pollution program. The following year, in 1963, the Federal Clean Air Act was formulated. It was a modest initiative that empowered the Public Health Service of the Department of Health, Education, and Welfare to engage in more extensive research, to provide financial stimulation to states and local air pollution control agencies in the form of project grants, and to take action to abate interstate air pollution. Congress introduced a legal process by which municipalities and states could regulate air pollution. With the passage of this act, attention shifted to automobile exhausts and in 1966, the first federal regulations of carbon monoxide and hydrocarbon emissions from new motor vehicles were established.[7] The federal government was becoming involved in regulating air pollution, but still primarily through assistance to the states. Congress continued to resist giving any real regulatory power to federal officials.

At the end of 1966, a four-day inversion in New York City killed an estimated eighty people. Concern mounted and calls for policy change emanated from more and more places. State control of pollution simply was not working. The next step in an incremental process of expansion of federal involvement in air quality control came with the passage of the Air Quality Act of 1967. Through this act, the federal government planned for the establishment of metropolitan air quality regions and states were authorized to establish air quality standards. If states failed to act, then the Department of Health, Education, and Welfare was authorized to enforce federal standards. Implementation of the measures, however, was limited.

Pressures mounted for more expansive and effective governmental involvement in pollution control and environmental protection. Arguments that pollution control was too costly, that it would impede economic development, that it was a local matter, and that scientific evidence was insufficient to warrant action were no longer effective. The environment entered national politics when Senator Edward Muskie, a strong environmental advocate, considered running for president. Almost overnight, the environment became one of the most salient political issues of the campaign and Richard Nixon and his administration responded with a set of remarkably strong environmental reforms.[8]

In 1969, Congress passed the National Environmental Policy Act (NEPA). The NEPA required detailed environmental impact statements

---

[7] Gary C. Bryner, *Blue Skies, Green Politics* (Washington, DC: Congressional Quarterly Press, 1995), p. 98.

[8] J. Brooks Flippen, *Nixon and the Environment* (Albuquerque: University of New Mexico Press, 2000).

on all major projects receiving federal assistance. It also established the Council on Environmental Quality to advise the president and Congress on environmental matters. The following year in a race between the administration and Congress to gain the lead in this now politically important issue area, major amendments were made to the Clean Air Act of 1967. The 1970 amendments contained far-reaching changes in existing approaches to air pollution control. It established national air quality and emissions standards for stationary sources and required that state implementation plans be designed to meet national air quality standards by 1975. Under the influence of Senator Muskie, a provision was also added requiring automobile emissions of carbon monoxide and hydrocarbons to be reduced by 90 percent of 1970 levels by 1975 and nitrogen oxide emissions by 90 percent of 1971 levels by 1976. The bill was signed into law on December 31, 1970. President Nixon also made provisions for the establishment of an EPA.

This was a period of sweeping policy change. New norms about the importance of environment protection became institutionalized and a pluralistic and diverse environmental policy community arose. Developments in the US were paralleled in other countries and internationally. In 1968 Sweden called for the world's first global Conference on the Human Environment.[9] Preparatory committee meetings for the United Nations (UN) conference were held in 1970 and 1971 and the meeting was held the following year. A large number of associated meetings and conferences also were convened which aided nations in gathering information, disseminating ideas, and coming to broad agreements about policy problems and solutions. Both Japan and Germany reacted to the environmental developments in the US and internationally, but they reacted in different ways, for somewhat different reasons, and with rather different results.

Economic miracles and pollution nightmares

Japan

The Liberal Democratic Party (LDP), a conservative, pro-growth party, has been in control for most of Japan's history as a modern democracy. In the immediate postwar years, there was a rapid shift away from agriculture to industry. A major push was made to develop steel and petrochemical industries, both of which are heavily polluting. So rapid was economic

---

[9] Lynton K. Caldwell, *International Environmental Policy: Emergence and Dimension*, second edition (Durham: Duke University Press, 1990); Stephen Hopgood, *American Foreign Policy and the Power of the State* (Oxford: Oxford University Press, 1998).

growth in Japan that by the late 1960s, Japan was one of the most heavily industrialized countries in the world.

Industrialization brought wealth, but also major problems. Japan's population is heavily concentrated in coastal regions because of the archipelago's mountainous terrain. Because of shortages of land suitable for agricultural, residential, and industrial needs, highly polluting industries were often located in or near densely populated residential areas. Little was more important to a nation defeated in war than to prove itself in peace through concentrating on economic development. In this rush to catch up, there was little room to pay attention to pollution problems or the environmental destruction that rapid urbanization, industrialization, and infrastructure development caused.

A handful of conservation organizations did emerge soon after the war. As an example, in 1949, volunteers formed the Oze Marsh Conservation Union to protest the building of a hydroelectric dam that would destroy marshland where birds nested and fed. They became the basis for the foundation of the Japan branch of the Nature Conservation Society (NCS) in 1951. The conservation movements achieved important successes, including the setting aside of tracts of land for protection from development, but they were limited in their goals. They were small in number and were primarily interested in protecting natural areas for recreational purposes and natural resources for economic reasons.

In the 1950s, the first cases of mercury poisoning were identified. Minamata and Niigata became the sites of environmental battles over mercury poisoning that were to have profound effects on Japanese politics. In Toyama prefecture, another debilitating pollution-related disease that eats away at the nervous system and is associated with cadmium waste was discovered. The name given to the disease, *itai-itai byô*, or literally "it hurts, it hurts sickness," speaks to the agony of the victims. Chronic asthma became a problem in many industrial and urban areas where photochemical smog levels were extremely high. So bad was the air that vendors sold oxygen on Tokyo's streets, and children wore masks on their way to school in a futile attempt to protect their young lungs. Japan may have been the world's most polluted country at this time, experiencing pollution problems not unlike many of the heavily polluted areas of India, China, and Southeast Asia today.

Germany

Like in Japan, in the immediate postwar years, German energies were largely focused on economic rebuilding. In the Federal Republic of Germany in 1949 a coalition between the CDU, their Bavarian sister party, the Christian Socialist Union (CSU), the small Free Democratic Party (FDP), and the short-lived German Party was formed after the first election for the Bundestag. The CDU dominated the coalition. Konrad Adenauer of the CDU became chancellor, a post that he maintained for the next fourteen years. Adenauer's economics minister, Ludwig Erhard, launched Germany on a program of *soziale Marktwirtschaft* or social market economics.

Growth rates under policies that promoted free enterprise with indirect government guidance of the economy were impressive. From 1952 to 1958, Germany's GNP grew by 7.6 percent per annum in real terms, and by the end of the decade, Germany ranked second only to the US in world trade. During the 1960s, Germany achieved an average annual GNP growth rate of 4.0 percent in real terms. Postwar recovery was so rapid and extensive that people started to talk of the West German *Wirtschaftswunder*, the economic miracle.[10] Like in Japan, rapid economic growth, however, also led to problems. Air, water, and noise pollution became increasingly bad in industrial regions. Infrastructure development threatened the scenic beauty of the countryside and the quality of life.

Several new nature conservation groups emerged shortly after World War II. In 1947, the Schutzgemeinschaft Deutscher Walt (Association for the Protection of German Forests) was established in reaction to the deforestation that was occurring throughout the country. Three years later, the Deutscher Naturschutzring (DNR) was formed. There were fifteen founding members. The World Wildlife Fund (WWF) set up its German branch office in 1961. These nature conservation groups, however, chose to remain relatively apolitical as a result of their prewar experiences. They did not play a major role in pushing pollution control on to the German policy agenda.[11]

The rise of the modern environmental movement and environmental policy change

Japan

As pollution problems grew increasingly severe throughout Japan, small, locally focused citizens' movements began to protest pollution from industry. Many of the citizens' movements formed because of pollution-related health problems. Initially these movements faced many hurdles.

[10] Karl Hardach, *The Political Economy of Germany in the Twentieth Century* (Berkeley: University of California Press, 1980).
[11] Der Rat von Sachverständigen für Umweltfragen, *Umweltgutachten* (Stuttgart: Verlag Metzler-Poeschel, 1996), p. 225.

They were viewed as left-wing radicals and as enemies of modernization. They were ostracized, lied to, and hampered in their efforts to restrict industrial activities. They also faced resource problems, both financial and knowledge-based. Many pollution victims, for example, did not understand that they were suffering from pollution-related problems, and it often took years before they decided to organize to speak in a collective voice. Even when causal connections between emissions from factories and health problems were theorized by university professors and medical doctors and victims started to come together in groups, they had problems in getting polluting industries and local governments to listen to their complaints. Industries were quick to deny responsibility even when evidence strongly suggested that their industrial effluents or emissions were to blame. Local governments claimed that it was not within their authority to act.[12]

There were only a handful of advocates of pollution control within the bureaucracy. An early example was in 1953 when the Ministry of Health and Welfare (MoHW) conducted a national survey of pollution that found that many Japanese were suffering from air, water, and noise pollution. On the basis of this survey and similar debates that were going on in the US, the UK, and Germany, the MoHW formulated a bill to prevent contamination of the "living environment." Other ministries, industry, and the LDP, however, opposed the bill.[13]

To the citizens' movements, the battles that they had to fight with powerful industries and the political and bureaucratic establishment must have seemed overwhelming. Still, their efforts were spurred on by occasional victories. One group, for example, received considerable press coverage and succeeded in preventing plans to build a new industrial complex in Mishima-Numazu in Shizuoka prefecture on environmental grounds in 1963. This was a major victory for anti-pollution activists and sent a strong warning signal to developers and the economic ministries.[14] In most cases, however, the citizens' movements achieved only partial victories in the form of limited compensation or minor modifications to construction plans with their petitions and sit-ins.

The four big pollution cases
It is critical to appreciate the role played by four major pollution cases that were brought to trial. Two cases were brought to court by victims

---

[12] See Jeffrey Broadbent, *Environmental Politics in Japan: Networks of Power and Protest* (Cambridge: Cambridge University Press, 1998); Margaret A. McKean, *Environmental Protest and Citizen Politics in Japan* (Berkeley: University of California Press, 1981); Jun Ui, *Kôgai Genron*, vols. I–III (Tokyo: Aki Shobo, 1990).
[13] Interview with Michio Hashimoto, 1991.
[14] See Michio Hashimoto, "History of Air Pollution Control in Japan," in Hajime Nishimura (ed.), *How to Conquer Air Pollution* (Amsterdam: Elsevier, 1989), p. 11.

of mercury poisoning in Kumamoto and Niigata prefectures. Another case involved the victims of *itai-itai* disease in Toyama prefecture. The fourth involved victims of asthma in Yokkaichi, an industrial city in Mie prefecture. The decision by victims to challenge government and industry in the courts was a major break with tradition in a political culture that shuns litigation. That citizens' movements turned to the courts shows just how unresponsive government and industry had been to years of efforts on the part of victims' groups to get the responsible industries to stop their polluting activities and the government to act to protect the public. Others have examined the four big pollution cases in much detail.[15] Here, for purposes of comparison with the German case, and in order to appreciate more fully how early air pollution laws were established in Japan, only one of these cases – the Yokkaichi asthma case – is briefly examined. The case illustrates just how closed the Japanese political system was to societal interests and concerns.

Yokkaichi asthma and the efforts of a citizens' movement   In many ways, the city of Yokkaichi symbolized the Japanese economic miracle. In 1955, the Japanese government designated Yokkaichi as a site for the development of a *kombinato*, a huge industrial complex of oil refineries and petrochemical and power plants. The Yokkaichi *kombinato* was opened in 1959; its lights provided Japan with a "million dollar night view."[16] It was the pride of the area. Soon after the *kombinato* began operations, however, there was a sharp increase in chronic respiratory problems among residents of the surrounding area and fishermen found that their catches could not be sold on the market because the fish smelled so foul.

Fishermen and local residents initially went to local and prefectural officials and then factory officials to request that something be done about the heavy fumes and water pollution, but their requests were ignored. As more and more citizens complained, the mayor of Yokkaichi established a City Pollution Countermeasures Council in 1960 to conduct a study. The council's report concluded that pollution was a serious problem in the region. The report, however, was not released to the general public. Instead, another survey was commissioned.

When months passed and the local government continued to say and do nothing, citizens began to lose faith. A local federation of village councils decided to conduct its own study. They found that close to half of all

---

[15] Julian Gresser, Kôichirô Fujikura, and Akio Morishima, *Environmental Law in Japan* (Cambridge: MIT Press, 1981); Norie Huddle and Michael Reich with Nahum Stiskin, *Island of Dreams: Environmental Crisis in Japan* (New York: Autumn Press, 1975); Frank Upham, *Law and Social Change in Postwar Japan* (Cambridge: Harvard University Press, 1987), pp. 28–77; McKean, *Environomental Protest and Citizen Politics*; Ui, *Kôgai Genron*.
[16] Huddle and Reich, *Island of Dreams*, p. 59.

young children were suffering from respiratory abnormalities. With their survey in hand, the citizens again approached the city demanding coverage of medical fees for those suffering from asthma. Eventually, their petitions convinced the prefectural governor to provide victims with free medical examinations, but nothing was done about the pollution.

The protests also had some impact on the national government. In 1962, MITI and the MoHW sent an interdisciplinary team of experts to study the pollution problem at Yokkaichi. The six-month investigation concluded with a report recommending the establishment of SO_x emission standards at Yokkaichi, the development of desulfurization technology for the petroleum refinery plant, and the construction of higher smokestacks. It took years before the full set of recommendations of this task force was implemented. In the meantime, in 1963, a second petrochemical complex began operations in the Yokkaichi area.

At the national level, the government passed a Smoke and Soot Control law. The formation of this 1962 law was spurred on by the Yokkaichi problem. A bill submitted to the Diet by the MoHW and MITI was based on studies of smoke and soot control laws in the US, Germany, and the UK. The new law regulated smoke, soot, dust, and SO_x emissions generated by combustion, heating, and melting processes. The effectiveness of the law, however, was severely limited by a clause calling for the harmonization of efforts at public health protection with the promotion of sound industrial development – a stipulation that was attached to subsequent environmental policies as well. Moreover, while the law succeeded in controlling dense pollutants such as smoke and heavy deposits, it did little to control SO_x emissions. It was made largely ineffective in regulating SO_x emissions because it applied only to designated areas, included no penalties for violators, and was based on a standard that could be met by simply building more stacks, using larger stacks, or diluting concentrations with fresh air.[17] Its emissions standards were attacked as being far too loose and its enforcement inequitable. Loopholes made effective implementation difficult.[18] It should be noted, however, that the law had the important effect of instituting an air pollution monitoring system, which gave the public important access to information about air pollution levels.

Increasingly frustrated by the limited government response, in 1963, pollution victims formed the Pollution Countermeasures Council to strengthen their ability to campaign against industry and the local pro-growth politicians. They received assistance from the Socialist and Communist Parties, the City Councilmen's Progressive Group, and labor

[17] Hashimoto, "History of Air Pollution Control in Japan," pp. 15–17.
[18] Gresser, Fujikura, and Morishima, *Environmental Law in Japan*, p. 18.

unions. Under mounting pressure, in 1964, the Yokkaichi city government took another step to appease residents by establishing a pollution disease compensation system. Under the system, the city agreed to pay the medical expenses of officially recognized pollution victims, but it still failed to do anything to control pollution.[19] Policy change was limited to incremental changes that did not seriously challenge the status quo.

Serious respiratory problems became increasingly commonplace and citizens became increasingly desperate. After one pollution victim committed suicide, other victims took a most unusual step and decided to seek redress in the courts. The situation was so bad that litigation appeared to be the only recourse left to victims. An association to support the pollution victims' legal case was established in 1967; this development was reported in great detail by the Japanese press. The association became a rallying cry for other citizens' initiatives that used "no more Yokkaichi" as a slogan to win support for their anti-development positions.[20] The case was to have profound impacts on environmental policy developments.

In the mid-1960s, rising public interest in environmental matters started to make pollution a campaign issue at the local level. Progressive scholars began to use a Marxist line in arguing that the LDP and big business were responsible for destroying people's living environment. Opposition party politicians began to win an increasing number of mayoral and gubernatorial elections on pollution control platforms. The LDP began to fear a similar loss of control at the national level.[21]

Local governments began to take action into their own hands. In 1969, for instance, the Tokyo Metropolitan government under the leadership of progressive Mayor Ryôkichi Minobe enacted the Tokyo Metropolitan Environmental Pollution Control Ordinance, which gave pollution control priority over economic growth and set stricter emissions standards than existed at the national level. At this time, local authorities did not have the right to establish stricter laws than those established nationally. While the Diet challenged the legitimacy of Tokyo's ordinance, public support was behind it. In doing this, Minobe was following the example set by California, which by taking a similar step had emerged as the most progressive regional standard setter in the US.[22]

In the mid-1960s, the *Asahi Shimbun*, one of Japan's leading national newspapers, began to run articles on pollution victims, and after a

[19] Huddle and Reich, *Island of Dreams*, pp. 72–7.
[20] OECD, *Major Air Pollution Problems: The Japanese Experience* (Paris: OECD, 1974); Huddle and Reich, *Island of Dreams*, pp. 51–77.
[21] Steven R. Reed, *Japanese Prefectures and Policymaking* (Pittsburgh: University of Pittsburgh Press, 1986), pp. 46–51.
[22] Reed, *Japanese Prefectures and Policymaking*, pp. 19 and 49–50.

42   Environmental Politics

photochemical smog incident in July 1970 in which students at a high school collapsed and had to be rushed to hospitals, the newspaper created a pollution reporters' team.[23] Articles on pollution appearing in the *Asahi* jumped from under 300 in 1969 to over 1,600 articles in 1970.[24] It is widely acknowledged that the media helped turn national attention to the plight of victims of pollution diseases in the 1960s and 1970s.[25]

There were also many individuals who played particularly important roles in disseminating scientific and policy information from abroad. Saburô Ohkita, a former minister of foreign affairs active in Third World development issues, and Yôichi Kaya, an energy and environment specialist at Tokyo University, for example, were instrumental in getting the Club of Rome report translated into Japanese. It painted a bleak picture of the future global situation based on rising population rates, growing resource and food demands, and rising levels of industrial production.[26]

The bureaucratic and political response   Reflecting the priority placed on industrial growth, the central government was ill equipped to deal with pollution issues. The MoHW, which had primary responsibility for environmental protection, had an Environmental Sanitation Section and a National Park Division, but had no office to deal with industrial pollution problems.[27] Due to the rising salience of the environment as an issue, slowly, a process of bureaucratic reorganization began. A Pollution Office was established within MITI in 1963 and in the MoHW in 1964. In 1965, at the behest of the MoHW, a law was passed establishing a Pollution Control Service Corporation (later renamed the Japan Environment Corporation) in order to help finance the construction of pollution-prevention facilities and to move polluting industries away from residential areas on a voluntary basis.[28] Special Standing Committees for Industrial Pollution were established in both Houses of the Diet, and an Advisory Commission on Environmental Pollution was created under the MoHW's jurisdiction.[29]

[23] Michael Reich, "Crisis and Routine: Pollution Reporting by the Japanese Press," in George DeVos (ed.), *Institutions for Change in Japanese Society* (Berkeley: Institute of East Asian Studies, University of California, 1984), pp. 114–47.
[24] From counts I made of the *Asahi Shimbun* newspaper index.
[25] Huddle and Reich, *Island of Dreams*, p. 171.
[26] Yutaka Tonooka, "A Short History of Global Warming Policy in Japan," unpublished paper shared with the author.
[27] Ichirô Katô, Tarô Kaneko, Keiichi Kihara, and Michio Hashimoto, "Kankyô Gyôsei 10 Nen no Ayumi," *Juristo* 749 (1981), 17–62.
[28] Japan Environment Corporation, 1994 brochure.
[29] Tsunao Imamura, "Soshiki no Bunka to Kôzô," in Kiyoaki Tsuji (ed.), *Gyôseigaku Kôza*, vol. IV: *Gyôsei to Soshiki* (Tokyo: Tôkyô Daigaku Shuppankai, 1976), pp. 37–82.

The 1967 Basic Law for Environmental Pollution Control

In 1965 reacting to growing citizen discontent, the Democratic Socialist Party (DSP) and the Japan Socialist Party (JSP) submitted basic pollution control bills to the Diet. These were the first attempts at major reforms to pollution policies at the national level (with the exception of water pollution control – a national water quality act was established in 1955 and was the first comprehensive national environmental law). While neither bill passed, they put the LDP on the defensive.[30]

Strong differences existed between the positions of the MoHW and MITI. The MoHW argued that comprehensive pollution control measures be adopted that give priority to health over industrial development and that polluting industries should be liable for damage even when they were not negligent. Although MITI argued that pollution control should be implemented, it insisted that pollution standards did not need to be fixed in law and that pollution control should not pose a burden to industry or the economy. As the traditionally stronger of the two ministries, MITI succeeded in eliminating the MoHW's proposals for strict liability for polluting industries. Pollution control obligations for industry were also purposely left vague. A "harmony clause" asserted that pollution control should be harmonized with the need for a sound, healthy economy. This clause called for the "preservation of the living environment in harmony with the healthy development of the economy," giving polluting industries an escape route from the environmental intentions of the law.[31] This clause effectively took the bite out of the bill and raised questions about how serious the government was about controlling pollution.

Despite its severe shortcomings, the Basic Law for Environmental Pollution Control made some important legislative and institutional changes that expanded formal participation in environmental pollution control. It was one of only twelve basic laws and one of the first of its kind in the world. A basic law outlines the broad principles upon which policy in a particular area is to be based. The Basic Law for Environmental Pollution Control outlined the responsibilities of different governmental levels, industry, and citizens in pollution control; called for the creation of a pollution monitoring and surveillance system and the development of science and technology for pollution control; and instructed the government to establish environmental quality standards for air, water, and soil

---

[30] Gresser, Fujikura, and Morishima, *Environmental Law in Japan*, pp. 19–27.
[31] See Gresser, Fujikura, and Morishima, *Environmental Law in Japan*, p. 18; and Margaret McKean, "Pollution and Policymaking," in T. J. Pempel (ed.), *Policymaking in Contemporary Japan* (Ithaca: Cornell University Press, 1977), pp. 201–39.

pollution.[32] It also established an interministerial Environmental Pollution Control Council.

The Basic Law for Environmental Pollution Control played an important role in expanding formal involvement in the newly emerging environmental policy community and prepared the way for further legislative changes. It required the establishment of air emission standards and ambient air quality standards. In 1968, an Air Pollution Control Law was passed by the Diet.[33] Similar to the US Air Quality Act of 1967, the Air Pollution Control Law set an emissions standard for SO_x, which placed a cap on the quantity of a pollutant that could be discharged from a specific source. The standard applied to all areas. In addition, the law established more stringent emissions standards for new sources of emissions. There were, however, some important differences with the US law. Whereas, for example, the US law established state automobile pollution inspection systems, opposition from the rapidly growing Japanese automobile industry kept such provisions out of the Japanese law.

In 1969, a Cabinet ordinance on ambient air quality standards for SO_x was established. As opposed to emissions standards, ambient air quality standards set levels for allowable concentrations of a pollutant in a designated region. The standards, however, were still too weak really to protect human health, and the government exempted industrial areas from meeting the standards. Industry had successfully argued that achieving the higher standards would require the introduction of desulfurization technology and that this would put industry at an economic disadvantage. Thus, a compromise was made.[34]

The effect of these new laws on air quality was minimal. To meet the new standards, many industries began to build higher smokestacks. The building of higher smokestacks was relatively inexpensive for industry and reduced pollutant loads near factories, but did not reduce total pollution levels and spread pollution problems over wider areas.

The pollution Diet of 1970
Despite the new pollution control legislation, grass roots demands for more significant action became stronger. The environmental movement in the US was also starting to win victories. Developments in the US lent

[32] See Imamura, "Soshiki no Bunka to Kôzô"; McKean, *Environmental Protest and Citizen Politics*; Gresser, Fujikura, and Morishima, *Environmental Law in Japan*, pp. 19–27 and 395–8; and Kankyôchô Kikaku Chôsei Kyoku, *Kankyôchô Kihonhô no Kaisetsu* (Tokyo: Gyôsei, 1994).
[33] See Hashimoto, "History of Air Pollution Control in Japan," pp. 20–4, and Takeshi Hayase, "Taiki Osen," inTsuji (ed.), *Gyôseigaku Kôza*, pp. 175–201.
[34] Hayase, "Taiki Osen."

legitimacy and support to the demands of Japan's environmental citizens' groups.

The LDP had to act. There was a sense of urgency behind the need for new environmental regulations. Thus, in July 1970, the Cabinet established a Special Headquarters for Pollution Control to formulate new policies and measures and a special Ministers' Conference for Pollution Control to coordinate ministerial views. This group met seven times in a three-month period to consider legislation for submission to a special Diet session. In November, the Ministers' Conference drafted a proposal for the revision of the Basic Law and just one month later, fourteen major anti-pollution bills and amendments were passed under the government of Eisaku Satô. The opposition parties and the LDP reached general consensus on emergency pollution measures.

Given the short period of time in which these laws were drafted, there was little time for study or debate. A policy window had opened; environmental activists quickly borrowed ideas about environmental regulations from abroad and then worked to get them enacted domestically.

Under the 1970 amendments, the "harmony clause" of the Basic Law was dropped. The 1968 Air Pollution Control Law was amended to include a national minimum SO_x emission standard. Lead in gasoline was targeted. Local governments were given the right to establish more stringent standards than were established nationally, as was the case with vehicle emissions standards in California in the US. Penalty provisions were also strengthened. An Environmental Pollution Crime Law was established making it a criminal offense to emit pollution that could cause health damages, and polluting industries were taxed to contribute to the costs of government pollution control programs.[35] One major difference with the US is that little progress was made in the area of environmental impact assessments because of strong industry opposition.[36] Under the new laws, companies planning to construct new emission sources were required to notify and submit details of their plans within sixty days from the date of the beginning of construction. The prefectural governor then had sixty days to respond with any specifications for changes in the plan. In practice, however, this gave local governments little chance to influence construction plans.[37]

Establishment of an Environment Agency   In May 1971, following Swedish and US examples, an Environment Agency was created under the Prime

[35] Hashimoto, "History of Air Pollution Control in Japan," pp. 27–9.
[36] Brendan F. D. Barrett and Riki Therival, *Environmental Policy and Impact Assessment in Japan* (London: Routledge, 1991).
[37] OECD, *Major Air Pollution Problems.*

Minister's Office. The Environment Agency began with a staff of 502, a little less than half of which were assigned to nature conservation. There were large staff increases in the first few years, stabilizing at around 900 by 1980.[38] When the Agency was founded, there was considerable debate about what its shape should be. The National Park and the Air Pollution Divisions were taken from the MoHW and protection of wildlife from the Forestry Agency and put in the new agency. The Environment Agency, however, was not given control of large budget items like energy, which stayed in MITI or sewerage projects, which stayed in the MoC. In the end, in addition to a director-general's section, four bureaus were created: air quality, water quality, nature conservation, and planning and coordination. Three advisory councils and two certifying bodies also were attached to the new agency. Particularly important was the Central Council for Environmental Pollution Control. The council was charged with informing the prime minister of environmental matters and consisted of academics, doctors, former bureaucrats, private enterprise representatives, and members of the press, labor unions, local governments, and women's organizations. In addition, three research institutes and a training institute were established. One of the research institutes, the National Institute for Environmental Pollution Research (later renamed the National Institute for Environmental Studies), accounted for over one quarter of the Environment Agency's staff.[39]

Pollution victims' compensation law   Pollution control remained on the agenda for several years and public opinion in favor of environmental protection remained strong. According to one estimate, by the early 1970s, an estimated 1,500 to 3,000 citizens' groups had organized to protest against industrial pollution in Japan.[40] In 1971 alone, local governments received over 75,000 pollution-related complaints – almost four times the number in 1966.[41] The call for stringent environmental regulations was also strengthened by the long-awaited verdicts in the four big pollution trials. In September 1972, the first of the trials came to a close. The court's decision in favor of the asthma victims in the Yokkaichi

[38] Kankyôchô 20 Shûnen Kinen Jigyô Jikkô Iinkai, *Kankyôchô 20 Nenshi* (Tokyo: Gyôsei, 1991), pp. 516–17.

[39] Tsunao Imamura, "Environmental Responsibilities at the National Level: The Environment Agency," in Shigeto Tsuru and Helmut Weidner (eds.), *Environmental Policy in Japan* (Berlin: Sigma, 1989), pp. 43–53.

[40] *Asahi Shimbun*, May 21, 1973. Cited in T. J. Pempel, *Policy and Politics in Japan: Creative Conservatism* (Philadelphia: Temple University Press, 1982), p. 232.

[41] Ellis S. Krauss and Bradford Simcock, "Citizens' Movements: The Growth and Impact of Environmental Protest in Japan," in Kurt Steiner, Ellis S. Krauss, and Scott C. Flanagan (eds.), *Political Opposition and Local Politics in Japan* (Princeton: Princeton University Press, 1980), p. 187.

air pollution case came as a blow to both industry and government. The court ruled that the six companies in the Yokkaichi petrochemical complex had been negligent in siting and operating the complex and in failing to use the best available technology to control emissions. The court also concluded that it was the responsibility of national and local governments to take administrative measures for air pollution control.

The Environment Agency's second director, Buichi Ôishi, formerly a practicing medical doctor, is credited for the Agency's successful use of these societal forces and this judicial support to enact several new environmental laws, including a Nature Conservation Law, a Chemical Substances Control Law, and a Pollution Victims Compensation Law, all of which were enacted by the end of 1973. The Pollution Victims Compensation Law was a polluter-financed, nation-wide compensation system for victims of designated air and water pollution diseases. This law was based on similar arrangements made by local governments in the late 1960s to compensate pollution victims. Various high pollution areas were designated as pollution zones and illnesses were classified as pollution-related diseases. Victims suffering from chronic bronchitis, bronchial asthma, Minamata disease or *itai-itai* disease, among others, who lived for a specified length of time in a designated pollution area became eligible for health and welfare compensation. As of December 31, 1984, there were about 94,000 recognized victims, most of whom suffered from air pollution related health problems.[42]

New strict ambient air quality standards for suspended particulates were established in 1972 and for sulfur dioxides (SO_2), nitrogen oxides (NO_x) and photochemical oxidants in 1973. In 1974, the government passed a law regulating plant sitings; a law requiring the establishment of a factory pollution-control manager system which would act as an internal policing force within industry; and total mass emission regulations for SO_x, which allowed companies to choose the most economical method of limiting discharges. The new SO_x standards were set at 0.017 ppm/year, and became the most stringent in the world.[43] In August 1972, the Central Advisory Council for Environmental Pollution Control Measures also proposed the adoption of the same NO_x standards as those in the US Clean Air Act. In October 1972, the Environment Agency formally issued NO_x standards for 1975 and 1976 that were equivalent to the US standards for 1976, essentially surpassing US regulations in terms of their stringency. By the end of this bout of legislative change, Japan had among the most stringent environmental regulations in the world.

[42] Michio Hashimoto, "The Pollution-Related Health Damage Compensation Law," in Nishimura (ed.), *How to Conquer Air Pollution*, pp. 239–98.
[43] Hashimoto, "History of Air Pollution Control in Japan," pp. 29–34.

In taking up the environmental cause and other social welfare issues, the LDP was able to stem its electoral slide at the local level. By responding to the environmental agenda of the citizens' movements, the LDP prevented the opposition from capitalizing on this issue more than it already had and helped limit future use of the courts as an arena for environmental law making.[44] Thus, in Japan, what T. J. Pempel has labeled "creative conservatism" helped to keep conservative political forces in power for many more years.[45] It also helped weaken movements of the left.

Germany

Early citizen protest

In the mid-nineteenth century, as air pollution grew more serious, the Prussian state empowered local authorities to restrict heavily polluting industrial facilities through the establishment of a permit system. The principles of these regulations were later adopted by the German Reich. In 1895, air pollution regulations were expanded with the passage of Technical Guidelines for Air Purity. The regulations gave local authorities the power to use licenses to control polluting industries.[46]

There were some "Not-In-My-Back-Yard" (NIMBY) protests against pollution in the postwar years. For example, in 1959, a concerned and angered doctor living near Essen in the Ruhr region, filed a legal complaint against a nearby metallurgy plant which he claimed was causing bodily injury. As evidence, he showed that the pollution affected the respiratory tracts of children. The court ruled in favor of the industry, however, on the grounds that customary levels of pollution did not merit legal redress.[47]

North Rhine–Westphalia is Germany's industrial heartland, and this is where the first efforts at strengthening pollution control began. A small expert community was the driving force behind policy change although there were some indications of growing public concern with air pollution in the region. The director of the Federation of Settlements in the Ruhr Coal District, for example, was concerned about research that showed a steady increase in pollution in the region and that problems were likely to get worse because of growing use of coal, higher levels of steel production, and a shift to the use of crude oil as a heating material in large combustion plants. The director asked the Land legislature to consider air pollution control legislation. He called for industry cooperation and

---

[44] Upham, *Law and Social Change in Postwar Japan*, pp. 28–77.
[45] See Pempel, *Policy and Politics in Japan*; and T. J. Pempel, *Regime Shift: Comparative Dynamics of the Japanese Political Economy* (Ithaca: Cornell University Press, 1998).
[46] Klaus-George Wey, *Umweltpolitik in Deutschland: Kurze Geschicte des Umweltschutzes in Deutschland seit 1900* (Opladen: Westdeutscher Verlag, 1982), pp. 181–94.
[47] Raymond H. Dominick, *The Environmental Movement in Germany: Prophets and Pioneers, 1871–1971* (Bloomington: Indiana University Press, 1992), p. 171.

the establishment of regulations in designated areas to deal with the air pollution problem.

In 1955, Dr. Schmidt, a CDU member of the North Rhine–Westphalia Land legislature visited the Center for Air Pollution Control Research at Carnegie Mellon Institute. Inspired by what he saw in the US, Dr. Schmidt acted upon the director's request and introduced to the North Rhine–Westphalia legislature a motion that would require it to draft legislation that would expand observation and research related to air pollution control. With air pollution a serious problem in the region, all parties agreed in principle to the resolution; the SPD and FDP argued, however, that ultimately only a federal government initiative would work. In the spring of 1956, the SPD proposed a similar resolution to the Bundestag pushing the issue of air pollution control on to the federal policy agenda for the first time.

The Bund der Deutsche Industrie (BDI) quickly criticized these developments, arguing that the concentration of power stations and coal mines in the region already had spawned the development of greatly improved smoke and soot control technologies over the previous two decades. They argued that despite higher production levels, they had managed over the past thirty years to reduce considerably smoke and gaseous emissions. They further argued that greater attention should be paid to smaller enterprises, household fuel use, and in particular transportation. Moreover, they suggested that it would be difficult to identify which industries were responsible for pollution and that pollution control would be cost prohibitive since it would require the building of new installations at each source. This would mean that even those who were already cooperating with the law would have to pay for pollution control equipment. They also argued that there were insufficient measurements being taken in the region to determine pollution levels. They agreed that there was sufficient evidence of a problem, however, to concede to the idea of expanding the list of installations requiring government licenses in order to operate and amendments to the Technical Guidelines for Air Purity to bring this sixty-year-old implementing legislation up to date.

In the spring and summer of 1957, the North Rhine–Westphalia and the federal governments both reported that air pollution was a serious problem in specific locales and that pollution monitoring and control measures should be strengthened. The similarity in the timing and content of their reports suggests that there was cooperation or learning between the two levels of government in their answers to parliamentary questions. The reports called for the expansion of the list of enterprises requiring licenses to begin operations and updating Technical Guidelines for licensing and control of new facilities that had been in place since the late nineteenth century. One big difference between the reports was related to the question of jurisdiction. The federal government called for all air pollution control issues to be legislated at the federal level. The North Rhine–Westphalia legislature did not intend to give up the right to attach additional requirements.

The Interparliamentary Working Group for Nature Appropriate Economics, a group that cuts across parties and federal and Länder parliaments, was instrumental in finding a compromise. They drafted legislation, which was then unanimously accepted by the Committee for Health. The Committee for Economics raised no major objections. The BDI, which initially had opposed the introduction of new environmental regulations, eventually chose to cooperate in order to influence the shape of legislation. The 1959 guideline legislation called for an expansion of the list of installations requiring licenses for operation and a revision of the Technical Guidelines that would require the use of "state of the art technology" for pollution control in new installations – primarily to deal with smoke, soot, and sulfur emissions. The Federal Emissions Control Law strengthened standards for enforcement and weakened to some extent a requirement that existed under the 1895 law that there be evidence of a link between emissions and damage to the public health before pollution control measures be enforced. The law, however, did not extend to transportation or household heating. To obtain industry cooperation, the Interparliamentary Working Group had to give up the extension of the list to the growing number of industries that were switching to crude oil for heating purposes. Their efforts to amend the nineteenth-century legislation in order to deal with these major producers of sulfur oxide emissions failed. There was strong opposition from the oil industry and industrial unions, which argued that the desulfurization of crude oil was far more expensive than desulfurization of waste gases and therefore would be cost inhibitive.

The CDU and FDP were supportive of the guideline legislation; the SPD accepted the new law but called for future amendments that would extend pollution control measures to the transportation sector and household heating. The Social Democrats also anticipated quick passage of implementation legislation. When this did not happen, the SPD decided to push the matter by turning air pollution into a campaign issue at the federal level.[48]

Blue skies over the Ruhr campaign
There was a noticeable rise in environmental reporting in German newspapers and magazines in the 1950s. Between 1951 and 1959, the coverage

[48] Wey, *Umweltpolitik in Deutschland*, pp. 152–229.

of environmental issues in the *Frankfurter Allgemeine Zeitung* rose from less than 100 articles per year to over 400 articles per year.[49] In 1957, the *Ruhr-Nachrichten*, a regional newspaper, ran a headline that warned its readers that "Many Diseases Nest Under Pollution Dome."[50] Capitalizing on what he thought would be a persuasive issue, in 1961, in what was to become a famous speech, Willy Brandt, the Social Democratic candidate for chancellor declared: "Frightening results from investigations show that an increase in leukemia, cancer, and ... [other diseases] are apparent in children where there is pollution of air and water. It is dismaying that this collective task, which affects the health of millions of people, has been completely neglected until now. The skies over the Ruhr territory must become blue again!"[51]

In conjunction with this campaign, *Der Spiegel* ran a cover story on air pollution entitled, "Toward Blue Skies."[52] The campaign, however, did not catch on. Years later, reflecting on the campaign, Willy Brandt bemoaned:

I made environmental problems part of my platform in my first Bundestag election campaign, thereby providing amusement for pragmatic politicians of all shades. When I spoke before the election – supported by American data – of the hitherto almost entirely neglected community task of protecting the environment, my principal argument was that the health of millions of people was at stake. Demands for pure air, clean water and less noise should not be left merely on paper. Later, when I spoke as the party's leading candidate in North Rhine–Westphalia, I concluded by wishing that the sky above the Ruhr might be blue again; this was made to sound ridiculous by lowbrow critics. It is hard to understand why people were so slow to perceive the great ecological threats of our time.[53]

Policy change in North Rhine–Westphalia   Brandt's campaign had little impact on politics at the national level, but it had important ramifications in North Rhine–Westphalia. In 1962 all the political parties submitted pollution control bills to the state legislature. North Rhine–Westphalia became the first Länder to adopt a comprehensive air pollution control law. It took more than a decade before similar legislation was passed at the federal level.[54] The North Rhine–Westphalian law included not only smoke and gas but also noise and vibration. Under the new law, the list of plants requiring permits for operation was extended to include small plants – a provision that went well beyond federal guidelines. In the next

---

[49] Wey, *Umweltpolitik in Deutschland*, p. 184.
[50] Cited in Dominick, *The Environmental Movement in Germany*, p. 170.
[51] Quoted in Dominick, *The Environmental Movement in Germany*, p. 171.
[52] Dominick, *The Environmental Movement in Germany*, p. 189.
[53] Willy Brandt, *My Life in Politics* (New York: Penguin Press, 1992), p. 254.
[54] Dominick, *The Environmental Movement in Germany*, p. 193.

two years, four other Länder governments followed suit. In 1964, the North Rhine–Westphalia government again took the lead over the federal government by enacting an ordinance that dealt with smog, establishing a comprehensive monitoring system, and developing clean air programs that sought to reduce pollution loads in heavily polluted areas.[55]

Policy change at the federal level

At the federal level, enactment of Technical Guidelines that were necessary to implement the 1959 Federal Emissions Control Law was delayed by opposition from the BDI and Economics Ministry and Länder governments that were concerned about the law and its implementation. Differences in opinion emerged between the Committees for Health and Economics within the Bundestag; the Ministry of Economics and the Ministry of Health within the federal government; and the Länder and the federal governments. Up until this point, pollution control had primarily been defined as a health matter. The Ministry of Economics used this to their advantage, arguing that there was no clear scientific evidence linking air pollution to health problems. They argued that it was therefore more important to take into consideration the economic impacts of pollution control and to consider the positive societal benefits that would come from strong economic growth.

The BDI also expressed its opposition to the criteria that "state of the art technology" for pollution control be required of plants seeking licenses. The BDI argued that requirements for "state of the art technology" went beyond the intentions of the 1959 Federal Emissions Control Law and were unnecessarily vague. They called for a long period of discussion and debate on technical and scientific aspects of pollution control.

Although the Clean Air Commission of the German Engineers Association produced a report in 1961 showing the adverse effects of sulfur dioxide on human health and the environment and recommended emissions levels that should not be exceeded, it was not until 1964 that the Federal Ministry of Health (newly established in 1961) succeeded in issuing the Technical Guidelines for maintaining air purity that were necessary to implement the 1959 Federal Emissions Control Law.[56]

This long delay showed the weakness of the environmental lobby within the German bureaucracy. Prior to the establishment of the Ministry of Health, air pollution control was under the purview of the Ministry of Labor, where there was only one official who spent half his time working

[55] Weidner, *Air Pollution Control Strategies*, pp. 49–51.
[56] OECD, *Case History from Germany on the Use of Criteria Documents in Setting Standards for the Control of Sulfur Oxides* (Paris: OECD, 1975).

on air pollution control and the other half working on labor protection issues. The new Federal Ministry of Health was a weak ministry and had little power to push initiatives over the opposition of more powerful ministries. Thus, it took years before the Technical Guidelines could be enacted.

In their final form, the Technical Guidelines included information on licensing procedures for industrial facilities seeking permits, ambient air quality standards for five air pollutants, and a stipulation that industries be equipped with the best technical control devices available.[57] They resulted in recommended short-time and long-time maximum ambient concentrations for sulfur dioxide.[58] The standards did not really take human health into consideration, however, and enforcement efforts were limited.

Further efforts by environmental advocates within the Ministry of Health and the Health Committee within the Bundestag to introduce a comprehensive federal air pollution control law that would set nation-wide emissions standards failed. In 1966, the Committee for Health requested that the government draft legislation for a law to regulate emissions. In 1968, the government presented draft legislation that would extend standards on emissions to cover not only air pollution, but also noise and vibration. With Germany in the midst of an economic recession, however, the Economics Ministry was able to kill this legislative effort.

The SPD–FDP coalition

In 1969, the SPD formed a coalition government with the FDP, ushering in a thirteen-year period that became known as the social-liberal era.[59] Throughout the early 1950s, the SPD had remained critical of the CDU's economic policies. It also attacked the CDU's strong Western orientation, which it claimed hindered possibilities for negotiating with the Soviet Union over the reunification of Germany. After electoral defeat in 1953 and 1957, however, elements within the SPD began to consider party reform for fear that the party's Marxist orientation would doom it to a position of perpetual opposition. In 1959, at a party congress held in Bad Godesberg, the SPD adopted a new party program. Under what became known as the Godesberg Program, the SPD announced its acceptance of private enterprise in an effort to transform itself from a working-class party to a party with a broader base of support. Willy Brandt was made

---

[57] Weidner, *Air Pollution Control Strategies*, pp. 49–51.
[58] OECD, *Case History from Germany*.
[59] Edda Müller, *Innenwelt der Umweltpolitik: Sozial-liberale Umweltpolitik (ohn)macht durch Organisation?* (Opladen: Westdeutscher Verlag, 1986).

their candidate for chancellor. Although the SPD did not win the 1961 election, it improved its standing in the Bundestag.

The shift in the SPD's stance was important. Although electoral victory again escaped the party in 1965, the party remained a viable contender. In contrast with the situation in Japan, where there was a slow but steady fragmentation of the opposition in the 1960s, first with the formation of the DSP in 1964 and then the Kômeitô in 1967, in Germany, the number of parties in the Bundestag declined from ten in 1949 to only three in 1961. The SPD's shift towards the center in its economic and foreign policies made possible the Grand Coalition between the CDU/CSU and the SPD in 1966 and the subsequent rise to power of the SPD.[60] In 1969, the SPD formed a coalition with the FDP, ending a long era of conservative rule.

Willy Brandt of the SPD became the chancellor at a time when the economy was relatively strong after a severe recession. It was also a period when extra-parliamentary opposition was rapidly growing in the form of student protests, opposition to Germany's close alliance with the US which was aggravated by the Vietnam War, and the formation of extremist parties on the left and right. With a policy window opened by their electoral victory, the SPD/FDP coalition reacted to these movements with promises of sweeping policy reforms. Willy Brandt challenged the coalition to "dare more democracy" and to be a party of "inner reforms."[61] In Brandt's first speech as chancellor in October 1969, he stated that, as part of its reformist policy package, the government would introduce bills that would provide sufficient protection against air, water, and noise pollution.

The SPD/FDP's decision to take on environmental issues involved a certain amount of opportunism. Internationally, the environment was becoming a big political issue just at a time when the new ruling coalition was looking for policy ideas that would appeal to voters. This was particularly important for a coalition that had only a narrow grip on a majority.

In contrast with Japan, where grass roots movements were a primary impetus behind policy change, in Germany, it was the SPD/FDP coalition that took the lead. In 1969, the jurisdiction of air, water, and waste disposal was moved from the Ministry of Health to the Ministry of the Interior, which also had jurisdiction for planning and urban development. The Interior Ministry also assumed direction of a Permanent Committee on Environmental Affairs, which coordinated environmental policy at the federal level and prepared decisions for a newly founded Cabinet

[60] Peter Katzenstein, *Policy and Politics in West Germany: The Growth of a Semi-Sovereign State* (Philadelphia: Temple University Press, 1987), pp. 36–7.
[61] Quoted in Saral Sarkar, *Green-Alternative Politics in West Germany* (Tokyo: United Nations University Press, 1993), p. 8.

Committee on the Environment. An FDP appointee, Günter Hartkopf, who saw in the environment a way to reform his party's image, assumed leadership of the Permanent Committee on Environmental Affairs in 1969, remaining in that post through 1982. He also directed a Conference on Environment Ministers of the Bund and the Länder, which was set up to coordinate environmental policy between them. This gave the FDP a particularly strong influence over environmental policy for the remainder of the decade.[62]

Citizens' initiatives

Growing environmental awareness in society certainly played some role in the SPD's decision to pick up the environment as an issue area. There are indications that the environment was becoming a more important issue. There was heightened awareness of pollution issues in Germany because of the Blue Sky over the Ruhr campaign. There was also a growth in the number of questions on the environment posed to the Länder legislatures and the Bundestag.[63]

Most of the citizens' initiatives in Germany at the end of the 1960s, however, were concerned with problems in the educational sector, social services, local housing, and traffic planning.[64] It was not until the beginning of the 1970s – after the SPD/FDP coalition announced its environmental plans – that environmental citizens' initiatives really mushroomed in number and began to consolidate. Edda Müller argues that outside events, including the environmental movement in the US, the passage of the NEPA in 1969 and the Clean Air Act amendments of 1970, and international activities including preparations for the 1972 Stockholm Conference, were the main reasons why the new government began to introduce environmental laws. In making these arguments, she noted a study by Küppers et al. of the *Süddeutschen Zeitung* and *Der Spiegel* that found that while a few issues were covered in the press prior to their politicization, most press coverage of environmental issues paralleled or followed government action. She also found that the environment played no role in the elections of 1965 and 1969.[65]

[62] Douglas Barnes, "Established Parties and the Environment in the Federal Republic of Germany: The Politics of Responding to a New Issue," paper presented at the American Political Science Association Annual Meeting, Palmer House Hilton, September 3–6, 1992.
[63] Wey, *Umweltpolitik in Deutschland*, pp. 154–5.
[64] Lutz Mez, "Von den Bügerinitiativen zu den GRÜNEN: Zur Entstehungsgeschichte der 'Wahlalternativen' in der Bundesrepublik Deutschland," in Roland Roth and Dieter Rucht (eds.), *Neue soziale Bewegungen in der Bundesrepublik Deutschland* (Frankfurt: Campus Verlag, 1987), pp. 263–76.
[65] Müller, *Innenwelt der Umweltpolitik*, pp. 49–55.

Dr. G. Dietrich Feldhaus, who was involved in early air pollution policy formulation first within the Ministry of Health and then in the Ministry of the Interior, similarly stated that in the early 1970s, policy change was not caused by political discussions in Germany but by President Nixon's sudden interest in environmental protection. According to Feldhaus, Hans Dietrich Genscher, "a very clever politician," picked up on Nixon's greening, adopted the environment as a theme and turned it into an important political issue.[66]

Federal environmental law

In September 1970, the SPD/FDP government issued an Emergency Program for Environmental Protection, which included measures for clean air, noise abatement, water pollution control, waste disposal and nature protection. In November, an Environmental Program Planning Division was established within the Interior Ministry and tasked with creating an Environment Program. Then in 1971, the SPD/FDP announced their Environment Program, which at least in name elevated environmental protection to the same status as other governmental responsibilities in education, social security, internal security, and defense, and became the basis of all environmental programs established since then by various political parties, associations, and social groups.[67]

Like the Basic Law for Environmental Pollution Control in Japan, the Environment Program covered and established important basic philosophies underlying pollution control, but established few concrete standards or timetables.[68] The three philosophical underpinnings of the new law were far sighted and remain important guiding principles. They include the polluter pays principle, the precautionary principle, and the cooperation principle. The polluter pays principle placed responsibility on polluters for clean-up costs as was becoming an accepted norm within the OECD by this time. The precautionary principle called on the state to take action to prevent environmental damage through precaution and planning. The cooperation principle established that environmental policy should be developed in close cooperation among all relevant parties through the use of hearings as well as international endeavors.[69] The law

---

[66] Interview with Dr. Feldhaus, May 17, 1993.
[67] See Helmut Weidner, "The Capability of the Capitalist State to 'Solve' Environmental Problems – The Examples of Germany and Japan," paper presented at the XVth World Congress of the International Political Science Association, Buenos Aires, July 21–5, 1991, p. 13; and Müller, *Innenwelt der Umweltpolitik*, p. 62.
[68] Müller, *Innenwelt der Umweltpolitik*, pp. 60–1.
[69] Jochen Hucke, "Environmental Policy: The Development of a New Policy Area," in Manfred Schmidt and Klaus von Beyme (eds.), *Policy and Politics in the Federal Republic of Germany* (New York: St. Martin's Press, 1985); Sonja Boehmer-Christiansen and Jim

also called for the development of technology that had little or no negative environmental impacts. The effectiveness of the polluter pays principle was modified to some extent, however, by a clause calling for the economic defensibility of pollution control measures. The statement read: "The capacity (*Leistungsfähigkeit*) of the national economy will not be overstretched by the practical implementation of the environment programme. Environmental protection shall be supported by financial and fiscal measures, as well as measures applied to the infrastructure."[70] In 1972, an amendment to the Basic Law was passed, granting the federal government jurisdiction in environmental matters, although implementation remained the responsibility of the Länder.[71] The Basic Law of 1949 had assigned the eleven Länder primary powers in the environment, including the implementation of laws.[72]

The amendment to the Basic Law meant that legislative jurisdiction over air, water, waste, and noise pollution were added to the federal government's existing responsibilities in the areas of nuclear safety and radioactive waste management. The federal government did not obtain full authority, but rather concurrent jurisdiction with the Länder in air pollution control. Länder retained the right to pass laws in this area when the federal government had not already done so. Federal laws, however, were allowed to replace existing ones at the Länder level.[73]

The establishment of an environmental administration   The change in the Basic Law made it possible for the government to begin passing legislation. Within the Interior Ministry, environmental protection matters became the responsibility of the Environmental Protection Division, which had sections dealing with general environmental affairs (planning, coordination, international affairs), water resource management, noise abatement, and air quality control.[74] The division started with forty-six personnel and increased to seventy-seven in 1974, at which point the number roughly stabilized.

Skea, *Acid Politics: Environmental and Energy Policies in Britain and Germany* (London: Belhaven Press, 1991), p. 163; William E. Paterson, "Environmental Politics," in Gordon Smith, William E. Paterson, and Peter H. Merkl (eds.), *Developments in West German Politics* (London: Macmillan Education Ltd., 1989), p. 273.
[70] Quoted in Weidner, "The Capability of the Capitalist State," p. 14.
[71] On the relation between the Basic Law and environmental politics see Dominick, *The Environmental Movement in Germany*, p. 120.
[72] Boehmer-Christiansen and Skea, *Acid Politics*, pp. 160–4 and Dominick, *The Environmental Movement in Germany*, p. 120.
[73] Boehmer-Christiansen and Skea, *Acid Politics*, p. 163.
[74] Weidner, *Air Pollution Control Strategies*, p. 62.

In 1972, the Interior Ministry also won jurisdiction of nuclear reactor safety. The Ministry of Agriculture, however, successfully prevented the transfer of jurisdiction over nature protection and land conservation.[75] Thus, like in Japan, environmental administration remained divided. The creation of a Federal Environment Agency with 450 personnel in 1974 was another big boost for environmental bureaucrats within the Interior Ministry. The Environment Agency acted as an advisory arm to the Ministry and was charged with conducting research on environmental problems. Its establishment increased the capacity of the state to conduct research into environmental protection.

Under the Brandt government, the environment was elevated to a new level of importance. Under the leadership of Interior Minister Genscher and the secretary of state responsible for environmental protection, Günther Hartkopf, several important environmental laws were passed, including the Act Against Noise from Air Traffic (1971), the Leaded Petrol Act (1972), the Waste Removal Act (1972), the DDT Act (1972), and the Federal Emissions Control Act (1974).[76]

The Federal Emissions Control Act provided the legal basis for setting air quality standards. In accordance with this law, the Technical Guidelines for Air Pollution Control of 1964 were revised and the SO_x standard was changed. The new directive established standardized procedures for the limitation of SO_x emissions through the licensing of new SO_x emitting installations and requirements for abatement measures in existing installations. New installations in principle were only to be granted a license when equipped with devices for limiting and diffusing the emissions in conformity with the latest advances in engineering and when operation of the plant would not lead to an increase in the ambient air quality standards of the surrounding area.[77] Retrofitting existing plants, however, had to be economically defensible, providing industry with a loophole that made enforcement difficult particularly in CDU/CSU-controlled Länder that were opposed to the new act.[78]

Asked to compare the stringency of these laws with Japanese air pollution laws at the time, an expert on air pollution policy suggested that Japanese standards in general were not stronger, but that the approach to air pollution control was quite different from in Germany. In Japan, local authorities often demanded more stringent controls than the regional policies that were established in Germany. Thus, the air pollution control

---

[75] Müller, *Innenwelt der Umweltpolitik*, pp. 56–67.
[76] Weidner, "The Capability of the Capitalist State," p. 13; and Müller, *Innenwelt der Umweltpolitik*, p. 16.
[77] OECD, *Case History from Germany*.
[78] Boehmer-Christiansen and Skea, *Acid Politics*, p. 163.

regulations established in Yokkaichi were more stringent than those found in any region within Germany, but at the federal level, German laws were comparable to those established at the national level in Japan. It should be noted that one major difference between Japan and Germany was in the control of nitrogen oxide emissions (NO_x). Whereas Japan adopted legislation that essentially mandated the use of catalytic converters, in Germany, no similar law was passed. At the time, SO_x and particulates were considered problematic, but NO_x were not yet on the agenda.[79]

With these changes, environmental protection efforts entered a new era in Germany. As was occurring throughout the industrialized world, new norms about environmental protection were emerging and these were accompanied by sweeping legislative and administrative changes.

As we will see in the next chapter, despite the many similarities in the laws that were passed at this time, in the course of the next decade, Japan, Germany, and the US developed very different environmental policy communities and policy-making processes.

[79] Interview with Dr. Feldhaus, May 17, 1993.

3 The institutionalization of environmental movements

The 1970s were the environmental decade in the US. Beginning with the sweeping changes to environmental laws that began with the passage in 1969 of the NEPA and the Clean Air Act amendments of 1970, Congress continued to pass one major new environmental law after the next. In 1972, Congress enacted the Federal Water Pollution Control Act; the Federal Insecticide, Rodenticide, and Fungicide Act; the Noise Control Act; the Coastal Zone Management Act; and the Marine Mammals Protection Act. The following year, the Endangered Species Act was passed and in 1974, the Safe Drinking Water Act. In 1976, Congress passed the Resource Conservation and Recovery Act, the Federal Land Management Act, and the National Forest Management Act. In 1977, the Clean Air and Water laws were expanded and in 1980, the Comprehensive Environmental Response, Compensation, and Liability Act (Superfund) was instituted.

As discussed in the previous chapter many changes also were made to environmental laws and institutions in Japan and Germany in the early 1970s, but the mid-1970s were a period of environmental policy stagnation. Over the course of the remainder of the decade, few new major environmental laws were established and there were several environmental setbacks. The Organization of the Petroleum Exporting Countries (OPEC) oil shock of 1973 was a major reason for the shift in attention away from the environment and back to the economy. Japan and Germany were especially heavily dependent on imported oil. Whereas in 1955, only 16.7 percent of Japan's energy supply was from oil, a shift away from coal to oil in the following decade meant that by 1973, 77.8 percent of Japan's energy was supplied by oil, close to 90 percent of which came from the Middle East. Germany also had a high dependence on oil. In 1973, 56.2 percent of Germany's energy was supplied by oil, essentially all of which was imported. The sudden sharp rise in imported oil prices dealt a sharp blow to both countries' economies. The US too, although less dependent than either Japan or Germany on imported oil, felt the impact of the embargo.

In response to the oil shock, Japan, Germany, and the US intensified efforts to diversify energy sources. Renewable energy sources gained some attention, but nuclear energy, an energy source that had been embraced with much enthusiasm in the previous two decades, was the real winner. The three governments heavily promoted nuclear as an energy source for the future. The share of nuclear energy as a percentage of total energy supply was still quite low at the time of the oil shocks. It rapidly increased after this time. In Japan, the share of total energy held by nuclear jumped from 0.8 percent in 1973 to 5.2 percent in 1979 and 11.7 percent in 1989. In Germany, nuclear energy accounted for 1.2 percent of total energy supply in 1973, 3.9 percent in 1979 and 13.8 percent in 1990.[1] In the US, President Nixon's Project Independence called for nuclear power to provide half of the country's electricity needs by the end of the century.[2] (See Figures 3.1–3.6.) Nuclear energy politics in the course of the 1970s became closely entwined with environmental debates and sparked anti-nuclear movements.

Another reaction to the oil shocks that was particularly prominent in Japan and Germany was a shift in policy makers' attention back to the economy. The Environment Agency in Japan was relatively powerless to act in the face of growing opposition to further expansion of environmental regulations on the grounds that it threatened Japan's economic viability. In Germany, there was a similar loss of interest in the environment on the part of the SPD when Helmut Schmidt became chancellor in 1974 and economic recession loomed on the horizon. The Interior Ministry was left to do what it could to defend recently passed environmental laws. In the US, the environmental fallout was not as pronounced, but there were amendments made to the Clean Air Act of 1970 to provide waivers for the automobile industry that kept failing to meet motor vehicle emissions standards. In this new climate, the strategies of the environmental movements in Japan, Germany, and the US diverged.

Environmental protection and the influence of the US

Over the course of the 1970s, there was significant growth in the membership of US environmental groups. Many movements emerged to address local environmental concerns resulting from development. In addition, many new national environmental groups formed and older groups,

[1] OECD, *Energy Policies of IEA Countries: 1991 Review* (Paris: OECD, 1991), pp. 431 and 436.
[2] Michael Smith, "Advertising the Atom," in Michael J. Lacey (ed.), *Government and Environmental Politics: Essays on Historical Developments since World War II* (Washington, DC: Woodrow Wilson Center, 1991), p. 253.

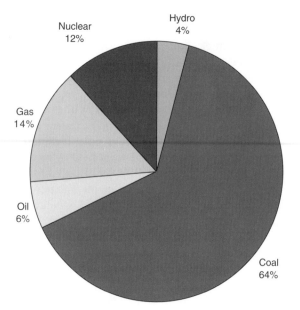

Figure 3.1   Germany: electricity by source 1980
Source: 2000 World Bank Development Indicators.

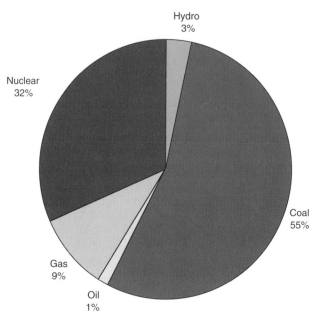

Figure 3.2   Germany: electricity by source 1997
Source: 2000 World Bank Development Indicators.

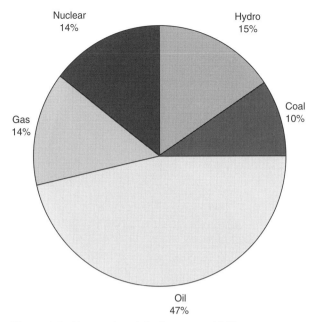

Figure 3.3   Japan: electricity by source 1980
Source: 2000 World Bank Development Indicators.

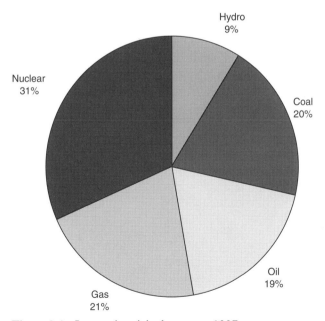

Figure 3.4   Japan: electricity by source 1997
Source: 2000 World Bank Development Indicators.

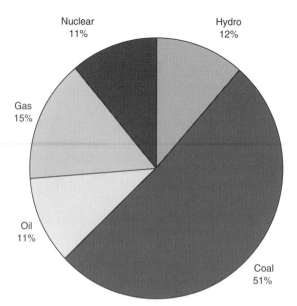

Figure 3.5   US: electricity by source 1980
Source: 2000 World Bank Development Indicators.

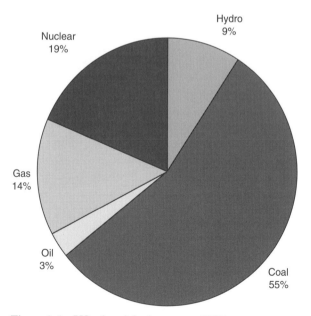

Figure 3.6   US: electricity by source 1997
Source: 2000 World Bank Development Indicators.

like the Sierra Club and the National Audubon Society, saw their membership swell. The Sierra Club went from a membership of approximately 15,000 in 1960 to 136,000 twelve years later. The National Audubon Society saw its 1960 membership of 32,000 increase by over seven-fold by 1972. By 1983, its membership was close to half-a-million. New groups, like FOE, EDF, and NRDC also saw their memberships explode. By 1983, respectively, just thirteen and fourteen years after their founding, FOE had 29,000 members and NRDC had 45,000 members. The combined membership of the nation's eleven largest national environmental groups went from 124,000 in 1960 to 819,000 in 1969 and almost 2 million by 1983.[3]

US environmental groups' success at membership expansion was the result of a number of factors. The appeal of their issues was important. Environmental awareness in the country was high as a result of the popularization of environmental books, the 1970 Earth Day extravaganza, and high media attention.

It is questionable, however, if the environmental groups could have attracted so many members without the special status accorded them by the state. It is relatively easy for environmental groups in the US to obtain legal standing as a public foundation and tax-exempt status under sections 501(c)(3) and 501(c)(4) of the tax code. Legal standing gives groups the right to enter into contracts, open bank accounts, and establish a name and an office. Tax-exempt status means that groups do not have to pay taxes on income derived for the maintenance of the group and that they can attract donations from individual contributors who can write them off of their own taxes and grants from foundations. In addition, 501(c)(3) status gives groups the right to lower postal rates, making mass mailings possible for educational purposes and to attract membership. Initially, there were strict limitations on the ability of public foundations to participate in lobbying activities. This was a great barrier to the environmental groups that clearly had an interest in lobbying Congress on legislation and in supporting some candidates with environmental views. The environmental community won a victory when a revision was made to the tax laws in 1976, allowing groups with 501(c)(3) status to spend up to 20 percent of their budget on lobbying. Many environmental organizations include both an arm of the organization set up under 501(c)(3) status and another under 501(c)(4).

The 501(c)(4) status is for groups that are engaged in substantial lobbying activities and thus have greater restrictions on their ability to receive

---

[3] Robert Cameron Mitchell, "From Conservation to Environmental Movement," in Lacey (ed.), *Government and Environmental Politics*, pp. 94–6.

non-taxable contributions and to avoid payment of taxes. 501(c)(4) status is for groups that are set up to promote social welfare; they may engage in substantial lobbying activities in order to gain legislation that is germane to the organization's purposes. Restrictions do apply on the ability of a 501(c)(4) organization to engage in direct or indirect participation or intervention in political campaigns on behalf of, or in opposition to, any candidate for public office, although some political activities are allowed. Expenditures made for political activities are usually subject to taxation.[4] The importance of these tax benefits to the US environmental community should not be underestimated. As the later comparison with the situation in Japan suggests, this institutional support can be assumed to have greatly aided the ability of environmental interests to organize, gain national recognition, and lobby policy makers.

US environmental groups have attempted to advance environmental quality through education, direct action, policy reform, and litigation. It is no accident that almost all of the major environmental groups and think tanks have offices in Washington, DC, where they can more easily try to push Congress and the administration to accept their views. Over the course of the 1960s and 1970s, US environmental groups became increasingly professional, relying less on volunteers and more and more on hired staff for legal activities, lobbying, and fund raising.

Another of the important gains made by US environmental groups in the 1960s was the expanded right of standing accorded them by the courts. In the past, groups only had the right to sue the government if it or its members had been harmed in a direct physical or economic way. This greatly limited the ability of environmental groups to work to protect the environment in general. These barriers were removed when the courts in a series of important cases in the mid-1960s expanded the class of interests that could seek judicial review and the set of issues for which a group could obtain standing. Environmental groups filed 1,900 lawsuits in the federal courts in the 1970s. Particularly active on the legal front have been NRDC, EDF, the Sierra Club Legal Defense Fund, and the National Wildlife Federation (NWF).[5] They based many of their challenges on the NEPA's requirement that environmental impact assessments be conducted for all federally funded projects. They also sued the government when it failed to enforce legislation or to bring regions into compliance with environmental standards. In sum, environmental

---

[4] http://www.irs.ustreas.gov/bus_info/eo/sw-exempt.html. See also Shaiko, *Voices and Echoes for the Environment*.

[5] Mitchell, "From Conservation to Environmental Movement," pp. 99–107.

NGOs were given powerful new rights and tools to use to try to influence environmental outcomes.[6]

Citizens' movements, democracy, and the environment in Japan and Germany

From a material perspective, the quality of life certainly had improved dramatically in Japan and Germany by the 1960s under the respective leadership of the LDP and the CDU. Economic recovery helped Japan's and Germany's new governments gain legitimacy. Yet, not all elements of society were equally pleased with the politics of the conservative governments. The electoral situation of the conservative parties became less certain. There were pockets of public dissatisfaction with aspects of the LDP's and CDU/CSU's economic and security policies and later with their social and environmental ones. Extra-parliamentary opposition became a thorn in the side of Japan's and Germany's otherwise remarkably successful postwar recoveries. Citizens began to challenge what they saw as the closed and secretive nature of governmental decision making. There were massive protests in Japan against the 1960 revision of the US–Japan Security Agreement, which was concluded by a highly questionable and rather undemocratic Diet maneuver by the LDP.[7] Protest groups emerged in both countries to challenge US and Soviet testing of nuclear weapons and there were active and at times violent student protests against the Vietnam War.[8] A primary goal of the extra-parliamentary movements was to expand citizen involvement in policy formation and to hold policy makers politically accountable. There were great concerns, particularly among youth, about whether or not their governments really were democratic in practice and not simply in name.

Ellis Krauss and Bradford Simcock suggest that the idea of environmental citizens' movements in Japan originated in the anti-security treaty movement. The rise of citizens' movements, they argued, signaled the transition from traditional and deferential political culture to the

[6] Norman J. Vig, "Presidential Leadership and the Environment: From Reagan to Clinton," in Norman J. Vig and Michael E. Kraft (eds.), *Environmental Policies in the 1990s: Reform or Reaction* (Washington, DC: Congressional Quarterly Press, 1997), pp. 98–101; Joel A. Mintz, *Enforcement at the EPA: High Stakes and Hard Choices* (Austin: University of Texas Press, 1995), pp. 40–83.

[7] Junnosuke Masumi (translated by Lonny E. Carlile), *Contemporary Politics in Japan* (Berkeley: University of California Press, 1995), p. 27.

[8] Andrei S. Markovitz and Philip S. Gorski, *The German Left: Red, Green and Beyond* (New York: Oxford University Press, 1993), pp. 47–9.

institutionalization of grass roots participatory democracy.[9] Kurt Sontheimer similarly argues that the growth of citizens' initiatives in Germany would have been inconceivable "without the transformation of political awareness brought about by the student protest movement and without the general tendency it triggered to represent civil rights, particularly those of minorities, in a more resolute, if not to say radical, fashion vis-à-vis the state."[10] Although it did not achieve many of its goals, the anti-authoritarian ideals of the student movement were a precursor to other new social movements that questioned the conservative politics of the Adenauer and Erhard years and the politics of the Grand Coalition between the SPD and the CDU. The student movement's concern with democratic decision making and the direction of national and foreign policies were later incorporated as central elements of the environmental movement.

As discussed in the previous chapter, beginning in the 1960s and into the 1970s, there was an explosion of grass roots environmentalism. It happened first in Japan and several years later in Germany. Citizens' movements (*jûmin undô* and *shimin undô*) in Japan and citizens' initiatives (*Bürgerinitiativen*) in Germany, as they are usually called, arose to protest development that threatened human health and the environment. The citizens' groups were similar in many ways, although the movements had more political impact in Japan a decade before they did in Germany. Margaret McKean described the citizens' movements she studied in Japan in the 1970s as "grass-roots movements independently organized by the members themselves (or founded by local opinion leaders acting in a private capacity), not by external forces and particularly not by established authority." They were groups "engaged in protest against established authority, as distinguished from 'cooperative' groups, often sponsored by neighborhood associations whose very raison d'être is to work with local government." Japan's citizens' movements, she suggested, were "concerned about a local problem (such as pollution) that affects the livelihood or well-being of ordinary people, as opposed, for example, to foreign policy issues."[11] Writing about the citizens' initiatives in Germany, B. Guggenberger similarly described them as

spontaneous, loosely organized association[s] of citizens, normally in existence for a limited period of time only, who directly affected by a specific issue, intercede outside the traditional institutions and participatory forms of representative party

---

[9] Krauss and Simcock, "Citizens' Movements," pp. 187–9.
[10] Quoted in Rob Burns and Wilfried van der Will, *Protest and Democracy in West Germany: Extra-Parliamentary Opposition and the Democratic Agenda* (New York: St. Martin's Press, 1988), p. 165.
[11] McKean, *Environmental Protest and Citizen Politics*, p. 8.

democracy and who seek, either by way of self-help or by way of influencing public opinion and exercising political pressure, to prompt action on the part of the authorities with regard to the citizens' particular concern.[12]

Many scholars saw the rise of citizens' movements as a sign of a new era in Japanese politics and the beginning of a new form of participatory democracy and even as "one of the most important and spectacular trends in contemporary Japanese history."[13] The citizens' movements were heralded as a sign of a civil society that was gaining power vis-à-vis the state.[14]

Similar arguments were made about developments in Germany. Carol Hager argues that grass roots groups emerged to challenge not only the construction of large technological projects (particularly power plants), but also the legitimacy of the bureaucratic institutions that created them.[15] This theme is a strong element in writings by German environmentalists. Sixty citizens' initiatives in Frankfurt portrayed themselves in a handbook: "The power of the bureaucrats, the unimaginativeness of the politicians, the overbearing attitude of the parties have begun to sway. A new power has formed itself in the country, right across the population, heterogeneous and diffuse, with the most varied goals, united only through the common will: we will now take our interest in our own hands."[16] The different fate of these movements in Japan and Germany is explored below.

Japan

The environment falls from the agenda

In contrast with the US and German cases and the predictions made by analysts of the period, by the late 1970s, Japan's environmental movement had been politically marginalized. There are many indications of the drop in political salience of the environment. Public and media attention to environmental issues dropped sharply. In the early 1970s, the newspapers were filled with pollution-related articles. There were over 1,600 articles on the environment in the *Asahi Shimbun* in 1970. In the mid-1970s, attention dropped off and by the end of the decade, although media attention was still higher than it had been throughout most of the 1960s, environmental reporting was far below its 1970 peak.[17]

---

[12] Quoted in Burns and van der Will, *Protest and Democracy in West Germany*, p. 164.
[13] Krauss and Simcock, "Citizens' Movements," pp. 187–8.
[14] McKean, *Environmental Protest and Citizen Politics*, pp. 213–36.
[15] Carol Hager, *Technological Democracy: Bureaucracy and Citizenry in the German Energy Debate* (Ann Arbor: University of Michigan Press, 1995).
[16] Quotation found in Sarkar, *Green-Alternative Politics*, p. 28.
[17] Count by Maharu Kitamura and Miranda Schreurs using indexes of the *Asahi Shimbun*.

Public opinion surveys also showed a drop in the percentage of the public that felt adversely affected by pollution. In 1973, the Prime Minister's Office conducted an opinion poll on the public's attitude towards pollution. Respondents were asked about the most serious pollution problem they had personally experienced in the last five years. Of those responding, 55.3 percent said they had not been affected by any problems, 15.8 percent complained about noise, and 10.2 percent complained about air pollution.[18] A very similar question asked in 1979 found that 68.7 percent had experienced no problems; 12.6 percent complained about noise and only 3.6 percent about air pollution.[19] The percentage of the public that felt personally affected by pollution had clearly dropped.

There is no available data on the actual number of environmental citizens' movements that still existed at the end of the 1970s. Still, there are many accounts that suggest that many of the groups disbanded.[20] This does not mean that there were no environmental citizens' movements left. NIMBY activities continued and some new environmental protection initiatives formed. There were still citizens' movements protesting developments that threatened their living environment or their health. For example, a citizens' movement in Musashino City, in western Tokyo, organized to protest high-rise construction that threatened to block all sunshine from residential areas in the early 1970s. Their efforts were later followed by other groups like those in Nishikamata in Tokyo, which made similar claims in the late 1970s.[21] Other groups continued to make demands for compensation on behalf of Minamata and other pollution disease victims.[22] In Zushi, a city that lies a short distance to the south of Tokyo, the Citizens' Association for the Protection of Nature and Children and the Ikego Green Operation Center formed in the early 1980s to protest against plans to build US military housing in the Ikego Forest. The mayor of the town initiated a lawsuit against the central government for starting construction in the river that runs through the area without first obtaining his approval. This was the first suit brought against the government on nature conservation grounds.[23]

[18] Sôrifu Naikaku Sôridaijin Kanbô Kôhôshitsu (ed.), *Kôgai Mondai ni Kansuru Yoron Chôsa*, *Chôsa 19*, October 1973.
[19] Sôrifu Naikaku Sôridaijin Kanbô Kôhôshitsu (ed.), *Kôgai Mondai ni Kansuru Yoron Chôsa Chôsa 20*, March 1979.
[20] Krauss and Simcock, "Citizens' Movements"; Broadbent, *Environmental Politics in Japan*.
[21] McKean, *Environmental Protest and Citizen Politics*, pp. 110–15.
[22] Michael Reich, *Toxic Politics: Responding to Chemical Disasters* (Ithaca: Cornell University Press, 1991).
[23] Kiichirô Tomino, "Wildlife and Environment: Citizens' Movement and the Environment: A Mayor's Experiments and Achievements," transcript of a speech presented at the Japan Society, November 4, 1991; and Huddle and Reich, *Island of Dreams*, pp. 15–19.

Domestic groups also successfully opposed the building of an airport on Ishigaki Island in a location that would have destroyed a precious blue coral reef. They failed, however, in their efforts to stop the damming of the Nagara River. Citizens' movements have pushed local recycling efforts, called for the greening of local environs, protested against the Resort Law, which promoted the building of golf courses and ski resorts, and opposed the expansion of airports at Narita and in Osaka.[24]

There also was considerable local opposition to the siting of nuclear power plants. Protest against the construction of the Hokkaido Electric Utility Company's Kyowa–Tomari nuclear power plant delayed construction by sixteen years. In this particular case, protest was organized by local fishermen who feared the impact that water pipes used for cooling by the plant would have on their catch. The JSP opposed construction both because of its general concerns about nuclear safety and its concerns about the impact a nuclear power plant would have on the coal industry in Hokkaido. There was also conflict within the prefectural assembly between those LDP members who supported production of nuclear energy and those who supported coal. In the end, the company was forced to modify its siting plans. Hayden Lesbirel calculated that, whereas the average lead-time to gain public acceptance for nuclear power plants in Japan was only two to three years in the 1960s, it reached fourteen to fifteen years in the 1980s.[25]

Unlike in Germany, the anti-nuclear movement in Japan, however, remained largely a NIMBY phenomenon. Anti-nuclear activities rarely moved outside of the towns and villages where nuclear power plants were to be located. MITI and industries' decision to site plants in remote coastal regions with small populations and low agricultural and economic productivity weakened the likelihood for intense opposition.

Proponents of a grievance-based model of social movement activity might argue that the decline in Japan's environmental movement occurred because the wind was taken out of its sails. There is some validity to this argument. As a result of earlier policy changes, Japan achieved one of the world's most rapid and successful air pollution control programs. Air pollution levels also showed some improvements in Germany, but they were far less dramatic than in Japan. A 1977 OECD report suggested that Japan was an example of how environmental regulation could be successfully integrated into a growing economy.[26]

[24] *Japan Environment Monitor*, 4, no. 7 (Nov./Dec. 1991).
[25] Hayden Lesbirel, "Implementing Nuclear Energy Policy in Japan: Top-Down and Bottom-Up Perspectives," *Energy Policy* (April 1990), 267–82; and Hayden Lesbirel, *NIMBY Politics in Japan: Energy Siting and the Management of Environmental Conflict* (Ithaca: Cornell University Press, 1998).
[26] OECD, *Environmental Politics in Japan* (Paris: OECD, 1977).

Policy implementation

It is interesting to reflect on why Japan was relatively successful in the implementation of many environmental laws when the environmental movement was weaker than in perhaps any other major industrialized state by the end of the decade. Understanding the primary reasons behind implementation success helps shed light on the environmental policy approach that was to come to dominate in Japan – one focused on administrative guidance, voluntary agreements, and a mix of incentives to improve performance and penalties for non-compliers.

Important in the implementation process was the support provided to industry by the government in the form of administrative guidance, research, and tax incentives. Also important was the role accorded to local governments. Typically, Japan is thought of as a country where local governments are weak relative to the central government. Yet, in the case of environmental protection, local governments have played a very important role in both the agenda setting and implementation process.

The central government permitted local governments to create extra-legal pollution control agreements with industries that resulted in the creation of more stringent pollution control standards than existed at the national level.[27] Pollution control agreements provided an avenue for citizen input into implementation at the local level that was by design, relatively non-politicized. Beginning in the 1960s, an extensive system of non-binding local agreements was established among industry, local governments, and citizens' movements that influenced control over development plans. The first such agreement emerged in 1964 between the City of Yokohama and two electric power companies in relation to the construction of a coal-fired power plant on reclaimed offshore land. Concerned with the health effects of pollution from the proposed plant in a densely populated urban region, the city succeeded in getting the companies to agree to pollution control measures that went beyond those existing nationally.[28]

There were only a few such agreements in the 1960s, but by 1970, over 800 had been established, and as of 1984, there were more than 25,000 agreements. Yamanouchi and Otsubo contend that these agreements are preferred by local governments to legally binding local ordinances because of their flexibility and speed. These agreements stipulate pollution

[27] Reed, *Japanese Prefectures and Policymaking*, pp. 63–87.
[28] Saburô Katô, "System for Regulation," in Nishimura (ed.), *How to Conquer Air Pollution*, pp. 197–238; Geoffrey W. G. Leane, "Environmental Contracts: A Lesson in Democracy from the Japanese," *U.B.C. Law Review* (1991), 361–85; Kazuo Yamanouchi and Kiyoharu Ôtsubo, "Agreements on Pollution Prevention: Overview and One Example," and Tokue Shibata, "Pollution Control Agreements: The Case of Tokyo and Other Local Authorities," in Tsuru and Weidner (eds.), *Environmental Policy in Japan*, pp. 246–51.

control standards that go at times far beyond those set nationally. They take various forms, being established between local government and industry, exclusively between citizens' groups and industry, and, at times, on a tri-partite basis. In response to air pollution control, these agreements limited emission concentration of pollutants, stipulated the installation of the latest pollution prevention technologies or even specified the type of facilities and technologies to be installed, and required industries to switch to low-sulfur fuels in air pollution emergencies. Enterprises were often forced to enter these agreements in order to get siting licenses or licenses to expand operations. They felt it necessary as well to maintain the peace with local citizens' groups. While these agreements are a form of administrative guidance and lack punitive measures, industries often had little choice but to abide by them or be subject to local boycotts or demonstrations or loss of a license. These agreements have given local governments considerable power over enforcement and in gaining industrial compliance with meeting national standards.[29] They may also have helped to keep environmental politics locally focused and to minimize the likelihood of environmental movement demonstrations.

The effectiveness of these local efforts was strengthened in the early 1970s by judicial involvement in the policy process. By establishing its willingness to adjudicate on environmental issues and to support the position of pollution victims, the courts sent a strong message to government and industry. Frank Upham has suggested that one reason why the LDP and the bureaucracy enforced the strict pollution laws passed in the early 1970s was that by doing so, they were able to take the momentum out of the citizens' movements and to dampen reliance on the courts as a means of dispute resolution.[30] Since the early 1970s, the government has encouraged citizen participation that is channeled through government-sponsored mediation. It is also important to note that the courts have not given citizens the same kind of broad rights of standing that are found in the US. The Japanese Supreme Court limits standing to plaintiffs whose legal right and duties are created or delimited by administrative acts. Many agency actions are not subject to judicial review. There is also no provision for class action suits. As a result, environmental litigation has "largely disappeared as a major political or legal factor in National policy."[31]

[29] Hiroshi Oda, "The Role of Criminal Law in Pollution Control," in Tsuru and Weidner (eds.), *Environmental Policy in Japan*, pp. 183–95.
[30] Upham, *Law and Social Change in Postwar Japan*.
[31] James V. Feinerman and Kôichirô Fujikura, "Japan: Consensus-Based Compliance," in Edith Brown Weiss and Harold K. Jacobson (eds.), *Engaging Countries: Strengthening Compliance with International Environmental Agreements* (Cambridge: MIT Press, 1998), p. 263.

The central government also encouraged research and development into pollution control technologies. Takashi Inoguchi argued that both the consensus decision-making culture of Japan and a government–business relationship which is close and strong but in which the government cannot impose its will makes for a system that is slow in reaching decisions, but effective at implementing them.[32] One way MITI and the Ministry of Finance could win industrial cooperation in investing in pollution control technologies was through favorable tax incentives. Private investment in pollution control reached an impressive 17.7 percent of total investment in equipment in 1974, after which point it dropped off somewhat, but remained at relatively high percentages: 13.3 percent in 1975 and 7.2 percent in 1976.[33]

The case of desulfurization technology is a good example of government–business cooperation in pollution control. While MITI and industry remained opposed to the establishment of SO_x emissions standards in the 1960s, behind the scenes, they were actively involved in developing desulfurization technology. The first large-scale project began in 1966. As a result of this project, a one-year desulfurization pilot project was set up in Yokkaichi in 1967 and an expanded pilot project began the following year.[34] Between 1966 and 1971, joint public–private research into desulfurization technology totaled over ¥2.6 billion. The government further promoted industrial efforts into research and development of heavy oil desulfurization and flue gas desulfurization with tax benefits and low interest financing from the Development Bank of Japan.

By 1970, the first five flue gas desulfurization units had been installed. By 1971, there were over 100 flue gas desulfurization units in place. An additional 1,000 units were installed at various plants, including oil refineries, thermal power plants, chemical plants, and iron and steel mills, in the next five years.[35] In contrast, it was not until 1977 that the first German plant was equipped with a flue gas desulfurization unit. In 1983, there were a total of ten plants equipped with flue gas desulfurization technology in Germany[36] compared with 1,405 in Japan. As of 1989,

---

[32] Takashi Inoguchi, "The Nature and Functioning of Japanese Politics," *Government and Opposition* 26 (1991), 185–98.

[33] Statistics cited in Ken'ichi Miyamoto, *Nihon no Kankyô Seisaku* (Tokyo: Ohtsuki Shoten, 1987), p. 27.

[34] Keizai Hôkoku Sentaa, Sangyô to Kankyô no kai, *Sangyô to Kankyô no Henyô*, August 1989.

[35] Environment Agency of Japan, *Japanese Performance of Energy Conservation and Air Pollution Control: How Japanese Performance Has Resulted in its Relatively Low Emissions of Greenhouse Gases among Industrialized Countries*, October 1990.

[36] Weidner, *Air Pollution Control Strategies*, p. 100. For data on desulfurization and denitrification units in Japan see Makoto Matsumura, "Challenging Acid Rain," *Journal of Japanese Trade and Industry* 2 (1991), 15–16.

Japan's 2,189 desulfurization and denitrification plants accounted for a remarkable 76 percent of the global total of such plants.[37] Japan made tremendous progress in implementing air pollution control measures and improving energy efficiency. These were areas where Japan excelled from a technological perspective. This is not to say that Japan was equally strong in all areas of environmental enforcement. Critics like Ken'ichi Miyamoto believed that the favorable 1977 OECD report on that status of environmental protection in Japan triggered a retreat in the government's environmental policies.[38] There certainly were still many environmental problems that needed to be addressed. These included the thousands of people waiting for certification as pollution victims in the late 1970s; the water pollution that was tied to the low percentage of homes having modern sewerage facilities and contamination from toxic wastes; and urban areas that suffered from very low ratios of green areas. In addition, the national parks remained sorely strained from heavy use and inadequate efforts devoted to preserving pristine areas. Wildlife and fragile coastal areas continued to be threatened by industrial expansion and the building of new roads and airports, including those in Osaka, Narita, and on Ishigaki Island. Asbestos regulations remained weak and illegal toxic dumping a serious problem. Moreover, as in Germany, an ambitious nuclear energy program was being pushed by the state.

The environmental movement in Japan, however, had arisen primarily as a victims' movement. These other environmental issues did not garner the same level of public attention as had the pollution problems that were threatening human health and welfare. This meant that the government did not feel as pressured to address these problem areas. It could focus on those areas where industry could excel – energy efficiency improvements, pollution control technology development, and production process improvements.

Environmental policy retreat

There were few new major environmental laws passed in Japan after the mid-1970s until the beginning of the 1990s. A major reason for this was the drop in public and media attention to the environment and the weakness of the Environment Agency. The drop in activities by environmental citizens' movements meant that the new Environment Agency was left without much support. After the first oil shock, resistance to further environmental regulation grew within industry and the LDP was pressured to ease up on environmental regulations.

[37] MoFA, *Japan's Environmental Endeavors*, April 1992.
[38] Miyamoto, *Nihon no Kankyō Seisaku*, p. 33.

In this milieu, the Environment Agency found itself on the defensive. The Environment Agency's budget stagnated, and then slightly declined. In 1977, the chairman of the LDP's environment division within the Policy Affairs Research Council suggested at a newspaper reporters' club that "in the future the Environment Agency should be scrapped." Nor was the Agency well liked by all environmental groups. A local newspaper reported an NGO representative at a meeting of pollution victims saying that such a useless Agency might as well be done away with.[39] Another problem for the Agency was its limited access to information, a form of power. Information tends not to flow freely among Japan's ministries and agencies. In addition, industry which is in control of much information relevant to environmental policy formation tended to share information only with MITI. This put the Environment Agency at a disadvantage.

The weakness of the Environment Agency is perhaps best illustrated by its failure in annual attempts beginning in 1975 to get an environmental impact assessment law passed over the objections of MITI and MoC.[40] For years, getting an environmental impact assessment law passed was a top priority of the Agency. Yet the Agency failed to get a law passed despite successive attempts at submitting a bill to the Diet. Finally, in 1984, the Agency gave in to a compromise solution. A Cabinet decision was made that before projects requiring government licensing or approval be carried out, contracting industries must conduct an assessment of the impact that the project will have on the environment, but there were no penalties for non-compliance. The Cabinet decision promoted essentially a form of administrative guidance.[41] Bemoaned an Environment Agency official, "Japan remains the only OECD member without an environmental impact assessment law."[42] (This changed in the spring of 1997.)

Germany

The environment falls from the agenda

When Helmut Schmidt succeeded Willy Brandt as chancellor in 1974, the environmental movement lost a powerful supporter. Whereas Brandt had made the environment an important part of his reformist policy package,

[39] Katô et al., "Kankyô Gyôsei 10 Nen no Ayumi," p. 40.
[40] Hirobumi Hatakeyama and Toshimitsu Shinkawa, "Kankyô Gyôsei ni Miru Gendai Nihon Seiji," in Ôtake Hideo (ed.), *Nihon Seiji no Sôten: Jirei Kenkyû ni yoru Seiji Taisei no Bunseki* (Tokyo: San'ichi Shobô, 1984), pp. 230–80.
[41] Brendan F. D. Barrett and Riki Therivel, "EIA in Japan: Environmental Protection v. Economic Growth," *Land Use Policy* (July 1989), 217–31; and Barrett and Therivel, *Environmental Policy and Impact Assessment in Japan*.
[42] Discussion with an Environment Agency official, June 22, 1995.

Schmidt showed little interest in furthering environmental protection efforts. Together with the new minister of economics, Hans Friederichs, Schmidt was a key figure in efforts to rollback the laws passed under his predecessor. They were seen as impediments to investment and general economic recovery. With the economy in recession and energy prices soaring as a result of the OPEC oil embargo, the environment took on a secondary role in the SPD's political strategy. Increasingly, the SPD left environmental protection to its junior coalition partner, the FDP.[43] Despite efforts on the part of the FDP's Günther Hartkopf to keep federal government support behind environmental initiatives, the junior coalition partner was able to do little more than to defend existing legislation. Symbolic of the shift in government attitude towards the environment was a conference held in Gymnich Castle in 1975. This closed gathering was organized by the Chancellor's Office and leading industrial interests to discuss environmental regulations and their effects on the economy. It was attended by officials from the federal government, several Länder governments, industry, labor unions, and, after protest by environmentalists at their exclusion – the Council of Environmental Experts. As a result of the new environmental regulations, participants argued that close to DM 50 billion had been lost in investments and that jobs in the energy sector and elsewhere were threatened. Because of the efforts of the Council of Environmental Experts, an agreement was reached to continue with environmental protection, but to try to reduce the costs of pollution control that industries had to shoulder and to simplify licensing procedures established under the Federal Emissions Control Act. In addition, industry won support for extended phase-in schedules for newly enacted environmental regulations and governmental agreement to strike down any further legislative initiatives that carried any financial burdens.[44] The meeting symbolized the change in the SPD's position on environmental protection and the opposition of industry to the stringency of the new laws.

As in Japan, the environment movement found itself on the defensive. The Ministry of the Interior managed to get an environmental impact assessment law enacted for public works' projects but not for private development plans.[45] Within the Ministry of Economics, also under FDP leadership, a special unit was established to check environmental policy initiatives for their economic costs, and a bill was drafted to take power plants out of the Federal Emissions Control Act. The FDP was divided

[43] Müller, *Innenwelt der Umweltpolitik*, p. 43.
[44] Weidner, "The Capability of the Capitalist State"; Barnes, "Established Parties"; Müller, *Innenwelt der Umweltpolitik*, pp. 97–102.
[45] Müller, *Innenwelt der Umweltpolitik*, p. 108.

between those who continued to support environmental protection initiatives and those with a strong tie to industry. While the bill did not pass, it was indicative of the Ministry of Economics' concerns about the effects of environmental regulations on the economy.[46]

An important case that reflected the strong pressures on the government to ease environmental standards centered around plans to expand the STEAG coal-fired power plant, one of the largest postwar investment projects in Germany. The plant was located in Voerde, a small town in the Ruhr district of North Rhine–Westphalia. STEAG argued that it had been granted approval for the construction before technical emissions and ambient air guidelines were tightened up under the 1974 Federal Emissions Control Law and the related Technical Guidelines, although it was granted approval in the same month that the new law came into effect. Moreover, STEAG argued that, upon request of the North Rhine–Westphalia government, it had agreed to adopt standards for a four-year transitional period established under the new Federal Emissions Control Law. It had also agreed to reduce existing pollution levels in the area by increasing the height of chimney stacks and reducing pollution emitted by a nearby coal-fired power plant.

Environmentalists challenged the licensing approval given to the power plant by the Industrial Supervisory Board of Duisburg on the grounds that the expansion of the plant would result in pollution levels higher than those permitted under the Technical Guidelines attached to the Federal Emissions Control Law. In September 1975, they won an injunction by the Administrative Court in Düsseldorf that blocked construction on environmental grounds. The court said that the project could only proceed if measures to reduce the pollution already in the area were taken and these steps guaranteed that expansion of the plant would not exceed the newly established ambient air quality standards. The Administrative Court did not accept the measures proffered by STEAG as sufficient. The Court also concluded that the standards that applied to the plant were those in the amended Technical Guidelines and not those for the four-year transitional period under the Technical Guidelines for the Federal Emissions Control Law.

In reaction, parliamentarians supportive of the project introduced a draft bill to the Bundestag. The STEAG bill removed some of the obstacles to construction of the power plant created by the court's decision. Specifically, amendments were made to the Federal Emissions Control Law that allowed the standards established for the four-year transitional period to apply to all plants for which a permit was required or for which

[46] Hucke, "Environmental Policy," p. 161.

approval was granted during the transitional period. The Bundestag made this bill its first amendment to the Federal Emissions Control Act.[47] When a Higher Administrative Court in Münster confirmed the decision by the Administrative Court to stop construction of the STEAG plant on the grounds that the projected plant would increase SO_x levels above those permitted under the Technical Guidelines of 1974, industry and trade unions demanded that the federal government clarify the requirements for the licensing of power plants so that individuals could not block economically important projects. This was an attempt on their part to prevent the tightening of restrictions at the Länder level through court actions undertaken by citizens' initiatives. They preferred federal regulations, since this would provide a uniform playing field for industry throughout the country. Efforts to impose such a standard made their way into the Ministry of Economics' Third Energy Program of 1978.

The federal Cabinet also called upon the Ministry of the Interior to prepare proposals for accelerating the licensing procedure for coal-fired power plants with the stipulation that greater consideration be given to the effects on employment and economic growth of environmental protection. The legislative initiative, however, lost much of its urgency after the federal Administrative Court in Berlin reversed the decision of the lower court and dismissed the challenge to the construction of the STEAG plant in 1978. The Bundestag ended its term before moving on the matter.[48]

Policy implementation

Numerous scholars have referred to Germany's implementation deficit (*vollzugs defizit*) in the environmental area in the 1970s.[49] Despite broad support for the 1971 Environmental Program, there was considerable opposition when it came to the passage of specific pieces of legislation. Many aspects of the proposed laws set forth in the Environmental Program of 1971 were weakened during the process of legislation. The Toxic Substances Act was reduced to a relatively weak procedure of registration for new toxic substances. The Federal Conservation Act exempted almost all agricultural activities and the Traffic Noise Law failed altogether because

[47] Heinrich Siegmann, *The Conflicts between Labor and Environmentalism in the Federal Republic of Germany and the United States* (New York: St. Martin's Press, 1985).
[48] Gabriele Knödgen, "The STEAG Coal-Fired Power Plant at Voerde or Changing German Clean Air Policy," paper from the International Institute for Environment and Society of the Science Center Berlin, November 1981.
[49] Renate Mayntz, "Intergovernmental Implementation of Environmental Policy," in Kenneth Hanf and Fritz Scharpf (eds.), *Interorganizational Policy Making: Limits to Coordination and Central Control* (Beverley Hills, CA: Sage Publications, 1978).

of local opposition. The Bundesrat opposed the extension of Federal powers in the areas of water quality, nature protection and conservation because of Länder opposition to any further centralization of government power.[50] Enforcement of legislation has remained highly fragmented in Germany and "is often identified as the weakest point in an otherwise ambitious system."[51] Several mechanisms were established to deal with the horizontal and vertical fragmentation. These included the establishment of a Working Group for Environmental Questions, a forum for information exchange among administrators, politicians, communities, and industry. The Working Group strengthened the position of the Ministry of the Interior in interministerial negotiations by providing it with access to information of a technical and scientific nature. Annual conferences among environmental ministers at the federal and Länder levels were also begun in 1972. This became an arena for bureaucrats with a common interest to strengthen their bargaining positions. These mechanisms, however, were more useful in achieving compromises in the formulation of environmental policy than they were in its successful implementation.

In the case of the Federal Emissions Control Act, for instance, the federal government gained the authority to issue ordinances and administrative rules related to air pollution despite early opposition from North Rhine–Westphalia and several southern Länder, all of which were under CDU/CSU governments. New Technical Instructions for Maintaining Air Purity were also established.[52] The Länder retained considerable power to influence standards and approaches to air pollution control, because their consent must be obtained in the Bundesrat before an air pollution control bill can be enacted. The new technical instructions replaced those of 1964 and provided instructions for implementation. Implementation, however, remained a Länder responsibility. The Länder, therefore, each determined their own institutional forms for enforcement of the Federal Emissions Control Act. Each Länder had its own system for dealing with the licensing of plants and at times this meant a delegating of responsibility to regional and local levels.[53] Enforcement depended greatly on the enthusiasm of different regions for the laws.

---

[50] Müller, *Innenwelt der Umweltpolitik*, p. 83; Hucke, "Environmental Policy," p. 62.
[51] Boehmer-Christiansen and Skea, *Acid Politics*, p. 178.
[52] Boehmer-Christiansen and Skea, *Acid Politics*; Weidner, *Air Pollution Control Strategies*, p. 51; U. E. Simonis, "The German Experience," paper presented at the International Conference on Ecology and Environment in the 90s, Aula des Jeunes-Rives, University of Neuchatel, August 26–7, 1991.
[53] OECD, *Environmental Performance Review: Germany* (Paris: OECD, 1993), p. 28.

Under the Federal Emissions Control Act, industries were required to use state of the art technology in pollution control, but the ambiguity of this requirement led to long negotiations between the government, industry, and the public over the precise meaning of state of the art or "appropriate technologies." By reference to technical difficulties or "excessive" economic costs, companies could avoid measures aimed at cutting down emissions in existing plants. Injunctions could be appealed in court, leading to lengthy delays in implementation. This contrasts with the situation in Japan where similar vagueness in laws is a means for the government to employ administrative guidance with industry to obtain desired policy goals. In the German judicial and legislative arena, however, the vagueness of terminology was as problematic as it would be in the US. The Länder and municipal governments in Germany felt that they had only limited means at their disposal to force existing plants to adopt measures to reduce emissions. Another weakness was that the law provided companies with few incentives to improve existing technologies from an environmental perspective. The legislation was primarily targeted at assuring that "state of the art technology" be employed in new facilities and not that improvements be made to existing equipment.

In contrast with Japan, power plant operators in Germany were opposed to licensing specifications that included flue gas desulfurization technology as part of the "state of the art technology" on the grounds of cost. In the STEAG coal-fired power plant case discussed above, the company argued that the technology was not sufficiently advanced. Interestingly, the North Rhine–Westphalia government rejected this appeal pointing to the successful operation of desulfurization units in Japan.[54]

While investment levels in pollution control increased in Germany in the 1970s, sharp increases did not occur until 1984. It is problematic to compare directly investment levels in air pollution control in Japan, Germany, and the US, due to differences in how these statistics are collected. Still, differences in their trend lines are noteworthy. Whereas investment levels in Japan showed a dramatic rise in the 1970s, a similar dramatic rise did not occur in Germany until a decade later, after the passage of the Large Combustion Plant Directive in 1983. Incentives to invest in pollution control appear to have been stronger in Japan than Germany during the 1970s. In the US, because older plants were grandfathered from emissions reduction requirements, investment levels in pollution control were also far less than in Japan.

An analysis by Helmut Weidner and Peter Knoepfel of air pollution control in Germany in the early 1980s concluded that, between 1966

[54] Knödgen, "The STEAG Coal-Fired Power Plant," pp. 54–60.

and 1978, sulfur dioxide emissions had changed only marginally. They concluded that, although Germany has the most restrictive air pollution control regulations in Europe, as well as the most developed administrative system for implementation and the most comprehensive licensing procedures for large polluters, there had been no progress in air pollution abatement.[55]

Grass roots activism

Whereas the activities of citizens' movements in Japan became less visible over the course of the mid- to late 1970s, in Germany, the environmental movement exploded in size and dramatically increased its visibility. The *Bürgerinitiativen* went through three distinct phases. Initially, they were primarily concerned with local environmental and quality of life issues. While their numbers grew quickly, they were not yet a powerful political force. The second phase coincided with the SPD's loss of interest in the environment soon after Helmut Schmidt came to power. The third phase began at the end of the 1970s, when green lists emerged at the local level, beginning a process that was to alter fundamentally how environmental opinions were brought into the policy-making process.

The German population was not all that "green" in the early 1970s. Indeed, a 1975 Eurobarometer survey found that Germans were less concerned about forming a common policy within the EC for the protection of nature and fighting pollution than individuals surveyed in any of the other eight members of the EC. At some point in the middle of the 1970s, however, that began to change. A Eurobarometer survey taken in 1976 found that the percentage of German respondents rating the environment as very important had doubled from its 1975 level of 33 percent to 66 percent.[56] This coincided with several major anti-nuclear and environmental protest activities.

By the mid-1970s, environmental movements were playing an increasingly visible role in German politics. Robert Burns and Wilfried van der Will suggest that, while citizens' associations had a long history in Germany, in the 1970s, there was such a proliferation in their numbers that "by the middle of the decade the *Bürgerinitiativen* had become an established feature of the West German political culture."[57]

Bürgerinitiativen began to expand their thematic interests and to consolidate organizationally at the regional and federal levels. They showed

---

[55] Peter Knoepfel and Helmut Weidner, *Luftreinhaltepolitik in internationalen Vergleich* (Berlin: Sigma, 1995).
[56] Commission of the European Community, "Euro-barometre, Public Opinion of the European Community," June–July 1975, Table 3, A 12.
[57] Burns and van der Will, *Protest and Democracy in West Germany*, pp. 163–4.

increasing awareness of the relationships between various problems, such as energy, traffic, urban planning, and environmental protection, and established new environmental groups to deal with them. These included the Citizen Action for the Coasts, the Citizens' Initiative for the Protection of the Lower Elbe, and the BBU. The BBU was formed by fifteen regional groups as an umbrella organization in 1972 and rapidly expanded in membership over the next few years. While many claim that the BBU peaked in membership in the late 1970s with 1,000 groups and a membership of somewhere between 300,000 to 1.5 million members, Rucht argues that these figures were largely exaggerated, in part because members themselves often made overly generous estimates. He suggests that there were instead some 450 direct member groups, with a total membership of 50,000 individuals.[58] Regardless of the actual numbers, this umbrella group was certainly large and very important in mobilizing and coordinating extra-parliamentary protest activities. The role of the BBU was particularly important in protests against nuclear power plant sitings.

It is difficult to get a good sense for just how many citizens' initiatives there were in Germany. U. Margedant estimated that their numbers fluctuated between 15,000 and 50,000 with between 40 and 45 percent engaged in environmental protests by 1975 and 1976.[59] Lutz Mez estimated that there were between 15,000 and 20,000 citizens' initiatives at this time, 3,000 to 4,000 of which were concerned with environmental problems.[60] Far more modest figures made by analysts suggest that there were only from 1,000 to 4,000 citizens' initiatives in the early 1970s, and far more than that after 1975. According to one estimate, after 1974, protection of the environment in urban and rural areas became the major concern of the *Bürgerinitiativen* with close to 40 percent of the citizens' initiatives considering themselves environmental.[61] The large differences in these figures reflect in part differences in the definitions used in counting groups as well as the difficulty of making such a count. Whatever the exact figures, what is clear is that, whereas the citizens' movements in Japan appear to have peaked in number in the first half of the 1970s, they continued to grow in number in Germany in the second half of the decade and to change dramatically their protest strategies. They expanded their interests and linked their concerns with those of the peace, anti-nuclear, and women's movements.

---

[58] Dieter Rucht, "Von der Bewegun zur Institution? Organisationsstrukturen der Ökologiebewegung," in Roth and Rucht (eds.), *Neue soziale Bewegungen*, p. 253.

[59] Cited in Weidner, "The Capability of the Capitalist State," p. 17; and Wey, *Umweltpolitik in Deutschland*, p. 171.

[60] Mez, "Von den Bügerinitiativen zu den GRÜNEN," pp. 263–4.

[61] Sarkar, *Green-Alternative Politics*, pp. 36–8.

In their study of the "red" and "green" elements of German society, Andrei Markovitz and Philip Gorski contend that Green Parties only emerged in countries where social democratic parties shared or were in control of government. In these countries, corporatist forms of conflict mediation were important. Reforms were extended into new domains by the social democratic parties in the early 1970s when economic growth rates were still relatively high. They found themselves in trouble, however, when the economic situation changed. They started to slash the very programs upon which their party support depended. In doing this, they provided fodder for the emergence of new political parties.

This appears to have been the case in Germany. In the wake of the energy crisis, the SPD and FDP further strengthened grass roots protest movements by supporting the nuclear energy industry. This alienated many of the SPD's and FDP's supporters. Both parties had won support from student groups and citizens' initiatives when they announced their reformist party platform. After the oil shock and with the transition from Brandt to Schmidt, however, the SPD turned its back on the more radical movements that had given it support, including the Maoist-inspired K groups (Communist groups) and young Socialists. The expulsion of these groups by the SPD/FDP coalition made them ready candidates for cooperation with anti-nuclear and environmental advocates. Their involvement added a radical and strongly pro-egalitarian element to the environmental movement.[62]

The anti-nuclear movement   The SPD's and FDP's support of the nuclear industry came to dominate the environmental debate. In 1975, protest against the building of a nuclear power plant in the town of Whyl in southwestern Germany culminated in the occupation of the construction site by citizens' initiatives and other protesters. When police forced the protesters from the site, a second larger demonstration occurred and an estimated 28,000 people set up camp to block construction. Protest remained non-violent. The protesters' efforts were rewarded when an administrative court called a halt to construction.

The Whyl demonstration spurred on other citizens' initiatives and opened the road for cooperation among different kinds of movements in their growing push to reform German political institutions. In 1976, thousands of citizens gathered in the village of Brokdorf in the north to oppose construction of another nuclear power plant. Protest turned violent when police and protesters clashed. There was also a

[62] Markovitz and Gorski, *The German Left*, pp. 14–28.

counter-demonstration of an estimated 7,000 employees of the largest German manufacturer of power plants, the Kraftwerk Union, pitting environmentalists against labor union members. Tensions between anti-nuclear activists and environmentalists, on the one side, and the energy industry and labor unions, on the other, remained high as protests against nuclear power facilities and coal-fired power plants spread. The violence in Brokdorf was repeated in protests against the building of a reactor in Grohnde. Hearings on plans to build a nuclear waste reprocessing plant in Gorleben in Lower Saxony coincided with the Three Mile Island reactor accident in the US and led to a march by an estimated 50,000 to 100,000 individuals. Later that year, an even larger number convened in Bonn to demonstrate against the government's nuclear program and in support of a reorientation of environmental policies.[63]

The government reacted to these large anti-nuclear demonstrations (as well as to a fear of terrorism) by restricting the right of demonstration. To the movement, this was a sign that Germany was not a true democracy. Already angered by the strong tactics used by authorities at the federal, Länder, and local levels against demonstrators, the environmental movement began to seek new strategies.

The rise of the Green Party

The protests against nuclear power were behind an emergent sympathy for ecological parties. A Batelle Institute Study conducted in 1975 found that 72 percent of the citizens in Freiburg and 63 percent of the people in Emmendingen, both election districts in the vicinity of Whyl, felt that the existing parties did not represent their interests and therefore they turned to citizens' initiatives. An opinion poll conducted in August 1977 found that 25.1 percent of the people questioned wanted to vote for an ecological party.[64]

The movement began to consider the need to reform the political system from within through the formation of an environmental party. This decision, however, was by no means unanimous. The environmental movement was never all that cohesive in its goals or unified in its support of pursuing change through parliamentary means. For many, the formation of an environmental party was antithetical to the democratic goals – the *Basis demokratie* – of the movement. Yet, there was a growing belief within the movement that large-scale demonstrations were having

---

[63] Siegmann, *The Conflicts between Labor and Environmentalism*, pp. 15–20.
[64] Reported in Mez, "Von den Bügerinitiativen zu den GRÜNEN," p. 268.

little real impact and that the only way to transform the state was to transform the system from within.[65]

The success of the French ecology movement in local elections in March 1977 provided encouragement to Germany's citizens' initiatives, as did the success of a *Bürgerinitiativ-Liste* in a district election in Berlin in March 1975 when it received 14.3 percent of the vote.[66] The *Bürgerinitiativen* continued their extra-parliamentarian activities, but they also began to work towards the establishment of a parliamentarian "green" branch. They were aided in these efforts by the organizational skills provided by SPD members who had become disenchanted with the pro-nuclear policies of Schmidt's government.[67] A few CDU members, such as Herbert Gruhl, also defected to the Greens. Gruhl was a founder of the first Green Party, the Grüne Aktin Zukunft.[68]

Ecological lists won in local elections in Lower Saxony in October 1977 and in Schleswig-Holstein in March 1978. Green lists won their first parliamentary seats at the Länder level in Bremen, Hamburg, and Hess in 1979. Soon afterwards, a Green Party was formed at the federal level by the merger of the Grüne Liste Umweltschutz, the Grüne Liste Schleswig-Holstein, the Grüne Aktion Zukunft, the Aktionsgemeinschaft Unabhängigger Deutscher, and several smaller groups. In January 1980, the Green Party was formally established at a conference in Karlsruhe in time to run for elections in the European parliamentary and Bundestag elections.

The Greens received 1.5 percent of the vote in the 1980 Bundestag election. Their strongest showings were in Hamburg, Bremen, and Hesse. They expanded their representation to seven of the eight Länder parliaments. In 1983, the Greens received 5.6 percent of the vote in the federal election and became a new force in German politics.[69] In 1981, representatives of the Green Party or various green–alternative lists held still only 1.4 percent of all local council seats in communities of over 20,000

---

[65] Helmut Fogt, "The Greens and the New Left: Influences of Left-Extremism on Green Party Organisation and Policies," in Eva Kolinsky (ed.), *The Greens in West Germany* (Oxford: GERG, 1989), pp. 89–121; and Horst Mewes, "History of the German Green Party," in Margit Mayer and John Ely (eds.), *The German Greens: Paradox between Movement and Party* (Philadelphia: Temple University Press, 1998), pp. 29–48.

[66] Mez, "Von den Bügerinitiativen zu den GRÜNEN," p. 270.

[67] Hucke, "Environmental Policy," p. 163.

[68] Elim Papadakis, *The Green Movement in West Germany* (London: Croom Helm, 1984), pp. 158–63.

[69] Katzenstein, *Policy and Politics in West Germany*, pp. 356–60.

inhabitants. By 1986, this figure had climbed to 7 percent.[70] The success of the Greens is the main reason why the established parties became active in the following years in addressing domestic and newly emerging international environmental issues.

Political opportunity structures, resource mobilization, and the development of environmental policy communities

The institutional structures of a state can influence the shape that environmental policy communities take. A nation's political opportunity structure is defined by Sydney Tarrow as "the dimensions of the political environment which either encourage or discourage people from using collective action."[71] Kitschelt suggests that institutional rules such as those reinforcing patterns of interaction between interest groups and government and electoral laws can facilitate or impede the institutionalization of new groups and claims. Kitschelt argues that systems tend to be more open to movement demands where there are more parties, the legislature is relatively powerful vis-à-vis the bureaucracy, and there are precipitating issues for individuals to mobilize around.

After analyzing anti-nuclear power movements of the 1970s in several countries, Kitschelt classified Germany's political output structure as closed on the input side and weak on the output side. He considered it closed on the input side because of a party system that drew parties to the center and where parties were organized along class and religious lines. Moreover, he argued, Germany's legislature was relatively weak and the executive inaccessible making it difficult for groups outside the system to influence policy outcome. On the output side Kitschelt suggested that the German state was relatively weak, particularly because of jurisdictional and territorial fragmentation and the problems that this caused for implementation.

The emergence of Germany's anti-nuclear movement and the Green Party, argues Kitschelt, can be considered as responses to the inability of anti-nuclear groups to effect change working within the system. The highly formalistic regulatory framework kept movements largely out of any direct participation in the environmental policy formation and implementation processes.[72] Although court cases often led to significant delays in construction, the courts rarely ruled in favor of plaintiffs. Activists

---

[70] Scharf, *The German Greens*, p. 72.   [71] Tarrow, *Power in Movement*, p. 18.
[72] Susan Rose Ackerman, *Controlling Environmental Policy: The Limits of Public Law in Germany and the United States* (New Haven: Yale University Press, 1995), pp. 10–12.

resorted to protests, but the state failed to respond to their demands. The state, argues Kitschelt, thus, "unwittingly fueled the movement's mobilization and thwarted the nuclear program."[73]

When the protest movements failed to alter the direction of government policy, the movement, which also feared being labeled as violent, began to search for other means to influence policy. An uneasy coalition formed among the peace movement, the anti-nuclear activists, the environmentalists, and the women's movement. The movements turned to the electoral system. They formed alliances as Green lists and parties at the local and then regional and federal levels.

While political opportunity structures may be considered to be relatively fixed, a successful movement can change institutions, opening the system to new actors and interests.[74] Baumgartner and Jones, for example, suggest that fundamental changes in how individuals view some aspect of the world can bring new actors into the policy-making process. As ideas are challenged and new actors enter the political arena, there can be changes to policy as well as to more basic formal or informal institutional structures.[75]

This is the case in Germany. Thus, whereas the system was relatively closed to environmental activists in the 1970s, as we will see in the next chapter, with the birth of the Green Party many changes to both formal and informal policy-making procedures were made considerably opening access channels to policy makers. Indeed, Germany can now be considered among the more open systems when it comes to environmental interest representation.[76]

The US electoral and political system is not conducive to the maintenance of third parties although it is generally viewed as relatively open to interest groups since they can lobby Congress and the White House, make use of the courts, or work up through the state level to influence policy change. Still, as with Germany, the system is more open today than it was in the 1970s. The court's decision to enhance the legal rights of environmental activists and subsequent changes to the laws governing non-profit organizations opened the system and enhanced the opportunity for movements to form as national environmental organizations.

---

[73] Kitschelt, "Political Opportunity Structures and Political Protest," 57–85, quotation on 76. See also Herbert S. Kitschelt, *The Logic of Party Formation: Structure and Strategy of Belgian and West German Ecology Parties* (Ithaca: Cornell University Press, 1989).

[74] Kitschelt, "Political Opportunity Structures and Political Protest," pp. 57–85.

[75] Baumgartner and Jones, *Agendas and Instability in American Politics*.

[76] Hanspeter Kriesi, "The Political Opportunity Structure of New Social Movements: Its Impact on their Mobilization," in J. Craig Jenkins and Bert Klandermans (eds.), *The Politics of Social Protest: Comparative Perspectives on States and Social Movement* (Minneapolis: University of Minnesota Press, 1995), p. 173.

Japan's case is quite different. Japan's political opportunity structure in the 1970s also was relatively closed to the demands of environmentalists and anti-nuclear activists due to the domination of politics by the conservative LDP and the weakness of the opposition parties. Moreover, the bureaucracy dominated policy making, and there was no obvious bureaucratic access point for activists to try to influence policy direction since there were so few officials in any of the ministries working on environmental matters. The system was, in short, unresponsive to victims' demands. This led to the kind of use of the courts and protest tactics witnessed in both Germany and the US. In response, the state felt pressured to respond to the growing power of the movement incorporating the movement's objectives into its policy platform. While not everyone will agree, it can also be argued that the bureaucracy performed quite well in terms of environmental policy implementation. Thus, the movement's *raison d'être* was weakened. Also important was that the state encouraged the formation of alternative channels for groups to influence the implementation process at the local level through locally formulated pollution control agreements. This reduced the potential for remaining groups to use the courts or to attempt change by mobilizing at the national level. This may not have been possible had the central authorities not delegated authority to local levels, permitting the establishment of emissions standards that went beyond those established at the national level. There was no serious effort on the part of Japan's environmental community to form a Green Party as occurred in Germany.

Movement resources

It is also important to think about the resources that movements can attract from constituent or non-constituent supporters. These resources might include information, media coverage, financial donations, leadership, or time – the elements necessary for movements to carry out their goals.[77] Also important are the laws governing the formation and operation of non-profit organizations, the availability of government grants and contracts, and the existence of private foundation support.[78] The US and Germany provided such support, albeit because of their different political systems in very different ways. In Japan's case, movement activists have been severely hampered by lack of access to basic resources necessary for groups to maintain themselves.

Germany's well-organized citizens' movements had the organizational skills, membership potential, and funding potential necessary to launch

---

[77] McCarthy and Zald, "Resource Mobilization and Social Movements," pp. 1212–41.
[78] Jack L. Walker, *Mobilizing Interest Groups in America: Patrons, Professions, and Social Movements* (Ann Arbor: University of Michigan Press, 1991).

a successful political campaign. While the 5 percent of the vote necessary to gain representation in the Bundestag was a formidable barrier to entry, it was not insurmountable. One could even argue that it provided considerable incentive to the diverse elements that merged to form the Green Party to work together to achieve their goals. Credibility gained through electoral success at the local level provided incentives to organize a Green Party at the federal level. The Green Party, moreover, received subsidies from the state, as do all "organizations" that receive at least 0.5 percent of the national vote. Thus, in addition to the benefits that movement organizations could accrue from non-profit status and the financial support that they could receive from members and other organizations, such as the churches, the political arm of the environmental community in Germany received substantial funding from the state. Environmental groups in the US could also relatively easily obtain non-profit status, raise tax-deductible donations from members, receive tax-deductible grants from private foundations, and obtain contracts and grants from government.

The situation was quite different in Japan. In her influential study of citizens' movements in Japan, Margaret McKean argued that one reason why the movements in Japan failed to form umbrella organizations as happened in Germany was their local orientation and local goals. The citizens' movements she interviewed feared being coopted by outsiders.[79] Another option that McKean did not consider was the role of the laws governing the formation of non-profit organizations in Japan. Until the Non-Profit Organization Law was amended in 1998, it was extremely difficult to gain tax-exempt status in Japan – considered almost a prerequisite to a group's survival in the US and Germany.[80] Based on Article 34 of Japan's Civil Code, which was promulgated in 1896, it was necessary to obtain approval from the "competent authorities" before an NGO could obtain non-profit status. The "competent authorities" were those local or national level government offices with some jurisdiction over an issue area. Obtaining approval from national ministries proved a tremendous barrier of entry for national level environmental groups.[81] Nancy London argues that "[t]he lack of predictability in the incorporation process often has a debilitating effect on smaller, private nonprofit initiatives...

---

[79] McKean, *Environmental Protest and Citizen Politics*.
[80] See Robert Pekkanen, "Japan's New Politics: The Case of the NPO Law," *Journal of Japanese Studies* 26 (2000), 111–48; Tadashi Yamamoto (ed.), *Deciding the Public Good: Governance and Civil Society in Japan* (Tokyo: Japan Center for International Exchange, 1999); and Lester M. Salamon and Helmut K. Anheier, *The Emerging Sector: An Overview* (New York: Manchester University Press), pp. 83–4.
[81] Toshirô Menju and Takako Aoki, "The Evolution of Japanese NGOs in the Asia Pacific Context," in Tadashi Yamamoto (ed.), *Emerging Civil Society in the Asia Pacific Community* (Tokyo: Japan Center for International Exchange, 1995), pp. 143–60.

[S]maller endeavors are often stymied at the start, not knowing where or how to begin and not able to commit time and money to a process whose outcome is so uncertain."[82] Yukio Tanaka, the founder FOE Japan, noted that, when he set up office in 1979, he did not even try to get approval from a ministry because he did not want the kind of control that would give the ministry over the organization. Nor did he think that he would receive approval. Instead, the group operated without non-profit status.[83] In the early 1990s, Greenpeace Japan similarly had not obtained status as a public-interest corporation and it operated with primary financing from Greenpeace International.

Akira Matsubara of the Research Institute of Civil Systems bemoaned:

It is highly troublesome for an NGO to acquire the status of juridical person . . . [T]here is a problem that the minimum fund required to establish a public interest organization is not officially defined. Some 30 million yen is said to be necessary for an incorporated association to operate, and 500 million is said necessary for an incorporated foundation (*zaidan hōjin*) to start with, but the true figures remain unclear. It sounds quite unfair, compared with the fact that a profit corporation can obtain the status of juridical person with only 3 million yen in capital.[84]

This adds another important element to the explanation of why informally organized citizens' groups were reluctant or unwilling to consider establishing more formal organizations.[85]

The discussion begun here will be resumed in Chapter 8, which compares environmental groups and their activities in Germany, Japan, and the US. The next chapter turns to an analysis of Japanese, German, and US responses to acid rain.

---

[82] Nancy London, *Japanese Corporate Philanthropy* (Oxford: Oxford University Press, 1991), p. 39.
[83] Interview with Yukio Tanaka, April 1994.
[84] Akira Matsubara, "NGOs in Japan: Problems of Legal Framework and Management Issues," Research Institution of Civil Systems paper.
[85] McCarthy and Zald, "Resource Mobilization and Social Movements."

4   Acid rain: signs of policy divergence

This chapter explores how Germany, Japan, and the US reacted in the 1980s to environmental issues, focusing on the emergence of acid rain as an international environmental concern. It also shows how their perceptions of environmental issues and policy approaches began to diverge. These differences are in part a reflection of the different geographical situations and environmental problems experienced by these countries. More importantly, however, the different policy responses to acid rain reflect the different kinds of formal and informal relationships that emerged among the environmental policy community, industry, and government in each country.

Acid rain

One of the first international atmospheric pollution concerns to gain scientific and political attention was acid rain. Acid rain has its roots in scientific understanding and policy responses related to local air pollution. Scientific research into the formation, transportation, and impacts of acidic rainfall followed upon decades of research related to classical air pollutants, and particularly SO_x and NO_x emissions. In the mid-nineteenth century, acidic emissions from local factories and mining operations were recognized as problems. In the mid-nineteenth century, when the Prussian state empowered local authorities to restrict heavily polluting industrial facilities, it did this in part to deal with acidic depositions. Acidic deposition was an ecological and health problem known to German scientists at least since the nineteenth century.[1]

Acidic deposition has been recognized as a problem for over a century, but it was not until 1968 that the long-range transport of acid rain over distances of tens and even hundreds of miles was seriously debated in the scientific and international policy communities. In that year, Svante

[1] Dominick, *The Environmental Movement in Germany*, p. 16.

Odén, a Swedish scientist, published a paper arguing that the long-range transport of acidic compounds from the European continent, and in particular the UK and Germany, was causing damage to Scandinavian lakes.[2] At the time, there was no scientific consensus that the long-range transport of acidic compounds was possible, and there was considerable skepticism that it could cause ecological damage. Nevertheless, the hypothesis was important enough that international research into the possibility of the long-range transport of acid rain was initiated within the OECD.

In 1971, the Environment Directorate of the OECD released a report that concluded that there had been a significant increase in the atmospheric content of sulfur compounds, that atmospheric processes lead to the transport of these compounds over long distances, and that for remedial action to be effective, it must be taken on an international basis.[3] There was considerable concern in Sweden that German and UK emissions from power plants and industry were to blame for the acid rain the country was experiencing, since there were few major emissions sources in Sweden. Both the UK and Germany scoffed at the idea.[4] The acid rain issue was a primary reason behind Sweden's proposal to the UN to hold the world's first international conference on the environment, the Stockholm Conference. In addition to promoting environmental protection efforts more generally, Sweden used the Stockholm Conference to draw attention to the plight of Scandinavian lakes and to apply pressure on Germany and the UK to take action. Sweden's scientific contribution to the UN Conference reflected its concern with acid rain. The paper was entitled "Air Pollution Across Boundaries."[5]

Also in 1972, after two years of preparatory work supported by the Scandinavians, the OECD launched a cooperative technical program to measure the long-range transport of air pollutants. Eleven countries, including Germany, participated in this program to measure sulfur deposition patterns throughout Europe. In 1977, the findings of this program

---

[2] Svante Odén, "The Acidification of Air and Precipitation and its Consequences in the Natural Environment," *Ecology Committee Bulletin*, No. 1 (Stockholm: Swedish National Science Research Council, 1968).

[3] OECD Environment Directorate, "Ad Hoc Meeting on Acidity and Concentration of Sulphate in Rain," May 1969 (Paris: OECD, 1971).

[4] See also Albert Weale, *The New Politics of Pollution* (Manchester: Manchester University Press, 1992), pp. 66–92; and Albert Weale et al., *Environmental Governance in Europe: An Ever Closer Ecological Union?* (Oxford: Oxford University Press, 2000), *passim*.

[5] Detlef Sprinz, "Why Countries Support International Environmental Agreements: The Regulation of Acid Rain in Europe," Ph.D. Dissertation, University of Michigan, 1992, p. 57.

were released confirming that acidic deposition in Scandinavian lakes was a result of the long-range transport of emissions from overseas.[6]

Despite growing scientific consensus that long-range transport of acidic compounds was a problem at the international level, Germany continued to express skepticism that its emissions were causing damage to forests and lakes in Scandinavia. Domestically, the SPD had supported a policy of building high smokestacks to disperse pollutants and decrease emissions concentrations near their source. The high smokestack policy improved local ambient air quality but spread pollutants over wider areas. While the use of desulfurization technology was suppose to replace the high smokestack policy, weak efforts at implementation meant that little progress was made. Instead, the high smokestack solution prevailed. Thus, a solution adopted to address a domestic air pollution problem in the 1960s became the source of international tensions between Scandinavia and Germany in the following decade.

Negotiations for an international agreement to address air pollution problems on the European continent began at the initiative of the Soviet Union in 1975. The Soviet Union was looking for an issue through which it could continue the process of détente begun with the 1975 Helsinki Conference on Security and Cooperation in Europe. The environment was one of the few areas where East–West cooperation was deemed safe from a security and technology perspective. Responding to the Soviet proposal, the UN Economic Commission for Europe ultimately decided that air pollution was a problematic area and one where cooperation with the Soviet Union was safe.

The Scandinavians used the negotiations for a Convention on Long Range Transboundary Air Pollution (LRTAP) to push for action on SO_x emissions. Together with the Eastern bloc countries, they introduced clauses into the draft treaty text calling for a cap on national SO_x emissions at current levels and percentage cutbacks in those emissions in subsequent years.[7] The Scandinavian effort failed, however, in the face of opposition from Germany, the UK, and the US, which were concerned about international liability. Even after the Nordic countries dropped their demands for regulations on SO_x emissions, Germany remained opposed to the convention. Germany was "the chief remaining opponent of the convention, apparently afraid that LRTAP might create principles that would cause countries to be held liable for future claims of damage

---

[6] OECD Environment Directorate, "The OECD Programme on Long Range Transport of Air Pollutants, Summary Report" (Paris: OECD, 1977).
[7] Thomas Gehring, *Dynamic International Regimes: Institutions for International Environmental Governance* (Frankfurt am Main: Peter Lang GmbH, 1994), pp. 63–194.

in Scandinavia."[8] Germany agreed to the convention only in the face of a united front by thirty-two other countries.

In 1979, the Geneva Convention on the LRTAP was established and became an important venue for the coordination of research efforts between European and North American countries on long-range transboundary air pollution. As a result of opposition from Germany and elsewhere, the convention simply required members to work to limit and gradually reduce air pollution through the use of the best available control technology without establishing concrete targets or goals.[9] In these negotiations, Germany insisted that the convention recognize that "the best available control technology" should be "economically feasible."[10] Mirroring the low priority that the SPD/FDP government placed on the environment, internationally Germany played the role of a foot dragger, opposing stringent environmental regulations.

The changing German political landscape

Prior to the late 1970s, acid rain was not seriously viewed as a political issue in any part of the world except Scandinavia.[11] This changed abruptly in the late 1970s and early 1980s, when acid rain became a big political issue, first in Canada and then in many other countries in Europe and North America. A 1981 cover story that appeared in *Der Spiegel* reported the hypothesis of a German scientist, Bernhard Ulrich, that large tracts of German forests might be dying as a result of acid rain.[12] The environmentally sensitized German public quickly showed their fears.

Acid rain struck a cord of concern with Germans – some argue because of German's cultural love for forests. Wrote Boehmer-Christiansen and Skea in their account of the formation of acid rain policy in Germany: "Forest death (*Waldsterben*) guaranteed the involvement of many powerful motifs in the acid-rain debate, motifs deeply embedded in culture and

---

[8] The treaty went into force in 1983. Marc A. Levy, "European Acid Rain: The Power of Tote-Board Diplomacy," in Peter M. Haas, Robert O. Keohane, and Marc A. Levy (eds.), *Institutions for the Earth: Sources of Effective International Environmental Protection* (Cambridge: MIT Press, 1993), pp. 75–132, quotation on p. 82. See also Gregory Wetstone and Armin Rosencranz, *Acid Rain in Europe and North America: National Responses to an International Problem* (Arlington, VA: Environmental Law Bookcrafter, 1983), p. 140.

[9] Boehmer-Christiansen and Skea, *Acid Politics*, p. 27.

[10] Wetstone and Rosencranz, *Acid Rain in Europe and North America*, p. 140.

[11] Clark et al. (eds.), *Learning to Manage Global Environmental Risks*, I, *passim*.

[12] Jeannine Cavender-Bares and Jill Jäger with Renate Ell, "Developing a Precautionary Approach: Global Environmental Risk Management in Germany," in Clark et al. (eds.), *Learning to Manage Global Environmental Risks*, I, pp. 63–4.

literature, ranging from the Grimm fairy tales through to Goethe and the Romantic poets."[13]

Acid rain emerged as a public issue at a time when the strength of the environmental movement in Germany was swelling. Greenpeace opened an office in Hamburg in 1981. That year, two Greenpeace members slipped into the Boehringer chemical factory in Hamburg and climbed up a 30-meter chimney to bring attention to the factory's emissions. The following year, a new environmental group, Robin Wood, formed. The founding members had left Greenpeace Germany dissatisfied with that group's strategies. Robin Wood resorted to radical, but non-violent protests against nuclear plants and air pollution. In Hamburg, they climbed the tower of the Michaels Church and unfurled a banner entitled "Save the Michaels" to bring attention to the acid rain that was believed to be destroying famous historical buildings. They also climbed chimneys of thermal power plants unfurling banners that read, "Stop acid rain" and "The forest is dead, long live politics." In Munich, the newly founded German Action Group, Struggle Against the Death of Forests, organized an estimated 23,000 people in November 1984 to protest against forest death from acid rain. Private foresters also began to demand compensation for their damaged investments. In December 1984, the president of the forest-owners' association predicted total losses at DM 1 billion.

The Greens as a political force

The electoral success of Greens at the local level and then in the federal elections elevated the environment to a new level of political importance in Germany. The Greens established themselves as a party at the federal level just as acid rain was emerging as an issue of growing public concern. In an effort to stem the influence of the Greens at the local level and to take up a cord that resonated with voters, the established parties began to pay new attention to the environment. These efforts had begun already in the year or two prior to the collapse of the SPD/FDP coalition as the Greens began exerting considerable influence at the local level. The CDU/CSU coalition started to show more interest in green issues and criticized the SPD-sponsored policy of building higher smokestacks in the coal-mining regions of North Rhine–Westphalia and the Saarland. The new interest in the environment of the CDU also was partly spurred on by the strong influence of its sister party, the CSU. The CSU was a Bavarian party. The southern Länder, including Bavaria, had the largest forest tracts in Germany but relatively low levels of industrialization.

---

[13] Boehmer-Christiansen and Skea, *Acid Politics*, p. 61.

Consequently, they began to perceive of themselves as victims of the long-range transport of pollutants from more industrialized Länder. As a champion of nuclear energy, moreover, the CSU had little to lose in pushing for stringent controls on fossil fuel-based industries.

In the 1983 electoral campaign, the Greens campaigned for an energy policy that was both anti-coal and anti-nuclear. They also campaigned against other emitters, including the automobile.[14] Their campaign posters included scenes of German industries billowing smoke into the air with subtitles that suggest unchecked industrial expansion was causing ruin.[15] The rise of the Greens strengthened the position of the pro-environmental group within the FDP that had remained strongly in favor of environmental protection initiatives. Their efforts to promote new environmental measures, including regulations to control emissions from power plants, were largely unsuccessful in the mid- to late 1970s. In 1981, however, the FDP's Josef Ertl, the minister of agriculture, was able to secure Cabinet approval for a more stringent Directive on Large Combustion Facilities, which would essentially require the use of desulfurization technology. Ertl had an interest in the issue because of his ministry's jurisdiction over forests. In 1982, the interior minister, the FDP's Gerhart Baum, was influential in convincing the Ministry of Economics to agree to the idea of the Large Combustion Plant Regulation.[16] This set the stage for a major change in Germany's international position on acid rain.

In 1982, the Swedes were still determined to win international recognition of the acid rain problem, and decided to host a conference on Acidification of the Environment as a ten-year anniversary to the Stockholm Conference. At the conference, Ulrich presented additional data that suggested that already 100,000 hectares of forests throughout central Europe, and especially in Germany, were dying because of acid rain and that up to a million hectares could be in danger.[17] Because of the SPD's desire to appear more pro-environment, German foreign minister Hans Dietrich Genscher was able to surprise the international community with his announcement that Germany would adopt a stringent technology-forcing domestic abatement program. This announcement was the first political indication that a major overhaul of German air pollution policies was imminent.[18]

[14] Sarkar, *Green-Alternative Politics*, pp. 88–96; and David Vogel, "Environmental Policy in the European Community," in Kamieniecki (ed.), *Environmental Politics in the International Arena* (Albany: State University of New York Press, 1993), pp. 191–6.
[15] Reproduced in Mayer and Ely (eds.), *The German Greens*, p. 219.
[16] Barnes, "Established Parties," pp. 9–10.
[17] Levy, "European Acid Rain," pp. 92–3.
[18] Boehmer-Christiansen and Skea, *Acid Politics*, p. 185.

In this changing political milieu, the environmental wing within the SPD regained some control over the direction of the party's platform. The SPD proposed a new environmental program. The proposal called for many important new measures: the introduction of German emission standards as international guidelines within the OECD and the EC; the enhancement of national efforts to reduce pollution; revision of the Technical Guidelines for Clean Air (TA Luft) to extend to the reduction of emissions from existing plants in heavily polluted areas; the issuance of a special regulation for large combustion plants that would set stringent limits for major pollutants emitted by large new fossil fuel-burning plants; the retrofitting of existing plants to comply with the new standards within ten years; and efforts to tighten vehicle exhaust standards at the EC level. The proposal also called for changes to water pollution control laws, nature conservation, chemical testing practices, as well as greater attention to research and development, global environmental problems, and economic development and the Third World.[19] This proposal would be a major advance in environmental protection regulations, although the stringency of the most important measure – the large combustion plant regulation – was weakened somewhat in negotiations due to successful lobbying by the utility industry.[20]

In the end, the plan was not put into action because the SPD/FDP coalition collapsed. Still, when the CDU/CSU–FDP coalition came to power, it took this SPD initiative and with some modifications, presented it as its own. The CDU/CSU–FDP formed a new coalition in October 1982. This meant that they had only a few months to formulate their own position on energy and environmental issues prior to new federal elections. Friederich Zimmerman, a staunch conservative, was appointed as the new head of the Ministry of the Interior and, to the surprise of many and the dismay of some, actively pursued an environmental program that was based largely on the SPD's environmental action plan. The new coalition was eager to develop a greener image prior to the upcoming election and the SPD had provided them with a plan of action. The party began plans for a Large Combustion Plant Regulation, vehicle emission limits, and large increases in research and development funding for the environment.

In February 1983, based on the CDU's new environmental plan, the Technical Guidelines for Air Pollution Control were amended. This amendment gave Länder authorities power to enforce limits on ambient pollution levels. Four months later, a Large Combustion Plant Regulation

---

[19] Weidner, "The Capability of the Capitalist State," pp. 23–5.
[20] Boehmer-Christiansen and Skea, *Acid Politics*, p. 192.

which set strict emission limits for seven major pollutants, including SO_x, NO_x, and particulates, was passed despite remaining opposition from the Economics Ministry. The regulation applied to plants of 50 MW or more. In the debate over the regulation, the Bundesrat rejected an attempt by the administration to relax the requirement by restricting the applicability of the law to individual units at combustion sites. The strong push coming from below was thus important to the bill's formulation. The regulations applied not only to new plants but also to existing plants. The implementation of the regulations was subjected to strict timetables and penalties for non-compliance. Existing plant operators had to propose how they planned to comply with the new regulations within a year's time. Their choices essentially amounted to retrofitting or closing down operations. As a result, there was a sharp jump in the number of flue gas desulfurization and denitrification units employed in Germany. A year later, a Small Combustion Plant Regulation also was issued. SO_x levels in Germany declined sharply after this time.[21] In the period from 1983 to 1993, the energy sector invested DM 22 billion in the installation of denitrification and desulfurization equipment.[22] SO_2 emissions dropped by more than 75 percent of 1970 levels by 1992 in the former West Germany.[23]

While the trade unions were initially opposed to the introduction of this new environmental protection plan, they began to change their tune as well. Many members of the trade unions had also become supporters of environmental protection initiatives. The trade unions began to portray environmental protection as a means of stimulating investment and employment. The unions also began to add environmental experts to their staff and began environmental education efforts of their membership. They began to build up expertise in environmentally friendly industrial processes and alternative products. In 1983, the Federation of German Unions issued a position paper on acid rain that called for the use of environmentally benign coal-burning technologies, energy conservation, the tightening of emission standards for SO_x, heavy metals, and NO_x if technically feasible, the introduction of ambient standards for noxious compounds, stricter emission standards for large power plants and industrial boilers, the provision of catalytic converters in cars, and the implementation of a government program that would secure employment while introducing measures to protect dying forests.[24] In a 1984 survey, 62 percent of the public agreed to the proposition that

[21] Weidner, "The Capability of the Capitalist State," pp. 23–5.
[22] http://www.bmu.de/UNBericht/partc2.htm
[23] http://www.bmu.de/UNBericht/partb1.htm
[24] Siegmann, *The Conflicts between Labor and Environmentalism*, pp. 40–1.

environmental protection requirements stimulated new technologies and thus new jobs. An even greater proportion of union members (76 percent) agreed to the proposition.

The Federation of German Unions' change of heart was influential in getting utility industries in North Rhine–Westphalia to agree to introduce modern pollution control technologies in their old coal-burning power plants before federal regulations were introduced. It was also important that the state governor at the time felt that the likely success of the Greens in the next state elections would lead to even more stringent requirements and there was a hope that early action would prevent this from happening.[25]

The entry of the Green Party into the Bundestag sent shock waves through an institution that had grown accustomed to particular ways of doing things. Not only did legislators have to get used to their new colleagues who wore jeans and tee shirts into the Bundestag, they had to react to the many legislative pressures that this new party produced. By July 1984, after just one year in parliament, the Green Party had suggested twenty-two draft bills out of a total of sixty from all parties.[26]

Germany and European environmental law

In the following years, Germany rapidly emerged as a European and international leader in pursuing international regulations for the control of acid rain-producing substances. In June 1984, the federal government organized an international conference in Munich on transboundary air pollution. This conference was important to the adoption in June 1985 of the Helsinki Protocol on the reduction of SO_x emissions by 30 percent between 1980 and 1993. At the Helsinki Conference, Germany announced its intentions to exceed the 30 percent reduction target with a unilateral pledge to reduce its own SO_x emissions by 60 percent by 1993.

Germany, together with Austria and Switzerland, pushed for an international agreement on NO_x, increasingly recognized as another major contributor to acid rain. These countries called for a 30 percent reduction of NO_x and hydrocarbon emissions. As a result of opposition to this plan, they agreed to a compromise position – a freeze on NO_x levels at 1987 levels by 1994. The Protocol to the 1979 Convention on Long-Range Transboundary Air Pollution Concerning the Control of Emission of Nitrogen Oxides or Their Transboundary Fluxes (the Sophia Protocol)

---

[25] Siegmann, *The Conflicts between Labor and Environmentalism*, p. 101.
[26] Weidner, "The Capability of the Capitalist State," p. 198.

was formed in 1988 and ratified in 1992. Importantly, Germany and several other countries that felt this reduced goal was inadequate formed a separate group that pledged to reduce their own emissions by 30 percent by 1998 in comparison to a base year chosen from between 1980 and 1986.[27]

After the Large Combustion Plant Regulation was enacted, the German government began to pressure the EC to adopt a directive that would introduce the German standards throughout the Community. Initially, the German initiative met with considerable resistance because of the different economic development levels and energy policies of countries as well as their lack of strong domestic pressures for policy change. Eventually, however, the German effort contributed to the establishment of an EC directive on Large Combustion Plants in 1988 that called for country-specific reductions.[28]

Efforts were also made to change EC legislation regarding the use of catalytic converters. EC technical norms could only be tightened in a legally binding form through EC legislation. Because of strong opposition from the UK, however, EC level policy change was not possible. Prior to the Single European Act of 1986, a unanimous vote was necessary to change policy. UK opposition, thus, prevented domestic policy change in Germany despite strong grass roots pressures. Instead, Germany had to resort to a voluntary program supported with fiscal incentives to promote environmentally friendly cars. Germany continued to apply pressure on its European neighbors and, finally, in late 1989, political agreement was reached at the EC level on standards for three-way catalytic converters for all new vehicles after 1992.[29]

Ironically, were it not for the German government's nuclear program and its political exclusivity, Germany may not have seen the rise of a movement that was eventually to turn the country into a far more environmentally minded state. The electoral challenge posed by the Greens awakened greater concern for the environment in the SPD, the CDU, and the FDP. When in the early 1980s the media picked up on scientific reports that Germany's forests were dying due to acid rain caused by emissions from domestic power plants and automobiles, the established parties were forced to become more sensitive to environmental considerations.

---

[27] Sprinz, "Why Countries Support International Environmental Agreements," pp. 61–2. See also, Detlef Sprinz and Tapani Vaahtoranta, "The Interest-Based Explanation of International Environmental Policy," in A. Underdal (ed.), *The Politics of International Environmental Management* (Dordrecht: Kluwer Academic Publishers, 1997) pp. 13–44.

[28] Boehmer-Christiansen and Skea, *Acid Politics*, pp. 230–50.

[29] Boehmer-Christiansen and Skea, *Acid Politics*, p. 186.

The United States

The 1980s has been called a decade of lost chances in the environmental realm in the US by various observers in large part because of the election of Ronald Reagan to office. Walter Rosenbaum writes:

Ronald Reagan and his advisors believed he had been elected to bring "regulatory relief" to the US economy, and environmental regulations were an early priority on the hit list of laws needing "regulatory reform." The environmental movement regarded the Reagan administration as the most environmentally hostile in a half century and the president's regulatory reform as the cutting edge of a massive administrative assault on the institutional foundations of federal environmental law.[30]

Similarly, Norman Vig argued:

The "environmental decade" came to an abrupt halt with the landslide victory of Ronald Reagan in 1980 . . . Reagan viewed environmental conservation as fundamentally at odds with economic growth and prosperity. He saw environmental regulation as a barrier to "supply side" economics and sought to reverse or weaken many of the policies of the previous decade.[31]

Some environmental gains were made during the decade. The US strengthened the Resource Conservation and Recovery Act in 1984, the Superfund Amendments and Reauthorization Act in 1986, the Safe Drinking Water Act in 1986, and the Clean Water Act in 1987. Also, in 1987, the US played a critical role in the formulation of the Montreal Protocol. Congress was fragmented on its environmental positions but when a strong enough coalition could be formed, policy change was possible. The coalitions that formed behind policy change did not simply pit environmentalists against industrial interests. At times, coalitions that cut across these two groups formed.

Still, the 1980s, and in particular, the first half of the decade, were hard ones for environmental advocates. The pace of legislative change was down relative to the 1970s, and the attacks on existing environmental regulations and on the EPA were harsh. US business succeeded in convincing the administration that environmental protection responsibilities had made the cost of doing business too expensive. Environmental regulations, they argued, were too complicated and inflexible. Industry complained heavily about the cost of complying with environmental regulations and lobbied hard to reduce the undue burden they felt was being placed upon them. There were few environmental laws passed under the

---

[30] Walter Rosenbaum, *Environmental Politics and Policy* (Washington, DC: Congressional Quarterly Press, 1998), pp. 11–12.
[31] Vig, "Presidential Leadership and the Environment," p. 98.

Reagan administration and, in an effort to promote regulatory reform, the administration attempted to reverse and weaken environmental regulations established in the previous decade, to trim environmental budgets, and to reduce the power of the movement.

Reagan appointed two attorneys known for their work in litigating against environmental regulations, Anne Gorsuch Burford and James Watt, to head up respectively, the EPA and the Interior Department. Environmentalists were infuriated by their efforts to reduce the size and scope of the EPA and to sell off public lands. Eventually, both were forced to resign, but not before the EPA had lost about one third of its operating budget and one fifth of its personnel. Reagan also attempted to dismantle the Council on Environmental Quality, but when that failed due to Congressional opposition, he cut its staff. He also set up a new Task Force on Regulatory Relief to review and propose revisions of regulations in response to complaints from industry.

The 1980s was a decade of environmental stalemate. Environmental groups saw their membership grow as a result of the attacks made on them by the administration. The Reagan administration succeeded in limiting new environmental regulatory initiatives and in rewriting hundreds of EPA regulations to reduce their impact on industry. On the international front, the US also retreated in several policy areas. The US opposed the Law of the Sea Treaty and stopped funding UN programs that promoted family planning and population control.[32]

There was also little policy activity in relation to acid rain even though by the late 1970s, reports had been issued implicating acid rain in the degradation of lakes in Canada and New England and in the health of forests.[33]

In 1981, authorization for the Clean Air Act terminated. Congress had to fund its implementation throughout the rest of the decade by passing appropriation resolutions until the act was finally amended again in 1990. The Clean Air Act of 1970 had been amended numerous times over the 1970s, strengthening the law in some areas but weakening it in others. The 1977 amendments, for example, mandated the use of scrubbers in new power plants and the use of local sources of coal in order to protect jobs, and prohibited switching from high sulfur coal to low sulfur coal in order to meet emissions standards. This was a case where environmental interests won Congressional support for stricter regulations on new power plants. It was also a case where Congressional support was obtained to

---

[32] Mintz, *Enforcement at the EPA*, pp. 40–83.
[33] William C. Clark and Nancy M. Dickson, "Civil Science: America's Encounter with Global Environmental Risks," in Clark et al. (eds.), *Learning to Manage Global Environmental Risks*, I, pp. 263–5.

prevent power plants from looking to western states for better quality coal at the cost of jobs in the mid-west where coal with a high sulfur content was mined. Thus, labor and mining industries plus environmental concerns combined to influence the shape of the 1977 amendments. This amendment was later to be criticized because of the high cost this imposed on industry to clean up air quality.[34] The amendments also provided waivers to the automobile industry, which kept failing to meet the requirements for auto tailpipe emissions standards. The auto industry argued that the emissions that had been established by the Clean Air Act and its amendments were too stringent and that technology to meet them did not exist.[35]

The debate over reauthorization of the Clean Air Act was complicated and brought in many different actors. The automobile industry and its Congressional advocates argued for further delays in the meeting of tailpipe emissions standards. Other industrial sources called for a weakening of regulations on stationary sources of emissions. Yet, others were interested in a tightening of standards. The Canadians pointed to mid-west utility plants as the source of much of the acid rain pollutants that were being deposited in northeastern Canada. Also, New England states began to be concerned about the death of their lakes and forests from acid rain.[36]

In the 1970s, in response to local air pollution concerns, power plants built higher and higher smokestacks much like they had in Japan and Germany. As a result, pollutants at times traveled hundreds of miles with the winds before they came back to the ground either in dry form or with the rain. Older power plants had been exempted from many of the regulations established under the 1970 Clean Air Act amendments. These areas, therefore, wanted new regulations that would address the emissions from the coal-burning utility plants. Many areas in the US were failing to meet national ambient air quality standards.

Bill after bill was introduced in the US Congress, some calling for stricter standards, others proposing a weakening of regulations. The divisions did not fall strictly along party lines. Rather, broadly speaking, they were regional, pitting representatives from coal-burning mid-west states against the northeast, and auto-producing states against more environmentally minded regions. Yet, the divisions at times became more

---

[34] Bryner, *Blue Skies, Green Politics*, p. 172.
[35] Bryner, *Blue Skies, Green Politics*, p. 101.
[36] William C. Clark and Nancy M. Dickson (eds.), *The Press and Global Environmental Change: An International Comparison of Elite Newspaper Reporting on the Acid Rain Issue from 1972 to 1992*, Environment and Natural Resources Program Working Paper No. E-95–06, Harvard University, John F. Kennedy School of Government, Center for Science and International Affairs, 1995.

complicated and unusual coalitions formed, such as when environmentalists and western states producing low-quality coal united to oppose a bill to amend the Clean Air Act being considered by Senator George Mitchell in 1988. The environmentalists felt that the bill was too weak. The western states felt that the bill favored high-sulfur coal-producing states over the low-sulfur coal-producing states of their own. Time after time, the bills were defeated either in committee or on the floor. Congressional gridlock led to a long period of policy stagnation. Reagan made no attempt to break this political stalemate. Instead, he called for more research into the matter.[37]

The gridlock was finally broken with the election of George H. W. Bush. Bush tried to distance himself from the Reagan approach to environmental issues in his first years in office. He was elected at a time when environmental concerns had been receiving much attention in the press. 1988 was a record hot year in the US and the media gave much attention to the threat of global warming. Stratospheric ozone depletion was also a major public concern, as more and more people came to learn about the ozone hole. The environment was an issue that resonated with the public. Bush responded, promising to be an "environmental president." By the end of his term in office, his promise was being questioned by environmentalists because of Bush's resistance to taking action on climate change.

In the first two years of his presidency, Bush helped push through the Clean Air Act of 1990 and raised the status of the EPA giving it Cabinet rank. Bush followed a bi-partisan coalition-building strategy in order to push the legislation through. This was necessary given that, at the time the 1990 Clean Air Act amendments were formulated, both houses of Congress were under the control of the Democrats. The 1990 Clean Air Act was among the most significant legislation passed during his administration. This act had as its main goals the reduction of acid rain, improvements in urban air quality, and a reduction in airborne toxic chemicals. Acid rain was to be addressed by cutting SO_2 emissions from coal-burning power plants almost in half in a decade's time. The Clean Air Act of 1990 was a significant achievement in terms of its ambitious policy goals. With the passage of this act, the US could again claim some international leadership in terms of policy content.

The most unique element of this new legislation was the adoption of market-based tools for implementation. Industry had long criticized US environmental regulations as being too inflexible and inefficient. Important in the bill's formulation was the interaction between environmentalists, represented by EDF, White House officials, representatives of

[37] Bryner, *Blue Skies, Green Politics*, p. 112.

the EPA, the Department of Energy, and the Office of Management and Budget (OMB). The president's bill was modified in Congressional debates, but important elements survived, including the introduction of an emissions trading and permitting system. This approach to environmental regulation deserves some attention. Because of its tremendous success in reducing SO_2 emissions, permitting and trading have been championed by US political leaders as approaches to employ in addressing environmental pollution.

Emissions trading has been employed in the US since the mid-1970s. In 1974, the EPA permitted within-firm emissions trading. Under this system, firms that reduced emissions below levels required by law could gain credits towards higher emissions elsewhere. At this time, the concept of "netting" emissions and "bubbles" were also introduced. Firms were permitted to trade emissions among sources within the firm as long as the firm's combined emissions stayed within an established aggregate limit. The offset program initiated in 1976 introduced the concept of allowing firms to establish operations in areas that were not in compliance with ambient standards by reducing existing emissions in the area by an amount greater than the amount that the firm's new operations would produce. Finally, the concept of banking, storing earned emissions reduction credits for future use, either to allow for expansion of the firm or for sale to another firm, was also introduced.[38] These ideas were employed to some extent in efforts to reduce the use of lead in gasoline and in phasing out CFCs. Los Angeles also initiated a tradable pollution permit system for nitrogen oxide emissions. Yet, while emissions trading has been in existence for many years, outside of a few cases, it was not extensively used until the formation of the Clean Air Act of 1990.[39]

Under the Clean Air Act of 1990, every stationary source of pollution regulated by the law was given an operating permit issued by the state. The permits specify how much each source can emit as well as monitoring and maintenance requirements. These permits provide the public with a paper trail that they can use in court against non-complying industries. In the case of acid rain, sharp emissions reductions of approximately 10 million tons of SO_2 per year were mandated. In contrast with traditional command and control approaches to regulation of industry, however, the sources of pollution were given considerable flexibility in how they were to achieve those reductions. Making use of the permit system did this.

Under Phase I of the act, each power plant was allocated pollution allowances based on the size of the plant and its historic emissions

---

[38] Robert W. Hahn and Robert N. Stavins, "Trading in Greenhouse Permits," in Henry Lee (ed.), *Shaping National Responses to Climate Change* (Washington, DC: Island Press, 1995), p. 184.
[39] Hahn and Stavins, "Trading in Greenhouse Permits," pp. 184–5.

levels. Anyone, however, can buy, sell, or own allowances. Over time, the number of allowances will decrease, as the states are required to phase in stricter standards. The power plants can determine for themselves whether it makes more sense to buy up pollution permits from other plants or to clean up their emissions and then sell their excess allowances. Industries that want to expand their operations might find it necessary to buy pollution permits. Industries may also find it cheaper to buy pollution permits than to control pollution. Conversely, as the price of the permits rise, industries may find it cheaper to switch fuel sources to cleaner fuels, to install scrubbers, or to introduce more fuel-efficient technologies and then to sell off their excess permits. Environmental groups that want to clean up the air might choose to buy up pollution allowances and retire them from the system, thus forcing up the price of the remaining permits. Utilities that exceed their SO_2 emissions allowances are fined heavily.

Big polluters that typically could more cheaply clean up their pollution than smaller emitters were encouraged under this system to clean up their pollution more than was required and then to sell their pollution allowances to other industries that found it more expensive to make marginal reductions in their emissions levels. The system has also stimulated competition among pollution control sources.

The system has been quite successful although it also has its opponents. Estimates are that the cost of complying with the goals of the act has been considerably cheaper than would have been the case under the more traditional command and control approach to regulation. Opponents argue that the law advocates pollution and that it gives too much discretion to the polluter.[40] The idea of using economic incentives (but not pollution taxes) to control pollution has gained a strong following in the US, and, as we will see in Chapter 6, became a major component of US and also international debates about how to address climate change.

Japan

Acid rain did not make it on to the political agenda in Japan in the early 1980s. This may simply have been because acid rain was not much of a problem. There were no dying forests. There were no dying lakes. In contrast with Germany and the US, Japan was not involved in international negotiations pertaining to acid rain abatement. Japan was not part of the international negotiations for LRTAP since this was primarily a European treaty with US and Canadian participation. Japan did, however, participate in the OECD's air pollution research programs.

[40] Bryner, *Blue Skies, Green Politics*, pp. 208–9.

As was the case in Germany and the US during the 1970s, attention to acid rain in Japan was limited to a small community of scientists and bureaucrats.[41] Acid rain did emerge as an environmental concern in a few local instances. On June 30, 1973 in Shimizu, Shizuoka, for instance, there were numerous complaints filed with the local government of eye and skin irritation from acid rain. This led local health offices to conduct studies to determine the pH level of clouds. Speculation followed that pollutants, at least in the case of the Shizuoka incident, had traveled from industrial areas in Tokyo to Shizuoka, since there were no factories in the vicinity that emitted SO_x.[42] Over the next few years, there were several similar reports. One described a case where hundreds had been injured by acid rain:

On the afternoon of the fourth (of July), residents of Kanagawa and Chiba prefectures and Tokyo reported to their prefectural or district environmental offices that their eyes hurt from the misty rain. By 2:00 PM, the number of victims had risen to 201. On the fourth, it was also discovered that over 4,000 residents of Tochigi, Gunma, and Saitama prefectures had suffered similar damage. The Tokyo District Pollution Office believes the cause to be SO_x and NO_x emissions from factory smoke stacks and automobiles that "melt" in the rain and form [formed] "acid rain."[43]

This event, however, did not trigger any calls for political action, although the Environment Agency did commission a study on the mechanisms by which acid rain forms and irritates the eyes.[44]

There were only a handful of articles on acid rain injuries that appeared in the print media in the early to mid-1970s, compared with hundreds of articles on other pollution-related health problems. Injury from acid rain was a minor issue among these far more serious pollution problems. Interestingly, some experts even speculated that some of the reports of eye damage from acid rain could be attributed to "mass psychogenic systemic illness" rather than to the poor ambient air quality.[45]

Although not a political issue, Japanese industry became interested in the acid rain issue as it was unfolding in Europe because they felt that they

---

[41] Miranda A. Schreurs, "Shifting Priorities and the Internationalization of Environmental Risk Management in Japan," in Clark et al. (eds.), *Learning to Manage Global Environmental Risks*, I, pp. 191–212.

[42] *Asahi Shimbun*, June 30, 1973, p. 23.

[43] *Asahi Shimbun*, July 5, 1974, p. 19. See also Miranda A. Schreurs, Patricia Welch, and Akiko Kôda, "Devil in the Sky," in Clark and Dickson (eds.), *The Press and Global Environmental Change*, pp. G1–36.

[44] Environment Agency of Japan, *Quality of the Environment in Japan* (Tokyo: Environment Agency of Japan, 1983), p. 192.

[45] Hitoshi Kasuga, "Health Effects of Air Pollution," in Nishimura (ed.), *How to Conquer Air Pollution*, p. 108.

had a technological solution to the problem. In the mid- to late 1970s, the European Community, France, West Germany, Canada, Yugoslavia, Czechoslovakia, and Poland were requesting environmental cooperation agreements with Japan. These countries wished to learn from Japan's success in applying advanced pollution control technology and in establishing and meeting strict SO_x emission regulations from stationary sources.

Nor could Japan help but notice the mounting concern with forest death in Germany and elsewhere in Europe and the emergence of tensions between the US and Canada due to acid rain. Thus, some efforts were made to increase bureaucratic capacity related to this issue and, after the fifth Japan–United States Environment Conference convened in Washington, DC, in November 1981, the Environment Agency began to consider the acid rain issue somewhat more seriously.[46] In 1982, the government's Quality of the Environment White Paper noted that acid rain was rapidly becoming an international problem in Europe and North America and urged precautionary action be taken in Japan.[47] In 1982, the Environment Agency established a Committee on Acid Rain Countermeasures within its Air Quality Bureau to survey existing scientific information on acid rain and to prepare plans for future surveys and research. The Water Quality Bureau also began to collect data on the acidification of lakes.

The following year, a new advisory Committee on Acid Rain Countermeasures was established to conduct research into acid rain in Japan as a precautionary step resulting from reports of acid rain damages in the forests and lakes of North America and Europe. It launched a five-year research program on the extent of acid rainfall in Japan and its effects on ecosystems. Explaining the formation of the committee, the Environment Agency stated that, although no ecosystem damage from acid rain had been reported in Japan, highly acidic rainfall had been observed and some cases of eye irritation reported. Therefore, the Agency explained, it was necessary to initiate measurements in Japan.[48] A 1987 interim report of the committee found that throughout Japan, there was acid rain with an average pH between 4.4 and 5.3. Industrialization in China and Korea was determined to be part of the cause of the acid rain. Moreover, it was reported that 35 percent of Japan's lakes were acidic or close to being acidic.[49]

---

[46] *Asahi Shimbun*, October 8, 1981 and November 3 and 10, 1981.
[47] Environment Agency of Japan, *Quality of the Environment in Japan* (Tokyo: Environment Agency of Japan, 1982), p. 211.
[48] Environment Agency of Japan, *Quality of the Environment in Japan* (Tokyo: Environment Agency of Japan, 1984).
[49] *Asahi Shimbun*, March 28, 1987, p. 3.

The idea that Japan might be affected by transboundary acid rain from China is an idea that appears to have been pushed by Americans and Europeans, and not initially by Japanese scientists or activists. In an informal meeting in Japan in February 1984, US EPA director William Ruckelshaus raised the issue of long-range transport of acid rain in the Asian area. Ruckelshaus suggested that China's reliance on high sulfur coal for fueling its rapid industrialization ultimately would increase transboundary emissions of SO_x and, as a result, in the future, Japan could suffer from acid rain. A French scientist also warned that acid rain damage in Japan from emissions in China could spread quickly due to Japan's warm climate.[50] These warnings initiated some interest in the link between China's pollution and Japan's environment. In 1985, there were a small number of articles on acid rain that appeared in the press. About half of these made mention of acid rain in China and the potential for its long-range transport to Japan. One article warned that 85 percent of China's rainfall was acidic and that, despite China's insistence that the impact on Japan was negligible, SO_2 emissions could transcend national borders, traveling distances of as much as 1,000 miles.[51] In the fall of 1986, the Environment Agency and the Ministry of Agriculture, Forests, and Fisheries produced a report announcing that cedar trees in the northwestern Kantô Plain, near Tokyo, were dying from acid rain.[52]

The main line coming from scientists and the small group of bureaucrats involved with this issue was that acid rain was not an immediate problem, but a potential problem for the future. The limited concern with acid rain was not an isolated response. With the recession of the mid-1970s, the automobile industry became increasingly vocal in its criticism of the ambient air quality standards for NO_x. Honda and Mazda quickly developed technology to meet the 1975 standard for reducing nitrogen oxide emissions, but resistance emerged to the more stringent 1976 standards. After US automobile manufacturers who were years behind Japan in development of this technology succeeded in successfully lobbying against the timetable for enforcement, Japanese automobile manufacturers also succeeded in getting a postponement in the enforcement of the 1976 standards. Their implementation was delayed until 1978. The 1978 standards were set at 0.6 g/km for small cars and 0.85 g/km for large cars.[53]

In general, there was limited Japanese environmental policy activity in the 1980s even though, or perhaps because, Japan had done much to

[50] *Asahi Shimbun*, January 19, 1985, p. 4.
[51] *Asahi Shimbun*, May 10, 1985, p. 1.
[52] *Asahi Shimbun*, October 3, 1986, p. 22.
[53] Katô et al., "Kankyô Gyôsei 10 Nen no Ayumi," 31–5.

improve its domestic environmental situation in the 1970s. Nor was Japan very active in following the international environmental issues that began to emerge in the 1980s. Embattled at home, the Environment Agency had few resources to use to stay abreast of international environmental developments. The extent to which this was true can be seen from a review of the government's annual White Paper for the Environment. This annual report prepared by the Environment Agency describes the state of the environment and policy activities. Prior to publication, the Agency circulates it to other agencies and ministries for review and modifications. In 1979, the White Paper devoted only 6 of 284 pages to international environmental cooperation, and these were tacked on to the end of the volume. There was no discussion of specific international environmental problems. Attention to global environmental issues remained limited until 1988. The 1982 volume made no mention of global warming, devoted one page to tropical deforestation in Asia, and mentioned stratospheric ozone depletion in two sentences. The 1986 and 1987 volumes dropped the section on the Global Environment altogether, including only brief sections on the promotion of international environmental cooperation and Japan's involvement in international efforts for the protection of international waters from oil and other pollution. The 1986 volume also included a brief section on transfers of environmental technology overseas. The Environment Agency was focused almost exclusively on domestic environmental matters.

Getting acid rain on to the policy agenda
The lack of real policy interest in acid rain did not change until the late 1980s. In 1988, a full eighty-six pages of the White Paper for the Environment, a third of the entire volume, was devoted to global environmental problems. In this volume, considerable discussion was given to the nature of various transboundary and global pollution problems, including acid rain, the extinction of wildlife species, atmospheric pollution problems, and marine pollution.[54]

In 1989, there also was a sudden jump in media attention to acid rain and other environmental issues. Media coverage of acid rain jumped to eighty-four articles in 1989, up from twenty-three the year before. A 1989 poll conducted by the Environment Agency's Pollution Research Center found that 87 percent of respondents considered global warming to be among the most serious environmental problems; 57 percent chose acid rain.[55] Compare this with polls conducted by the Prime Minister's

[54] The Environment Agency of Japan, *The Quality of the Environment in Japan* (Tokyo: Environment Agency of Japan, 1972–93).
[55] *Asahi Shimbun*, October 3, 1989, p. 6.

Office in 1981 and 1984. The 1981 poll was the first government poll in which questions on global atmospheric issues were raised. Given a list of problems, respondents were allowed two selections. In both polls, by far the most concern was accorded pollution of the environment by chemical substances – a domestic policy concern in Japan – followed by concern over deforestation and concern for pollution of the oceans by oil. Atmospheric pollution issues were not high on the list. In 1984, acid rain was only perceived as a big problem by slightly over 3 percent of respondents and stratospheric ozone depletion by less than 10 percent.[56]

Why then did acid rain and global environmental issues get on to the agenda in the late 1980s? It was not because there was a serious acid rain problem as had been the case in Germany. A 1989 Environment Agency report based on a five-year research program on acid rain found that the pH of rain in Japan averaged from 4.4 to 5.5. All twenty-nine areas where measures were taken have some degree of acid rain; however, it went on to say that there had been no serious damage as of yet. It simply warned that, in the future, damage could be expected as a result of acid precipitation coming from the Asian continent.[57] The tone of the report was serious, but did not speak of an immediate or impending disaster, as was the tenor of reports related to German forests in the early 1980s.

Yet, soon hereafter the Japanese government began to pay more and more attention to acid rain problems from China, initiating monitoring programs and educational and scientific cooperation.[58] As we will see in the next chapters, in the end of the 1980s, there was a more general change in the stance of policy makers in Japan towards global environmental issues. The reasons for these changes and their implications for the policy-making process, the environmental policy community, and environmental laws will be discussed in later chapters.

Explaining divergent approaches to pollution control

During the 1970s, powerful industrial voices prevented Germany from taking a proactive stance in the LRTAP negotiations. Although stringent air pollution control regulations were established in the early 1970s, as noted in the previous chapter, there was a gap between promises made by the SPD in its environmental program and what was actually

---

[56] Sôrifu Naikaku Sôridaijin Kanbô Kôhôshitsu, "Kôgai ni Kansuru Yoron Chôsa," *Yoron Chôsa Nenpô, Chôsa 11.*

[57] Kankyôchô, *Ichiji Sanseiu Taisaku Chôsa Kekka ni Tsuite* (Tokyo: Kankyôchô, 1989). See also *Asahi Shimbun*, August 15, 1989, p. 1. A second report with similar findings was released three years later. Kankyôchô, *Dai Ni Sanseiu Taisaku Chôsa no Chûkan Torimatome ni Tsuite* (Tokyo: Kankyôchô, 1992).

[58] Kenneth Wilkening, "Culture and Japanese Citizen Influence on the Transboundary Air Pollution Issue in Northeast Asia," *Political Psychology* 20 (1999), 701–23.

implemented. The incentives that the government established for industry to improve their pollution control efforts proved insufficient. The German government failed to provide industry with the same kinds of fiscal incentives to introduce pollution control technologies that the Japanese government did. The German coal and oil industries, moreover, expressed their strong opposition to newly created air pollution control regulations and succeeded in delaying the introduction of new laws. Domestic industrial opposition to air pollution control regulations were mirrored at the international level in Germany's opposition to international regulatory action on transboundary air pollution.

Faced with a serious recession and high unemployment rates in the post-oil shock years, industry and labor unions grew increasingly concerned about the economic costs of environmental regulation. Moreover, with the election of Helmut Schmidt, an economist took the helm of the German political system. It was not until the political climate changed as a result of the emergence of the Greens that environmental issues were again pushed on to the political agenda.

Once this happened, however, the transition was dramatic and affected not only domestic environmental politics but Germany's position in European Community environmental negotiations. In their bid for parliamentary representation, the Greens, together with the environmentalists who supported them, picked up acid rain as an issue to highlight the failures of the established political parties in environmental protection. It was a powerful issue that resonated with the population. The established political parties suddenly felt compelled to address air pollution issues in an effort to win back the votes lost to the Green Party.

The CDU did this by introducing control policies that hit the worst polluters – the energy producers. There had been earlier, unsuccessful attempts by the Ministry of the Interior to pass laws that would tighten controls on these polluters, but they had run into too much opposition. The 1983 election provided a window of opportunity to push through policy changes. The preceding decade of growing environmental activism helped instill new environmental norms in society. Essentially, the electoral victories of the Greens, first at the local level and then at the federal level, and the rise of the environmental movement helped to push environmental concerns on to the agendas of other policy actors. Policy priorities changed and new environmental institutions were created. This process occurred as transboundary environmental issues, beginning with acid rain, began to emerge as policy concerns.

The Large Combustion Plant Directive and the Small Combustion Plant Directive both employed command and control approaches to emissions reductions, establishing heavy penalties for plants that failed to comply with the law. In the case of acid rain, there were two main reasons why Germany's position on international regulatory action changed. The first is that acid rain became a domestic and not just a foreign problem. The second, and most important, is that in the interim period, the environmental movement succeeded in making inroads into the political party system and, in the process, forced almost every other actor in society to turn a little greener. This suggests that the rise of the Green Party did influence significantly policy outcome even if the biggest influence was not in terms of direct impact but rather in forcing the major political parties to address the issue more actively than they might have otherwise. Attention to the acid rain problem was brought first by the Scandinavians and then by German scientists.

The Japanese experience with acid rain is less complicated. It was not much of a political issue. In the early 1970s, there was little Japanese response to Swedish efforts at Stockholm to make acid rain an international policy matter. Japanese scientists were involved in research related to the effects of emissions on humans, plants, animals, and materials and the long-range transport of pollutants. Technologically, because of its own bad air pollution problems in the 1960s, Japan became a world leader in the control of SO_2 emissions; Japan took advantage of this fact by becoming an exporter of air pollution control equipment and technological know-how to Europe and elsewhere. Over the course of the 1970s, Japan developed a system of pollution control that it has continued to embrace. The system combines administrative guidance, in which government and industry have worked together to determine means for complying with environmental laws, and a system of local government control through the use of pollution control agreements. These controls are often quite stringent, but provide a degree of flexibility to industry in meeting goals.

Japan's domestic policy successes in air pollution control did not translate into a proactive international environmental policy position. There was no restructuring of the political landscape in the 1980s. Environmental protection remained domestic in focus and policy change remained incremental in nature. The 1980s was a quiet decade in terms of environmental policy developments.

In some ways, this parallels the situation in the US, where there was also limited environmental policy change. The reasons for Japan's limited activity, however, differ significantly from the case in the US. In Japan, the environmental NGO community was weak and relatively limited in its scope of activities. Without much public attention to environmental issues, the Environment Agency could achieve little.

In the US, in contrast, environmental NGOs became increasingly strong in terms of numbers and budgets. This was especially true after the Reagan administration launched broad-sided attacks on the environmental gains of the previous decade. Yet, despite the growing strength of the environmental NGO community and their interest in addressing acid rain, little happened at the policy level. This was primarily because of the lack of support of the White House and strong fragmentation within Congress among those favoring and opposing different kinds of regulations on automobile emissions, coal-burning power plants, and other sources of toxic air pollutants.

Policy change became possible in the US only after there was a strengthening of public concern about the state of the global environment in the end of the 1980s. This appears to have influenced the position of George H. W. Bush on acid rain. The response of the administration to acid rain became the largest experiment to date with the use of tradable emissions permits.

It is useful to consider why the US has become the leading advocate of a tradable permit system for the control of certain kinds of pollution. In the US, since the era of deregulation initiated under the Reagan administration, there has been considerable momentum behind reducing the size of government and using market forces to allocate the least-cost approach to pollution control. Far more than appears to be the case in Germany and Japan, in the US, there is a relatively strong level of antagonism between government and industry. The frequent use of litigation to resolve environmental disputes in the 1970s and the costs of this litigation led to growing concerns in the 1980s about the effectiveness and efficiency of command and control approaches to pollution control. This set off a series of efforts to reformulate US approaches to pollution control and prevention. One has been the adoption of processes that try to limit use of the courts. In some cases, judges acting as intermediaries urge opposing parties to reach a compromise before a case goes to trial. The EPA has increasingly turned to the use of environmental dispute resolution mechanisms that bring environmental groups and business interests together to discuss their differences and seek out mutually acceptable solutions.[59] A tradable emissions permit system also reduces the role of the federal government in pollution control and provides industry with more flexibility in meeting federal emissions standards.

The next chapter examines the case of stratospheric ozone depletion and the formation of an international agreement to deal with it. It is an example of how despite differences in environmental programs and movements, cooperation for environmental protection can be achieved.

---

[59] Lettie McSpadden, "Environmental Policy in the Courts," in Vig and Kraft (eds.), *Environmental Policy in the 1990s*, pp. 170–1.

5   Stratospheric ozone depletion

Damage to the ozone layer was the first truly global atmospheric pollution issue to face countries around the world. The issue had major economic ramifications for Japan, Germany, and especially the US, for they were among the largest producers and consumers of ozone depleting chemicals in the world. The process leading up to the formation of the Montreal Protocol and its subsequent amendments took years. The US, Japan, and Germany differed in their level of interest in, and willingness to act in relation to, stratospheric ozone depletion. These differences stemmed in no small part from the differences in the strength of their environmental policy communities and the core environmental paradigm operating in each.

The formation of the Montreal Protocol was a major success. Subsequent amendments to the Montreal Protocol have essentially called for a complete phase out of ozone depleting chemicals, including five haloginated CFCs that were commercially available (CFC-11, CFC-12, CFC-113, CFC-114, and CFC-115), halons, and methyl bromide. In Japan, CFCs are often referred to as Freon (Flon), a trademark for CFC-12 which is used as a refrigerant. A partially halogenated CFC that has replaced the use of CFCs in some commercial products is hydrochlorfluorocarbon (HCFC)-22. It has a lower ozone depleting potential than the fully halogenated CFCs, but has a high global warming potential.[1]

The formulation of the Montreal Protocol was a remarkable achievement on a number of grounds. CFCs represented a huge industry; they were used in aerosol sprays, as refrigerants, in air conditioning, as solvents for cleaning circuit boards, in styrofoam packaging, and in many other materials and processes. There was tremendous industrial opposition to the establishment of an international regulatory agreement. Finally, there were considerable differences among states in their interpretations of how much of a threat ozone depletion was.

---

[1] Karen Litfin, *Ozone Discourses: Science and Politics in Global Environmental Cooperation* (New York: Columbia University Press, 1994), pp. 58–61.

This chapter presents an analysis of the evolution of German, Japanese, and US positions on ozone layer protection. This case illustrates how international negotiations narrowed the differences among these states and helped them to reach compromise and, in the end, a highly successful agreement. Helpful to this process was the sense of international environmental crisis produced with the discovery of the ozone hole. Thus, while this chapter also deals considerably with issues of divergence, it is a good example of how states can reach agreement on policy goals and options despite differences in national interests.

The ozone depletion case is also very important in terms of Japanese domestic environmental policy making. Much as acid rain proved to be a pivotal case in Germany and was associated with the rise of the Green Party and dramatic policy transformation, the formation of the Montreal Protocol was a crucial turning point for environmental policy making in Japan. It is with this issue and the rapid subsequent emergence of climate change on to the policy agenda that a process of domestic political transformation began in Japan. The Japanese case, moreover, has received little attention in the literature on this otherwise well-studied policy issue.

In terms of Germany, there was a change in policy position along with the greening of the German political landscape much as occurred with the acid rain case. The US was a key player in pushing for international action to deal with ozone layer depletion. As we will see in the next chapters, this contrasts with its subsequent behavior in the climate change negotiations.

The rise of stratospheric ozone depletion as a policy concern

The US takes the lead

In the troposphere, the level of the atmosphere closest to the earth's surface, ozone is produced by NO_x emissions from automobiles, industry, and waste disposal. In sunlight, the NO_x reacts with hydrocarbons and other gases to produce ozone. Ozone is extremely toxic and even very small amounts can irritate the eyes and throat, lower resistance to respiratory infections, and cause damage to vegetation. Twenty to thirty kilometers above the earth's surface in the stratosphere, however, ozone is produced naturally and has the important function of protecting living species from the sun's ultraviolet rays. It is one of nature's paradoxes that ozone, which is harmful to humans and plant life close to the earth's surface, provides a natural protective shield in the upper atmosphere so that plants and animals can survive.

Ozone layer depletion first became a political concern after scientists theorized that NO_x produced by high flying planes could damage stratospheric ozone. In the early 1970s, the US was considering plans for a large supersonic transport (SST) fleet. Concern about the potential damage to the ozone layer that a large fleet of supersonic planes might produce led the US Department of Transportation to initiate a Climatic Impact Assessment Program. Scientific theories that NO_x might destroy ozone in the stratosphere became the basis of a battle between environmentalists, who called on the government to ban Concorde flights into the US and to abandon its own plans to build a supersonic fleet, and those who wanted to go ahead with both plans. The issue quickly became an international one as Britain and France charged that the NO_x theory was simply being used as a smoke screen behind which to protect the US airline industry from European competition once the SST program was abandoned in the US.[2]

Other chemicals became suspect as well. Plans for the development of a space shuttle elevated scientific interest in the effects of chlorine on the earth's atmosphere. Concern that hydrogen chloride emitted by the booster rockets would put chlorine directly into the stratosphere became an incentive for scientific research on the potential effects of this chemical. In May 1974, R. J. Cicerone and R. S. Stolarski of the University of Michigan were the first to theorize that, through a catalytic chain reaction, chlorine atoms could diminish stratospheric ozone. A month later, Sherry Rowland and Mario Molina of the University of California at Irvine published a paper in *Nature* that came to similar conclusions and pointed to CFCs as a potential large source of chlorine. CFCs were widely used as propellants in spray cans and as refrigerants.[3]

The Rowland–Molina theory triggered a sudden rise in scientific interest in the stratospheric ozone layer.[4] There still was considerable uncertainty about ozone depletion – there was no evidence that the stratospheric ozone layer had declined or that CFCs were even accumulating in the atmosphere. There were also uncertainties about the rate at which CFCs would destroy ozone. Nevertheless, the CFC–ozone link quickly became a political issue.

By the fall of 1974, many of the major US newspapers had run stories linking CFCs and ozone destruction to the household spray can.

[2] Lydia Dotto and Harold Schiff, *The Ozone War* (New York: Doubleday, 1978), p. 116.

[3] Mario J. Molina and F. Sherwood Rowland, "Stratospheric Sink for Chlorofluoromethanes: Chlorine Atomic Catalysed Destruction of Ozone," *Nature* 249 (1984), 810–12.

[4] Assembly of Mathematical and Physical Sciences, National Research Council, *Halocarbons: Environmental Effects of Chlorofluoromethane Release* (Washington, DC: National Academy of Sciences, 1976).

Environmental groups, and especially the NRDC, started lobbying for legislation both at the state and federal levels. They challenged industry to stop producing a chemical that destroys the protective ozone layer and thereby increases rates of skin cancer. As early as December 1974, ozone depletion was being discussed in Congress and funds were requested for research into ozone layer depletion and consequent harm to public health.

The six manufacturers of CFCs in the US and the approximately twenty-five companies involved in producing aerosol sprays that used CFCs were immediately put on the defensive. The US aerosol industry, which consumed about half of the CFCs being produced in the US in 1975, challenged the theory that was gaining widespread attention. A DuPont official, the largest manufacturer of CFCs in the world, remarked, "I doubt that we would continue to manufacture or sell a product that poses a hazard to life."[5] Industry began a campaign to discredit the new theory on the basis that it was based on insufficient evidence and called for more time to advance scientific understanding.[6]

Yet, domestic political pressures intensified behind the call for a ban on CFC use in aerosol sprays. By 1976, it was becoming clear that the days of the CFC-containing aerosol spray can were numbered. There was the pressure from many sides to act – from interest groups, the attention given to the issue by the media, and the legislative moves taken by some state governments (in 1976, the Oregon legislature voted to ban the sale of spray cans containing CFCs, and New York passed legislation requiring a warning label to be put on all spray cans containing the chemical). Also, consumers' buying habits began to change, and sales of aerosols dropped sharply. Industry was fighting a losing battle despite concerns about what unilateral action would mean for the competitiveness of the US industry. Pro-regulatory forces won the first round at the domestic level. In August 1977, the US Congress passed amendments to the Clean Air Act authorizing the administrator of the EPA to regulate "any substance . . . which in his judgment may reasonably be anticipated to affect the stratosphere, especially ozone in the stratosphere, if such effect may reasonably be anticipated to endanger public heath or welfare."[7] The Federal Drug Administration, the EPA, and the Consumer Product Safety Commission jointly announced that a ban on the use of CFCs as propellants in spray cans would go into effect in 1978.

[5] Quotation provided by James Walker in a talk entitled, "Lessons on the Ozone Wars," University of Michigan, April 13, 1992.
[6] Dotto and Schiff, *The Ozone War*, p. 235.
[7] Quoted in Richard Benedick, *Ozone Diplomacy: New Directions in Safeguarding the Planet* (Cambridge: Harvard University Press, 1991), p. 23.

Internationalizing the problem

Getting the issue on to the agendas of other CFC producers, including Japan and Germany, was important to the US for scientific, environmental, and economic reasons. Research into the stratosphere was extremely expensive; a ban on the use of CFCs in aerosols in the US alone would have minimal impact on protecting stratospheric ozone; and finally, failure to adopt a similar policy by the other major CFC producers and consumers (i.e., Germany, the EC, and Japan) would put US industry at a disadvantage.[8]

Several efforts at internationalizing the problem were made by different US actors for different reasons. Industry was one of the first to act. In 1973, the US Chemical Manufacturers' Association (CMA) invited members of manufacturers of CFCs from other countries, including Japan and Germany, jointly to establish a Fluorocarbon Technical Panel. Its mandate included funding studies of the impact that fluorocarbons might have on the atmosphere, plants, and animals. Contracts appear to have been biased in favor of scientific work that would show that CFCs were not a problem.[9] Japanese scientists were not actively involved in CMA research efforts although in October 1978, there was an international CMA study group in Tokyo.[10] Nor were German scientists big players. Of the principle investigators on CMA Fluorocarbon Panel Research Contracts as late as 1990, there were only three Japanese and nine German researchers compared with ninety-one US researchers.[11]

Although the US accounted for half of all global production of CFCs in 1974, other countries produced substantial amounts. The US produced 376,000 metric tons. Germany was the second largest producer at 88,300 metric tons. Japan was the sixth largest producer at 34,200 metric tons. Japan eventually moved its way up to the second rank position.[12] Thus, the State Department initiated a program for international exchange of information, cooperative research, and proposals for unified international action.

Two international meetings were held in Washington in March and April of 1977, the first organized by the United Nations Environment

---

[8] Markus Jachtenfuchs, "The European Community and the Protection of the Ozone Layer," *Journal of Common Market Studies*, 28, no. 3 (March 1990), 263–75.

[9] Litfin, *Ozone Discourses*, p. 64.

[10] Tsuushôsangyôshô Kisosangyôkyoku Ozonsô Hogo Taisakushitsu, *Ozonsô Hogo Handobukku* (Tokyo: Kagaku Kôgyô Nippôsha, 1994), p. 515.

[11] Chlorofluorocarbon Manufacturers' Associations Fluorocarbon Panel, "Searching the Stratosphere," 1990 pamphlet.

[12] Thomas B. Stoel, Jr., "Fluorocarbons: Mobilizing Concern and Action," in David Kay and Harold Jacobson (eds.), *Environmental Protection: The International Dimension* (Totowa, NJ: Allanheld, Osmun & Co., 1983), p. 48.

Programme (UNEP) and the second by the US EPA. No consensus was reached among participants on action, but the conferences ended with participants recognizing that "the ozone layer is a global resource, and that current knowledge is adequate to give cause for concern about effects of chlorofluorocarbon use on the ozone shield. At the same time, there is still much to be learned – especially in the effects area."[13]

Two important follow-up meetings were convened in Germany at the initiative of the Ministry of the Interior in late 1978. The first was a meeting of the Coordinating Committee on the Ozone Layer formed at the 1977 UNEP meeting. The committee issued an assessment of the scientific evidence that found consistency in model predictions about the impact of CFCs on the ozone layer, but noted that large uncertainties remained. In the following month, another meeting was held in Munich, assembling members of all CFC-producing nations, except Japan.[14] The purpose of the meeting was to discuss regulatory action. Due to opposition from France and the UK, however, no quantitative goals on CFC reduction were reached.[15] The meeting ended with a statement that "there should be a global reduction in the release of fluorocarbons." Furthermore, the participants called upon "all governments, industry and other bodies to work towards the goal of achieving a significant reduction . . . in the next few years in relation to 1975 data."[16]

While consensus behind an international agreement was not achieved, several states began to take domestic steps to reduce CFC use. In 1976, Canada initiated a voluntary reduction plan for industry, which was made into law in 1979. Sweden banned the manufacture and importation of CFCs in aerosol cans in December 1977. In 1977, the German Ministry of the Interior negotiated an informal agreement with industry to reduce CFC use by 30 percent. Slowly, these efforts began to spread. In 1978, the EC Commission recommended that the production of CFC-11 and CFC-12 not be expanded and that research into alternatives be encouraged. Then, in April 1980, the UNEP Governing Council approved a non-binding resolution for the reduction of CFC use, although no quantitative targets were set. Under growing international pressure, in the spring of 1980, the EC heads of state went beyond their 1978 decision and agreed to a freeze on production capacity of CFC-11 and CFC-12. They also agreed to a reduction in the use of these chemicals by at least 30 percent in aerosol sprays by the end of 1981.

---

[13] Quoted in Stoel, Jr., "Fluorocarbons: Mobilizing Concern and Action," p. 57.
[14] Umweltbundesamt, *Internationale Konferenz über Flurochlorkohlenwasserstoffe*, Conference Proceedings, December 6–8, 1978, Munich.
[15] Benedick, *Ozone Diplomacy*, p. 41.
[16] Stoel, Jr., "Fluorocarbons: Mobilizing Concern and Action," p. 58.

In December 1980, Japan also announced that it would use administrative guidance to get producers to freeze production capacity of CFCs:

The government does not feel that the scientific knowledge which is behind this problem is clear enough, but it is necessary to take a global perspective on the issue. Thus, as a preventative measure, we will conduct research on substitutes and work to reduce CFC release from aerosols. We have taken measures to freeze the production capacity of CFC-11 and -12 and feasible steps to reduce the use of CFC-11 and -12 in aerosol products.[17]

There was an international diffusion of action related to CFCs, but the timing and quality of national responses to ozone depletion varied.[18] The US, Canada, and the Scandinavian countries were the first to act and focused on reducing CFCs in aerosol sprays. The EC took a different approach. Instead of a complete aerosol ban, the EC suggested that a freeze on production capacity and a reduction of CFC use by 30 percent of 1976 levels in aerosols would be sufficient. Japan eventually took a position similar to that of the EC. It relied on administrative guidance rather than regulations to achieve industry compliance.

Markus Jachtenfuchs concluded that the 1980 EC decision "comprise[d] only a minimum solution conceived out of the need to demonstrate to the United States that the EC was willing to act against the depletion of the ozone layer." Moreover, he noted that the EC only called for a production capacity freeze and a reduction in CFC use that had already been obtained by changing consumer buying patterns at the time it was initiated.[19]

The German response

Within the EC, Germany was more proactive in its early response to ozone depletion than it was to acid rain, but ozone depletion was not a particularly big political issue in the 1970s.[20] There were some signs of concern that ozone layer depletion could lead to skin cancer. Consumers also became aware of the Rowland/Molina hypothesis and a Consumers Association together with the BUND called for a consumer boycott of aerosol sprays. There was also limited newspaper attention to the issue. Compared with the US, however, grass roots activity was limited.

[17] Tsuushôsangyôshô Kisosangyôkyoku Ozonsô Hogo Taisakushitsu, *Ozonsô Hogo Handobukku*, p. 39.

[18] Thomas B. Stoel, Jr., Alan S. Miller, and Breck Milroy, *Fluorocarbon Regulation* (Lexington, MA: Heath, 1980).

[19] Jachtenfuchs, "The European Community," 263. See also Ian Rowlands, "EU Policy for Ozone Layer Protection," in Jonathan Golub (ed.), *Global Competition and EU Environmental Policy* (New York: Routledge, 1998), pp. 38–9.

[20] See Stoel, Jr., Miller, and Milroy, *Fluorocarbon Regulation*, pp. 117–29.

A report issued by Battelle Institut-Frankfurt in 1976 argued for further scientific research, but predicted that the economic consequences of regulation would be grave. After the report was issued, the German government increased somewhat funding for research on the ozone layer.[21] The German government also initiated talks with industry about voluntary reductions in the use of CFCs. After intensive negotiations, the industry (primarily the cosmetic industry) agreed to reduce CFC use in aerosols by 25 percent of 1975 levels by 1979. There was a projected reduction of 50 percent by 1981. This was not a big concession since consumer buying patterns were changing.[22] After the international conference on CFCs hosted by the German Ministry of the Interior, the Bundestag's Home Affairs Committee was briefed on the results. Members of the Home Affairs Committee became convinced that a reduction of CFCs in aerosols was necessary and that corresponding EC action should be a goal. The committee questioned why the informal agreement between industry and the Ministry of the Interior had been limited to a relatively small reduction goal. The decision was justified based on consumption trends in CFCs that already showed a 17.5 percent reduction in the total consumption of CFCs in aerosols between 1975 and 1977 and the significant economic costs that would be incurred by regulations.

Calls for a ban on CFC use in non-essential aerosol uses similar to those initiated in the US and Sweden did not materialize due to industry opposition. At a March 1980 meeting of the Home Affairs Committee, a unanimous resolution was passed that stressed the need to reduce CFC use still further. The committee called on the German government to study the effects of a ban and proposed a future total ban on the use of CFCs, including in areas where substitutes for CFCs were not yet available or practical (e.g., in refrigerants).

The federal minister of the interior submitted a report on CFCs and the environment in May 1980. The report noted that a total ban on CFCs in aerosols had proved feasible abroad but that in Germany it could lead to a loss of sales totaling DM 180 million for Germany's two producers of CFCs (Hoechst AG and Kali-Chemie) and DM 50 million for their suppliers, or 0.3 percent of the chemical industry's total sales in 1977. It also suggested that there were no good alternatives to CFCs given the state of the art of refrigerator design and that similar problems existed for other industrial uses.

[21] German Bundestag (ed.), *Protecting the Earth's Atmosphere: An International Challenge*, Interim Report of the Study Commission of the 11th German Bundestag, *Preventive Measures to Protect the Earth's Atmosphere*, vol. I (Bonn: Deutscher Bundestag, 1989), p. 189.
[22] Stoel, Jr., "Fluorocarbons: Mobilizing Concern and Action," p. 61.

With resistance to further action in Brussels and in the absence of strong domestic pressures for further action, policy change in Germany remained limited. The government justified its position by arguing that the global nature of ozone damage made it desirable to adopt a supranational approach, working together with other countries within the framework of the EC.[23] The government did, however, call for more drastic reductions in the aerosol sector as a way of compensating for the growing use of CFCs in other applications.[24]

In the following years, some scientists suggested that ozone depletion was occurring less rapidly than earlier believed. Producers and users used this to oppose spending large amounts of money in finding CFC substitutes. Thus, the EC determined in May 1983 that it was not necessary to amend the policies that the EC had pursued to date and that no additional assessments would be necessary before the end of 1985. The German government supported this view. The German aerosol industry responded to this shift in the scientific debate with the following press release:

Ozone hysteria – did it really have to be? Environmental relevance of aerosol propellants put back in perspective – popularity of sprays keeps growing. What environmentalists saw as a warning was scientifically disputed from the very beginning and has now proven to be a miscalculation . . . In the Federal Republic of Germany, the authorities should avoid over-hasty measures when it comes to handing down administrative regulations and they should take into account current scientific findings.[25]

Initially, Germany used its EC membership as a way of reducing domestic and international pressure to take additional regulatory steps. The Dutch environmental minister Peter Winsemius critically suggested that it was the most economically advanced states within the EC, and in particular Germany, France, and the UK, which clung to the 1980 EC policy on CFCs as a way of protecting their domestic chemical industries.[26]

The Japanese response

Japan, France, and the UK rejected initial US-led calls for an international agreement on reducing CFC use. Only a few years back, the US had similarly warned of damage to the ozone layer from supersonic transport, a theory which later lost some of its salience when it was determined

---

[23] German Bundestag (ed.), *Protecting the Earth's Atmosphere*, pp. 194–7.

[24] Helmut Breitmeier, *Wie entstehen globale Umweltregime? Der Konfliktaustrag zum Schutz der Ozonschict und des globalen Klimas* (Opladen: Leske & Budrich, 1996), p. 111.

[25] Cited in German Bundestag, *Protecting the Earth's Atmosphere*, pp. 199–200.

[26] Jachtenfuchs, "The European Community," 265.

that the amount of NO_x emissions that would be released into the stratosphere by a fleet of SSTs was negligible. There was some concern that
perhaps US companies had already developed new technologies and were
pushing new regulations to benefit US industry.[27] Japan, France, and the
UK remained skeptical of the latest ozone theory.

Japan had five producers of CFCs and three producers of halon: Shôwa
Denkô KK (CFCs), Daikin Industries, Ltd. (CFCs and halon), Asahi
Glass Co., Ltd. (CFCs and halon), Central Glass Co., Ltd. (CFCs),
DuPont–Mitsui Fluorochemicals Co., Ltd. (CFCs), and Nihon Halon
(halon). Together, they produced slightly under one tenth the amount
of CFCs being produced in the US and somewhat under one half
the amount being produced in Germany in 1974. In 1973, the Japan
Flon (Freon) Gas Association (JFGA), an association of CFC-producing
companies, joined the Fluorocarbon Technical Panel. This international
panel provided an avenue for the CFC manufacturers to stay abreast of
pertinent international research findings. The JFGA, however, was not
actively involved in research efforts, although from 1973 to 1989, it
contributed annually between 5.5 and 9 percent of the Fluorocarbon
Technical Panel's annual budget.[28] Outside of these cooperative international projects, there was limited Japanese industry support for research
on CFCs and the ozone layer.[29]

In sharp comparison with the US and even with Germany, there
were no domestic actors trying to get ozone layer protection on to the
agenda. There was almost no media attention to ozone depletion or the
Rowland/Molina hypothesis and, despite much searching, I have been
unable to identify any NGOs in Japan that picked up on the issue in
the 1970s. The first NGO activity appears to have begun in 1981 by
the Greater Osaka Consumer Association, which later gave birth to the
Citizens' Alliance for Saving the Atmosphere and the Earth (CASA).[30]

There was little scientific research in Japan on the stratospheric ozone
layer prior to 1980.[31] Japanese atmospheric scientists concentrated their
energies on understanding ground level air pollution. The Environment
Agency's main research contribution in relation to stratospheric ozone
depletion was a three-year project that it initiated in 1978 to test levels
of CFCs in the stratosphere using jumbo aircraft carriers flying between

[27] Hidefumi Imura and Hikaru Kobayashi, "Kagakuteki Fukakujitsusei no moto ni Okeru
Ishi Kettei," *Kankyô Kenkyû* 68 (1988), 26.
[28] Chlorofluorocarbon Manufacturers Associations Fluorocarbon Panel, "Searching the
Stratosphere."
[29] Interview with representatives of the Japan Flon Gas Association, May 1992.
[30] CASA, pamphlet.
[31] On the early history of stratospheric ozone science in Japan see Kôji Kawahira and Yukio
Makino, *Ozon Shôshitsu* (Tokyo: Yomiuri Kagaku Sensho, 1989), pp. 208–16.

Narita, Anchorage, and San Francisco.[32] In September 1980, the Environment Agency's Environmental Health Department also prepared a very brief report on the "CFC Problem" that primarily introduced the research program that the agency had launched.[33]

Still, as a result of international pressures, MITI felt pressured to act. The ministry issued guidelines to reduce CFC emissions in September 1980 and three months later announced at the 28th OECD Environmental Committee meeting that it would work to freeze production capacity of CFC-11 and CFC-12 at 1980 levels and to decrease them further through administrative guidance.[34]

MITI objected, however, to any further action reasoning that: (1) Japan consumed only one fourth the amount of aerosols on a per capita basis that were consumed in other advanced industrialized countries; (2) restrictions on the use of liquid petroleum gas meant that it could not be used as a substitute for CFCs in aerosols as was done in the US; and (3) in 1979, consumption of CFCs in Japan was already down approximately 25 percent from 1973 levels.[35] Ironically, after 1979, CFC production increased sharply in Japan.

Despite these objections to further policy action, in 1981, MITI established a Policy Committee on Chlorofluorocarbons and the Environment within the Basic Industry Division and another Committee on Chlorofluorocarbon Modeling. MITI also began to conduct yearly surveys on fluorocarbon production capacity and the potentials for alternatives.

The 1981 Environmental White Paper noted: "The threat of chlorofluorocarbons damaging the ozone layer, has touched off extensive debates among Europeans and Americans, whose skin is particularly sensitive to ultraviolet rays."[36] There was a general feeling that ozone layer depletion was more a problem for Caucasians than Japanese who are less prone to skin cancer.

A period of limited international activity

The efforts made in several states to reduce CFC use in aerosols as well as changing consumer preferences led to a drop in world CFC production by almost 25 percent between 1974 and 1982. The problem of CFCs in the environment, however, was not solved. The drop in worldwide

[32] *Nihon Keizai Shimbun,* March 11, 1979.
[33] Kankyôchô Kankyô Hokenbu Hoken Chôsa Shitsu, "Furon Gasu Mondai ni Tsuite," September 1980.
[34] Takashi Ôshima, "Furongasu," *Kankyô Kenkyû* 33 (1981), 128–9.
[35] *Nihon Keizai Shimbun,* December 15, 1980, p. 1 (evening edition).
[36] Environment Agency of Japan, *Quality of the Environment in Japan* (Tokyo: Environment Agency of Japan, 1981), p. 37.

production of CFCs was short lived. By 1982, production levels were again rising because of the chemical's growing importance as a cleaning solvent (CFC-113), in foam, and refrigerants. Tonnage of CFC-11 and CFC-12 by EC producers rose rapidly after 1982. Production and sale of CFC-113 and CFC-114 steadily rose from 1976.[37] Scientific assessment of the status of the stratospheric ozone layer continued but no consensus was achieved, and some scientists argued that earlier projections had been overblown. A 1981 National Academy of Sciences report found no evidence of ozone layer depletion but predicted a loss of 5 to 9 percent by the second half of the twenty-first century. Industry read this to mean that there was no serious problem and used it to argue against further regulations, even though other scientific reports suggested that there was indeed a problem at hand.

In the US, after the appointment of Anne Gorsuch Burford as EPA administrator, administrative support for further regulatory efforts largely dried up. Burford had made it clear that she did not think that ozone layer depletion was a serious threat. DuPont stopped its research on replacements for CFCs.[38]

Ozone layer protection also fell off the agenda in Germany – not that it fell very far since it had not been a big priority up to this time and engendered nowhere near the same kind of public concern that acid rain had in the early 1980s. A May 1983 European Commission report to the Council stated that, based on current scientific understanding and economic data, there was no need to amend the EC's policy on CFCs. Pushed by industry, the German government supported this position. The German aerosol industry issued a press release in 1984 that stated:

Since February 1984, there has been another argument in favour of aerosol sprays – their environmental compatibility . . . German industry responded with voluntary self-restraint to the hasty legislative measures, which in the United States, Canada, Sweden and Norway even went so far as to ban the controversial CFCs, consequently leading to considerable restrictions in the European Community as well . . . In the Federal Republic of Germany, the authorities in charge of environmental matters should avoid over-hasty measures when it comes to handing down administrative regulations and they should take into account current scientific findings. In this way, it would be possible to avoid both unnecessary worry for the environmentally-minded consumer and considerable consequential economic costs resulting from precipitative measures.[39]

There were few actors in Germany challenging the statement.

---

[37] German Bundestag (ed.), *Protecting the Earth's Atmosphere*, pp. 176–7.
[38] Litfin, *Ozone Discourses*, p. 70.
[39] German Bundestag (ed.), *Protecting the Earth's Atmosphere*, pp. 199–200.

The road to the Vienna Convention

Although the sense of political urgency for further action was sharply diminished, at a conference of UNEP held in Montevideo, the ozone layer was made a priority action area for UNEP. Mostafa Tolba, head of UNEP, initiated work towards an international agreement to protect the ozone layer. There were seven working group meetings between 1982 and 1985 at which negotiations were initiated for a framework convention on ozone depletion. A major issue that had to be resolved in these negotiations was the negotiating rights of the EC. After much debate and initial US objections, the EC was permitted to participate along with its member states in the international negotiation.

In these deliberations, two main proposals emerged for a framework convention: the "Toronto" group (the name deriving from the city where a meeting was held by the group), which included Canada, Finland, Norway, Sweden, Switzerland, and the US – which joined the group only after Anne Gorsuch Burford was forced to resign as the head of the EPA – advocated a worldwide ban on non-essential uses of CFCs in spray cans as well as additional regulations. These states had already instituted bans on aerosol sprays containing CFCs because substitutes for CFCs in aerosol sprays (but not for other applications) were already available.

An EC group, backed by Japan and the Soviet Union, strongly opposed this proposal. Instead, the EC came up with an alternative draft protocol text that would require each nation to freeze its CFC-11 and CFC-12 production capacity (as opposed to total production) and reduce the use of CFCs in aerosols sprays by 30 percent. This position required no additional measures above those already taken by Japan and the EC in 1980, since production levels were still well below capacity and a 30 percent reduction in CFC use in aerosols had already been achieved. The EC maintained that a total ban on CFCs in aerosols was jumping ahead of what current science warranted. The US countered that a production capacity cap would allow major EC producer countries, because of their excess capacity (about 35 percent), to expand production well into the future.

The Toronto group made several proposals: a total ban on CFC use in aerosols, an 80 percent cut of CFC use in aerosols, a 20 percent reduction of all CFC use in four years, and, finally, 70 percent reduction related to aerosol use plus a production cap. The EC group argued that these proposals did not take into account the expected long-term growth in CFC production as demand rose. Eventually, the US was to come to agree with the EC on this issue.[40]

---

[40] Litfin, *Ozone Discourses*, pp. 73–5.

In March 1985, representatives of forty-three countries convened in Vienna for an ozone convention. With a stalemate among participating states over what kind of measure to adopt – a worldwide ban on the non-essential use of CFCs in aerosols or a production capacity freeze – the Vienna Convention simply created a general obligation for signatories to take "appropriate measures" to protect the ozone layer. Signatories included all the major CFC-producing nations except Japan. Japan's formal justification for its decision not to sign was that the agreement lacked any concrete measures. Internationally, this was seen as a delay tactic.[41] Indicative of the issue's low priority, the Environment Agency failed to send a representative to the meeting. Stated an Environment Agency bureaucrat: "In the 1980s we were more concerned with domestic environmental issues than international ones."[42]

The Montreal Protocol

At the close of the Vienna Convention, there was an agreement to meet again in two years to negotiate a protocol if warranted. International efforts to meet this deadline were spurred on by subsequent scientific findings. First, in May 1985, two British scientists published their findings of a hole in the ozone layer over Antarctica. Then in 1986, three US agencies, the World Meteorological Organization (WMO), UNEP, the Commission of the European Communities, and the West German Federal Ministry for Research and Technology published a major international scientific report on the stratosphere. The report was the most comprehensive of its kind and represented a close approximation to a broad international scientific consensus on the condition of the ozone layer. Based on various models, the report suggested that at 1980 rates of CFC-11 and CFC-12 releases, the ozone layer would decline by 40 percent or more.

International negotiations for a protocol began the next year. There still was considerable scientific uncertainty about the real rates of ozone layer depletion and even about levels of CFC production, but there was now a much greater sense of urgency behind the negotiations as a result of the discovery of the ozone hole.

The big differences that existed at the negotiating table at the time of the Vienna Convention between the Toronto group and the EC group carried over into negotiations for a protocol. The EC group maintained its support for a production capacity cap. The US, as a result of changes in leadership in the EPA and control within the EPA over the ozone

[41] Imura and Kobayashi, "Kagakuteki Fukakujitsusei," 27–8. See also Kankyôchô Ozonsô Hogo Kentôkai (ed.), *Ozonsô o Mamoru* (Tokyo: NHK Books, 1990).
[42] Interview with Environment Agency official, summer 1991.

layer issue, came out with a proposal calling for a far more drastic cut than that proposed by the EC – a near term freeze on consumption of CFC-11, CFC-12, and CFC-113 and halon-1211 and halon-1301. In addition, the US proposed 95 percent reductions of these compounds to be phased in by the year 2000. Industry and industrial representatives in the US government opposed the US negotiating position, which they had had little say in formulating. Because the 95 percent reduction goal had already been tendered internationally, it was not revoked, but the US delegation to the negotiations was instructed to push only for a 50 percent reduction in CFCs and a freeze on halons.[43]

US leadership had waned in the early 1980s, but in the negotiations leading up to the Montreal Protocol, the US played a forceful role in pushing for an international agreement. Domestically, support for action was strengthened based on the discovery of the "ozone hole" and the growing belief that delayed action would have serious long-term consequences. There also was concern within industry that the US government might take unilateral regulatory action in response to public demands. A level international playing field was preferred by industry. In September 1986, DuPont and the Alliance for a Responsible CFC Policy, a lobby group of CFC users and producers, announced their support for an international agreement. DuPont also felt confident about its ability to produce substitutes.[44]

In the initial negotiations in December 1986, the EC balked at the US position but eventually its opposition broke down. There were internal differences within the EC. On the one hand, the UK, France, and Italy, all CFC producers, continued to favor a production capacity cap that would require no further regulatory actions. Japan sided with this group which argued that significant ozone depletion would not occur for decades and that there was need for more scientific research before taking drastic regulatory measures. Germany, the remaining major producer of CFCs within the EC, on the other hand, joined the Netherlands, Denmark, and Belgium in calling for stricter regulations. This meant that by the February 1997 negotiations, the US position had gained strength. In the end, the Montreal Protocol stipulated a freeze on production and consumption of controlled CFCs at 1986 levels and then stepped reductions to 50 percent of 1986 levels by 1998. It also included a freeze on the production and consumption of controlled halons at 1986 levels. Developing countries were allowed some exceptions to these rules.

With the US pushing internationally and Germany pushing within the EC, in September 1987, twenty-five countries including Japan, Germany,

[43] Litfin, *Ozone Discourses*, pp. 82–106.
[44] Kauffman, "Domestic and International Linkages," p. 78.

and the European Community agreed to the Montreal Protocol. Japan ratified the Montreal Protocol and the Vienna Convention on September 31, 1988. Germany ratified the Montreal Protocol on November 9, 1988. The roles of Germany and Japan in the unfolding negotiations are discussed below.

Germany's evolving leadership within the EC

As a result of a strengthened international scientific consensus on the need for action after the Vienna Convention and a growing domestic consensus behind the need for action, the German government's position within the EC became markedly more proactive than it was earlier in the decade. In the early 1980s, in an effort to protect Hoechst, the largest German CFC producer, from costly regulations, the government had opposed any international regulatory agreements that would go beyond the EC's 1980 pledge.

By the time of the first round of international negotiations for the Montreal Protocol in December 1986, however, the German position had changed dramatically. The shift in the German stance reflected the importance of German involvement in the formation of an international scientific consensus on the need for action, the greening of the domestic political landscape, and the heightened power of environmental bureaucrats after the Chernobyl nuclear accident. The Chernobyl nuclear accident not only heightened domestic awareness of the international nature of many environmental concerns; it also empowered environmental interests within the governmental system. Seizing an opportunity to show his support for environmental initiatives and to respond to calls by the SPD and the Greens for an immediate halt to Germany's nuclear energy program, in June 1986, Chancellor Helmut Kohl proposed that a Federal Ministry for Environment, Nature Protection, and Reactor Safety be created. This institutional change strengthened the position of those in the bureaucracy calling for a stronger regulatory position on ozone layer protection and other environmental issues. In the past, questions related to CFC use and the ozone layer had been handled by the Ministry of the Interior, which had the advancement of the nation's economic goals as its primary goal. With the creation of the Ministry for Environment, the issue was put into the hands of a ministry that had environmental protection as its primary goal.[45]

Reflecting the changed political landscape, the German government strongly criticized a November 1986 report of the European Commission

[45] Kauffman, "Domestic and International Linkages," p. 84.

that stated that no further action beyond the measures taken in 1980 would be necessary – a position which Germany had itself maintained just a few years earlier.

The improved electoral performance of the Greens in the 1986 elections strengthened the position of environmentalists who renewed their 1976 campaign for an aerosol ban and a CFC phase out.[46] Prevention of further ozone depletion was first dealt with along with other air pollution issues. When in early 1986, the German government amended its Clean-Air Regulation (TA Luft) and the Regulation Limiting Emissions of Volatile Halogenated Hydrocarbons, it included a provision, which defined emission limits for CFC emitting installations. It was estimated that this provision would lead to a reduction of about 90 percent in CFC emissions from plants producing polyurethane foams. Pressures quickly grew, however, for a total ban on aerosols using CFCs.

Reacting to these pressures, in March 1987, Kohl called for national and international action to address the growing global threats to the earth's atmosphere. In May 1987, the Bundesrat adopted a resolution calling for a general ban on the production and marketing of CFCs. The ban was to cover the production and use of CFCs as propellants for aerosol sprays (except where used for medical purposes) and their use in products where substitution of other chemicals was possible. A few months later, in May 1987, the German parliament called for consideration of a national ban on CFC use in aerosols and sharp reductions in other areas. The aerosol industry reacted by making a commitment voluntarily to reduce CFCs in spray cans.

Protection of the ozone layer was on the political agenda and prevention of global climate change was rapidly being linked to this issue. The SPD proposed a motion in August 1987 calling for an immediate ban on CFC use in aerosols, their reduction in other applications, and study of restrictions on the production and consumption of long-lived chlorinated and brominated hydrocarbons. The following month, the Green Party's Parliamentary Group proposed a ban on CFCs in aerosols to begin in July 1988.

The German government responded by noting that a voluntary agreement already had been established with industry that would lead to a phase out of CFCs in aerosols by the end of 1990. The government also argued that international measures were more critical than isolated national ones and that a national ban on the production of aerosols with CFCs would not be immediately possible because of EC regulations regarding the free movement of goods within the community.

[46] Litfin, *Ozone Discourses*, p. 110.

The Committee for the Environment, Nature Conservation, and Nuclear Safety turned down the motions proposed by the SPD and the Greens. Instead, it called for meeting the objective of the Montreal Protocol through voluntary restrictions by industry. The argument proposed was that this would be more flexible and would not require legislative measures. The committee also called for the speedy implementation of the Protocol by the EC. Finally, the committee agreed unanimously to establish an Enquete Commission on Preventive Measures to Protect the Earth's Atmosphere, with the mandate to study the ozone problem and make proposals for action.[47]

As a rule, Enquete commissions are composed in such a way that half of its members are representatives from all the parties and the other half are experts. Because of the popularity of this commission, eleven parliamentarians, as opposed to the normal nine, were appointed – five from the CDU/CSU, four from the SPD, and one each from the FDP and the Green Party. The purpose of the Enquete commission was to incorporate scientific findings more rapidly into the political process by bringing parliamentarians face to face with scientific experts. After eleven months, the commission presented a 600-page report to parliament that expressed its opinion that the Montreal Protocol is "far from sufficient in order to reduce the damage already caused, or yet to be expected," to the stratospheric ozone layer. Because CFCs damage the ozone layer and account for 17 percent of the greenhouse effect, the Enquete Commission announced its feelings that the production and use of these substances should be reduced by at least 95 percent by 2000. The Commission urged the German government to press internationally for a 95 percent reduction in controlled substances at the latest by 1997 based on 1986 levels. It also urged the EC to act regardless of the outcome of international negotiations. Finally, the study commission felt that Germany should take the lead by reducing by at least 50 percent ozone depleting substances listed in the Montreal Protocol based on 1986 levels by 1990 at the latest, a 70 percent reduction by 1992, and a 95 percent reduction by 1995.

The report concluded: "it is indispensable that efforts made to obtain self-restraint commitments from industry should extend over a limited period of time only. If no agreements are reached by a given date, legal regulations should be proposed to [the] German parliament without any further delay."[48]

Between 1986 and 1988, CFC use as a propellant in spray cans dropped by almost 85 percent. Initially, the German government

[47] German Bundestag (ed.), *Protecting the Earth's Atmosphere*, pp. 202–8.
[48] German Bundestag (ed.), *Protecting the Earth's Atmosphere*, pp. 54–61, quotation on p. 59.

relied completely on informal agreements with industry to reduce the emissions of CFCs. In August 1987, the aerosol industry, for instance, made a binding agreement with the Ministry for Environment (newly established in 1986) that it would reduce the use of CFC-11 and CFC-12 in aerosols by 90 percent by December 1989. Failure on the part of the CFC industries to meet fully with reporting commitments under this voluntary restriction plan led to demands for a ban.

The need to negotiate with other EC members on a joint plan for action prior to formulating domestic policy regulations was a central element of the policy-making process in Germany. The UK, like Japan, remained opposed to the formulation of an international agreement. As was true for the Benelux countries, Germany's newly proactive domestic policy position was constrained to some extent by its membership within the EC.

In response to a mid-1987 proposal for an immediate ban of CFCs in aerosols by a group of Green Party representatives in the Bundestag, the German government said that it was "more effective to control a possible depletion of the ozone layer by an agreement providing for medium CFC reduction rates that was signed and respected by a large number of countries, than by an agreement providing for higher reduction rates but signed only by a few countries."[49] The change in Germany's stance shifted the balance of pro- and anti-regulatory views within the European Council in the direction of stricter regulations, and allowed for agreement between the EC and the US on a proposal to take an initial step to reduce CFC production and consumption by 20 percent. By February 1987, Germany was advocating unilateral cuts of 50 percent and urging other EC members to follow suit.

Germany took over the EC presidency in 1987, giving it a chance to exert additional pressure on reluctant member states. Germany put ozone layer protection on the top of the EC agenda and played a pivotal role in getting France and the UK to agree to the provisions of the Protocol.[50] In May 1988, the German federal Cabinet approved the Montreal Protocol, and a month later under the German presidency, the EC Council of Ministers for the Environment also signed the agreement.

Japan's reluctant acceptance

The story of Shigeru Chûbachi and his colleagues in making the first discovery of an unprecedented decline in the ozone layer over Antarctica is a good starting point for our discussion of Japan. Chûbachi, a specialist on the stratospheric ozone layer in the Meteorological Agency's

---

[49] German Bundestag (ed.), *Protecting the Earth's Atmosphere*, p. 208.
[50] Jachtenfuchs, "The European Community," 267.

Aerological Observatory, was a member of a winter research team sent annually to the Shôwa base, a meteorological observation outpost on East Ongul Island, about 5 kilometers from the Antarctic mainland. On September 4, 1982, Chûbachi's data showed that the amount of stratospheric ozone was significantly less than the previous day's measurement. It was also extremely low when compared with data from the previous sixteen years of measurements. For the next month and a half, the data continued to show a decrease in the ozone layer that was considerably higher than estimates based on previous measurements would predict. Not only was the depletion rate unexpectedly high, but at a height of 20 kilometers where ozone levels were supposed to be ten times as high as at the earth's surface, they were surprisingly low. At the time, scientists were talking about ozone depletion due to CFCs above a height of 40 kilometers, believing that ozone depleting chemical reactions would not occur at a height of 20 kilometers. Such low levels of ozone at this height had never been reported. Chûbachi and his colleague, Ryôichi Kajiwara, were worried about their findings. So unusual was their data that they felt that if they reported it and they were wrong, their careers would be over. Could their data be right when the National Aeronautics and Space Administration (NASA) had made no such reports? Their first reaction was concern about their equipment. They feared that the Dobson meter that they had newly brought to the base might be to blame, but when they returned to Japan and tested the meter, they found that it was operating properly.

Chûbachi first reported his findings in the spring of 1983 at the Ministry of Education's Polar Research Institute and elsewhere in Japan. He then traveled to Greece and reported his findings at the 1984 International Ozone Symposium.[51] There were only seven other Japanese at this meeting of 300 scientists. Kôji Kawahira, who was among them, expressed his concern at the meeting to Chûbachi about the Dobson meter. How could Chûbachi be right? Chûbachi's findings received little reaction in Japan or internationally.[52]

Chûbachi noted that, at the time he made his discovery, others within the Meteorology Agency showed little support for his work.[53] This conclusion differs from that of James Feinerman and Koichiru Fujikura who

---

[51] See Shigeru Chûbachi, "Watashi ga Ozon Hôru o Hakkenshita Koro," *Nihon Butsuri Gakkaishi* 48 (1993), 815–18; and Shigeru Chûbachi, "A Special Ozone Observation at Syowa Station, Antarctica from February 1982 to January 1983," in C. S. Zerefos and A. Ghazi (eds.), for the Commission of the European Communities, *Atmospheric Ozone: Proceeding of the Quadrennial Ozone Symposium Held in Halkidiki, Greece, 3–7 September 1984* (Dordrecht: D. Reidel Publishing Co., 1985), pp. 285–9.

[52] Kawahira and Makino, *Ozon Shôshitsu*, pp. 20–4.

[53] Interview with Shigeru Chûbachi, August 1994. See also Kawahira and Makino, *Ozon Shôshitsu*.

argue that after "a Japanese research team stationed at the South Pole first observed and reported an unusal depletion of the ozone layer... [t]he matter caught public attention and accelerated international efforts to arrest the depletion."[54]

There was also little awareness of the issue among the public or political leaders. Prior to 1987, the Environment Agency had only one official working part time on the subject. In annual intergovernmental meetings that occurred between the US EPA and the Environment Agency, US officials brought up the ozone problem several times. Reflecting on these discussions, two Environment Agency bureaucrats wrote: "It was a mystery to us why the US side was so concerned with this issue."[55]

It could also be argued that industry had an interest in maintaining a perception that CFCs were not a big problem. Industry was concerned that regulation of CFC-113 would have serious implications for the semi-conductor industry at a time when Japan dominated worldwide production. Production of CFCs in Japan had steadily increased from their 1980 level of 94,291 tons to 209,434 tons by 1987. As of 1986, Japan accounted for approximately 11 percent of world production and 12 percent of world consumption of CFCs. Moreover, while in 1980 only two kinds of CFCs – CFC-11 and CFC-12 – were targeted for regulation; in the meantime, numerous other substances, including among others CFC-113 and various halons, had made it on to the list of ozone depleting substances.[56] This meant that such important industries as the semi-conductor, electronics, refrigeration, food, packaging, and automobile industries had a direct stake in any policy decision.

Japan's position was relatively safe as long as other major CFC producers, such as the UK and France, opposed regulations. Once the EC's position began to change, however, it became harder for Japan to oppose the establishment of an international agreement. The US began a series of bi-lateral initiatives to convince Japan and other countries that opposed international regulations to change their position.[57] With scientific uncertainty becoming less of a possible excuse for non-action, it became increasingly difficult to remain opposed to action. Japan also was concerned with the economic implications of non-cooperation.

At several points in the on-going international negotiations for the formulation of a legally binding protocol, the US had introduced specific

---

[54] Feinerman and Fujikura, "Japan: Consensus-Based Compliance," p. 282.

[55] Imura and Kobayashi, "Kagakuteki Fukakujitsusei," 26.

[56] Greenpeace, "Furon Repôto: Nihon ni Okeru Omona Ozonsô Hakaibusshitsu no Seisan, Shôhi Dôkô," May 1991.

[57] See Kazuaki Mori, "Ozonsô Hogo Mondai no Kagakuteki Chiken ni Kansuru Nichibei Senmonka Kaigô ni Tsuite," *Kankyô Kenkyû* 65 (1987), 53–8; and Yoshinori Komiya, "Furon Kisei Mondai to Nihon no Taiô," *Kôgai to Taisaku* 24 (1988), 46–53.

proposals to restrict trade in CFCs and other controlled substances to non-parties. Furthermore, as an incentive to get countries to ratify the Protocol, it had bargained hard to introduce restrictions on imports of products containing or produced with CFCs or other substances that were to be controlled. Richard Benedick, the chief US negotiator in the international process, stated that: "One rationale for such limits was to provide another incentive for potential holdouts to join the protocol, lest they lose their markets (for example, Asian electronic products using CFC 113 as a circuit cleaner)."[58] While many of these proposals were eventually watered down and were never all that close to being adopted, they must have caused concern in Japan and elsewhere. Alan Miller, a long-time observer of Japanese CFC policies, noted that in early 1987, Senator John Chafee introduced a bill to ban imports of CFC-containing products from countries that were not in compliance with international agreements or that had not taken action equivalent to the US. Richard Benedick publicized this bill in Japan during a satellite press conference, which Miller said, "received attention disproportionate to its likely legislative prospects."[59]

Also at this time, Dupont, the world's largest producer of CFCs supplying about 25 percent of the world market, announced its intentions to phase out completely CFCs by early next century. This must have worried Japanese producers.

These activities helped to expand levels of participation in Japan, heightening the likelihood that policy change would occur. Beginning in 1987, a few Kômeitô and Socialist Party members began to raise questions about Japan's policy. In March 1987, Dietwoman Wakako Hironaka (Kômeitô), who had recently met with US EPA director Lee Thomas, in Diet interpellations asked officials from the Environment Agency, MITI, and the MoFA to explain Japan's stratospheric ozone policy and why Japan was not yet a signatory to the Vienna Convention. Thomas had asked Hironaka to encourage Japanese cooperation.[60] Similarly, in May 1987, at a meeting of the Lower House's Environmental Committee, Kômeitô Dietman Kazuyoshi Endô noted that Japan's production of CFCs was rising sharply and that Japan was becoming the object of international criticism. He urged that Japan take positive action.[61] These developments mark the beginning of a period of rapid expansion of

[58] Benedick, *Ozone Diplomacy*, p. 92.
[59] Alan Miller's comments to the author.
[60] Record of the 108th Diet, House of Councilor's Foreign Affairs Committee meeting, March 26, 1987.
[61] Record of the 108th Diet, House of Representative's Environmental Committee meeting, May 15, 1987.

interest in international environmental issues in Japan that were to be accompanied by dramatic policy and some institutional changes.

In February 1987, MITI's Chemical Substances Committee produced an influential report that provided the foundation for Japan's Law Concerning the Protection of the Ozone Layer through the Control of Specified Substances and Other Measures. The Environment Agency also established a Stratospheric Ozone Protection Research Group and in October, reorganized this as the Upper Atmosphere Protection Policy Room. The Environment Agency had a lot of catching up to do. Given the lack of cooperation between MITI and the Environment Agency, the limited original scientific data coming out of Japan on this issue, and the Environment Agency's difficulties in getting information from industry, the members of the Research Group had to rely almost completely on research findings made abroad to produce a report. Using this foreign language material, in May 1987, the Research Group issued a thin interim report summarizing the science behind the ozone hole predictions.[62]

As a result of international exchange of information, application of heavy US pressure, and changing policy dynamics in Japan, the government warmed to the idea of joining the international agreement. The sticky point remained the question of restrictions on CFC-113. In the end, Japan agreed to the protocol once a compromise was made. In the compromise, CFC-113 was included but as a concession, parties to the convention were permitted to transfer among themselves portions of their allowable levels of production of a controlled chemical so long as their combined level of production did not exceed permitted totals (a basket approach). Importantly, under the terms of the protocol, production was calculated not just in terms of raw numbers, but also in relation to a chemical's ozone depleting potential. The protocol, thus, recognized that different chemicals presented different levels of hazard for the ozone layer.[63]

It is interesting to see how this process was reported in the Japanese press. A September 18, 1987 article in the *Nihon Keizai Shimbun* reported:

On the 16th UNEP decided on a policy to freeze CFCs at current production levels and then in ten years to reduce their level by half in steps. But this did not even come across the minds of Japan's relevant ministries and agencies. If you look at the negotiations until now, Japan was pushed by the US with its overwhelmingly strong basic research. Japan looked like it had to be dragged into the process of making a regulatory plan . . . After ten years what is still the same is the indecisive response of the administration and industrial world. Compared

---

[62] Environment Agency of Japan, "Seisôken Ozonsô Hogo ni Kansuru Kentôkai Chûkan Hôkoku," May 1987.
[63] Litfin, *Ozone Discourses*, p. 114.

with the US government, which was moved to act by strong arguments made by environmental scientists and NGOs in US environmental groups, Japan had no clear reaction, and slithered into retreat. In the negotiations, because of the doubts of the electric goods industry, which was the original CFC user and producer, MITI entered the negotiations with caution. It expected the same from the US and Europe, but it predicted incorrectly . . . The US government came to Japan to hold a meeting on Cooperation in Ozone Layer Protection. Japan neither agreed, nor disagreed, but said it would make positive contributions with data from Japanese surveys without proposing any plans . . . According to Kyoto University Professor Takasaki Masataka, "The homework that the CFC problem has left behind is tied to the big theme of how to get Japan to internationalize."[64]

In the end, Japan adopted the provisions of the Montreal Protocol as considered sufficient by MITI.[65] The Environment Agency which had wanted Japan to go beyond the Montreal Protocol provisions achieved only a small victory. It managed to get a tax incentive for CFC emissions control equipment included in a tax reform package and to convince LDP politicians to include a provision for the control of emissions into domestic law.

The Montreal Protocol amendments: moves towards a total ban of ozone depleting substances

An important element of the Montreal Protocol was its provision for periodic reviews of new scientific, technical, and economic understandings so that the treaty could be amended based on new knowledge. Indeed, international efforts to phase out completely the uses of CFCs and other ozone depleting substances progressed rapidly as new evidence emerged that the ozone layer was being destroyed more rapidly than previously thought.

Almost immediately after the Montreal Protocol was signed, environmental groups in Europe and the European parliament began to demand the strengthening of the EC and German policies. The European parliament joined the European Environmental Bureau, a coordinating body for environmental NGOs in Europe, and the European Bureau of Consumers' Unions in calling for an 85 percent reduction in the use of CFCs within ten years. The European Commission did not immediately respond to these calls, arguing that it was first necessary to get member states to ratify the Montreal Protocol as it had been negotiated. The Commission was concerned that any amendments would imperil the

---

[64] *Nihon Keizai Shimbun*, September 18, 1987, p. 2 (evening edition).
[65] Shin'ichi Kudô, "Ozonsô Hogohô o Furikaette," *Kankyô* 14, 44–8.

French and British willingness to ratify.[66] Pressures for the EC to modify its position, however, continued to build.

In early March 1988, the Ozone Trends Panel announced that ozone depletion was occurring over the northern hemisphere. After the report was released, DuPont announced its plans to work on a total phase out of halogenated CFCs as quickly as possible. Soon afterward, the European Fluorocarbon Technical Committee, ICI, and the US Alliance for a Responsible CFC Policy all announced their support for a phase out.[67] The Germans and the Danes called on the EC to speed up the phase out of ozone depleting substances.[68]

To this effect, the German government passed a resolution in March 1989, calling on the EC to reduce its CFC consumption and production by 95 percent by 1997 and for Germany to reduce domestic emissions by 95 percent by 1995.[69] After Canada stated its aim of banning CFCs and halons within ten years, the EC Environmental Council announced that the EU would reduce CFCs by 85 percent by 1995 and if possible completely by the end of the decade. The US then announced that if substitutes became available, it would consider a complete phase out based upon international agreement by the end of the century. Japan made no concrete commitments, but said that it would study the strengthening of regulations and announced that it would host a Pacific Asia Seminar on Ozone Layer Protection to facilitate bringing developing countries into the agreement.[70]

At the first official meeting of the parties to the Montreal Protocol in Helsinki in May 1989, the Helsinki Declaration was formed calling for a phase out of CFCs by 2000 at the latest, a phase out of halons, and control of other ozone depleting substances. In January 1990, the European Commission proposed that CFCs be eliminated by 1997, although the EC Council of Ministers later changed this proposal with the qualifying phrase "or no later than 2000."[71]

Compared with the strong leadership role the US had played during the Montreal Protocol negotiations, going into the Second Meeting of the Parties in London in 1990, the US joined the Soviet Union and Japan in opposing a total phase out of CFCs by 1997. The US also put up

---

[66] Jachtenfuchs, "The European Community," 267–8.
[67] Litfin, *Ozone Discourses*, pp. 125–6.
[68] Jachtenfuchs, "The European Community," 270.
[69] Der Bundesminister für Umwelt, Naturschutz und Reaktorsicherheit, Bericht der Bundesregierung an den Deutschen Bundestag über Maßnahmen zum Schutz der Ozonschicht, 11/8166, October 22, 1990, p. 4.
[70] Tsuushôsangyôshô Kisosangyôkyoku Ozonsô Hogo Taisakushitsu, *Ozonsô Hogo Handobukku*, p. 48.
[71] Litfin, *Ozone Discourses*, pp. 148–9.

obstacles to plans to create a funding and technology transfer mechanism to the developing world to assist them in meeting the obligations of the protocol. Policy makers were expressing their concerns about economic costs. Only after the Alliance for Responsible CFC Policy announced that industry in fact supported the international proposals were key policy makers in the White House (particularly, John Sununu and Richard Darman) persuaded to take a stronger stance.[72]

At the London meeting, a phase out date of 2000 for CFCs was agreed upon. Methyl chloroform was also added to the list of chemicals slated for phase out, with a 2005 complete phase out date. Developing countries were given ten additional years to meet the phase out targets. At the London meeting, despite initial US opposition, a decision was reached on a funding mechanism to assist developing countries in transitioning away from CFC use. Japan enacted the 1990 London Amendment to the Protocol in September 1991.[73] At the Third Meeting of the Parties in Nairobi in June 1991, Germany joined several other northern European countries in committing to an earlier phase out than stipulated by the London amendments. The group committed to phase out CFCs by 1997 and to phase out methyl chloroform as soon as possible, but no later than 2000. They also announced plans to restrict use of HCFCs by 1995.[74]

When new scientific reports were released by NASA suggesting that an ozone hole could form over the heavily populated regions of the northern hemisphere, the process of amending the protocol gained new momentum. In the US, George H. W. Bush, who had only shown lukewarm support for many of the amendment proposals, announced that the US would move up the phase out date of CFCs, halons, methyl chloroform, and carbon tetrachloride except for "essential uses," by the end of 1995. He also announced that the US would reexamine the 2030 phase out date for methyl bromide as stipulated in the 1990 Clean Air Act because of its ozone depleting potential. In Germany, the Bundesrat demanded an earlier phase out of CFCs and halons.[75] The EC announced that it would move up its phase out date to 1995 as well, with an 85 percent phase out target by 1993.[76] In May, MITI requested that industry phase out CFCs

---

[72] Kauffman, "Domestic and International Linkages," p. 87.
[73] OECD, *Environmental Performance Review: Japan* (Paris: OECD, 1994), p. 169.
[74] Third Meeting of the Parties to the Montreal Protocol on Substances that Deplete the Ozone Layer, Nairobi, June 19–21, 1991.
[75] Christiane Beuermann and Jill Jäger, "Climate Change Politics in Germany: How Long Will Any Double-Dividend Last?," in Tim O'Riordan and Jill Jäger (eds.), *Politics of Climate Change* (New York: Routledge, 1996), pp. 186–227.
[76] Litfin, *Ozone Discourses*, pp. 167–8.

and methyl chloroform by 1996.[77] Japan also decided to contribute $9.6 million to the Montreal Protocol Multilateral Fund.[78] Reacting to the heightened sense of concern, further revisions to the agreement were made at the Fourth Meeting of the Parties in Copenhagen. At the meeting, it was agreed to eliminate CFCs, carbon tetrachloride, and methyl chloroform by 1996 and halons by 1994. In addition, restrictions were added for several additional chemicals. Environmentalists, however, criticized the meeting for failing to hasten the phase out of HCFCs, which the US had objected to because of their widespread use in air conditioners. In response to the Copenhagen meeting, in July 1993, MITI used administrative guidance to request industry to cooperate in meeting a 1995 phase out date.[79] The process of fine tuning the Montreal Protocol and bringing new countries into the agreement continued in subsequent Meetings of the Parties. As of the time of this writing, CFC production and consumption has been virtually eliminated in these three countries.

Analysis

There are now many accounts of the formation of this international agreement although few that really pay much attention from a comparative perspective to how national systems influenced negotiating positions or how involvement in the negotiations influenced domestic institutional arrangements.

Richard Benedick argued that the agreement was possible because of the leadership roles played by UNEP and the US government. Benedick suggests that it was largely the efforts of UNEP that brought countries to the bargaining table and the US that pushed a regulatory solution first at the domestic level and then internationally.[80] His account is more descriptive than it is explanatory of the action of countries like Japan and Germany. Peter Haas sheds some light on the changes in the stance of Japan, Germany, and other states towards the ozone depletion issue. He argues that the formation of an international scientific consensus provided the epistemic community cooperation that was needed to get policy makers to recognize the need for policy action.[81] Yet, we are still left with

[77] Tsuushôsangyôshô Kisosangyôkyoku Ozonsô Hogo Taisakushitsu, *Ozonô Hogo Handobukku*, p. 59.
[78] OECD, *Environmental Performance Review: Japan* (1994), p. 169.
[79] Tsuushôsangyôshô Kisosangyôkyoku Ozonsô Hogo Taisakushitsu, *Ozonô Hogo Handobukku*, p. 64.
[80] Benedick, *Ozone Diplomacy*.
[81] Peter Haas, "Banning Chlorofluorocarbons: Efforts to Protect Stratospheric Ozone," in Haas (eds.), *Knowledge, Power, and International Coordination*, pp. 187–224.

the question of why states differed in their interpretation of the seriousness of the threat posed by ozone depletion and why they took different positions in international negotiations.

Karen Litfin provides the most persuasive analysis, suggesting that science, politics, and economics are integrally linked. She argues that actors perceive science in different ways because of their different political and economic positions. She argues that the treaty was not fundamentally based in consensual knowledge. Litfin argues instead for a more nuanced approach that speaks to how scientific uncertainty opened the door for actors within states and in different countries to develop contending interpretations of what the science meant:

The acceptability of specific forms and interpretations of knowledge is partly a function of political and economic institutional factors. The domestic structures of the states involved in the Montreal Protocol negotiations influenced the extent to which scientific knowledge was available and appreciated. The nature of relations between industry and government and the structure of the various national CFC industries were also important factors in setting the political context. Another key element was the strength of domestic environmental pressure groups.[82]

The comparison of the Japanese, German, and US cases suggest that this was indeed the case. The significance of the Montreal Protocol negotiations, however, was to run deeper than just this case. They triggered a process of political and institutional change in all three countries, but especially in Japan, that was to accelerate with the climate change negotiations. In Germany's case, the negotiations helped push the country in a direction that it had already begun to move. The US, in contrast, was to take a far more hesitant position in relation to the climate change negotiations.

[82] Litfin, *Ozone Discourses*, p. 80.

6   Global climate change: the road to UNCED

There is perhaps no environmental issue that is more important than climate change. It is also among the most complex environmental issues policy makers ever have been asked to confront. The scale of the problem, both in terms of its potential causes and ecological and economic consequences, is enormous. Uncertainties about climate change, however, have opened the door for intense domestic and international political debates. Japan, Germany, the EU, and the US as the leading industrial players in the world, have been at the center of the first decade of these debates. They have each taken a distinctly different position on climate change with the US on one end of the spectrum, Germany and the EU on the other, and Japan taking a position in between.

The goal of this and the next chapter is to examine how domestic politics influenced their negotiating positions. The chapters do not attempt to retell the full and extremely complex history of the international climate change negotiations. Instead, the chapters focus on understanding national politics in these countries as they influenced and were affected by the international negotiations.

This chapter deals with the period through the United Nations Conference on Environment and Development (UNCED) and the formation of the Framework Convention on Climate Change (FCCC) in 1992. The UNCED, also known as the Earth Summit, was one of the largest gatherings of heads of state in history. They met to address the threats of climate change and biodiversity loss and the need to promote sustainable development. The FCCC was the legal instrument drawn up to address climate change. It is the second major international agreement to address a global-scale environmental problem based on the principle of precautionary action. In other words, it was a convention drawn up to win national commitments to action to solve a problem before its full scale or impacts were known.

Climate change

Changes in the seasons and variations in weather patterns have raised human curiosity throughout the ages. Our understanding of human ability to alter the earth's climate is more recent. The planet absorbs some of the energy that the sun radiates to the earth, and some is reflected back to outer space by clouds, water, and snow. Greenhouse gases capture some of the long-wave radiation that is reflected back to space and reradiate it back to the surface. This warms the temperature of the earth's surface and makes life on earth possible.

Greenhouse gases include water vapor, CO_2, methane, nitrous oxide, tropospheric ozone, and various industrial chemicals, like CFCs. The concentration of the greenhouse gases in the atmosphere has been increasing. Greenhouse gases are produced naturally, but can also be produced by human activities. The most important is carbon dioxide (CO_2), which is believed to account for about half of the greenhouse effect. CO_2 is produced primarily by the decay of vegetation, but also by volcanic eruptions, breathing, the burning of fossil fuels, and deforestation. CO_2 is removed from the atmosphere during photosynthesis. Phytoplankton in the oceans and forests act as a huge reservoir of CO_2. The oceans and forests are, therefore, commonly referred to as carbon sinks. Other greenhouse gases account for somewhat less than half of the greenhouse effect. The greenhouse gases vary in their global warming potential. HCFCs, for instance, have a very high global warming potential. Small quantities of a gas with a high global warming potential can contribute significantly to the greenhouse effect.

Since the beginning of the industrial revolution, levels of CO_2 and other greenhouse gases in the atmosphere have been increasing. Scientists have found that global mean surface temperatures have increased between 0.3 and 0.6 degrees Celsius over the course of the last century. This could simply be part of a natural variation in global temperatures, but there is significant reason to be concerned that this temperature change is linked to human activities. The consequences of a global rise in average temperatures are not well understood but could cause a rise in ocean levels if the polar ice caps melt, a shift in weather patterns, and an increase in natural weather disasters. The economic implications of global warming as societies are forced to adapt to rapidly changing weather conditions are also poorly understood.[1]

---

[1] See the IPCC, *IPCC Third Assessment Report: Climate Change 2001: The Scientific Basis* (vol. I); *Impacts Adaptations, and Vulnerability* (vol. II); and *Mitigation* (vol. III) (Cambridge: Cambridge University Press, 2001).

By the end of the 1970s, rising levels of CO_2 at the Mauna Laoa observatory in Hawaii helped to raise levels of concern about the greenhouse problem. Internationally climate change also began to gain greater political attention as a result of a number of workshops and conferences. In 1979 the WMO in Geneva organized the first World Climate Conference and created a World Climate Research Program. The US was a major force behind this initiative. Both Japan and Germany expanded their research capacities related to climate change at the urging of the WMO. Important workshops of concerned scientists were later convened in Villach, Austria, in 1985 and 1987 and in Bellagio, Italy, in 1987.[2] These workshops are often seen as a critical point in the process of moving climate change on to the political agenda.[3]

International preparations for UNCED

Global warming became a political issue in the wake of international efforts to address stratospheric ozone loss. Unusual weather events, including the record hot summer in the US in 1988, helped focus media attention on related global warming theories (see Figures 6.1, 6.2, 6.3). In June 1988 the first World Conference on the Changing Atmosphere was held in Toronto, Canada. At the conference governments were urged by scientists and environmentalists to set energy policies that would reduce the emissions of CO_2 by 20 percent from 1988 levels by 2005 as a preliminary measure. Also in this year the IPCC was established by UNEP and the WMO in order to give governments some assurance about the impartiality of the scientific reports being issued on climate change. The IPCC was to report back to the Second World Climate Conference scheduled for Geneva in the fall of 1990.[4]

Acting upon the suggestions made at the Toronto Conference, the Dutch government convened an international ministerial conference on climate change in Noordwijk in November 1989. At the conference the Dutch proposed that as a first step to combating global climate change, industrialized countries agree to stabilize CO_2 emissions at the latest by the year 2000. Germany on the one hand, and Japan and the US on the other, differed in their response to the Dutch proposal. German Environment Minister Klaus Töpfer declared: "The time to act is now, even if we have not yet reached any definitive scientific certainty about

[2] "The Scientific Consensus: Villach (Austria) Conference," in Dean Edwin Abrahamson, The Challenge of Global Warming (Washington, DC: Island Press, 1989), p. 64.
[3] Clark et al. (eds.), Learning to Manage Global Environmental Risks.
[4] J. T. Houghton, G. J. Jenkins, and J. J. Ephraums (eds.), IPCC, Climate Change: The IPCC Scientific Assessment (Cambridge: Cambridge University Press, 1990).

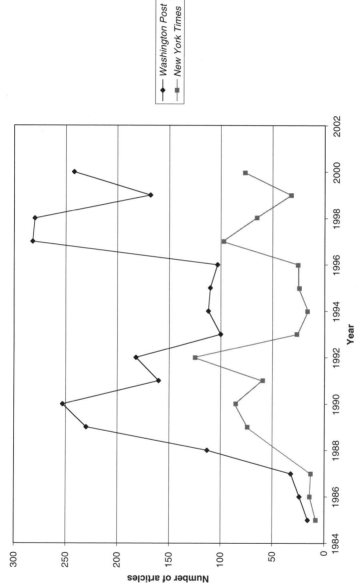

Figure 6.1 US media coverage of climate change

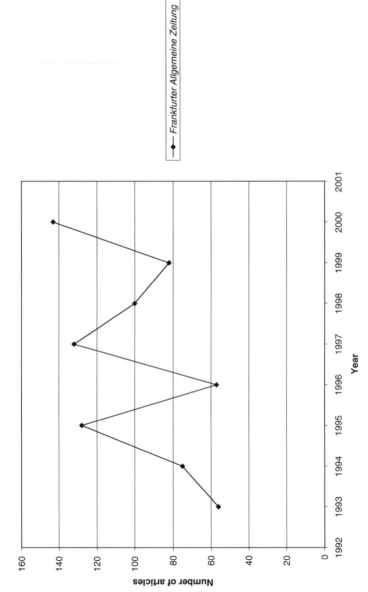

Figure 6.2   German media coverage of climate change

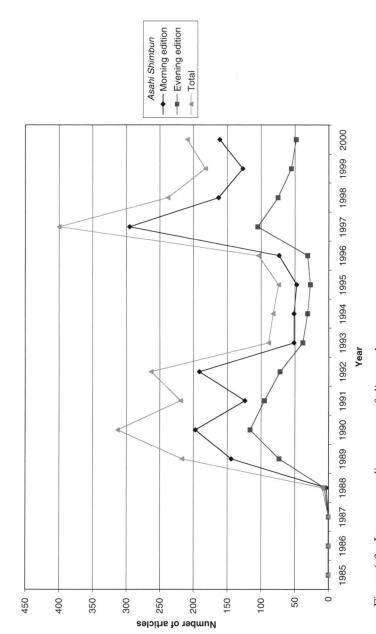

Figure 6.3 Japanese media coverage of climate change

the causal interrelations and the future development of climatic changes...We believe it is necessary to stabilize CO_2 emissions by the year 2000. A 20% reduction by the year 2005 must be urgently examined."[5] Töpfer also argued that "gaps in knowledge must not be used as an excuse for worldwide inaction."[6]

Japan initially sided with the US, the Soviet Union, and China in calling such a step premature.[7] At the convention, William Reilly said that the Bush administration recognized the CO_2 problem but believed that further study was necessary before binding controls could be proposed.[8] Although in his presidential election of 1988 George H. W. Bush had talked about the power of the "White House effect" to address the "greenhouse effect," at a climate change conference convened at Bush's initiative in Washington, DC, in April 1990, he stated that no action should be taken until the science was more certain. The Japanese response was similar. Environment Agency Director-General Setsu Shiga announced that he agreed in principle to stabilization but that concrete targets should wait until the IPCC made its report in the fall of 1990.[9] Concerns about the economic implications of policy action led to familiar calls by government and industry to delay action while waiting for further scientific research.

Despite considerable skepticism and opposition to action in various quarters, formal international negotiations on a climate change convention began in February 1991. This decision was driven by the scientific and environmental communities as well as international organizations, which felt climate change needed to be addressed with an international agreement. An Intergovernmental Negotiating Committee (INC) was established by the UN General Assembly to prepare a framework convention that would spell out internationally agreed upon understandings of the problem and the general actions to be taken. This would be followed by the formation of protocols that would address specific commitments. Five preparatory meetings spread over two years were held and a June 1992 date was chosen for the UNCED.

In the first INC meetings, the US staked out its position. The US delegation expressed their opposition to establishing quantifiable targets

---

[5] Statement of Klaus Töpfer at the Ministerial Conference on Atmospheric Pollution and Climate Change, *Noordwijk Conference Report, Vol. 1*, November 6 and 7, 1989.

[6] Cited in Matthew Paterson, *Global Warming and Global Politics* (New York: Routledge, 1996), pp. 38–9.

[7] Miranda A. Schreurs, "Nihon ni Okeru Kankyô Seisaku no Kettei Katei," *Journal of Pacific Asia* 2 (1994), 3–38; and *Nihon Keizai Shimbun*, November 8, 1989.

[8] *New York Times*, November 7, 1989.

[9] Setsu Shiga, "Norutoveiku Kaigi no Kotonado," in Kankyôchô 20 Shûnen Kinen Jigyô Jikkô Iinkai, *Kankyôchô 20 Nenshi* (Tokyo: Gyôsei, 1991), pp. 426–8.

for emissions reductions arguing that the science of climate change was still too uncertain and that there were still no reliable inventories of all the sources of greenhouse gases, especially in the developing world, or of sinks, making it difficult to establish credible baselines from which to establish targets or measure compliance. The administration also argued that the economic costs and benefits of different response strategies needed to be better understood. Similar to the US approach to the acid rain issue, the administration's position was that it was better to develop cost-effective national mitigation strategies than to focus on internationally agreed upon short-term targets and timetables.

The themes evident in this early US response were to be repeated again and again over the course of the next decade. They reflect the strong influence of not only industrial interests in shaping the negotiating team's position but also the growing strength of an underlying neo-liberal economic paradigm on environmental policy making in the US. The Bush administration followed a "no regrets" policy that basically said that action to address global warming should only be taken when that action would pose but minimal costs to society and would be beneficial on other grounds as well, such as energy conservation.

The US position was challenged by other industrialized countries and by the domestic environmental NGO community. EPA Director Reilly was supportive of a stronger US role, but he did not have Bush's ear. Despite the calls by environmental groups for the US to establish emissions reduction targets, no action was taken.

In the negotiations, Germany, in contrast, argued for quantifiable targets and timetables for action and as is discussed in more detail below was among the first nations to establish a domestic emissions reduction target of 25–30 percent of 1987 levels by 2005. The stance that Germany took domestically on climate change was critical in determining what the EC position in negotiations could be. The EC subsequently adopted the objective of stabilizing CO_2 emissions at 1990 levels by 2000. Germany and the EC favored early action. Environmental interests had stronger sway over negotiators in Europe than was the case in the US.

Japan had to determine if it should follow the Bush administration's "no regrets" policy or follow the European call for concrete emissions targets. Japan like the US opposed a firm reduction commitment even though by the time of the first INC, Japan like Germany had committed unilaterally to controlling CO_2 emissions domestically. Japan's ambiguous position adopting a domestic emissions reduction target, but siding with the US in the negotiations was a pattern that repeated itself many times in the next years. It reflected the desire of Japan's economic and political leaders to be perceived as being environmentally sensitive at the same time that they were concerned about costs and competitiveness. Japan far more than Germany was also concerned about pleasing the US.

Progress at the INCs was slow because of the US reluctance to commit to concrete terms of action. Political uncertainty at the international level was exacerbated by intense domestic political debates that took on rather different flavors in the US, Germany, and Japan. These differences are examined in more detail below.

The US waivers on the road to UNCED

George H. W. Bush announced that he would not attend the UNCED if emissions reduction targets were to be included in a framework convention. There were several reasons for this. Particularly important was that several of Bush's key advisors on environmental issues, including his chief of staff, John Sununu; the director of the OMB, Richard Darman; and the chairman of the Council of Economic Advisors, Michael Boskin, were skeptical of climate science and concerned about the economic costs of CO_2 reduction.[10] Behind this skepticism was considerable industrial concern about what regulatory action on climate change would mean for industrial competitiveness and the opposition of the coal, oil, and automobile industries.[11]

There were also institutional factors that influenced the relative balance of power among departmental interests in the development of the US position. When the Montreal Protocol was negotiated, the State Department and the EPA had much more influence over outcomes than domestic agencies that would be affected by their decisions. As a result following the Montreal Protocol negotiations, the Reagan administration shifted responsibility for the coordination of international environmental negotiations to a working group of the White House Domestic Policy Council. The EPA was included in this group, but had to compete with other departments such as Energy, Interior, Commerce, the OMB, and the Council of Economic Advisors. These departments on the whole tended to be less prone towards action on climate change for scientific or environmental reasons than the EPA, and were instead more concerned with the domestic economic ramifications of action.[12] The 1990 Economic Report of the President cited estimates made by Alan Manne and

---

[10] Vig, "Presidential Leadership and the Environment," pp. 102–3; Paterson, *Global Warming and Global Politics*, p. 62.

[11] Shardul Agrawala and Steinar Andresen, "The United States in the Climate Treaty Negotiations," *Global Governance* 5 (1999), 457–82.

[12] Daniel Bodansky, "Prologue to the Climate Change Convention," in Irving M. Mintzer and J. A. Leonard (eds.), *Negotiating Climate Change* (Cambridge: Cambridge University Press, 1994), p. 51.

Richard Richels that reducing CO_2 emissions by 20 percent would cost the US between $800 billion and $3.6 trillion.[13]

Nor was the US completely isolated in the period leading up to the UNCED in terms of its opposition to environmentalists' calls for significant action. A coalition formed among several industrialized states prior to the UNCED that opposed the formation of stringent commitments on CO_2 reductions in the climate change talks. The name given to this coalition, which included Japan, the US, Canada, and Switzerland was JUSCANSZ. There was also significant opposition from the oil producing OECD countries.

Sununu resigned in December, a half-a-year prior to the UNCED. This produced some openings for a slight shift in the US position during the negotiations. As part of a negotiating strategy to push the EC to concede on the issue of concrete targets and timetables, Bush's attendance at Rio was made contingent on the guarantee that concrete targets and timetables would not be included in an agreement.[14] In the months leading up to the UNCED, it remained uncertain whether or not Bush would attend.

EC President Jacques Delors met with President Bush at the end of April, just a little more than a month before the UNCED, to discuss the politically sensitive differences between the EC and the US on the issue of targets and timetables. Shortly afterwards, the lead US negotiator, Robert Reinstein, James Baker's deputy Robert Zoellick, and UK Environment Minister Michael Howard worked out compromise language that made it possible for Bush to attend. The language called upon each of the Parties to adopt national policies that would demonstrate that the developed countries were taking the lead in addressing anthropogenic emissions with "the aim of returning individually or jointly to their 1990 levels of these anthropogenic emissions by sources and removals by sinks of greenhouse gases not controlled by the Montreal Protocol."[15]

There were other contentious issues for the US as well. These dealt primarily with issues of providing financial assistance to developing countries, the use of the Global Environment Facility to overseas financial transfers, and issues pertaining to intellectual property rights. On these issues, however, disagreements were not so much with European and Japanese states as they were with developing countries. The OECD states opposed committing large funds to a climate fund, and instead chose to

---

[13] Paterson, *Global Warming and Global Politics*, p. 81.
[14] Hopgood, *American Foreign Policy and the Power of the State*, pp. 155–68.
[15] William A. Nitze, "A Failure of Presidential Leadership," in Mintzer and Leonard (eds.), *Negotiating Climate Change*, p. 194, and United Nations Framework Convention on Climate Change, Article 4(2).

make available smaller amounts to help developing countries determine and measure sources of greenhouse gas emissions and absorbing sinks, develop national plans of action, and work on specific projects.[16]

One additional point deserves attention. An important addition to the convention was the adoption of the idea of initiating joint implementation projects, a proposal forwarded by the Norwegians, and subsequently embraced by the US and other countries. The idea behind joint implementation is that developed countries be allowed to achieve some of their emissions reductions through cooperative projects in other countries. The plan was urged as a means of promoting economic efficiency in emissions reductions since energy efficiency improvements can be achieved more cost effectively in countries that are typically less energy efficient.[17] This was to become one of the "flexible mechanisms" later to be incorporated into the Kyoto Protocol.

Germany leads on the road to UNCED

Climate change was a concern to only a small, specialized community in Germany until well into the 1980s.[18] Climate change science was largely dominated by the US, but it was Germany that became the champion of major action on climate change. Climate change became an increasingly important political issue in Germany in the late 1980s and early 1990s as suggested by several institutional changes. In 1990 the German Federal Environment Foundation was formed with DM 2.5 billion to fund environmental protection programs. In 1992 the German Advisory Council on Global Climate Change was set up. The Federal Environment Agency also came to play an increasingly vital role in policy research and development.[19]

One of the first major reports on climate change of political significance was prepared for the Bundestag by the Enquete Commission on Preventive Measures to Protect the Earth's Atmosphere. The Enquete Commission completed its first report reviewing the state of scientific knowledge about the earth's atmosphere and regulatory proposals to deal with ozone layer depletion in September 1988. The report was based on discussions

[16] Nitze, "A Failure of Presidential Leadership," p. 194.
[17] Delphine Borione and Jean Ripert, "Exercising Common but Differentiated Responsibility," in Mintzer and Leonard (eds.), *Negotiating Climate Change*, pp. 86–8.
[18] See Cavender-Bares and Jäger with Ell, "Developing a Precautionary Approach"; and Beuermann and Jäger, "Climate Change Politics in Germany," pp. 186–227.
[19] Helmut Weidner and Martin Jänicke, "Vom Aufstieg und Niedergang eines Vorreiters, Eine umweltpolitische Bilanz der Ära Kohl," in Göttrik Wewer, ed., *Bilanz der Ära Kohl, Christlich-liberale Politik in Deutschland 1982–1998*, special edition of *Gegenwartskunde* (Opladen: Leske and Budrich, 1998), pp. 201–13.

with ecological and consumer protection groups, international organizations, and experts from within and outside of Germany. It came to the noteworthy precautionary statement that:

There is growing evidence suggesting that the expected changes in the Earth's atmosphere and in the climate . . . will have serious consequences for human living conditions and for the biosphere as a whole – consequences which preventive measures can prevent to a limited extent only. Dramatic developments cannot be precluded . . . In the energy sector, the Federal Republic of Germany accounts for about 3.6 percent of global CO_2 emissions from commercial fuels. So, even if national reduction strategies go beyond international reduction targets, their direct contribution is very small on a global scale. It can be assumed, however, that measures initiated in the Federal Republic of Germany may indirectly induce larger reductions. These indirect reductions might attain a relevant order magnitude, e.g., if national German measures push ahead the development within the EC, if they lead to competitive advantages in the world market, if energy-efficient innovations which are ready to be marketed are rapidly launched in the market place, if they help to improve the innovation potential of the industrialized nations as a whole, if they lead to appropriate development assistance, etc.[20]

Enquete Commissions typically have majority and minority opinions. In this case, however, the report received unanimous support. According to a member of the Secretariat, this particular commission was unusual in its ability to achieve an early consensus on the need for action. Bernd Schmidbauer of the CDU/CSU, who headed the commission, was an effective consensus-builder who had the support of Chancellor Kohl. Kohl had signaled his concern about climate change in a March 1987 policy speech. The ability of the Enquete Commission to achieve a consensus was in part a reflection of the consensus on the need for action held by the scientific members, each of whom had been picked to sit on the commission by the four different political parties. Their consensual position helped to build a sense of urgency into the commission's mission.[21]

The commission also was aware that most relevant societal actors could be persuaded to take action. Public opinion was supportive of environmental action. A June 1990 poll reported in the *Frankfurter Allgemeine Zeitung* found that at the end of November 1990, just prior to the first elections for a united Germany, 51 percent of those surveyed said that environmental degradation was the political problem that concerned them most. This was just below the 54 percent who answered that their biggest concern was the danger of war in the Middle East.[22] Public support for

[20] German Bundestag (ed.), *Protecting the Earth's Atmosphere*, pp. 439–41.
[21] Interview with Martina Etzbach, Federal Environment Ministry, May 21, 1993.
[22] Cited in H. G. Peter Wallach and Ronald A. Fancisco, *United Germany: The Past, Politics, Prospects* (Westport: Praeger, 1992), p. 92. See also Tad Schull, *Redefining Red and Green: Ideology and Strategy in European Political Ecology* (Albany: SUNY Press, 1999), pp. 22–3.

environmental protection was high; the political climate was right for action.

Moreover, there were many win-wins. For the pro-nuclear CDU/CSU, for example, climate change was seen as an important issue because of the high societal sensitivity to environmental threats in the post-Chernobyl period. Climate change could be a way to gain support for the embattled nuclear energy industry and to justify reducing subsidies to the German coal industry, a supporter of the rival SPD. After the Chernobyl nuclear accident, public support for nuclear energy was greatly weakened. The global warming problem was one that the nuclear industry tried to use to bolster its own position, arguing that atomic energy was "clean" from a greenhouse gas emissions perspective. An official in the Ministry of Economics also suggested that the CDU hoped that by taking a strong stance on climate change, they would be able to drive the Green Party out of the parliament.[23] For the opposition SPD, calling for action to address global warming was a means to pursue a green image. In contrast with the CDU, the SPD did not support nuclear energy, but instead the promotion of energy conservation and promotion of non-nuclear alternative energies.

Also important was the fact that this commission was setting a course for action and not ironing out the specific details of implementing a CO_2 reduction policy. Agreement on the need for action was relatively easily achieved. No specific greenhouse gas reduction goal was established and the sensitive issue of nuclear energy was left for further study.[24]

The Ministry for Environment was made responsible for formulating the outline of a climate change policy in consultation with other relevant ministries. Apparently, officials working in the Ministry for Environment had lobbied colleagues in the Chancellor's Office on the advisability of the German government preparing a statement of its intentions to establish a reduction target. An official working in the Ministry for Environment at the time claims that the support from the Chancellor's Office was very important in winning over other ministries for a reduction target.[25]

The Ministry for Environment took advantage of the political support coming from the Chancellor's Office and with its right of first draft, in June 1990, prepared a proposal calling for an ambitious reduction in Germany's CO_2 emissions and outlined various emissions reduction potentials.[26] The report served as a working proposal for the June 13

---

[23] Interview with Economics Ministry official, June 8, 1993.
[24] German Bundestag (ed.), *Protecting the Earth's Atmosphere*, p. 487.
[25] Interview with Federal Environment Ministry official, May 18, 1993.
[26] Bundesministerium für Umwelt, Naturschutz und Reaktorsicherheit, "Bericht des Bundesministers für Umwelt, Naturschutz und Reaktorsicherheit zur Reduzierung

Cabinet resolution announcing that Germany intended to reduce its CO_2 emissions by 25 percent of 1987 levels by 2005. The road to a target was not without its bumps. The Ministry of Economics opposed the establishment of a concrete CO_2 reduction target. In this case, though, public support was behind the Ministry for Environment.[27] The Ministry of Economics argued that a 25 percent reduction target was a political decision that did not take economic cost calculations into consideration: "In Toronto a reduction in global CO_2 emissions of around 20 percent of 1988 levels by 2005 was proposed. It is important to know that this '20 percent figure' was the outcome of negotiations among conference participants – mainly scientists and journalists. In other words: the reduction figure was what was ecologically necessary, not what is economically feasible."[28] Still, the Ministry of Economics could be won over to the general goal of reducing emissions as long as it meant doing away with subsidies for German coal and promoting nuclear energy.

The June 13, 1990 Cabinet Resolution established a Climate-gas Reduction Strategies Interministerial Working Group. Environment Minister Töpfer was appointed chairperson of this working group. Five study groups, each headed by a separate ministry, were established to determine greenhouse gas reduction potentials in the areas of energy supply, transportation, the building sector, agriculture and forest management, and through new technologies.

Meanwhile, German unification in 1990 significantly altered domestic political priorities and led to changes in Germany's global climate change policies. Environmental degradation in East Germany was severe. Air, water, and soil pollution in many areas were at acute levels. The gap between the former East Germany and the former West Germany in terms of energy efficiency and air quality control was huge. As a result of unification, Germany found itself in the strange position of being the wealthiest and most powerful state within the EU, at the same time that it had the poorest and environmentally most degraded regions within the EU.

To give a few examples, Bitterfeld, a chemical center of the former GDR was one of the world's most polluted cities. Strip mining in the Bitterfeld–Wolfen area, which supplied Bitterfeld with brown coal to

der CO_2-Emissionen in der Bundesrepublik Deutschland zum Jahr 2005: Erster Bericht auf der Grundlage des Beschlusses der Bundesregierung zu Zielvorstellungen für eine erreichbare Reduktion der CO_2-Emissionen 13 Juni 1990," (Bonn, June 13, 1990).

[27] Interview with Federal Environment Ministry official, June 9, 1993.

[28] Knut Kübler, "Die Energiepolitik zum Schutz der Erdatmosphäre," *Energiewirtschaftliche Tagesfragen* 41 (1991), p. 21.

power its chemical plants, resulted in what can best be described as an environmental nightmare. Together the chemical and coal-mining industries contaminated the air, soil, and groundwater. The chemical producers dumped 50 million tons of wastes into the mines. Open-cast lignite mining sites deeply scarred the central German region. In the decade beginning in 1990, the federal, Länder, and local governments spent about DM 1 billion just to clean up these sites.[29]

Clean up of the environment in the East was a daunting problem. Yet, unification also provided Germany with some leeway in meeting its CO_2 reduction target because of the potential to reduce substantially emissions in the East. Improvements in energy efficiency, a shift away from high reliance on poor quality brown coal, and the shutting down of major polluters helped to improve the environment in the new Länder although unemployment problems emerged as a result.

In October 1990 the Enquete Commission for Preventative Measures to Protect the Earth's Atmosphere produced its third report to the Bundestag entitled *Protecting the Earth: A Status Report with Recommendations for a New Energy Policy*. In this report, in light of unification and the potential rapidly to reduce greenhouse gas emissions in the former East Germany, the commission proposed a reduction that went beyond that already proposed by Töpfer. The commission supported a call for a 30 percent reduction in CO_2 emissions in Germany by 2005; a 20–5 percent reduction for the EC, and a 5 percent reduction worldwide.

Officials in the Ministry of Economics and the Ministry for Environment shared a common opinion as to why the commission came up with a 30 percent reduction target rather than the 25 percent reduction target decided upon in interministerial negotiations. It was clearly related to unification, but it also reflected a rivalry between the commission's chairman Bernd Schmidbauer of the CDU/CSU and Environment Minister Töpfer, both of whom wanted recognition as leaders in the setting of Germany's environmental goals. Apparently, Schmidbauer had originally thought a 20 percent reduction goal adequate, but then Töpfer had proposed 25 percent to the federal Cabinet. By pushing for a 30 percent reduction goal, Schmidbauer outdid Töpfer.[30]

Unlike the first Enquete Commission report, the third report showed signs of growing conflict among actors with different visions of how this new policy goal should be implemented.[31] The nuclear question was particularly controversial. Given the political momentum behind greenhouse

---

[29] Federal Ministry for the Environment, Nature Conservation, and Nuclear Safety, "Common Ground," January 1999, p. 8.
[30] Interviews were conducted in May and June 1993.
[31] Reinhard Loske, *Klimapolitik: Im Spannungsfeld von Kurzzeitinteressen und Langzeiterfordernissen* (Marburg: Metropolis Verlag, 1997), p. 287.

gas reduction measures, the best the Ministry of Economics could do was to push for policies it and its constituents favored – promotion of alternative energy technologies, the manufacture of energy efficient appliances and lighting systems, and nuclear energy.

One group of commission members representing the CDU/CSU and FDP argued that nuclear plants were cheaper to operate than power plants fueled by domestic hard coal and that their safety record would improve with new technological developments.[32] Opposition to nuclear energy promotion, however, came from many sides. SPD members had a different opinion. They wrote:

The dangers of a worldwide climate change and the risks associated with the use of nuclear energy are representative of the technical and ecological risks of modern industrial societies. They are the two faces of one and the same development: nuclear energy as the symbol of questionable large-scale technologies and environmental destruction as primarily the result of an immense increase in energy conversion.[33]

They went on to argue that nuclear energy systems lead to certain organizational structures and technologies that block more efficient energy use, co-generation, and technologies based on renewable energy sources. The Green Party representative took the debate even further, arguing for a shut down of existing nuclear power plants since these are "the most immediate peril" and argued instead for a decentralized energy structure which would maximize energy saving potential and renewable energy sources consistent with local needs.[34]

The Enquete Commission also recommended a CO_2 tax within the framework of the EC, reduction in transport volumes and a shift to low-emissions transport, improvement in power plant efficiency, and an increase in the use of alternative energies, promoting district heating, and reducing energy consumption by small-scale consumers.

In November 1990, the Climate-gas Reduction Strategies Interministerial Working Group released an interim report for submission to the Cabinet that took into account the added energy reductions potentials in the East. Acting on this report, the federal Cabinet altered its reduction target to a 25 percent reduction in CO_2 emissions by 2005 over 1987 levels for the old Länder, and to a considerably higher extent in the new Länder (no target was specified). Concrete measures for how the goal was to be achieved still needed to be ironed out.

[32] German Bundestag (ed.), *Protecting the Earth: A Status Report with Recommendations for a New Energy Policy*, Third Report of the Enquete Commission of the 11th German Bundestag, *Preventive Measures to Protect the Earth's Atmosphere*, vol. II, (Bonn: Deutscher Bundestag, 1991), pp. 315–17.
[33] German Bundestag (ed.), *Protecting the Earth*, pp. 318–19.
[34] German Bundestag (ed.), *Protecting the Earth*, p. 325.

One year later, the Interministerial Working Group produced a second interim report. On the basis of this report, the federal government confirmed its previous resolutions but decided on a reduction for all of Germany of CO_2 emissions by 25 to 30 percent of 1987 levels by 2005. Chancellor Kohl in Rio de Janeiro reconfirmed this goal. Reinhard Loske of the Green Party criticized this shift as a relaxation of the government's mitigation goal since the collapse of the East German economy could now be used to help all of Germany meet its CO_2 emissions reduction goal rather than having separate goals for the East and the West. Indeed, between 1990 and 1995 there was a reduction in CO_2 emissions for the whole of Germany of 13 percent, but a rise of about 2 percent in the emissions of the old Länder in the West.[35]

Within the Interministerial Working Group that was drafting concrete recommendations for policy alternatives, there was agreement on measures that dealt with energy saving and the promotion of new energy efficient technologies. There were conflicts, however, over the nuclear issue, the idea of a carbon/energy tax, and possibilities for reductions in the transportation sector.

While the Ministry of Economics argued strongly for a sentence stating that nuclear energy was necessary to meet a reduction target, the Ministry for Environment was against it. On this particular issue, the Ministry for Environment won support from the Chancellor's Office, because of the sensitive pre-election timing – the first elections for unified Germany were scheduled for December 2, 1990. The Ministry for Environment, however, was unable to push through a national CO_2 tax, over the Ministry of Economics' contention that such a tax should only be introduced if it were done at the EC level. The SPD was also unwilling to have the tax turned into an energy tax since this would raise costs for the coal industry, a key supporter of the party. Thus, although the Ministry for Environment had the support of manufacturers of energy technologies, the German energy sector and energy-intensive industries had made it clear that they were opposed to an energy/CO_2 tax because the financial burden would reduce capital resources for investments to promote energy efficiency and concerns about international competitiveness. Instead, measures focused on improving energy efficiency became the mainstay of the report's proposals.

The Ministry for Environment was not in a strong position to push forward its goals once discussions moved to implementation questions. This reflected in part the Ministry for Environment's lack of jurisdiction over the energy and transportation sectors where primary reduction

[35] Loske, *Klimapolitik*, p. 285.

measures would have to take place. It also reflected a change in the political milieu. German unification drained government coffers. In post-unification Germany, new issues quickly rose to the top of the political agenda. Also, the West German Green Party for the first time since 1983 was not represented in parliament; voters had viewed the party's opposition to unification under Kohl's terms negatively. The Green Party had opposed unification because they feared the effects of nationalism and supported many of the ideals of a socialist state. The party also campaigned independently of the environmental parties that had formed in the East because they opposed the absorption of East German parties by Western ones.

In this changing political milieu, the Ministry for Environment found that it could not push through important items on its agenda, like the introduction of a carbon tax at the national level. The more powerful ministries with jurisdiction over the economy, transportation, agriculture, and housing ironed out the details of policy measures for meeting reduction targets.

An official at the Ministry of Transport remarked that the Ministry for Environment has a lot of people that were taken over from scientific institutions who lack practical administrative experiences. Transportation is the sector where CO_2 emissions are increasing most rapidly. Within the Ministry of Transport officials assigned to finding measures to reduce CO_2 emissions tend to be more sympathetic to the Ministry for Environment's perspective. But the technical departments raise concerns about economic feasibility. This same official was surprised that the opposition was not making more of the fact that there were big gaps between official announcements and what was actually being implemented. Another official at the Ministry of Economics remarked that as far as his ministry was concerned, the reduction targets had been established without their approval and that from an economic standpoint it would be virtually impossible to reach the reductions.[36]

Germany within the European Community

Because of the rules of the EC, climate change politics in Germany had a wider European dimension to them as well. Indeed, it was not Germany but the EC that negotiated on behalf of its member states in the negotiations. Thus, Germany had an interest in influencing EC negotiating positions in order to protect its own domestic interests. Germany joined the Netherlands in pushing the EC to play a leadership role in the

[36] Interview with Economics Ministry official, June 8, 1993.

international negotiations. Certainly the EC could not propose a stabilization target for CO_2 emissions for 2000 based on 1990 levels were it not for the large domestic emissions reduction goal established by Germany. There were concerns within Germany, however, about how a reduction goal would be met. The only way that German industry would support a carbon/energy tax was if it was harmonized across the EU. This initiative failed, however, due to staunch industrial opposition to the idea.

Japan divided on the road to UNCED

Much as was the case with ozone depletion, there was initially little domestic pressure for any kind of regulatory action on global warming in Japan. Prior to 1989 there was little NGO, scientific, or media interest in international environmental issues.[37] Furthermore, contrary to the case with ozone depletion, there was little pressure on Japan to take policy action from the US where there were many powerful opponents to greenhouse gas regulations.

One of the earliest political indications of concern about global environmental issues occurred in the early 1980s. Upon the urging of Environment Agency Director-General Kujiraoka, Prime Minister Zenkô Suzuki ordered the establishment of an Ad Hoc Committee of Global Environmental Problems, which was chaired by Saburô Ohkita, a former minister of foreign affairs. The committee argued that threats from rapid deforestation, desertification, global warming, and other global environmental problems warranted greater international attention.[38] On the basis of their 1982 report, "International Responses to Environmental Problems of a Global Scale," Environment Agency Director-General Bunbei Hara proposed the establishment of the World Commission on Environment and Development (WCED) to UNEP at the tenth anniversary meeting of the Stockholm Conference.[39] The WCED was set up in 1984 and is better known as the Bruntland Commission, which produced the highly influential 1987 report, *Our Common Future*.[40]

The publication of *Our Common Future* was an important turning point for the Environment Agency. The Environment Agency took seriously the report's warnings that a rapidly expanding world population and rising economic activity would result in increased emissions of greenhouse gases

[37] Giichi Yamamoto, "Taiki Osen to Kikô Hendô," *Taiki Osen Gakkaishi* 10 (1975), 1–3.
[38] Kankyôchô Chikyûteki Kibo no Kankyô Mondai ni Kansuru Kondankai, *Chikyûteki Kibo no Kankyô Mondai he no Kokusaiteki Torikumi ni Tsuite: Kokuren Ningen Kankyô Kaigi 10 Shûnen ni Atatte*, 1982.
[39] Bunbei Hara, "Statement to the Session of a Special Character of the Governing Council of the United Nations Environment Programme," Nairobi, May 11, 1982.
[40] WCED, *Our Common Future* (Oxford: Oxford University Press, 1987).

and this could, in turn, have very serious consequences for the health of the planet. The Environment Agency moved quickly to strengthen its global environmental research and policy-making capacities. In 1987 global climate change research was initiated at the Environment Agency's National Laboratory of Pollution (later renamed the National Institute for Environmental Studies). In 1988 the Agency set up a Research Group on Global Warming and in 1989 it established a Global Environment Protection Office, which was elevated to the status of a division in 1990, the first new division created within the Agency since 1974 and one that rapidly became one of its most important.[41] Then, in July 1989 Prime Minister Sôsuke Uno made the Environment Agency director-general global environmental minister in a newly established Ministerial Council on Global Environmental Protection. The Ministerial Council was established to facilitate intra-governmental coordination of policies that would have to be negotiated internationally. Both MITI and the MoFA had sought the leadership of this Council. The Council was to play a central role in the formulation of Japan's "Action Plan to Arrest Global Warming," in which the government announced its CO_2 stabilization target.[42]

Some of the strongest voices for policy action on climate change came from the national government and from within the LDP. Perhaps most important and unexpected was Prime Minister Noboru Takeshita. Takeshita had not been an environmentalist before this, but he played a crucial role in turning the LDP – or at least his faction within the party – green. For foreign relations reasons, Takeshita turned international contributions into a major theme for the government. In a February 1989 meeting with President Bush, Takeshita made a point of explaining how Japan was going to increase its international cooperation efforts. ODA became a pillar of this new policy and environmental protection an important component thereof.[43] Consistent with this new policy direction, at the G-7 meeting in Paris in the summer of 1989, Japan announced that it would spend ¥300 billion in foreign aid to be targeted specifically for environmental measures over the FY 1989 – FY 1991 period.[44] In October 1989 Prime Minister Toshiki Kaifu announced that Japan should share its past experience with severe domestic air pollution and its technological know-how to assist developing countries in combating their own environmental problems.[45]

[41] Kankyôchô 20 Shûnen Kinen Jigyô Iinkai, *Kankyôchô 20 Nenshi*, pp. 112–16.
[42] *Asahi Shimbun*, July 8, 1989. [43] *Time*, October 23, 1989.
[44] Pat Murdo, "Japan's Environmental Policies: The International Dimension," *Japan Economic Institute Report*, March 9, 1990; and David Potter, "Assessing Japan's Environmental Aid Policy," *Pacific Affairs* 67 (1994), 200–15.
[45] *Nihon Keizai Shimbun*, October 3, 1989, p. 7.

Upon his resignation due to a political scandal in June 1989, the still enormously powerful Takeshita announced that he would make the environment his "special issue area." For a man tainted by political scandal and with his eyes still on a second term as prime minister, supporting environmental issues could serve as a way to clean up his image.[46] Kosugi Takashi, a long-term LDP Dietman and member of the small environmental *zoku*, noted that after Takeshita greened, the environment became popular among LDP politicians.[47] When an Investigator Committee on Basic Environmental Problems was set up, former Finance Minister Ryûtaro Hashimoto was made its chairman and such influential figures as Toshiki Kaifu, Masaharu Gotôda, Hiroshi Mitsuzuka, Keizô Obuchi, and Girô Hayashi became members.[48] In the absence of strong grass roots pressures for policy change, the emergence of a powerful politician as a policy sponsor can be what is necessary for major policy change. The shift in stance by a few key LDP politicians was very important for environmentalists.

Eager to be seen as a major international player, in the fall of 1989 Japan together with the UNEP hosted the Tokyo Conference on Global Environmental Protection. Chaired by Saburô Ohkita the conference was organized to gather the most recent scientific knowledge concerning such key environmental issues as climatic change, tropical forests, and related problems of development and environmental protection in developing countries, as well as to explore possibilities for international cooperative action. Participants included forty experts from overseas and seventeen from Japan.[49]

The public's interest in the environment was also growing. From 1987 to 1989, there was a five-fold increase in the coverage of ozone depletion in the *Asahi Shimbun*. Global warming coverage jumped from a mere 6 articles in 1989 to 98 in 1990 and 328 in 1991. Public opinion polls also began to reflect greater concern in global environmental problems. A March 1990 survey of public opinion on the environment gave respondents a choice of up to three issues that could be selected as issues of special concern. Global environmental issues ranked as the issues of greatest concern.[50]

---

[46] Interview with Ken Takeuchi, April 19, 1991.
[47] Interview with Takashi Kosugi, May 1991.   [48] *Asahi Shimbun*, April 28, 1992, p. 4.
[49] See IFIAS, ISSC, UNU, "Report of the Tokyo International Symposium on the Human Response to Global Change," Tokyo, Japan, September 19–22, 1989.
[50] Sôrifu Naikaku Sôridaijin Kanbô Kôhôshitsu (ed.), "Kankyô Hozen Katsudô ni Kansuru Yoron Chôsa," *Yoron Chôsa Nenkan* (March 1990), survey no. 21, question 1. Survey of 5,000 individuals over the age of 20. 75.1 percent response rate.

There were also growing signs of interest in the global environment on the part of politicians. One measure of this interest is the number of questions raised in the Diet on specific environmental issues. According to an index of Diet proceedings, politicians asked nine questions related to the ozone layer in 1987 and eighty-six in 1988. Questions on global warming went from zero in 1988 to eighteen in 1989 and thirty-six in 1990.[51] There were even more questions asked on global scale environmental issues more generally.

The NGO community initially was slow to react. In contrast with the US and the Europeans, there was no Japanese NGO at the first INC meeting to prepare for the UNCED. CASA was the only Japanese NGO present at the second INC. Japanese NGOs were not mobilized on the climate change issue. This quickly changed. A year later by the time of the UNCED the Japanese NGO community had rallied sufficiently to be able to set up ten booths at the Japan People's Center in Rio de Janeiro.[52] Numerous new environmental groups began to form as is discussed more fully in Chapter 8.

It was in this changing domestic political milieu that the Japanese government formulated its Action Plan to Arrest Global Warming. Representatives from the Environment Agency supported the idea of international cooperation and the establishment of a CO_2 reduction target called for by the Dutch in Noordwijk. MITI officials also expressed some concern about possible climate change, but like their German counterparts, they were more concerned about the economic implications of "premature action" and the division that existed between the US and EC positions on CO_2 stabilization. Instead of a concrete target, MITI sought a plan that would promote energy conservation, the transfer of energy efficiency know-how, and research and development in new technologies. Energy efficiency and the promotion of alternative energies fit in well with MITI's existing interests in energy supply diversification and improving energy security. Moreover, MITI felt that Japan's past successes in improving energy efficiency warranted some recognition.[53]

For Japanese industries, as long as unwanted regulations and carbon taxes could be avoided, global climate change was seen as a kind of "Green Gold."[54] Private sector investment in the environment doubled between 1987 and 1990. It stood at ¥974 billion in 1990.[55] Pollution control

[51] My count from the index to the Diet committee hearings.
[52] Tsunetoshi Yamamura, *Kankyô NGO* (Tokyo: Shinyama Shuppan, 1998), pp. 22–56.
[53] OECD, *Environmental Performance Review: Japan* (1994), p. 144.
[54] Miller and Moore, *Green Gold*, passim.
[55] OECD, *Environmental Performance Review: Japan* (1994), pp. 98–9.

equipment represented 5.7 percent of industrial machinery production in Japan in 1991; this was primarily air pollution control and waste treatment equipment targeted for Southeast Asia.[56]

Industry in Japan, like Germany, saw some lucrative possibilities in addressing global warming. For Japan's utility companies, global climate change was as much an opportunity to gain support for its nuclear energy policies as a problem because its thermoelectric plants are heavy CO_2 emitters. In a 1990 document Tokyo Electric Power Company stated: "The most important point here is the promotion of nuclear power."[57] Tohoku Electric Power, Tokyo Electric Power, Chubu Electric Power, and Kansai Electric Power began collaborating on the development of new CO_2 fixation technology.[58] Japan's automobile manufacturers were somewhat more cautious calling for international cooperation and further scientific research at the same time that they initiated research into alternative energy vehicles, automobile recycling, and improvements in fuel efficiency. In June 1990 the Japan Automobile Manufacturers' Association produced a position paper in which it called for scientific confirmation of global warming theories, comprehensive international environmental conservation efforts, balancing economic growth and environmental conservation, and improving further the fuel efficiency of motor vehicles.[59]

At the White House Conference on the Global Environment in April 1990, MITI first announced its ideas for New Earth 21: Action Program for the Twenty-First Century. The plan, the brain child of MITI's Sôzaburô Okamatsu, called for international cooperation in establishing a 100-year plan for environmental clean-up after 200 years of pollution caused by the industrial revolution. The plan called for the accelerated introduction of "clean" energies, including the building of safer nuclear power plants (beginning in 1990), the introduction of new and renewable energies (beginning in 2000), and the development of environment friendly technologies (including CFC substitutes, CO_2 fixation and re-utilization technology) and environment friendly production processes.[60] Research and development related to this plan was started at the Research Institute of Innovative Technologies for the Earth (RITE), a semi-private institution.[61]

[56] OECD, *Environmental Performance Review: Japan* (1994), p. 97.
[57] Masayuki Hatsushika, "Environmental Protection and TEPCO," Environmental Protection Department, Plant Siting and Environmental Protection Administration, Tokyo Electric Power, September 1990, p. 19.
[58] Yoshirô Yanagawa, "The Greening of Corporate Japan," *Journal of Japanese Trade and Industry* 5 (1992), 14–16.
[59] Japan Automobile Manufacturers' Association, Inc., "Basic Position on Global Warming and Related Issues," June 1990.
[60] MITI, "New Earth 21: Action Program for the 21st Century," 1990.
[61] Research Institute of Innovative Technology for the Earth, pamphlet.

MITI preferred this kind of long-term technology-driven approach to action over short-term targets and timetables and thought that the US would embrace the idea. Much to MITI's surprise, however, the New Earth 21 plan was initially looked upon with skepticism and received little attention overseas or domestically. The plan had been formulated with US objections to a short-term CO_2 stabilization target in mind. The initial cool reception meant that MITI had to bide its time and do some public relations work before reintroducing the plan several months later at the Houston Summit. This time around it received the blessing of EPA Director William Reilly. It was at this point that the plan won approval from the Japanese Interministerial Council on Global Environmental Protection as well.[62] MITI was clearly working to develop an approach that would satisfy Washington.

The delay on New Earth 21, however, gave the Environment Agency a chance to push hard on a stabilization plan and win support from within the LDP. The Environment Agency backed the European idea of CO_2 stabilization. MITI, however, was opposed to the idea. The Energy Agency, which is heavily influenced by MITI, prepared a long-term energy demand estimate that showed that to maintain Japan's 3–4 percent level of economic growth while keeping CO_2 emissions from rising above current levels would require the building of 100 nuclear power plants. If CO_2 levels were to be stabilized at current levels without building any more nuclear plants than the existing thirty-seven, then, the Agency argued, economic growth rates would fall to 0.8 percent. Once a population growth rate of 0.5 percent per year was taken into consideration then the growth rate would be really only 0.3 percent. Thus, MITI initially maintained the position that CO_2 emissions could at best be kept to a 16 percent rise over 1988 levels by 2000.[63] The Environment Agency borrowing ideas from developments in Europe responded by suggesting that with the implementation of various energy saving measures, fuel switching, and co-generation, stabilization would be possible. For months neither MITI nor the Environment Agency proved willing to budge on their respective positions.

Reaching a compromise was difficult and might not have happened if the Environment Agency had not gained support from several other ministries, including Foreign Affairs; Transportation; and Agriculture, Forests, and Fisheries. It also won the backing of the LDP. The LDP was anxious to have a CO_2 reduction target to bring to Geneva and thus, the ministries were forced to find a compromise.

---

[62] Interview with Keiichi Yokobori, August 1994.
[63] *Nihon Keizai Shimbun*, November 8, 1989.

A compromise became possible with some fancy number juggling. MITI's estimates were based on the long-term energy forecast produced by the Energy Agency. The Agency's initial estimates had been based on the sharp rise in energy demand seen in the 1988–9 period. The 16 percent forecasted rise in CO_2 emissions could be adjusted downward to a 9 percent increase in CO_2 emissions by 2000 when 1990 was used as a base year instead. Due to the recession, energy demand was lower than expected. A further 1 percent decrease to an 8 percent rise in CO_2 emissions over 1990 levels by the year 2000 became possible when the Ministry of Transportation announced a revised long-term energy plan for the transportation sector. This revision reflected plans to shift more goods transports to rail and to increase mileage efficiency standards. Finally, the 6 percent figure settled upon by MITI was within the room for error provided by the forecast. This figure, moreover, equaled stabilization on a per capita basis given an estimated 6 percent rise in the population by 2000.[64] Director of MITI's Environment Division, Keiichi Yokobori, was confident that if plans went smoothly total CO_2 emissions could be reduced after 2013 or so. Thus it was conceivable that with further efforts, stabilization by 2000 would be more or less possible on a per capita basis![65]

The Environment Agency, however, stuck to its position of a flat stabilization target. This difference between MITI and the Environment Agency was not bridged. Thus, at the October 23 meeting of the Ministerial Council on Global Environmental Protection two plans for CO_2 stabilization were announced for the Action Plan to Arrest Global Warming.[66] The first was MITI's revised plan calling for stabilization of CO_2 emissions at 1990 levels by 2000 on a per capita basis. The Action Plan then went on to say that if technological developments in new energies and CO_2 fixation went faster than predicted, the Environment Agency's plan would be put into effect. The Action Plan also stated that the emission of methane gas should not exceed the present level. Japan announced its CO_2 stabilization target at the Second World Climate Conference in November 1990. For the Environment Agency, the outcome of this struggle had great symbolic importance.

There was still, however, the divide between the US and the EU to worry about. Japan was uneasy that the US was being isolated in the negotiations. At the second INC in preparation for UNCED held in Geneva in June 1991, the Ministry of Foreign Affairs therefore proposed

---

[64] Compiled from *Enerugii to Kankyô, Shukan Enerugii to Kankyô* 1125, October 18 (1990), 2–3; 1126, October 25 (1990), 2–3; and 1127, November 1 (1990), 2–3.
[65] Interview with Keiichi Yokobori, August 1994.
[66] Naikaku Sôri Daijin, "Chikyû Ondanka Bôshi Kôdô Keikaku," February 10, 1990.

the adoption of a Pledge and Review system, formulated apparently in part to try to help bring the US into an agreement. The idea of the Pledge and Review system was that countries would be allowed unilaterally to make pledges that consisted of national strategies and response measures to limit their greenhouse gas emissions. An international team of experts would then periodically review these pledges. France and the United Kingdom proposed similar ideas.[67]

This proposal too, however, immediately came under attack from NGOs, developing countries, and most surprisingly, the LDP. MITI and the Foreign Ministry had made a huge miscalculation. The two ministries had proposed the Pledge and Review system at an important international meeting without first getting agreement from Kazuo Aichi, the minister responsible for global environmental affairs, or other members of the LDP. This was a dramatic instance of power politics between the ruling LDP and two powerful ministries. LDP politicians were not pleased that they had first learned about the Pledge and Review system from foreign governments and NGOs and not from the ministries. In a clear move to punish the ministries, the LDP's Special Committee on Global Environmental Problems (chaired by Masahisa Aoki), criticized the ministries for "going it alone" and refused to give its approval to the Pledge and Review plan.[68]

According to explanations made to the committee by a representative of the Foreign Ministry, the proposal was made to take into account the different capacities that countries have to reduce CO_2 emissions and to bring the three largest emitters of CO_2 – the US, China, and Russia – into the treaty. Moreover, he claimed that it was uncertain whether or not the EC would put a CO_2 target into practice. The plan was made as a way of getting countries to stick to their promises. Another opinion is that this plan was made to appease the US, which was holding out on any kind of concrete international commitments on CO_2 reductions.[69]

Whether the LDP would have been so upset with the idea if it had been brought into the decision-making process is not clear. The proposal was made just a couple of weeks prior to a three-day conference in Tokyo of an international body of parliamentarians concerned with the environment, GLOBE. At this meeting, US Congressman Gerry Sikorski (whose views differed from the Bush administration) strongly criticized the Pledge and Review system.[70] In a letter to Jean Ripert, chairman of the UN organization on climate change, GLOBE members wrote, "Statements supporting a 'pledge and review' mechanism will frustrate attempts to achieve

[67] Bodansky, "Prologue to the Climate Change Convention," pp. 45–74.
[68] *Asahi Shimbun*, July 26, 1991, p. 4.   [69] *Asahi Shimbun*, July 26, 1991, p. 4.
[70] GLOBE, "Sekai Sôkai Tôkyô Kaigi Hôkokusho," Tokyo, Japan, July 1–3, 1991.

meaningful commitments to reduce emissions."[71] The Special Committee on Global Environmental Problems decided that the plan would have to be revised. Chairman of the committee Aoki stated that "at a minimum the EC's stabilization target for 2000 should be agreed to."[72] Days later, the Environment Agency Director-General Aichi announced in Washington that Japan planned to agree to a firm target.

The shifting and somewhat conflicted Japanese position at this early stage of the climate change negotiations suggests a process of domestic political change dominated by competing ideologies. The Environment Agency, environmentalists, and green politicians leaned towards the European approach to climate change mitigation and environmental protection more generally. MITI and industry were willing to take some actions, but they were more sympathetic to the Bush administration's no regrets policy.

A new basic environment law

Another important debate was whether Japan should follow the northern European states that were calling for the introduction of CO_2 taxes. Takeshita was a primary supporter of enhancing Japan's institutional capacities for protecting the environment both domestically and overseas; he pushed for the establishment of a new environmental basic law, elevation of the Environment Agency to ministerial status, and consideration of CO_2 taxes. A coalition to support this idea formed between the Environment Agency and the Ministry of Finance, which proposed a carbon tax for Japan in January 1991 following similar discussions within the OECD and the European Community.[73] For the Environment Agency a carbon tax on oil, coal, and natural gas was a necessary instrument for assuring that the CO_2 stabilization target be met. From the Ministry of Finance's point of view, a carbon tax would help pay for the large rise in environmental expenditures that began in 1989 with the government's plan to increase spending on environmental programs in its ODA.

Takeshita hosted an international eminent persons meeting on Financing the Global Environment and Development in Tokyo in April 1992 to promote international discussion of the idea of carbon taxes and environmental taxes. Then, in May 1992, the Environment Agency issued a report entitled "An Appraisal of Instruments to Prevent Global Warming." The report argued that while CO_2 stabilization at 1990 levels by 2000 was possible, it would be necessary to introduce a carbon tax to ensure that the target was met.[74]

---

[71] *Japan Times*, July 4, 1991, p. 4.   [72] *Asahi Shimbun*, July 26, 1991, p. 4.
[73] *Yomiuri Shimbun*, January 8, 1991, p. 1.   [74] *Yomiuri Shimbun*, May 25, 1992, p. 3.

Takeshita, however, did not have the backing of Japanese industry. MITI and business argued that the introduction of a carbon tax would hurt business, which was already suffering under a recession.[75] The *Keizai Dantai Rengôkai* (*Keidanren*, the Japan Federation of Economic Organizations) stated its general support of the idea that Japan should shoulder a large share of the burden of global environmental initiatives, but proposed that instead of a carbon tax, the consumption tax be raised. This they argued would be a better measure of resource use and would be a fairer tax since it would be spread more widely. Many within the LDP opposed the idea, which they feared would cost the party public support.[76] Backed by Takeshita, however, some politicians within the LDP pushed for a carbon tax.

The idea of a carbon tax was incorporated into discussions over the revision of Japan's Basic Law for Environmental Pollution Control. It was widely agreed that the existing law, formulated two decades earlier, was too narrow in its scope and did not adequately address the global nature of many environmental problems. In February 1992 at Takeshita's urging the LDP established an Investigatory Committee on Basic Environmental Problems. Close Takeshita ally, and future prime minister, Ryûtarô Hashimoto was appointed its chairman. A few months later, Prime Minister Kiichi Miyazawa announced that he had instructed concerned government agencies to work towards creating a new Basic Environment Law.

Another important debate regarded incorporating an environmental impact assessment requirement into the law. The idea had the backing of environmental groups, opposition parties, and LDP members of the new environment *zoku*. To gain support from the rest of the party, Takeshita included representatives from the Diet's Policy Affairs Research Council's committees for Construction, Foreign Affairs, Agriculture, and Commerce in Hashimoto's group.[77] There was, however, strong opposition from MoT, MoC, MITI, and *Keidanren*. These opponents argued that the existing Cabinet decision and voluntary efforts on the part of industry made such a law unnecessary. Moreover, they argued that such a law could trigger countless lawsuits by residents opposed to construction projects, delaying development, and making it difficult, if not impossible, to undertake large construction projects.

In mid-May 1992 the Environment Agency established a team to work on the fundamentals of a new law. Two months later the team submitted its proposals for a new environment basic law to the Central Council for

[75] *Asahi Shimbun*, May 24, 1992, p. 1.   [76] *Yomiuri Shimbun*, April 18, 1992, p. 7.
[77] *Asahi Shimbun*, March 10, 1993, p. 4.

Environmental Pollution Control and the Nature Conservation Council. The proposal called for environmental impact assessments for new projects and the introduction of economic measures, including taxes and surcharges, that would help spread the cost of environmental protection across society.[78] These two councils, in turn, submitted a recommendation to Environment Agency Director General Shôzaburô Nakamura.[79] Regarding an environmental tax, the report stated that:

[I]t is important to incorporate [the] idea of economic instruments into the basic law on the environment, for the promotion of measures against urban and household-generated pollution, increased waste discharge, and global environmental problems . . . On the other hand, . . . [a]s there are areas in which extensive, careful discussion have not resulted in a national consensus, it would be inappropriate to incorporate the economic instruments as [a] whole into the basic environmental law.

Regarding environmental impact assessment the report was similarly ambiguous.

The Environment Agency did not give up. In January 1993 the Agency issued its proposal for a Basic Law on the Environment, which included the idea of a carbon tax and an environmental impact assessment clause, for negotiation among the various ministries. MITI meanwhile had sent its own bill to the Diet to promote energy-saving efforts by industries through financial incentives. When the Cabinet approved the bill for a Basic Environment Law on March 12, 1993 the bill simply stated that the government would seek public understanding and cooperation in introducing economic sanctions as a way of preserving the environment. Both the environmental tax and environmental impact assessment legislation were essentially written out of the bill. In fact, the *Yomiuri Shimbun* reported that the Environment Agency had to agree to sign an official memorandum stating that an environmental assessment requirement would not be introduced soon in order to get MoC and MITI to approve the rest of the bill.[80]

The key reason why the Environment Agency's bill was watered down as much as it was is that it was an unfortunate victim of the *Sagawa Kyûbin* scandal of March 1993, a case of immense political corruption in which Takeshita's mentor, Shin Kanemaru, was implicated in accepting huge bribes. Takeshita's political influence dropped precipitously because of his close ties to Kanemaru. The scandal triggered the splintering of his

---

[78] *Mainichi Shimbun*, July 15, 1993, p. 13.
[79] Central Council for Environmental Pollution Control and the Nature Conservation Council, "Establishing a Basic Law on the Environment," October 20, 1992.
[80] *Daily Yomiuri*, March 29, 1993, p. 2.

faction. Both Hashimoto and Takeshita, important advocates of a pro-gressive new environment basic law, became too preoccupied with other issues to continue to pay attention to the bill. This meant that ministries and agencies that had backed off on their criticism of the Environment Agency's earlier draft felt free once again to state their objections and both the ideas of an environmental tax and environmental impact assessment were essentially dropped from discussion for the time being.

What this discussion illustrates is that the ambiguous position Japan often takes in international environmental negotiations reflects some deep ideological divisions that exist among relevant policy actors. The divide that exists between the US and the EU internationally is mirrored in some ways in the divisions that exist between MITI (now METI) and the Environment Agency (now Environment Ministry). This also helps explain why despite Japan's desire to play the role of an effective policy mediator, it is often difficult for Japan to do so effectively because of the difficulty of building sufficient consensus among the ministries about which course to follow.

The UNCED and the Framework Convention on Climate Change

The UNCED negotiations took place over close to a two-week period in Rio de Janeiro, Brazil in June 1992. Representatives from 172 countries were present for the meeting. Three important agreements were estab-lished at the conference: (1) the FCCC, (2) the Biodiversity Convention, and (3) Agenda 21, a non-binding action plan for achieving sustainable development. Here only the FCCC is considered. The FCCC was signed by over 150 nations in Rio de Janeiro. By 2001, 185 states and the Euro-pean Community had become parties.

The FCCC provides a framework, or set of broad guiding principles, for how nations are to work together to address climate change. Because of US opposition, the agreement did not set specific greenhouse gas emis-sions reduction targets or timetables for achieving reductions. Rather, the FCCC called for the "stabilization of greenhouse gas concentrations in the atmosphere at a level that would prevent dangerous anthropogenic in-terference with the climate system. Such a level should be achieved within a timeframe sufficient to allow ecosystems to adapt naturally . . . and to en-able economic development to proceed in a sustainable manner."[81] Each developed country party to the convention also agreed "to adopt national policies and take corresponding measures on the mitigation of climate

[81] United Nations Framework Convention on Climate Change, Article 2.

change, by limiting its anthropogenic emissions of greenhouse gases and protecting and enhancing its greenhouse gas sinks and reservoirs."[82]

The FCCC established two groupings of nations: Annex 1 and Annex 2 parties. An Annex 1 party is a developed or transitioning economy that agreed to take measures "to mitigate climate change, by limiting its anthropogenic emissions of greenhouse gases and protecting and enhancing its greenhouse gas sinks and reservoirs." It also agreed to regular national inventories of greenhouse gas sources and their removal by carbon absorbing sinks (e.g. forests, agricultural land, wetlands) and to report national mitigation measures to the UN FCCC secretariat. Japan, Germany, the European Economic Community, and the US were classified along with other European states, Canada, Australia, and the transition economies of central and eastern Europe as Annex 1 parties. The Annex 2 parties were a subset of the Annex 1 parties that also agreed to provide financial and technical assistance to developing countries, and especially highly vulnerable countries, to help them deal with the impacts of climate change. Japan, Germany, the European Economic Community, and the US were also included as Annex 2 parties.

Following the example set by the Montreal Protocol, the FCCC called for regular review of the goals of the FCCC based on scientific and technological developments. To assure that progress on addressing climate change continue the FCCC also established a Conference of the Parties (COP) that would meet annually (unless otherwise determined by the Parties) to work towards establishing a climate change protocol that would spell out national and international commitments and implementation procedures.

There were many technical details of the convention that would need to be worked out in a future protocol. The FCCC made mention of sinks and joint implementation, for example, but left for future negotiations definitions of what qualified as a sink and how joint implementation was to work. Common methodologies for measuring and reporting also needed to be established as did issues pertaining to financial and technology transfers.

A close look at the FCCC shows that the differences in the positions of Germany/the EU, the US, and Japan were never fully bridged. There were no major shifts in the US negotiating position and in many areas the US position prevailed. The FCCC simply outlined major concerns and vague goals pertaining to climate change mitigation. The US did agree to special mention of the need for control of CO_2 even though it had originally objected to this idea. It maintained its opposition, however,

[82] United Nations Framework Convention on Climate Change, Article 4, section 2 (a).

to the establishment of targets and timetables for emissions reductions. Instead, the US pushed for a system under which states would be required to establish national strategies and plans of action to reduce their own greenhouse gas emissions. This was to lead to a requirement for nations to produce National Strategy reports outlining their goals and plans for action.

The US did not come out of the UNCED negotiations winning many friends. The US was the only industrialized country to refuse to sign the Biodiversity Convention arguing that it did not adequately protect the pharmaceutical industry and intellectual property rights. US industry feared what signing the treaty could mean in terms of the power of interpretation that a vaguely worded agreement would give to the US courts.[83] The US also was viewed as a blocking force in the negotiations on climate change because of its resistance to the idea of establishing targets and timetables. Still, having succeeded in modifying the wording of the FCCC, the US signed the climate convention and became one of the first countries in the world to ratify it. Also, consistent with its interest in national reporting, the US announced $25 million in new aid to help developing countries draw up national inventories of greenhouse gas sources and sinks.

Japan signed the FCCC and the Biodiversity Treaty in Rio de Janeiro. It also reconfirmed its pledge to stabilize CO_2 emissions at 1990 levels on a per capita basis by the year 2000 (a goal that was not achieved), and promised substantial support for international efforts to promote environmental protection in the developing world. Although Japan usually follows the US in international negotiations, domestic politics had pushed Japan in a different direction from the US on this crucial environmental issue.

Germany played the role of an advocate of strong action within the EC and internationally. Aided in its goal of reducing domestic greenhouse gas emissions by the collapse of the heavily polluting eastern German economy, the Germans were able to maintain their position as a leading voice for strong developed country action. The next chapter continues the discussion of climate change politics begun here.

---

[83] Kal Raustiala, "The Domestic Politics of Global Biodiversity Protection in the United Kingdom and the United States," in Schreurs and Economy (eds.), *The Internationalization of Environmental Protection*, pp. 42–73.

7 Global climate change: the battle over Kyoto

At the UNCED it was agreed that there should be regular COPs to the FCCC in order to continue to assess scientific developments and the need for additional action. It was also agreed that a climate change protocol should be established in which developed country commitments would be spelled out. This occurred in Kyoto, Japan, in 1997. Three-and-a-half years later the US decided to withdraw from the Protocol. In a historic move that left the US internationally isolated, Japan and the EU decided to move forward with the Protocol even without the US.

This chapter examines these highly politicized debates from a comparative national perspective focusing on the US, Japan, and Germany, respectively the first, fourth, and sixth largest CO_2 emitting countries in the world (see Table 7.1). The US throughout the decade after UNCED showed great resistance to committing itself to an international agreement that would require it to make major cuts to domestic CO_2 emissions. It also opposed an agreement that did not include China, India, or other major developing countries that in coming years will become the world's largest polluters as a result of population growth and economic development. Germany and the EU pushed for an agreement that would require nations to begin a process of domestic emissions reductions. They argued that it was the developed countries' responsibility to act first especially since when viewed on a per capita basis it is the inhabitants of the rich countries that are the big polluters. Japan continued in its uncomfortable role as the middleman, seeking a way to find a compromise between the EU and the US. In the end, it did what it seldom does. It chose to side not with the US, but instead with the EU.

The Clinton–Gore administration: a new US approach to climate change?

There were high expectations that the US position might change as a result of the election of William J. Clinton and his running mate, Albert Gore. Gore, after all, had written the best selling book, *Earth*

Table 7.1 *The world's top carbon dioxide emitting countries in 1998[1]*

Rank	Country	CO_2[a]	% global total
1	United States	1,489,801	24.0
2	People's Republic of China	848,266	13.7
3	Russian Federation	391,535	6.3
4	Japan	309,353	5.0
5	India	289,587	4.7
6	Germany	225,208	3.6
7	United Kingdom	148,011	2.4
8	Canada	127,517	2.0

[a] CO_2 emissions from fossil fuel burning, cement production, and gas flaring. Emissions are expressed in thousand metric tons of carbon.
Source: G. Marland, T. A. Boden, and R. J. Andres, "Global, Regional, and National Fossil Fuel CO_2 Emissions," in *Trends: A Compendium of Data on Global Change*, Carbon Dioxide Information Analysis Center, Oak Ridge National Laboratory, US Department of Energy, Oak Ridge, Tenn., USA, 2001.

in the Balance, in which he wrote in a foreword revised in September 1992:

At a crucial moment in history, when the rest of the world was requesting and eagerly expecting American leadership – not to mention vision – our nation found itself embarrassed and isolated at Rio . . . [L]ong before the summit, almost every other industrial nation in the world had stated its willingness to set binding targets for reducing and stabilizing carbon dioxide (CO_2) emissions. But the Bush administration threatened to torpedo the entire Earth Summit in order to prevent the adoption of targets and timetables for CO_2 reductions . . . Japan signaled early in the process that although it was willing to adopt targets and timetables, it would eventually follow the U.S. lead on this issue. By contrast, several European nations – led by Germany – attempted to pressure and persuade the United States to change its views . . . Tragically, as a direct consequence of U.S. insistence on having no binding agreement to reduce CO_2 emissions in industrial countries, the developing nations of the world abandoned their willingness to negotiate an international treaty to protect endangered rain forests and other fragile ecosystems.[1]

Gore was considered the greenest politician to enter the White House in decades. Expectations among environmentalists were high; fear among industry was also real. Early indications were that the Clinton–Gore team planned to shift US positions on key international environmental issues. Clinton, for example, signed the Biodiversity Convention on his first Earth Day as president. He declared, moreover, that the country would voluntarily stabilize its greenhouse gas emissions at 1990

[1] Al Gore, *Earth in the Balance* (New York: Plume, 1993), pp. xiii–xvi.

levels by 2000 even though the administration initially remained opposed to legally binding targets and timetables. Furthermore, one of the first policy initiatives of the Clinton–Gore team in 1993 was to propose a tax on the energy content of fuels, known as a British Thermal Unit (BTU) tax, in an effort to penalize heavy greenhouse gas polluters.

Yet, Congress stymied the leadership role that Gore wanted for the administration even though the Democrats were in the majority in the House of Representatives in the first two years of the Clinton presidency. The proposed BTU tax, for example, was defeated in Congress as a result of the effective lobbying skills of the coal, oil, utility, and auto lobbies. Instead, only a modest 4.3 cents a gallon tax on gasoline was passed.[2]

Congressional opposition to major policy changes that would affect energy policies tied Clinton's hands. The White House took action, but not the kind of steps that many environmentalists would have liked to see. Clinton's 1993 Climate Action Plan, thus, focused heavily on voluntary measures to be taken by industry and government to improve energy efficiency, reduce greenhouse gas emissions, and promote renewable energies, but no major regulatory measures were proposed. The Climate Action Plan, in other words, basically had no teeth. It should be noted, however, that the plan did lead to the formation of the US Country Studies Program to help developing countries assess their greenhouse gas emissions sources and sinks and the US Initiative on Joint Implementation, a non-regulatory pilot program to promote international partnerships to combat greenhouse gas emissions.[3]

The Republican electoral landslide in November 1994 simply made matters more difficult for the administration. One of the first moves of the Congress was to express its unwillingness to ratify the Biodiversity Convention that the Clinton White House had signed. They also made clear their dislike of the direction of the climate change negotiations. The 104th Congress devoted itself to reducing the size of government as part of its Contract with America and environmental regulations were a visible target.

The Conferences of the Parties: from Berlin to Kyoto (1995–1997)

The FCCC went into force in 1994 after fifty states had ratified the agreement. This opened the door for the first COP, which Chancellor Helmut Kohl had offered to host in Berlin. There is no doubt that the

[2] Agrawala and Andresen, "The United States in the Climate Treaty Negotiations," 462.
[3] Neil E. Harrison, "From the Inside Out: Domestic Influences on Global Environmental Policy," in Paul G. Harris (ed.), *Climate Change and American Foreign Policy* (New York: St. Martin's Press, 2000), pp. 100–1.

international negotiators had an immensely complex task before them. The technical details of an agreement were difficult enough simply to understand and in addition they had to worry about national economic, social, and political constraints.

As was the case in the pre-UNCED period, the INC met numerous times in preparation for the first COP. Germany as a strong advocate of climate change mitigation both domestically and internationally made early moves. The German interministerial working group on climate change came up with a list of 109 measures that Germany could take to reduce its CO_2 emissions domestically.[4] It also proposed a carbon energy tax for the EU as a whole during its EU presidency in the second half of 1994. The proposal failed, however, to gain sufficient support outside of Scandinavia and the Netherlands.[5]

In August 1994 in the run-up to the first COP, the German delegation also proposed a protocol on CO_2 emissions. The proposal called on industrialized states to reduce "their CO_2 emissions by the year (x) individually or jointly by (y) percent." There was, however, considerable opposition to this proposal. Environmentalists felt it did not go very far while some member states of the EU felt it premature to form a protocol at the first COP. The Association of Small Island States (AOSIS), however, built on the German idea and several months later submitted a proposal calling for a 20 percent reduction of emissions from 1990 levels by 2005. Germany supported the AOSIS proposal.[6]

At the first COP held in Berlin in 1995 the parties to the FCCC did not accept the German or AOSIS proposals, but they did agree that the commitments in the FCCC were inadequate and that there was a need to start a process aimed at strengthening the commitments in time for the third COP. The Parties to the FCCC agreed to negotiate a 'protocol or other legal instrument' that would "set quantified limitation and reduction objectives" for the Annex 1 countries "within specified time frames, such as 2005, 2010, and 2020, for their anthropogenic emissions by sources and removals by sinks of greenhouse gases not controlled by the Montreal Protocol" to be ready for agreement at the third COP which was scheduled to be held in 1997.[7] This came to be known as the Berlin Mandate.[8]

---

[4] Beuermann and Jäger, "Climate Change Politics in Germany," p. 200.
[5] Beuermann and Jäger, "Climate Change Politics in Germany," pp. 203–4. On UK opposition to the EC carbon tax idea see Tim O'Riordan and Elizabeth J. Rowbotham, "Struggling for Credibility: The UK," in O'Riordan and Jäger (eds.), *Politics of Climate Change*, p. 246.
[6] Paterson, *Global Warming and Global Politics*, p. 68.
[7] Sebastian Oberthür and Hermann Ott, *The Kyoto Protocol* (Berlin: Springer Verlag, 1999), pp. 47–8.
[8] Michael Grubb with Christiaan Vrolijk and Duncan Brack, *The Kyoto Protocol: A Guide and Assessment* (London: Royal Institute of International Affaris, Earthscan, 1999), pp. 47–8; Paterson, *Global Warming and Global Politics*, p. 70.

In Berlin an agreement was also obtained to initiate pilot Joint Implementation projects (Activities Implemented Jointly or AIJ) but without explicit crediting of emissions reductions to the donor country.[9] At the close of the meeting, Japan offered to host the third COP in its ancient capital, Kyoto.

In preparation for the Kyoto Conference, there were eight meetings of the Ad Hoc Group to the Berlin Mandate (AGBM). Bonn became the permanent location of the AGBM secretariat. The group's main function was to produce a draft protocol prior to the third COP. There were many issues under discussion. Should there be one flat emissions reduction or stabilization target for all industrialized countries or should differentiated targets be allowed for countries based on national circumstances? Which greenhouse gases should be covered by any agreement? Should sinks – that is, forests and agricultural land that can sequester carbon effectively removing CO_2 from the atmosphere – also be counted? What emissions ceilings should be established? Also very important was the question of the extent to which flexible mechanisms could be used to meet targets. Finally, there was disagreement about what the role of developing countries should be and how much responsibility the developed countries should bear for paying the cost of improving pollution control in developing countries.[10]

The negotiators were reminded of the importance of their work at numerous occasions. One such occasion was with the release of the IPCC's Second Assessment Report in December 1995. The report stated that to stabilize CO_2 emissions at 550 ppm in the atmosphere, a level believed necessary to arrest global warming, global CO_2 emissions would have to be reduced by 50 percent. This was a target far higher than what the negotiators were attempting. The IPCC also came out with the strongest statement yet by the body on the level of consensus achieved by scientists regarding climate change: "the balance of evidence suggests a discernible human influence on the climate."[11]

This report did not bring an end to the skeptics' questioning of the threat of climate change, but it did provide fodder to the Clinton White House. By this time, the Republican Congress's Contract with America was coming under considerable scrutiny by an increasingly skeptical public. The White House deep in an election campaign effectively portrayed the Republican Congress as being out of touch with the American population and an enemy of the environment. Secretary of State Warren

[9] Jorge Antunes, "Regime Effectiveness, Joint Implementation and Climate Change Policy," in Harris (ed.), *Climate Change and American Foreign Policy*, pp. 183–6.

[10] Oberthür and Ott, *The Kyoto Protocol*, p. 49.

[11] IPCC, *Climate Change 1995*, pp. 4–5.

Christopher announced that further cuts in greenhouse gas emissions were a top priority for the US.[12]

COP 2 was held in Geneva, Switzerland, in July 1996. The big surprise at COP 2 was a speech by Undersecretary of State for Global Affairs Timothy Wirth who was heading the US delegation. In his speech he recognized the integrity of the IPCC's findings and called for "realistic, verifiable and binding medium-term commitments ... met through maximum flexibility in the selection of implementation measures, including the use of reliable activities implemented jointly, and trading mechanisms around the world." This was the first time any of the major state actors had called for binding commitment targets and suggested a major shift in the US negotiating position. The speech made possible a Ministerial Declaration that instructed negotiators to accelerate work on text for a legally binding protocol.

With a little over a year left before the Kyoto Protocol several major debates needed to be settled. The EU and Japan were pushing for a system of internationally agreed upon policies and measures for reducing greenhouse gas emissions. The EU provided a particularly long list of policies and measures (nineteen pages in total), including such possibilities as minimum fuel excise taxes, broader environmental taxes, improvements in energy efficiency, and fuel switching. With decades of experience in harmonizing national regulations and other policy measures, this was an approach favored by the EU. The US, however, flatly rejected the idea and instead pushed the idea of flexibility in meeting national commitments.[13]

Another big issue that needed to be worked out regarded commitment targets and timetables. Numerous proposals were made over the course of the next months. Germany went into COP 2 with a proposal for a 10 percent reduction in CO_2 emissions of Annex 1 countries to the FCCC by 2005 and a 15–20 percent reduction by 2010.[14]

After the meeting, Japan felt pressured to develop its own proposal. The Japanese MoFA, the Environment Agency, MITI, and MoT began interministerial negotiations on a Japan proposal in August 1996, but there was considerable disagreement among them. The main point of contention regarded a fixed CO_2 emissions reduction target. The Environment Agency advocated a target that would require the advanced industrialized states to reduce emissions beginning in 2000. With this as a precondition, the Environment Agency then went on to support differentiated

---

[12] Harrison, "From the Inside Out," p. 104.   [13] Grubb, *The Kyoto Protocol*, pp. 54–68.
[14] Peter Newell and Matthew Paterson, "From Geneva to Kyoto: The Second Conference of the Parties to the UN Framework Convention on Climate Change," *Environmental Politics* 5:4 (1997), 729–35.

targets among states. If the precondition could not be met, then the Environment Agency supported a fixed target. MITI and the Ministry of Transportation supported differentiated targets. Both felt that a reduction would be impossible domestically and thus Japan should not make a reduction proposal. The MoFA felt that Japan could not present a proposal that did not work towards a reduction, but also felt that the country could not present a proposal that it could not meet. MoFA was also concerned about US participation in a protocol and thus was reluctant to push for the kind of standardized CO_2 reduction target by 2010 across the industrialized countries that was being pushed for by the Germans and the EU. MoFA instead favored differentiated targets for the Annex 1 countries. The MoFA backed a Pledge and Review type system.

After two months of interministerial negotiations, the MoFA drafted a proposal to be submitted to the fifth AGBM meeting in Geneva on December 9, 1996.[15] The vagueness of the Japanese proposal reflected the differences that existed among the major domestic players and interpretations of what might be acceptable internationally. The proposal called for differentiation in the establishment of targets and timetables among the Annex 1 parties. It stated that each party included in Annex 1 should select one of two quantified limitation or reduction objectives for its anthropogenic emissions of CO_2. The two proposed objectives were for each country:

a. To maintain its anthropogenic emissions of CO_2 over the period from [2000+x] to [2000+x+{5}] at an average yearly level not more than p tons of carbon per capita, or
b. To reduce its anthropogenic emissions of CO_2 over the period from [2000+x] to [2000+x+{5}] at an average yearly level of not less than q per cent below the level of the year 1990.[16]

The proposal was intended to establish a flexible system. As had earlier been the case with Pledge and Review, however, the proposal did not get a particularly warm reception. Instead, it raised concerns among environmentalists and other nations since the x, p, and q values were all left unspecified. The typically conservative *Yomiuri Shimbun* ran an article that was highly critical of the proposal stating that Japan was avoiding pushing a large reduction target by proposing instead a per capita

---

[15] Interview with government official, January 1997.
[16] Government of Japan, "Proposals on the Elements to be Included in the Draft Protocol to the United Nations Framework Convention on Climate Change." See also Toshiaki Tanabe, *Chikyû Ondanka to Kankyô Gaikô: Kyôto Kaigi no Kôbô to Sonogo no Tenkai* (Tokyo: DaiNippon Insatsu, 1999), pp. 66–70, 107–11.

emissions reduction target (expecting that the Japanese population would be increasing).[17]

In January 1997 the US submitted a framework for a draft protocol that included proposals for emissions budgets, joint implementation, emissions trading, banking, and borrowing.[18] The US also pushed for commitments to be made on a voluntary basis by developing countries as an initial step and for firm commitments by all parties by 2005. The US supported broader, multi-year target dates, rather than a single target year as called for by the EU and also wanted there to be a system in which states could "bank" unused emissions and borrow from future emission allocations in order to meet their commitments.

They also supported a larger basket of greenhouse gases than the three (CO_2, methane, and nitrous oxide) being suggested by Japan and the EU. The US wanted to include three other gases as well: HCFCs, perfluorocarbons, and sulfur hexafluoride. Adding these gases to the mix would target gases with high global warming potentials but would also make it easier for the US to meet a reduction goal since dependence on these gases in the US was expected to decline rapidly for other reasons.

The EU proposes a bubble

At the sixth meeting of the AGBM in Bonn in March 1997, the EU Environment Council proposed that industrialized countries cut the combined emissions of three greenhouse gases – CO_2, methane, and nitrous oxide – by 15 percent in 2010. The EU called for flat emissions reduction targets for all industrialized states, but produced much controversy by then also proposing a special internal-burden sharing arrangement for EU member states. Essentially, the proposal was for an emissions target for the EU as a whole that would be the same as for all other industrialized states, but it would also allow for differentiation within the EU. Some states would be allowed to increase their emissions while others would have to reduce their emissions sufficiently to assure that the EU target be reached. Thus, Spain would be allowed to increase its emissions by 17 percent, Greece by 30 percent, and Portugal by 40 percent since these states were still considered less developed than the northern states of Europe and were expected to require more energy in the future as their economies developed. Other states would make up for this growth in southern European emissions through substantial reductions. Germany,

---

[17] *Yomiuri Shimbun*, November 1, 1996, morning edition.
[18] Oberthür and Ott, *The Kyoto Protocol*, p. 55.

Austria, and Denmark were to decrease emissions by 25 percent each, the UK by 15 percent and the Netherlands by 10 percent. The US strongly criticized the EU bubble proposal, which called for a form of differentiation within the EU but a flat target for the rest of the industrialized world. The EU justified this approach because of its status as a political unit with its own parliament and regulatory rules.[19] The EU was to lose this debate.

The 15 percent reduction figure also elicited strong reactions. Kathleen McGinty, the top White House environmental advisor, announced in early October that the US considered the EU proposal for a 15 percent reduction "unrealistic and unachievable."[20] Japan also expressed its concern over the EU position as being both unfair and unrealistic.[21] They both argued that the EU had not shown how it could meet the reduction target, especially given its failure to pass a carbon tax over internal opposition. The EU responded to these criticisms in June 1997, under the presidency of the Netherlands, with a proposal for an intermediate cut of greenhouse gas emissions of 7.5 percent of 1990 levels by 2005 for industrialized countries.[22]

The US pushes flexible mechanisms

Wary of how far the Clinton White House might go in the up-coming Kyoto negotiations in the face of bold European calls for major cuts in emissions, the US Senate took action into its own hands. The Senate voted 95–0 on July 25, 1997 on a nonbonding bi-partisan resolution authored by Senators Robert Byrd and Chuck Hagel that any treaty signed by the US must also include meaningful commitments to action by developing countries. Hagel saw the treaty as an impingement on US sovereignty.

There was also much opposition coming from powerful industries. A prominent voice in the US on climate change has been the GCC. The GCC is an organization that was formed by business trade associations in 1989 to coordinate business participation in the scientific and policy debates about global climate change. Its membership is broad, including electric utilities, railroads, transportation, mining, manufacturing, small

---

[19] Sebastian Oberthür and Stephan Singer, "Die internationale Klimapolitik am Scheideweg: Ein Bericht über den Stand der Klima-diplomatie am Vorabend des entscheidenden Kyoto-Gipfels in Dezember 1997" (Frankfurt: World Wide Fund for Nature, November 1997).

[20] *Washington Post*, October 6, 1997, p. A4.

[21] Yasuko Kawashima, "Japan's Decision-Making about Climate Change Problems: Comparative Study of Decisions in 1990 and 1997," *Environmental Economics and Policy Studies* 3 (2000), 45.

[22] Oberthür and Ott, *The Kyoto Protocol*, p. 56.

businesses, oil and coal industries. The GCC in 1997 claimed 230,000 firms as members, explaining its political weight on Capitol Hill. It has been a very vocal opponent of regulatory action arguing that "it is imperative that climate change policies focus on voluntary actions, including further research, innovation and deployment of current and potential future technologies in developed and developing nations to address concerns about the climate. Unrealistic targets and timetables, such as those called for under the Kyoto Protocol, are not achievable without severely harming the US economy."[23]

Another influential industry association is the American Petroleum Institute (API), which represents the entire petroleum industry. The API argued that "the targets and timetables... would exact too heavy an economic price given our current understanding of the evolving science of climate change."[24]

In September 1997, an alliance of business and trade groups launched a $13 million media campaign warning of painful energy cost increases if a treaty was approved. In an advertisement placed in the *Washington Post* critical of the Kyoto Conference outcomes the Mobile Corporation raised such questions as: "What about jobs?... Since U.S. emissions have climbed by 9 percent through 1996, how will the nation reach this new goal without sharply cutting energy consumption and closing the door on economic growth?"[25] In another advertisement covering three full pages in the *Washington Post*, the Business Roundtable urged "the Clinton/Gore administration not to rush to policy commitments until the environmental benefits and economic consequences of the treaty proposals have been thoroughly analyzed."[26]

The White House was in a difficult position. In the end sandwiched between the international community and the Senate, the administration decided its best bet would be to focus on making sure that any agreement reached would allow for maximum use of flexible mechanisms and would win some form of developing country commitment. As a result, three kinds of flexible mechanisms became increasingly important elements in the development of a US position: joint implementation, the clean development mechanism, and emissions trading.

Joint implementation, a concept written into the FCCC, is the term used to describe when an Annex 1 party agrees to offset its emissions by reducing emissions in another Annex 1 party, such as a transitioning economy where emissions reductions can be achieved more economically. The

---

[23] http://www.globalclimate.org/policy-000301%2021St%20century.html.
[24] http://www.api.org/globalclimate/apipos.htm.
[25] *Washington Post*, December 21, 1997, p. C5.
[26] *Washington Post*, June 10, 1997, pp. A7–A9.

clean development mechanism is similar but refers instead to assistance by Annex 1 parties to developing countries in their efforts to reduce emissions through, for example, the provision of pollution control technology. Both parties would gain some credit towards their emissions reductions goals (actual or in the case of developing countries, projected) through these flexible mechanisms.

Another important flexible mechanism is the concept of emissions trading under a cap and trade system similar to the sulfur dioxide emissions trading system being used for acid rain control in the US.[27] A cap refers to a limit on emissions established for a large unit (like a corporation, a nation, or a group of nations). Permits are allocated to polluters within that unit who then can engage in trade among themselves in pollution rights. If a firm wants to expand, it must first obtain a permit that will allow it to pollute more. To do this, it must find a seller willing to give up some of its pollution rights, which might occur when a firm upgrades its production process. The cap can be lowered over time reducing allowable total pollution levels. At the international level, if a country establishes an emissions cap but has trouble reducing emissions domestically, it might look abroad for projects it could engage in to reduce CO_2 emissions elsewhere, conceivably at lower cost, and gain credit towards its own emissions reduction goals that way.[28] Countries that have exceeded their emissions reduction targets (the case of Russia's hot air) might sell their excess pollution rights.

Reliance on flexible mechanisms would reduce the need for use of traditional regulatory approaches. This, it was believed, would also make them more acceptable to US industry. The basis behind this line of reasoning was that command and control approaches are relatively inflexible because they do not differentiate between firms in their ability to reduce emissions or the costs involved in reducing emissions. They also do not typically create incentives for firms to exceed set performance standards.[29] Thus, the flexible mechanisms would give firms in the aggregate greater room to decide how best to reduce emissions. This line of reasoning, however, was not very well received in Europe.

Japan struggles to determine a position

With the conference date rapidly approaching, Japan was under considerable pressure to take on a leadership role. There were still strong divides between the positions of the EU and the US going into the negotiations.

---

[27] Hahn and Stavins, "Trading in Greenhouse Permits," p. 206, fn. 2.
[28] Suzi Kerr, "Introduction: Trading Toward a Stable Climate," in Suzi Kerr (ed.) *Global Emissions Trading: Key Issues for Industrialized Countries* (Cheltenham, UK: Edward Elgar, 2000), pp. 1–24.
[29] Hahn and Stevins, "Trading in Greenhouse Permits," pp. 179–80.

Kyoto Conference Chairman Estrada suggested that as host of the conference Japan should come up with a plan that went beyond its $p\&q$ formulation and propose concrete figures.[30]

MITI, MoFA, and the Environment Agency, however, were at a stalemate over what Japan's stance should be. The Environment Agency wanted Japan to propose at a minimum a 5 percent reduction in CO_2 emissions by 2010 and claimed that a 6–8 percent reduction was feasible. MoFA argued for a 6.5 percent reduction within five years of 2010 for industrialized countries with a smaller obligation for those that had already achieved high levels of energy efficiency. MITI was reluctant to act as it was unsure of what the US position would be, making it difficult for Japan to know what to propose. They also did not want to see anything more than a stabilization target for 2010. The internal consensus building process was not working.

With the conference date fast approaching, Prime Minister Hashimoto was forced to intervene and push the ministries to find common ground. Japan was feeling the heat of international criticism (particularly from Germany and the EU) that as the host country to the third COP it was failing to take on a leadership role. Hashimoto pushed the bureaucracy to come to a compromise. The support of members of the environmental *zoku* plus the research work of the National Institute for Environmental Studies which showed that reductions of CO_2 emissions of as much as 7.6 percent of 1990 levels in 2010 was feasible, helped to throw some support behind the position of the Environment Agency.[31]

Just two months before the Kyoto Conference after much interministerial wrangling, Japan proposed a 5 percent reduction target for 2010, far more than what MITI initially had claimed feasible. The proposal was not for a flat 5 percent target for all industrialized countries, but rather was based on a differentiated formula for reducing emissions of a basket of CO_2, methane, and nitrous oxide adjusted for each country according to their per capita emissions, emissions per unit of GDP, and expected rate of population growth. This would have meant a 2.5 percent reduction for Japan, a 1.8 percent reduction for Australia, and a 3.7 percent reduction for Germany.[32]

The US announces a position

With the negotiations fast approaching and Japan's position already announced, in October 1997, the Clinton administration announced that

[30] Tanabe, *Chikyū Ondanka to Kankyō Gaikō*, p. 77.
[31] Kawashima, "Japan's Decision-Making about Climate Change Problems," 44–6.
[32] Oberthür and Ott, *The Kyoto Protocol*, pp. 56 and 116–117; *Washington Post*, October 8, 1997, p. A23.

domestically, the US would embark upon a five-year, $5 billion plan to reduce emissions to 1990 levels by 2008 through tax incentives and research and development. The plan was also to initiate a domestic emissions trading scheme that would give industries that reduced their emissions credits that they could reclaim when (and if) pollution permits were issued in the future.[33]

The US also then announced its international negotiating position on October 22. The US called for returning a basket of six, rather than three, greenhouse gases to 1990 levels by a budget period of 2008–12 with further reductions in the following five years. The US also demanded meaningful participation by developing countries although what this exactly meant remained unclear.[34] The position was a clear effort on the part of the administration to make some kind of positive commitment to the international negotiation process while trying somehow to win over the Senate.

The Kyoto Conference (COP 3) and the formation of the Kyoto Protocol on Climate Change

In December 1997 delegates from 159 states met in Kyoto. The meeting was also attended by tens of thousands of NGO representatives, journalists, industrial representatives, scholars, and others. Paralleling the international negotiations, workshops were held, information booths were set up, and NGO rallies were held.

After eleven days of exhaustive negotiations that many thought could end in failure, the official representatives at the meeting concluded a protocol of measures that the industrialized states agreed to take. The last-minute appearance of Albert Gore three days before the close of the scheduled ten-day meeting appears to have been critical to moving the stalled negotiations forward. The US negotiators shocked the world by announcing that the US was willing to reduce emissions by a full 7 percent of 1990 levels within a 2008–12 budget period. The reason why the US position shifted so dramatically appears to be because of Gore's personal intervention. With what appears to have been a genuine belief that climate change was a serious problem and the environmental credibility of the administration on the line, Gore pushed hard for a compromise.

In the negotiations, the US argued strongly for the unlimited inclusion of market-based mechanisms in the agreement. The EU argued against heavy reliance on flexible mechanisms on the basis that they effectively

---

[33] Gary C. Bryner, "Congress and the Politics of Climate Change," in Harris (ed.), *Climate Change and American Foreign Policy*, p. 117.

[34] Oberthür and Ott, *The Kyoto Protocol*, p. 57.

diminished the responsibility of the industrialized states to take action to address emissions domestically. The US and the EU dominated the negotiations and it is doubtful that they would have been successfully completed without the skillful leadership of the conference chairman, Raúl Estrada-Ouyela. Japan found itself caught between the US and the EU.

In the end substantial compromises had to be made by all parties. The US proposal for a basket that included six, rather than three, greenhouse gases was accepted. Under the basket approach all gases are measured in CO_2 equivalents. Countries can meet their targets by adjusting their total CO_2 equivalent of the six gases. This gives each party the opportunity to determine which gases it is going to reduce by what amounts based on national circumstances as long as they add up to the emissions target.

The US also succeeded in having use of flexible mechanisms written into the protocol as means for achieving targets. Joint implementation was to be allowed between Annex 1 countries to the protocol. The clean development mechanism would allow Annex 1 countries to the protocol to invest in projects in non-Annex 1 countries and use the emissions reductions accrued from the year 2000 to comply with their commitments in the first commitment period (2008–12).

In addition, against EU opposition, a provision to include sinks was added to the Protocol. The US had successfully argued for sinks to be included for the calculation of emissions targets since they act to absorb carbon and can encourage activities like afforestation and reforestation, and because they can provide the private sector with low-cost opportunities to reduce emissions.

Another win for the US was that it convinced the EU to agree to a five-year budget period, rather than a single year. This is why there is reference to the 2008–12 period. Since emissions can be averaged across this budget period, it provides greater flexibility to nations given the potential for short-term fluctuations in economic performance or weather conditions, which could affect emissions levels quite sharply in any given year. The US also avoided a short-term 2003 target year that was proposed during the negotiations.

The US was pushed, however, to go far beyond the stabilization target announced by Clinton in October. While some argue that the 7 percent reduction figure for the US really only amounted to about a 3 percent reduction requirement because of technicalities in how the emissions were to be calculated, even this was substantially more than the US had said would be feasible going into the negotiations.[35]

---

[35] United States State Department, Bureau of Oceans and International Environmental and Scientific Affairs, "The Kyoto Protocol on Climate Change," January 15, 1998.

Table 7.2 *Kyoto Protocol emissions targets*

Country	percent
Austria	−13
Belgium	−7.5
Denmark	−21
EU bubble	−8
Finland	0
France	0
Germany	−21
Greece	+25
Ireland	+13
Japan	−6
Luxembourg	−28
Netherlands	−6
Portugal	+27
Spain	+15
Sweden	+4
United Kingdom	−25
United States	−7

Source: Kyoto Protocol to the United Nations
Framework Convention on Climate Change.

The EU gave in to the US proposal to address the larger basket of greenhouse gases. Under this mix, a 15 percent reduction for the EU would have been extremely difficult to meet. The EU bubble target, thus, was brought down to 8 percent. Some argued that in the end the EU achieved substantial public relations points with its strong 15 percent reduction proposal, but in the end could walk away with far lighter obligations.

Fearing that the negotiations might otherwise collapse, Japan agreed to a target that went beyond Japan's bottom line. Apparently, a call from Vice President Gore to Prime Minister Hashimoto helped lead to the change in Japan's position.[36]

The final emissions targets set at Kyoto are listed in Table 7.2.[37] A fact sheet released by the State Department summed up the agreement in this way: "The Kyoto Protocol in key respects – including emissions targets and timetables for industrialized nations and market-based measures for meeting those targets – reflects proposals advanced by the United States."[38]

[36] *Washington Post*, December 13, 1997, pp. A1 and A20.
[37] Miranda A. Schreurs, "Competing Agendas and the Climate Change Negotiations: The United States, the European Union, and Japan," *Environmental Law Reporter*, 31, 10 (2001), 11221.
[38] United States State Department, "The Kyoto Protocol on Climate Change."

The rules governing the design and use of flexible mechanisms, however, were left for subsequent negotiations. The protocol did not specify how the private sector and the government were to design, finance, or secure approval for jointly implemented projects or to conduct emissions trading.

Establishing rules for implementing the Kyoto Protocol: the negotiations continue

The formation of the Kyoto Protocol was only the beginning of a long and conflict-ridden process. The Protocol called for a reduction in emissions of the developed countries by 5.2 percent of 1990 levels by the 2008–12 budget period. This is only a small step towards the much larger reduction that scientists warn must be made if climate change is to be arrested. Moreover, for the Protocol to enter into force, fifty-five states with combined emissions of at least 55 percent of all industrial CO_2 emissions have to sign it. Although the White House had signed the agreement, the Senate made it clear that it had no plan to ratify the agreement in the form negotiated at Kyoto. Without US ratification, essentially all other major industrialized states would have to ratify in order to achieve the 55 percent target since US emissions alone accounted for a quarter of the global total. Thus, the US was in a powerful negotiating position.

The search for compromise on implementation strategies

Depending on what package of implementation tools was agreed upon, the costs of meeting Kyoto Protocol obligations could vary enormously. The US was interested in a package that would place few or no restrictions on the use of flexible mechanisms. This reflected the strength of support for the cost-benefit analysis approach and interest in market-based mechanisms. The EU was opposed to allowing a country to meet more than half of its reduction goals through the use of these flexible mechanisms since it would mean that there would be little pressure on countries actually to reduce their own emissions domestically.

The extremely complex details of how the flexible mechanisms were actually to work and how countries were to monitor compliance and assure compliance were at the heart of follow-up meetings held in Buenos Aires (COP 4), Bonn (COP 5), The Hague (COP 6, Part I), Bonn (COP 6, Part II), and Marrakech (COP 7).

At the Buenos Aires convention in November 1998 negotiators from over 160 countries agreed to set a deadline of late 2000 for setting the rules to enforce the protocol and to come up with guidelines for use of the flexible mechanisms. Going into COP 4, the new German Environment Minister Jürgen Trittin and the UK Environment Minister Michael Meacher jointly wrote an article calling on the world community to avoid "creating loopholes" in the treaty that "might allow some countries to avoid real domestic action."[39] The US argued against placing a cap on the use of emissions trading.[40] The disagreement across the Atlantic was sharp and neither side appeared willing to budge.[41]

Eager to keep the negotiations moving forward, but still hand-tied, the Clinton administration signed the Buenos Aires accord on November 12, 1998. It did not, however, send the Kyoto Protocol to the Senate for ratification because it was clear that there was not sufficient support to get the two-thirds majority that is necessary for Senate ratification of a treaty.

Senate opposition to the Protocol was not complete, but it was strong. In the 105th Congress, the late Senator John Chafee introduced a bill to authorize the president to enter into agreements to provide credit for early voluntary actions by industry so that they could gain credits if the Kyoto Protocol eventually was ratified. No action, however, was taken on the bill.[42]

Earlier in the year, the White House had also demonstrated its interest in action with its announcement of financial support for a Climate Change Technology Initiative, which included $2.7 billion for research and development and $2.6 billion in tax credits for energy efficiency.[43] This also reflected the growing call in the US for a long-term solution to climate change that would invest funds into a new generation of environmentally friendlier technologies rather than using those funds to make marginal short-term cuts to emissions.

In contrast with the political stalemate that characterized the US situation, the new SPD/Green Party coalition (formed after the September 1998 federal elections) in Germany suggested that it planned to go beyond the position that Kohl had maintained on climate change. Trittin announced that the government planned to meet Germany's target to reduce CO_2 emissions by 25 percent of 1990 levels by 2005 as established by the Kohl government, but that the new government would alter the mix of policies to meet this goal. Germany would meet the goal through energy savings, ecological tax reform, and placing strong emphasis on the use of renewable energy sources, in particular,

---

[39] *Environment Daily*, September 4, 2000.
[40] *Washington Post*, November 15, 1998, p. A6.
[41] Reuters News Service, November 14, 2000.
[42] Larry B. Parker and John E. Blodgett,"RL30155: Global Climate Change Policy: Domestic Early Action Credits, Congressional Research Service Report," July 23, 1999 (Washington, DC: Committee for the National Institute for the Environment, 1999).
[43] Bryner,"Congress and the Politics of Climate Change," p. 118.

wind, solar, and biomass. The new coalition also was a firm supporter of EU leadership in the negotiations.

Negotiations on technical details continued in Bonn (COP 5), a meeting that attracted little international attention. It was at COP 6 in The Hague, the Netherlands, in November 2000 that events turned highly political once again.

The negotiations collapse: COP 6 in The Hague

The goal of the sixth COP was to reach final agreement on how to implement the Kyoto Protocol. The meeting, however, ended in failure because of the different outlooks of the US and its umbrella partners (Japan, Canada, Australia, New Zealand, and Russia) on the one hand, and Germany and other EU member states, on the other.

Differences in the success of the EU and the US in reducing emissions relative to 1990 levels was large. As of 2000, the European Union had cut its greenhouse gas emissions by 4 percent relative to 1990 levels. Granted, this was largely because of the collapse of the East German economy (resulting in a 18.7 percent cut in German emissions) and the switch in the UK from coal to natural gas (resulting in a 14 percent cut). Since these two states account for 40 percent of EU emissions, the entire EU was able to benefit from their reductions. In contrast, the US had seen an 11 percent increase over the same time period.[44] Japan's emissions too were on the rise. These figures were on the minds of the negotiators (Figures 7.1, 7.2).

One of the main points of disagreement was whether or not countries should be allowed to count existing carbon sinks and the expansion of carbon sinks (e.g. through the planting of forests and maintaining of cropland and rangeland) towards their emission reduction targets. The US and Japan favored carbon sinks both as an offset for the amount of emissions reduction required domestically and in the clean development mechanism so that credit could be earned towards the emissions reduction target by expanding carbon sinks in developing countries. For the US negotiators, including carbon sinks in the agreement was seen as politically necessary to win the support of agricultural states. Without such support ratification of the agreement in the Senate was believed to be next to impossible given the strong opposition to the agreement coming from states with oil, gas, and coal industries.

The support that Japan provided the US on this issue reflected its own perceived difficulties in meeting reduction targets set in Kyoto and the

---

[44] *Agence France Presse*, April 21, 2001.

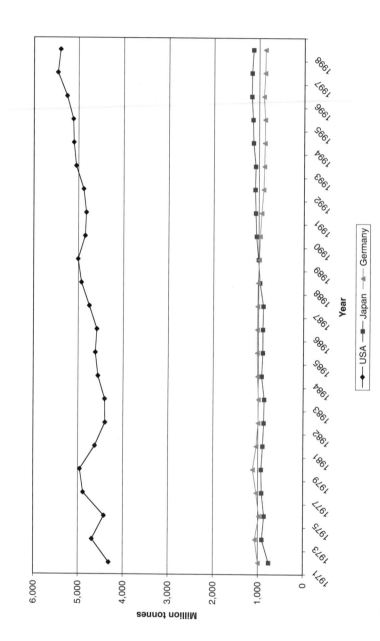

Figure 7.1   Carbon dioxide emissions
Source: as for Table 7.1.

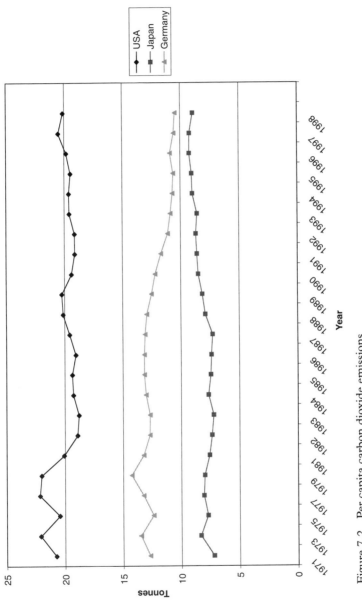

Figure 7.2 Per capita carbon dioxide emissions
Source: as for Table 7.1.

fact that Japan is a heavily forested nation. If management of sinks were permitted as a means of offsetting emissions, then there was a chance that Japan could meet its Kyoto target. Japanese negotiators argued that Japan should be allowed to get credit for more than half, and as much as 3.8 percent of the 6 percent emissions reduction goal, through management of sinks.[45] The Japanese decision to side with the US also reflected its desire to keep the US involved in the negotiations. Japan, heavily dependent on the US for both economic and security reasons, was reluctant to criticize the US position too strongly. Moreover, in contrast with the pre-Kyoto period when there was a strong group of green politicians in the LDP, by the time of The Hague Conference their numbers had fallen. Prior to COP 6 several key environmental supporters in the Diet either lost their seats in elections (e.g. Kazuo Aichi and Takashi Kosugi) or passed away (e.g. Noboru Takeshita). While this by no means decimated the green support within the Diet or the LDP, it did weaken it somewhat, meaning that Japanese environmentalists had fewer allies on their side to pressure the government to take a firmer stance.

The EU argued that if carbon sinks were included in the agreement and as part of the clean development mechanism, this would reduce the amount of emissions reductions that would have to be made by heavily forested countries (like the US and Japan). The position of the EU was that countries should be pressured to reduce their own greenhouse gas emissions without finding loopholes to get around doing so.[46]

In the end the negotiations collapsed when the EU failed to convince the umbrella group to accept the idea of a 50 percent cap on the percentage of emissions reductions a country could get credit for by means other than reducing emissions domestically. Within the EU, Germany and France particularly strongly opposed the idea of heavily depending upon sinks to offset emissions reductions.

When the differences between the two sides could not be bridged despite desperate last-minute efforts by Conference Chairman Jan Pronk, the meeting was cut short and a COP-6, Part II, was scheduled to be held in July of the next year in Bonn. Subsequent developments in the US, however, rocked the international negotiating community and for a time looked like they spelled the death of the Kyoto Protocol.

The George W. Bush administration's withdrawal from the Kyoto Protocol

On March 13, 2001 President Bush announced that he would not treat CO_2 as a pollutant and would not regulate CO_2 emissions of power plants

---

[45] *Daily Yomiuri*, July 25, 2001, p. 6.
[46] Peter N. Spotts, *Christian Science Monitor*, November 13, 20, and 27, 2000.

despite his campaign pledge to do so.[47] Two weeks later Environment Agency Director Christine Todd Whitman announced that as far as the administration was concerned, Kyoto was dead: "No, we have no interest in implementing that treaty. If there's a general agreement that we need to be addressing the global climate change issue, (the question is) how do we do it in a way that allows us to make some progress, instead of spending our time committed to something that isn't going to go." She also noted, "We are not the only ones who have problems with it."[48] These comments appear to reflect a view in the White House that the EU was not really that serious about Kyoto, and that because it would also have difficulty fulfilling the targets established in the agreement, it would in fact be quite happy to see the treaty collapse.

Days later in Bush's second news conference, President Bush stated: "We will not do anything that harms our economy, because first things first are the people who live in America. That's my priority. And I'm worried about the economy, I'm worried about the lack of an energy policy."[49] Ari Fleischer, the president's spokesperson, elaborated: "The president has been unequivocal. He does not support the Kyoto treaty. It exempts the developing nations around the world" and implementation will entail "huge costs... disproportionate to the benefits."[50]

The administration's position engendered immediate and harsh responses from Japan, the EU, and many other countries, including China. Chancellor Schröder used his official visit to the United States the next day to tell Bush of the EU's concerns about the US announcement. He requested that Bush reconsider his position.[51] The embattled Japanese Prime Minister Yoshihiro Mori wrote to Bush expressing "deep concern" and accusing the US of "backtracking." Reports were also issued challenging the Bush administration's economic reasoning. Norbert Walter, chief economist for Deutsche Bank Group, argued that if the US economy operated as efficiently as the Japanese and European economies, US energy consumption would fall by about 30 percent.[52]

The Bush administration's position also engendered a quick reaction by US environmentalists who initiated internet and other campaigns to protest the action. *Time* published a special edition on climate change, including a letter signed by Jimmy Carter, Mikhail Gorbachev, George Soros, Walter Cronkite, Stephen Hawking, and a group of prominent scientists urging the president to take measures to deal with climate

[47] *New York Times*, March 14, 2001, p. A1.   [48] *Washington Post*, March 28, 2001, p. A1.
[49] *Washington Post*, March 30, 2001, p. A1.
[50] *Washington Post*, March 29, 2001, p. A1.
[51] *New York Times*, March 29, 2001, p. A9.   [52] *New York Times*, June 13, 2001, p. A33.

change.[53] Fourteen US Senators signed a letter to Bush criticizing his decision to abandon the Kyoto Protocol and fifty-seven Democrats in the House of Representatives sent another letter urging the president to reconsider his decision to not regulate CO_2 emissions from power plants.[54] The Senate also approved a bi-partisan amendment to the fiscal 2002 budget resolution restoring $4.5 billion in funds for climate change programs for the next decade that the Bush administration had sought to cut.[55]

Commenting on the Bush administration's handling of the affair, Stuart Eizenstat, chief US negotiator under the Clinton administration during COP 3 in Kyoto, lamented the Bush administration's decision and especially the lack of consultation with other nations regarding the decision.[56] There are also indications that not everyone in the Bush White House was happy with the idea of abandoning the agreement. Secretary of State Colin Powell apparently wanted to find a way to modify the agreement and Christine Todd Whitman had urged Bush in a March 6 memo to demonstrate his commitment to cutting greenhouse gas emissions.[57] Just days before the Bonn negotiations began, at a GLOBE International meeting held at the Wye River plantation, two US Congressmen, one Republican, the other Democrat, expressed their dismay with the Bush administration's position and urged their Japanese and European counterparts to move forward with Kyoto even if it meant doing so without the US.[58]

Despite considerable lobbying from many environmental quarters in the US, the administration appears to have felt that there was sufficient support for its position to stand firm. The decision to abandon the Kyoto Protocol reflected Bush's personal dislike of the agreement, intense lobbying efforts by the oil and coal lobbies, and the efforts to kill Kyoto by several conservative Congressmen. The coal industry warned the president that requiring coal-burning power plants to reduce CO_2 emissions could "kill coal." Publicly, Bush said he was persuaded to make the decision based on an Energy Department report that concluded that CO_2 regulations would drive up the cost of electricity.[59]

There were also conservative skeptics in the administration who questioned the science behind global warming, such as the president's

---

[53] *Time*, April 9, 2001, vol. 157, no. 14.   [54] *USA Today*, April 5, 2001, p. 3.
[55] *Washington Post*, April 7, 2001, p. 5.
[56] Comments made to ambassador designates. "Conference on the European Union," Meridian International Center, Washington, DC, June 5, 2001.
[57] *Financial Times*, March 30, 2001, p. 13, and *Washington Post*, March 27, 2001, p. 7.
[58] GLOBE meeting, Wye River plantation, Maryland, July 14, 2001.
[59] *Washington Post*, March 25, 2001, p. 5, and March 27, 2001, p. 7.

economic advisor, Larry Lindsey, and others such as the chief economist of the American Council for Capital Formation who said that the Kyoto Protocol was an effort by Europeans to force US companies to adopt processes that were expensive and would made US products less competitive.[60] Robert J. Samuelson wrote an editorial in which he praised Bush's decision for discarding "all the convenient deceits." Samuelson noted that according to estimates by the Energy Information Administration global emissions of carbon would rise 34 percent to 7.8 billion tons if nothing were done. With Kyoto the rise would be held to 26 percent or 7.3 billion tons. These reductions, however, would be more than offset by emissions increases from developing countries. Moreover, the US, he argued, would face higher population increases than Europe (estimated at 20 percent compared to 6 percent for Europe between 1990 and 2010) and because of higher economic growth rates in the US than Europe over the 1990s, the US would have to make a 30 percent cut in emissions relative to 1990 levels to meet the Kyoto commitments. Samuelson thus concluded that "barring technological breakthroughs – ways of producing cheap energy with few emissions or capturing today's emissions – it's hard to see how the world can deal with global warming."[61] David Victor, in a book that received much attention in the US, called the Kyoto Protocol an unworkable sham.[62] The bottom line of these arguments was that Kyoto was unworkable for the US from an economic perspective and untenable from an environmental one because it would not really result in global reductions in greenhouse gases. Any reductions in the developed countries would be offset by increases in the developing countries.

Also important to note is that the new administration wanted to push through a new energy policy that focused on the development of domestic energy sources. As one of the first moves of the new administration, Vice President Richard Cheney was put in charge of an energy task force that was to consider America's energy needs into the future. After months of closed-door meetings, they released their plan, "Reliable, Affordable, and Environmentally Sound Energy for America's Future," in May 2001.[63]

Climate change policy is closely tied to energy policy. The report outlined an energy policy that critics argued was biased towards the fossil fuel and nuclear energy industries and gave short shrift to energy conservation and renewable energy potential. It was also criticized for its lack of concern with greenhouse gas emissions. Concerned that the process leading

---

[60] *Financial Times*, London, March 30, 2001, p. 13.
[61] *Washington Post*, June 21, 2001, p. A25.
[62] David Victor, *The Collapse of the Kyoto Protocol* (Princeton: Princeton University Press, 2001).
[63] The White House, "Report of the National Energy Policy Development Group, National Energy Policy," May 2001.

to the development of the report was too secretive and biased towards fossil fuel industries, at the end of the summer the General Accounting Office (GAO) demanded that Vice President Cheney release the names of the individuals who advised the National Energy Policy Development Group.[64] The Vice President's Office refused the GAO's request arguing that the Agency did not have this authority. US Comptroller General David M. Walker, head of the GAO, was considering litigation against the White House for its failure to release records relating to the development of its energy policy.[65]

The road to Bonn 2001: the EU and Japan respond

There was intense international condemnation of the Bush decision and, in particular, the unilateral manner in which it was made. Learning from its mistakes, the administration softened somewhat the tone of its statements. The administration announced that it was giving the issue "high-level attention" and was not "opting out of the process."[66] Yet, despite almost three months of sustained international efforts to convince the Bush administration to reconsider, the administration did not budge.

This left both the EU and Japan in a quandary. Under the rules of the Kyoto Protocol, in order for the agreement to come into force, fifty-five nations representing 55 percent of Annex I countries' CO_2 emissions must ratify the deal. By the time of the Bonn meeting thirty-six countries had ratified Kyoto, but all but one of these (Romania) were developing countries and had no obligations to reduce emissions under the agreement. It was difficult to see how the agreement could be put into force. Nevertheless, resolve quickly grew in Europe to push forward even without the US.

On March 31, 2001 the EU environment ministers agreed to pursue ratification of the agreement even without the US. This commitment was reconfirmed at the Gothenburg meeting of EU heads of state in June.

With the EU more or less united in its support for Kyoto, attention shifted to Japan. Japan was the big wildcard and for months sent out mixed signals. On the one hand, Japan showed its eagerness to keep the Kyoto Protocol alive; it was, after all, the only major international agreement to bare the name of a Japanese city. On April 9 at a Japan–EU environmental Cabinet level meeting, the two sides agreed to cooperate in trying to bring the US back to Kyoto.[67] On April 18, 2001 the Japanese Upper House passed a resolution urging the US to reconsider: "We strongly urge the

---

[64] GAO Statement, August 6, 2001.   [65] *Washington Post*, September 8, 2001, p. A13.
[66] *Financial Times*, London, March 31, 2001, p. 1.
[67] *Nihon Keizai Shimbun*, April 10, 2001, p. 3.

United States, which is the world's largest emitter of greenhouse gases, to continue to take part in negotiations on the Kyoto Protocol." It also called upon the Japanese government to "show international leadership in achieving the goal of implementing the accord."[68]

Japanese officials also joined the EU in lobbying the US administration to reverse its position. Just days before the Bonn meeting, for example, Environment Minister Yoriko Kawaguchi (subsequently appointed foreign minister in February 2002) traveled to Washington to try for a second time to find a point of compromise between the EU and the US. Diet-woman Wakako Hironaka also made a trip to Washington at this time to meet with GLOBE members and sharply criticized the US position.[69]

Yet, the prime minister made several statements that raised questions regarding his resolve to join the EU in pursuing Kyoto without the US. In his first visit as prime minister to the US just a few weeks before the Bonn meeting, Junichiro Koizumi met with Bush at Camp David. He told reporters that Japan did not "presently" intend to push ahead on the Kyoto Protocol without US support: "I believe if the United States were to cooperate in dealing with environmental issues we will be able to create more effective means in dealing with the global warming issue and also in reducing our gas emissions." He also later said, "I do not have the intention of proceeding without the cooperation of the United States."[70] Foreign Ministry official Yoshiji Nogami also raised doubts about Japan's willingness to move without the US when in Genoa he said,

Hard-liners in European countries say the European Union and Japan should ratify the protocol without the U.S., but it is meaningless. Because the protocol is favorable for the EU, European countries want to ratify it without changes, but the United States has been firm in its refusal. It is not known how deeply the discussion at the summit will progress.[71]

There was also some pressure from economic interests in Japan urging the prime minister to be cautious on moving forward with Kyoto without the US. *Keidanren* issued an official statement a month before the Bonn negotiations began saying that the participation of the US was essential for effective enforcement of the protocol. Hideo Takahashi, director of the Environment, Science, and Technology Bureau for *Keidanren* considered the US position "quite understandable because it calmly and objectively looked at the real picture and then took the most appropriate measures."[72] A Foreign Ministry official involved at the highest level in the climate

[68] Reuters News Service, April 19, 2001.
[69] GLOBE conference, Wye River Plantation, Maryland, July 14, 2001.
[70] *New York Times*, July 2, 2001, p. A9.
[71] *Daily Yomiuri*, July 21, 2001, p. 3.   [72] *Yomiuri Shimbun*, July 13, 2001.

change negotiations in Kyoto noted that the press was forgetting that the targets set in Kyoto were not written in stone, suggesting that he felt some sympathy for the US position.[73]

These and subsequent statements made at the G-8 meetings in Genoa, Italy, that suggested Japan was uneasy about moving ahead on the deal without the US had the EU worried. Leaders from Germany, France, and Britain warned Bush that public opinion in their countries was so emotionally charged over the issue that unless the US took action, the transatlantic relationship could suffer.[74]

Strong EU lobbying efforts were made in Japan with numerous EU delegates, German delegates, and others pressing Japan to follow the EU in resolving to ratify Kyoto. Chancellor Schröder and Environment Minister Trittin spoke frequently with their counterparts, Prime Minister Koizumi and Environment Minister Kawaguchi to persuade them to stay with Kyoto. Schröder telephoned Koizumi urging Japan to "play a constructive role" in the negotiations.[75]

Some pressure also started to build in Japan for Koizumi to stick with the Kyoto process. Members of the environmental *zoku* pressured Koizumi to take a strong stance and Environment Minister Kawaguchi and Foreign Minister Makiko Tanaka both spent much time and effort trying to make sure that the Protocol would survive.[76] New Kômeitô leader Takenori Kanzaki, whose party is in coalition with the LDP, urged the prime minister to push the US to support the protocol and went on to say that if the US did not accept, Japan should ratify nevertheless. Opposition leaders, including Yukio Hatoyama of the Minshutô, also joined in demanding that Japan ratify even without the US. Their statements were jointly released and reflected the opinions of the Minshutô, Jiyutô, the Japanese Communist Party, and the Social Democratic Party.[77] Prime Minister Koizumi, a conservative LDP politician, may himself not have had a strong personal stake in Kyoto, but public opinion suggested that the population was firmly behind ratification and angry with the US withdrawal. Koizumi, although immensely popular in Japan at the time, was also starting to be painted by some in the press as being overly beholden to US interests.[78] With an Upper House election scheduled for shortly after the Bonn negotiations and desiring a strong LDP victory in the election, Koizumi at the last minute chose to move ahead with Kyoto even without the US. At 6.00 a.m. July 23 with time to strike a deal running out and with negotiators weary after days of long negotiations and sleepless

[73] Conversation with a Japanese Foreign Ministry official, June 2001.
[74] *Washington Post*, July 22, 2001, p. A1.   [75] *Financial Times*, July 7, 2001, p. 8.
[76] Discussion with Wakako Hironaka, July 4, 2001; *New York Times*, June 16, 2001, p. A9.
[77] *Daily Yomiuri*, June 30, 2001, p. 3.   [78] *Mainichi Shimbun*, July 8, 2001, p. 11.

nights, word surfaced that Koizumi had instructed his negotiating team to find a deal. Without this last-minute intervention the negotiations may have collapsed a second time, effectively killing Kyoto.[79]

The *Washington Post* reported on the day after the deal had been struck: "Negotiators at the world conference on climate change in Bonn clapped and cheered following an all-night bargaining session when Japan and the European Union struck a compromise resolving the final terms for implementing the 1997 Kyoto Protocol and clearing the way for the ratification process. The United States was alone among major nations opposing the rules."[80] The *New York Times* was similarly critical of the US role in the conference:

A wallflower at what might have been its own victory party, the US could only watch yesterday as 178 countries agreed on a deal that salvages the 1997 Kyoto Protocol. The huge irony is that this agreement was tailored in many respects to American specifications – and with an eye to reducing the putative burdens on America's economy that Mr. Bush used as an excuse to abandon not only the protocol but also his campaign pledge to impose mandatory controls on carbon dioxide.[81]

Seldom in recent history has the US played such a minor role in such a major way as in Bonn.

Bonn 2001: the agreement

Japan was in the driver's seat at Bonn and was able to use its clout to push for concessions from the EU. In the end Japan got everything it had bargained for unsuccessfully in The Hague. The EU was so determined to strike a deal and keep the Kyoto Protocol alive that the agreement ended up being greatly watered down. The goal of reducing emissions in the industrialized states by an average of 5.2 percent of 1990 levels by 2008–12 was weakened and according to estimates made by the WWF now stands at less than 1.8 percent (the difference is to be offset by emissions trading and absorption by carbon sinks, including forests and agricultural land).[82]

Yet, from a political perspective the agreement showed that the EU can lead the international community and that Japan can act without the US. Frequently US officials have pointed to the weakness of the EU and its inability to stand strong as an entity and of Japan's lack of an independent foreign policy. In abandoning the Kyoto Protocol, the US expectation was

---

[79] *Christian Science Monitor*, July 24, 2001, p. 1.
[80] *Washington Post*, July 24, 2001, p. 1.   [81] *New York Times*, July 24, 2001, p. 1.
[82] *Deutsche Presse-Agentur*, July 24, 2001.

that this would lead to splits in the EU. They assumed that Japan would follow the US.

The Bonn negotiations showed otherwise. The Bush announcement galvanized Europe, strengthening its resolve to act. Japan after months of failed efforts to play the middleman between Europe and the US decided to join the EU in pushing forward with Kyoto. Japan continued to be concerned about the US, however, and in the negotiations made sure to strike a deal that would be attractive to the US. The parties intentionally "left the door wide open" should the US choose to rejoin the Protocol.[83]

The broad outlines of the agreement were based on a draft prepared by conference chairman Jan Pronk, the Dutch environment minister. After a week of intense bargaining an agreement was finally hammered out that gives countries considerable room to meet reduction targets through the use of the various flexible mechanisms. Use of a carbon emissions trading system similar to the sulfur emissions trading system described in Chapter 4 was agreed upon. Once the system is established and initial permit allocations are determined, companies will be allowed to trade in carbon permits. The system will be structured in such a way that the cost of permits will rise with time giving companies an incentive to reduce their carbon emissions. The US as a non-party, could be excluded from the carbon trading system if the protocol goes into effect.[84]

Countries can further offset their emissions by exporting clean technology (solar, wind, energy efficiency, and other renewable energy sources) to developing countries for up to 1 percent of existing emissions. To the dismay of some in Japan, nuclear energy was not allowed under the clean development mechanism although countries will be allowed to use nuclear energy development domestically as an offset to domestic CO_2 emissions. Japan was successful, however, in bargaining to allow countries to get credit under the clean development mechanism for planting trees in developing countries (so long as this is done in a way that protects biological diversity and is not simply the development of biologically sterile plantations).[85]

Under the agreement reached in Bonn, Japan will be able to get credit for up to 13 million tons of carbon per year (Mt C/yr) through forestry management and domestic farming activities. Germany will be able to get up to 1.24 Mt C/yr, Russia 17.63 Mt C/yr and Canada 12.00 Mt C/yr. Thus, Germany will be able to use afforestation projects in developing countries and domestically to reduce its emissions reduction

---

[83] Europe Information Service, *Europe Energy*, July 24, 2001, no. 586.
[84] *Daily Telegraph* (London), July 24, 2001, p. 4.
[85] *Christian Science Monitor*, July 24, 2001, p. 4.

requirements within the EU by as much as 4.5 Mt C/yr or almost 1.4 percent.[86]

The EU succeeded in having written into the agreement that parties not meeting their Kyoto emissions reduction targets will be penalized by having to reduce more from domestic sources in future periods (an extra 1.3 percent for every 1 percent shortfall). Countries that fail to meet their targets could also be denied the right to be involved in carbon trading in the future.

Developing countries such as China and India, which are not required under the agreement to meet emissions targets but are still encouraged to work towards reducing the growth rate of their emissions, were persuaded to sign by the promise of $530 million in technological aid. The US committed to this aspect of the deal.

From Bonn to COP 7 in Marrakech

In early September 2001 the European parliament expressed its delight with the lead that the EU took in the negotiations by a vote of 398 to 9 with 3 abstentions. The parliament urged rapid ratification of the agreement and the establishment of a Directive instituting an EU emissions trading system by the end of the year. They even criticized the limited goals agreed to in Bonn. Various EU parliamentarians, for example, expressed their criticism of the lack of stringent sanctions in the agreement for non-compliance and concern about the inclusion of carbon sinks and flexible mechanisms with few restrictions on their use.[87]

Michael Mueller, a deputy leader of the SDP in Germany, called the deal a "mini-step forward" even though it is still far from being a solution to global warming. Ulrike Mehl, spokesperson for the parliamentary SPD complained that the treaty was full of loopholes "as big as a barn-door." Reinhard Loske of the Greens said the treaty was "at best, a small first step" and that he hoped it would lead to pressure on the US to accept Kyoto.[88]

There was considerable hope in both the EU and Japan that the US would change its mind in the post-Bonn period and agree to work within the Kyoto Protocol framework at the COP 7 in Marrakech in November 2001. This hope was not unjustified. Pressures were building in the US as Congress and numerous businesses began to ascertain the depth of the US isolation on Kyoto. There were also many uncertainties regarding

---

[86] *Frankfurter Allgemeine Zeitung*, July 24, 2001, p. 1.
[87] "EU/UN Climate Change: MEPS Press Commission to Present Concrete Proposals," *European Report*, No. 2616, September 8, 2001.
[88] *Frankfurter Allgemeine Zeitung*, July 24, 2001, p. 1.

the potential ramifications for the US if the agreement went forward and the US as a non-party to the agreement was excluded from the use of the very flexible mechanisms that it had pushed so hard for in earlier rounds of the international negotiations.

There were numerous calls for a US response to the Bonn negotiations. Environmental NGOs had the White House on the defensive. They were effectively portraying President Bush as an enemy of the environment pointing at his support of oil drilling in the Arctic National Wildlife Refuge, efforts to rescind numerous environmental executive orders that Clinton passed in his last days in office, and rejection of the Kyoto Protocol. Public opinion polls suggested that the president's anti-environmental stance was hurting him. A *Washington Post* and ABC television network poll conducted in June found that 50 percent of those polled disapproved of Bush's environmental policies (compared to 41 percent that approved) and 58 percent disapproved of his handling of the energy problem.[89]

Opposition to the administration's position could be found at many levels. Vermont Governor Howard Dean, for example, argued that the Bush administration's voluntary approach to dealing with greenhouse gas emissions would not work.[90] Maryland Governor Parris Glendening strongly criticized the administration's decision to withdraw from the agreement.[91] In August the Senate Foreign Relations Committee unanimously approved a non-binding resolution calling upon the White House to participate in the climate change negotiations either through a proposal for a revised Kyoto Protocol or with a new binding agreement for reducing greenhouse gas emissions.[92] Several Senators and House members came out and criticized the Bush administration's decision. Senator James Jeffords, who, after bolting the Republican Party and becoming an independent earlier in the year, was made chairman of the Senate Environment and Public Works Committee, began work on a "four-pollutant" bill that would set government limits on industrial emissions of carbon dioxide, mercury, sulfur dioxide, and nitrogen oxides. This was in obvious opposition to the administration's support for a three pollutant bill that did not include CO_2. Senators John McCain and Joseph Lieberman called on the administration to address CO_2 emissions and supported the formation of a nationwide "cap and trade" system.[93]

[89] EFE News Service, June 5, 2001.
[90] *Associated Press State and Local Wire*, November 1, 2001.
[91] Interview, Annapolis, Maryland, August 28, 2001.
[92] *Washington Post*, August 2, 2001, p. A14.
[93] *Associated Press State and Local Wire*, November 1, 2001.

Yet, the tragic events of September 11 drastically altered the policy agenda in the US. The nation's attention was suddenly riveted to media reports of the attacks on the World Trade Center in New York and the Pentagon in Washington DC and the subsequent US war on terrorism in Afghanistan. Bush's public opinion ratings soared to well over 80 percent. This put environmentalists in a difficult position. They could no longer easily criticize the president at a time of war. Thus, the next COP, which was held in Marrakech, Morocco, in the first two weeks of November passed with little attention in the US. This was despite an Energy Department report released in parallel with the meetings that US CO_2 emissions had jumped 3.1 percent since the previous year and that total CO_2 emissions were almost 14 percent higher than in 1990.[94]

The purpose of COP 7 was to take the fourteen pages of agreements reached in Bonn and turn them into legal text. In Marrakech, 165 nations (minus the US) worked out implementation details that had been left unfinished in Bonn. The White House did little more than to send a delegation to observe the negotiations and to protect US interests. At the meeting, Paula Dobriansky, undersecretary of state for global affairs, suggested that the US preferred a "tapestry" of national and regional approaches rather than a single global system like that provided by Kyoto.[95] The White House maintained its position that it did not favor the Kyoto Protocol and instead supported voluntary measures by industry and a long-term science and technology research program. Halan Watson, US representative to the conference, told the plenary session, "if the United States were to ratify a climate change treaty it would have to be 'based on science,' must encourage technological innovation and 'profit from market forces.' It should include global participation and 'guarantee the economic growth and prosperity of the entire world.'"[96] The *Washington Post* wrote that Marrakech "marked an important victory for European and environmental leaders in rallying the international community behind a document that was rejected earlier this year by President Bush."[97]

The Bush administration responds

In February 2002 the "Economic Report of the President" was released. It dealt briefly with climate change and distanced the US even further from the Kyoto Protocol. The document questioned the scientific basis for action and then stated: "an important element of a reasonable climate change approach must be more research into both the science of

[94] *Associated Press*, November 10, 2001.   [95] *Washington Post*, November 11, 2001, p. A2.
[96] *Washington Times*, November 3, 2001, p. A7.
[97] *Washington Post*, November 11, 2001, p. A2.

climate change and mitigation technologies, in order to learn more about the risks and the appropriate response."[98] The report also questioned the advisability of an international emissions trading system even though this is what the US had long championed under the Clinton administration. Reflecting Vice President Cheney's opposition to a CO_2 emissions trading scheme,[99] the report stated that such approaches: "fail to recognize the enormous institutional and logistical obstacles to implementing any sweeping international program. Institutionally, it is important to learn to walk before trying to run."[100] Instead, the report calls for policy action based on "sound science," a "flexible, gradual approach," and "reasonable, gradual goals." It calls for a long-term technology-based solution to what it sees as a problem of uncertain magnitude. The approach outlined in the report goes strongly against what has been argued for by Germany, the EU, and Japan.

The EU and Japan ratify the Kyoto Protocol

Proving their resolve to keep the Kyoto Protocol alive both the EU and Japan ratified the agreement. On February 6, 2002 the European Union parliament in a landslide majority (540 to 4 votes) voted in favor of ratifying the agreement. The EU Environment Council followed suit giving its support to the agreement on March 4, 2002. Germany ratified the agreement on March 25 and by the end of May all fifteen EU member states had done the same. On May 31, 2002, the EU ratified the Kyoto Protocol in an official ceremony at the United Nations in New York. Paralleling developments in the EU, the Japanese Diet approved the agreement on May 31, 2002 and the Cabinet accepted it on June 4.

Conclusion

Few thought that the Kyoto Protocol could move forward without the US, but the EU and Japan proved otherwise. At the time of this writing, the future of the Kyoto Protocol is still not certain and many issues regarding the implementation and monitoring of the agreement remain to be worked out. Still, it is striking that the majority of industrialized states decided to join the EU's call to support the Protocol even after the US decided to abandon it. There are now two competing paradigms governing how the industrialized states are responding to global warming.

[98] "Economic Report of the President," Washington, DC: United States Government Printing Office, 2002, p. 245.
[99] *New York Times*, February 6, 2002, p. 5.
[100] "Economic Report of the President," p. 246.

Whether or not a bridge can be built between them remains to be seen. The struggle that played out among the industrialized states is now likely to shift to the developing countries as the US on the one side, and the EU and Japan on the other, try to convince them of the superiority of their own approaches.

The next chapter considers what the implications of the Montreal Protocol and Kyoto Protocol negotiations have been for the domestic environmental policy communities in Japan, Germany, and the US.

8 Global environmental politics and environmental policy communities

This chapter differs from the earlier chapters in that it does not explore a specific environmental issue. Instead, it examines how environmental groups have reacted to the globalization of environmental policy making. It first compares the membership, staff, and budget of environmental groups in Japan, Germany, and the US, and then examines how the strategies, goals, and organization of environmental policy communities have been affected by the emergence of new kinds of environmental problems and policy-making processes. Three trends are noteworthy. First, the Japanese environmental NGO community, though very small, is growing and institutional barriers to its activities are being removed. Second, the German environmental policy community, and especially the Green Party, is facing a crisis that stems from its own success. Third, the US environmental NGO community finds itself at a low point in terms of its ability to influence US foreign environmental policy.

Comparing environmental NGO resources in Japan, Germany, and the US

The difference in the size and resources of the NGO communities in Japan, Germany, and the US is really quite astounding (see Table 8.1). The largest and oldest internationally oriented group with a predominately environmental focus in Japan is WWF Japan. In 2000, it had a membership of 50,000, up from 37,370 in 1992. In comparison, the World Wildlife Fund (WWF) Germany had 180,000 members and the World Wildlife Fund (WWF) United States 1 million. Greenpeace had a membership of 5,000 in Japan in 1998 compared to 250,000 in Germany and 520,000 in the US. FOE Japan had a membership of 380 in the late 1990s; FOE Germany had 240,000.

The small membership size of Japanese NGOs means that they cannot rely on membership donations for financial support or for political weight. Indeed, of the 187 NGOs listed in the Japanese NGO Center for

Table 8.1 *Select list of environmental NGOs in Japan, Germany, and the US*

	Year established	Membership size (date of information 1997–2000)
JAPAN		
Wild Bird Society of Japan	1934	53,798
WWF Japan	1971	50,000 + 1,500 organizations
The Nature Conservation Society of Japan	1951	15,275 + 939 groups
JATAN	1987	600 + 100 groups
Greenpeace	1989	5,000
FOE	1980	380
Japan International Volunteer Center	1980	1,720 + 20 groups
OISCA, International	1961	5,482 + 3,048 groups
A SEED Japan	1991	290 + 35 groups
Rainforest Foundation Japan	1989	727
Sarawak Campaign Committee	1990	180 + 40 groups
The Japan Association for Greening Deserts	1991	1,309 + 65 groups
Action for Greening Sahel	1991	425 + 11 groups
Institute for Himalayan Conservation, Japan	1986	350
Association Sahel	1987	477 + 3 groups
Global Voluntary Service	1992	4,000 + 37 groups
Plan International Japan	1983	1,000 monthly supporters 54,698 foster parents
Japan NGO Center for International Cooperation	1987	990 + 141 groups
GERMANY		
DNR	1950	108 NGOs as member representing 5 million individuals (2000)
Naturschutzbund Deutschland (NABU)	1899	260,000
WWF	1963	180,000
FOE	1975	240,000
Greenpeace	1980	510,000; 1,800 groups members organized into 85 local groups
Bund fur Umwelt und Naturschutz Deutschland	1975	340,000
Forum Umwelt und Entwicklung	1992	35 NGOs
NaturFreunde Deutschland	1905	100,000
Robin Wood	1982	2,300
GERMANWATCH	1991	500 personnel

(cont.)

Table 8.1 (cont.)

	Year established	Membership size (date of information 1997–2000)
UNITED STATES		
EDF	1967	300,000 (2000)
National Audubon Society	1905	550,000 (2000)
NWF	1936	4,000,000 (2000)
The Nature Conservancy (TNC)	1951	1,000,000 (2000)
Greenpeace	1975	250,000 (2000)
Sierra Club	1892	600,000 (2000)
NRDC	1970	400,000 (2000)
WWF	1961	1,000,000 (2000)

Source: individual organization websites, email communication, and JANIC, *Kokusai Kyôryoku NGO Dairekutorii 2000* (Tokyo: JANIC, 2000).

International Cooperation (JANIC)'s international environmental NGO directory, only 28 had achieved incorporation and thus official non-profit status. The majority of NGOs in this listing had to support the bulk of their activities through membership donations, but because membership is so small, most groups had only very limited funds to work with.[1] In contrast, US and German NGOs are very well off.

Carrying this comparison further, I looked into the membership size of the groups that were members of the Climate Action Network (CAN), an international umbrella group of NGOs set up in March 1989 to facilitate information exchange and to promote governmental and public action to mitigate climate change (see Table 8.2). As of the time of this writing, CAN had a global network of over 287 NGOs. In 1998, there were 7 Japanese, 13 German, and 41 US environmental NGO members. The combined individual membership numbers of the Japanese NGOs was under 50,000. In comparison, the combined individual membership of the German and US NGOs stood in the millions in both countries.

The staff size of the largest CAN members also differed significantly. The US NGOs and think tanks had by far the largest staffs. The Sierra Club had 150, NRDC 190, NWF 500, and Greenpeace 65. The largest German NGO and think tank staffs were WWF (100), BUND (30), the Wuppertal Institut (120), and Öko Institut (80). WWF Japan had only 30 staff; FOE Japan 8; and Greenpeace Japan 17.

The financial resources available to the groups also differed enormously. Most Japanese environmental NGOs are strapped for cash.

---

[1] JANIC, *NGO Dairekutori, 1994* (Tokyo: JANIC, 1994). The data is based on a 1992 survey conducted by JANIC.

Table 8.2 *Climate Action Network member organizations*

Japan	Germany	United States
CASA	BUND	CAN
Staff 2	Staff 30	Staff 1
Volunteers 75	Members 340,000	EDF
Member organizations 60	27 million DM	Staff 194
Individual members 500	DNR	Volunteers 60
Center for Nuclear	Staff 11	Members 300,000
Information (CNIC)	Volunteers 5	Environmental Energy
Staff 10	Organizations 100	Solutions
Volunteers 10	(5 million individuals)	Staff 1
Individual members	Ecologic	Environmental Media
1,600	Staff 38	Services
FOE	EUROSOLAR	Staff 7
Staff 8	Staff 12	Volunteers 2
Volunteers 50	Volunteers 5	FOE
Individual members 600	Organization members	Staff 35
Greenpeace	12	Individual members
Staff 17	Individual members	35,000
Volunteers 20	25,000	Greenpeace
Individual members	Forum Umwelt &	Staff 65
5,000	Entwicklung	Volunteers 2
JATAN	Staff 5	Individual members
Staff 4	Organization members	300,000
Volunteers 30	100	International Council on
Individual members 650	GERMANWATCH	Local Environmental
Kiko Network	Staff 18	Initiatives
Staff 4	Volunteers 3	Staff 7
Volunteers 50	Personnel 500	Volunteers 2
Individual members 320	International Council	Member organizations
Volunteers 50	for Local	252
Organization members	Environmental	Alliance for Affordable
150	Initiatives	Energy
WWF	(ICLEI)	Staff 4
Staff 30	Staff 30	Volunteers 100
Volunteers 10	Organization members	Individual members 600
Individual members	350	Alliance to Save Energy
41,000	Klima Bündnis	Staff 40
Corporate members 500	Staff 9	Individual members 60
	Volunteers 1	Corporate & trade
	Member communities	associations 75
	850	American Council for an
	Individual members 38	Energy Efficient
	NABU	Environment
	Membership 260,000	Staff 15
	Öko Institut	
	Staff 80	

(cont.)

Table 8.2 (*cont.*)

Japan	Germany	United States
	Volunteers 50	Americans for Sustainable
	Individual members 5,000	Economy
	Weltwirtschaft, Ökologie	Staff 7
	& Entwicklung e.V.	Biodiversity Action Network
	(WEED)	Staff 2
	Staff 4	Volunteers 2
	Volunteers 1	Organization members 125
	Individual members 133	Center for a Sustainable
	Wuppertal Institute	Economy
	für Klima, Umwelt,	Staff 2
	Energie	Center for Clean Air Policy
	Staff 120	Staff 20
	WWF	Center for International
	Staff 100	Environmental Law
	Volunteers 50	Staff 20
	Organization members 28	Volunteers 5
	Individual members	Center for Sustainable
	180,000	Development in the
		Americas
		Staff 3
		Climate Institute
		Staff 6
		Volunteers 8
		Individual organizations
		1,200
		Climate Solutions
		Staff 5
		Volunteers 20
		Individual members 1,100
		Conservation Law
		Foundation
		Staff 40
		Volunteers 12
		Individual members
		10,000
		Conservation Law
		Foundation of New
		England
		Staff 35
		Organization members 150
		Individual members 8,000
		Environmental & Energy
		Study Institute
		Staff 20
		Volunteers 4

Table 8.2 (*cont.*)

Japan	Germany	United States
		International Institute for Energy Conservation
		Staff 55
		Volunteers 5
		Minnesotans for an Energy Efficient Economy
		Staff 3
		Organization members 15
		Individual members 200
		National Environmental Trust
		Staff 70
		Individual members 1,000
		NRDC
		Staff 190
		Individual members 400,000
		NWF
		Staff 500
		Organization members 31
		Individual members 4,000,000
		Ozone Action
		Staff 5
		Pacific Institute for Studies in Development, Environment, and Security
		Staff 15
		Associates 50
		Physicians for Social Responsibility
		Staff 20
		Individual members 20,000
		Redefining Progress
		Staff 20
		Volunteers 5
		Renewable Energy Policy Project
		Staff 9
		Volunteers 1
		Rocky Mountain Institute
		Staff 9
		Volunteers 1

(*cont.*)

Table 8.2 (*cont.*)

Japan	Germany	United States
		Safe Energy Communication Council Staff 6 Organization members 10 Sierra Club Staff 150 Individual members 600,000 Texas Fund for Energy and Environmental Education Staff 4 Volunteers 2 Individual members 2,000 TNC Staff 2,782 Individual members 1 million Foundations and corporations 1,900 The Woods Hole Research Center Staff 30 Union of Concerned Scientists Staff 60 Individual members 50,000 WRI Staff 125 Worldwatch Institute Staff 30 WWF, International Staff 370 Organization members 29 Individual members 1 million (US), 1.5 million (international including US)

Source: information as provided by the organizations, 1998–2000.

Even the richest are poor in comparison to their German and, especially, their US counterparts. At the end of the 1990s, WWF USA had a budget of over $110 million. WWF Japan, the richest predominantly environmental group in Japan, had a budget of about $8.4 million. Even the most active environmental groups working on international environmental issues in Japan must do with much smaller budgets. FOE Japan worked with about $480,000; Japan Tropical Action Network (JATAN) with $150,000; Kiko Network with $240,000, and A SEED Japan with $120,000. Greenpeace Japan's budget of about $1.5 million was very large in comparison. It should be noted, however, that for years Greenpeace International heavily supported Greenpeace, Japan financially. Considering that Japan is the world's second largest economy this should raise some eyebrows.

In contrast, there are numerous environmental groups in the US with budgets in the millions. EDF has a budget of over $31 million; the Sierra Club has assets of $45 million; NRDC $30 million; Greenpeace USA $8 million; the Alliance to Save Energy $4.5 million; and the Union of Concerned Scientists $6.8 million, to give just a few examples.

Environmental groups in Germany are considerably poorer than their US counterparts as well, but somewhat better off than they are in Japan. The NABU had a budget of DM 27 million (about $14 million) in 2000. The DNR reported a budget of 500,000 Euro (about $500,000) and GERMANWATCH of DM 800,000 (about $400,000).[2] In contrast with many other NGOs in Germany, which accept support or contracts from the federal and Länder governments, Greenpeace Germany only takes in private contributions and donations. Its budget in 1999 was DM 63.7 million or approximately $32 million US.

Chapter 3 explored some of the reasons behind the different size of the environmental NGOs in Japan, Germany, and the US. Here additional data on the situation of NGOs in the three countries is presented along with analysis of how, to what extent, and why their situation in the larger policy-making system is changing.

Japan's changing environmental policy community

The weakness of environmental NGOs in Japan has been a recurrent theme in previous chapters. There are some signs, however, that their position may be improving as some of the institutional barriers inhibiting NGO formation and maintenance are removed.

In an intriguing process that has been more top-down, than bottom-up, Japan has tried to become a larger player in international environmental

---

[2] Figures were obtained from annual reports, direct email contact, and from websites.

protection. Environmental NGOs have played only a relatively limited role in pressuring the government to change policy, mobilizing public opinion, or providing alternative policy options. Although citizens' movements, the courts, local governments, and the opposition parties were very important in getting environmental issues on to the Japanese policy agenda around 1970, they were not the ones which played the most active agenda-setting role in the late 1980s and early 1990s when global environmental issues began to attract more attention. As noted previously, it was the Japanese government, in response to international pressure, that chose to make global environmental protection one of the pillars of its foreign policy. Japanese industry could accept this development since it sees some win-win possibilities in environmental protection and energy efficiency improvements. Yet, the government has also come under pressure to enhance the role of environmental NGOs.

Japan's new concern for the global environment has resulted in changes in institutions, policies, and values that are slowly making Japan a larger player in the realm of global environmental matters. Comparing the situation in Japan in the early 2000s, with the 1980s, the changes are quite dramatic. Various actors in society have reorganized in order to have a greater influence on this policy area and to benefit from its greater political salience. Businesses, the bureaucracy, and the political parties have become increasingly environmentally savvy. New kinds of environmental groups have emerged and are forming or joining national and international networks. Japanese politicians, NGOs, and think tanks are taking advantage of international communication networks to disperse information about their environmental laws and programs and to promote international exchange for environmental protection. Some "greening" can be seen in virtually every actor group. Still, the situation for environmental activists in Japan remains complex. The environmental NGO community in Japan remains weak and its acceptance by governmental and industrial actors mixed.

Environmental NGOs
In the 1980s only a very small handful of environmental groups in Japan had activities even remotely related to addressing stratospheric ozone depletion, global warming, desertification, or tropical rainforest destruction. Surveys conducted by the JANIC in 1992, 1996, or 2000 suggest that there has been some growth in the number of NGOs involved in international environmental protection. The 1992 survey identified sixty groups and the 1996 survey eighty-eight groups that had international environmental protection as at least a sub-set of their activities. The 2000 survey changed its categories for reporting. Under the new categories

thirty-seven groups considered their activities to be partly related to global environmental protection, fifty-eight to reforestation or forest preservation, seven to biodiversity, and ten to alternative energies.[3]

Despite the remarkable constraints they face, since the late 1980s, the environmental NGO community has worked to strengthen its voice in the policy-making process. In July 1989, for example, CASA called on the Japanese government to initiate a complete ban on CFCs and participated in the March 1989 London Conference.[4] In May 1990, Greenpeace Japan surveyed industries about their production and consumption of CFCs, and publicized the "Greenfreeze," a refrigerator that uses hydrocarbons as a refrigerant and in insulation foaming in place of the CFC substitute chemicals that industry was promoting, HCFC-134a and HCFC-141b, both of which have high global warming potentials. The idea for the refrigerator came from Greenpeace in Germany, which got the idea from East Germany.[5]

Another way that groups are starting to try to increase their voice in the policy process is by forming umbrella organizations, much as the *Bürgerinitiativen* did in Germany in the early 1970s. For example, Shunsuke Iwasaki, who had served as president of the Japan International Volunteer Center, was instrumental in organizing Japanese NGOs into the People's Forum for the UNCED. The aim of this umbrella organization was to bring Japan's community of environmental activists together in order to present a united voice at the UNCED. The NGO People's Forum represented consumer groups, rainforest activists, lawyers, Minamata victims, climate experts, and many others. They produced an alternative national report to UNCED, which provided a different perspective on Japan's past progress, and future plans for the environment than the one presented by the government's report. The NGO report argued that Japanese corporations and official development aid have had a negative impact on the global environment and discussed the important role that grass roots movements can play in changing Japan into a more environmentally friendly society.[6]

In November 1993 members regrouped as People's Forum 2001. The group's goals were to participate in UNCED follow-up activities, to collect and disseminate information, conduct surveys, and make reports and issue statements to influence government policy on environment and development issues. People's Forum 2001 critiqued the draft proposal of

---

[3] JANIC, *Kokusai Kyōryoku NGO Dairekutorii* (Tokyo: JANIC, 1992, 1996, 2000).
[4] CASA pamphlet.
[5] Greenpeace Japan, "Guriin Furiizu no Jidai ga Kita" (pamphlet). See also, *Economisuto*, February 8, 1994, p. 84.
[6] *Asahi Shimbun*, January 23, 1992, p. 17.

the National Action Plan for Agenda 21. As a result of their critiques, over 100 modifications (albeit not always as far reaching as the environmental groups and the public wanted to see) were made to the plan. This is a major break with how policies were formulated in the past.[7] A study group on climate issues also was formed within Forum 2001; they produced a collection of reports critical of the government's slow response to climate change and its environmental budget reporting procedures.[8] Iwasaki left the organization to run for election, but failed in his first election bid.

The climate change negotiations also brought NGOs and citizens' organizations together. Several Japanese NGOs, including Greenpeace Japan, WWF Japan, People's Forum 2001, CASA, and Kankyô Shimin participated in international follow-up meetings to the UNCED. A German NGO umbrella group that was active at COP 2, Klimaforum '95, inspired members of these Japanese NGOs to launch a counterpart. In December 1996, Kiko Forum '97 (the Citizens' Forum for Preventing Climate Change/Global Warming) was established by a group of concerned citizens and approximately seventy NGOs. This group was set up as a clearing house for the press and the public on climate change. In the pre-Kyoto Conference period, the group worked to educate the public on climate change, fund raise, and provide logistical support for environmental NGOs, especially those from the south, so that they could participate in the COP 3.

A primary goal of the forum was to influence the shape of the protocol to be adopted at COP 3 in Kyoto. In doing this, they tried to learn from the experiences of their German counterparts. At the first meeting of the forum, Ulrike Wiehr from Germany gave a talk on the experiences of the Klimaforum at COP 1 in Berlin. In a big change from the past, the government also recognized the work of this group by participating at the highest level in the meeting. Environment Agency Director General Michiko Ishii gave a speech on the common goal shared by government and NGOs to prevent global warming. There was an audience of 400.[9] A network of 225 Japanese environmental NGOs, agricultural cooperatives, youth groups, and local living cooperatives attended the Kyoto Conference.

Kiko Forum reorganized as Kiko Network in April 1998. The network continues to hold information and research seminars, conferences, and

---

[7] Miranda A. Schreurs, "Japan: Law, Technology, and Aid," in Lafferty and Meadowcroft (eds.), *Implementing Sustainable Development*, pp. 112–41.

[8] Shimin Forum 2001 Chikyû Ondanka Kenkyûkai, *Shôsetsu: Chikyû Ondanka* (Tokyo: Shimin Forum 2001, 1998).

[9] Shimin Forum 2001 Chikyû Ondanka Kenkyûkai, *Ima, chikyû ondanka mondai ha hataraiteiru!!* March 15, 1996. Interview with Sumino Setsuko, January 1997.

prepares policy papers. Major goals of the network are to expand the input of citizens in the political decision-making process. They had a little over 300 individuals and about 150 organizations as members in 1998. Another network, Green Energy Law Network, was established to promote renewable energy use in Japan. The network's founder, Tetsunari Iida, had spent considerable time in Europe where he studied efforts to promote renewable energies. When he returned to Japan, he decided to work to promote renewable energy in Japan as well. He chose to distance the network from any kind of direct anti-nuclear activism, and sought legislative change that will promote renewable energies. One of the network's great successes was its ability to form an alliance with 256 politicians, the National Parliamentarians' Association for Promoting Renewable Energy, which formed in November 1999, to push for a renewable energy promotion law that maps out rules for electric power companies to purchase electricity generated from renewable energy sources. Kazuo Aichi headed up the parliamentarians' alliance. Although the effort failed in its first attempt at legislative change and Aichi lost his seat in the summer's Lower House elections, the development is significant. It suggests that a new era is emerging in Japan in which politicians and NGOs can form alliances.[10] It is also important to note that whereas efforts to promote this renewable energy law failed, a bill to promote nuclear energy construction passed in the Diet. Thus, while NGO support is growing in Japan, there are still strong lobbies representing traditionally powerful interests.

In the 1990s, several new Asia-focused environmental networks emerged as well. The Environment Agency helped to form the Environmental Congress for Asia and the Pacific (Eco Asia), which brings together environmental ministers from throughout Asia to discuss environmental issues and priorities. The Environment Agency also helped form the Asian Acid Rain Monitoring Network to further understanding of the state of the acid rain problem in the region.[11] NGOs from China, Hong Kong, Japan, Mongolia, Russia, South Korea, and Taiwan established the Atmospheric Action Network of East Asia in 1995 to improve citizen awareness of regional atmospheric pollution issues.[12]

Yet another way in which environmental activists are making their voices heard on environmental matters is through local referendum. Local

---

[10] Discussion with Tetsunari Iida, February 3, 2001.

[11] See Peter Hayes and Lyuba Zarsky, "Environmental Issues and Regimes in Northeast Asia," *International Environmental Affairs* 6 (1994), 283–319.

[12] Esook Yoon and Hong Pyo Lee, "Environmental Cooperation in Northeast Asia: Issues and Prospects," and Miranda A. Schreurs, "The Future of Environmental Cooperation in Northeast Asia," in Miranda A. Schreurs and Dennis Pirages (eds.), *Ecological Security in Northeast Asia* (Seoul: Yonsei University Press, 1998), pp. 67–88 and 195–219.

referenda have been used to block nuclear power plant construction and waste incineration plants and to test public opinion towards US military bases.[13] One area where there is likely to be much controversy in the future regards the role to be played by nuclear energy. The fatal accident at the Tokai uranium processing plant in September 1999 has heightened public concerns about the safety of Japan's nuclear energy plants and raised questions about the lack of transparency of the industry and adequate independent oversight of plants. This and a series of other more minor incidents has forced the government to reconsider its energy policies and its plans to build sixteen to twenty new nuclear power plants. In March 2000, MITI announced that it plans a comprehensive study to review the nation's energy policies.[14] Citizen activism is clearly a reason behind this.

Inter-actor cooperation

Japanese industry also is showing signs of becoming somewhat more sensitive to global environmental protection issues and supportive of NGOs if for no other reason than that being green is now perceived as good business sense. By the time of the UNCED, most of Japan's major corporations had established global environment offices and were actively involved in green advertising (even if they still had yet really to green their own operations). In July 1996 *Keidanren* announced an "Environmental Appeal" to industries to develop voluntary action plans to address environmental conservation in the twenty-first century. By June 1997, 37 industries and 137 industrial organizations had drawn up plans with yearly review plans. Many of the plans include measures for reducing greenhouse gas emissions.[15] Japanese corporations also began moving in record numbers to obtain the International Standards Organization's (ISO) 14,000 environmental management series certification. By December 1998, 1,542 firms had acquired ISO 14,001 certification in Japan, the highest level of any country in the world. In comparison, there were 1,100 acquisitions in Germany and 210 in the US. (German companies were actually ahead of their Japanese counterparts, however, when you take into consideration the fact that as of the same date 1,795 German firms were participating in the EU's Environmental Management and Audit System [EMAS], wich requires that they publish information about their environmental performance and management.)[16]

[13] *Los Angeles Times*, August 5, 1996, pp. A1 and A6.
[14] *Japan Times*, March 11, 2000, p. 1.
[15] Keizai Dantai Rengôkai, *Keidanren Kankyô Jishu Kôdô Keikaku*, June 17, 1997.
[16] Institute for Global Environmental Strategies, *Business and Environmental Governance*, March 1999. On German firms and the Environmental Management and Audit System

Certainly some of these developments are no more than an effort on the part of Japanese corporations to avoid new regulations and eco taxes. Also important is the desire to develop a more environmentally friendly image and to prevent the kinds of boycotts of Japanese products that have been called for in the past because of environmentally destructive activities. Yet, in other cases the changes represent a more fundamental change in corporate outlook. They also mean the potential for the development of cooperative channels between industry and NGOs.

In fact, a good number of individuals employed in major corporations have become members of environmental networks, like Green Energy Law network and Kiko Forum, in order to express their interest in environmental matters. While they participate in these groups as individuals and not as representatives of their firms, this kind of networking among representatives of industry and NGOs is intriguing given the kinds of adversarial relationships that existed between these actor groups in the past.

Another good example of the slowly changing dynamics between NGOs and industry was a meeting sponsored by Greenpeace in November 1996. Greenpeace, long viewed in Japan as an extremely radical environmental group, held a seminar attended by representatives of sixty Japanese companies, including banks, construction companies, energy utilities, insurance corporations, and chemical firms. At the seminar, Greenpeace discussed business chances that would be provided by efforts to prevent climate change and developments in US and European industries. This form of NGO–industry communication would have been unheard of in the 1980s.

Another important ally for Japan's fledgling environmental community is the new crop of green politicians to be found in the Diet. There was a noticeable growth in interest in environmental issues among politicians across all political parties in Japan during the 1990s. One indication of this is how many politicians have become members of the inter-parliamentary group, GLOBE. GLOBE was established to facilitate international cooperation for the environment among parliamentarians in the US, Europe, and Japan. In May 1997 in the months leading up to the Kyoto Conference, GLOBE International had 140 active members from the European Union, Japan, Russia, and the US. There were 25 Japanese among this group. A few months later in July 1997, the number had climbed to 33. In August 1997, GLOBE Japan hosted a meeting, Towards the COP3: Policy Making and Action, on the occasion of German Environment

see Klaus Fichter, "Competitive Advantages through Voluntary Environmental Reporting," Institut für ökologische Wirtschaftsforschung GmbH. On Japanese firms see Eric Welch, Midori Aoyagi-Usui, and Sukehiro Gotoh, "Greening Activity of Japanese Companies: An Application of Organization Theory," manuscript.

Minister Angela Merkel's visit to Japan. The symposium provided GLOBE Japan members with an opportunity to discuss the issue of climate change with business representatives, academics, bureaucrats, and citizens' groups.[17]

Funding concerns

A critical factor for the future of the environmental NGO community in Japan will be whether or not they can improve their access to funding. As discussed above, Japanese NGOs are cash strapped. In signing Agenda 21 at the UNCED, governments agreed to its provisions. Chapter 28 of Agenda 21 calls for involving different interests and minorities in the process of preparing national reports. UNCED elevated consensus-building approaches to new levels. Within Japan, this has helped NGOs to gain some legitimacy. The international community expects NGO participation in international negotiations, environmental decision making, and implementation.

This international normative expectation has created an interesting dilemma for the Japanese government and industry. They are now trying to figure out how they can work with NGOs to increase their size and status at the same time that they do not yet fully appreciate environmental groups' potential role in policy making and implementation. Several private corporations have found it in their interest to assist NGOs. The AEON Group Environmental Foundation for example was set up to support NGOs active in environmental conservation activities in developing countries. A *Keidanren* Nature Conservation Fund was established to provide financial assistance to NGO-operated nature conservation, education, and human resource capacity-building projects in developing countries.[18] In addition, there are several institutions promoting international research for environmental preservation such as the Center for Global Partnership, the Japan Foundation and the US–Japan Foundation.[19]

The Japanese government also began to create mechanisms to try to help raise funds for NGOs. A "Green Donation" program was established by law. Donations that are collected mainly on Green Day (April 29) and during Green Week (April 23 to 29) are directed towards NGO projects

---

[17] GLOBE meeting, August 25, 1997, Tokyo, Japan.

[18] Japan Council for Sustainable Development, *Japan Report for Rio + 5 Process*, March 1997.

[19] Kim D. Reimann, "Building Networks from the Outside In: International Movements, Japanese NGOs and the Kyoto Climate Change Conference," paper presented at the 1999 Annual Meeting of the Northeastern Political Science Association (NPSA) and International Studies Association-Northeast, Philadelphia Crown Plaza Hotel, November 10–14, 1999.

for forest management, reforestation, and international reforestation promotion and cooperation. A Postal Savings for International Voluntary Aid system was established by law. This fund assists NGOs working for the social welfare of people in developing countries by making contributions of up to 20 percent of the after-tax interest on Post Office ordinary deposit accounts tax-deductible. A Charity New Years Card system was also set up. Funds from this support non-profit organizations working to conserve the global environment.[20]

In 1993, the founding law of the Japan Environment Corporation was amended to establish the Japan Fund for the Global Environment. This fund promotes NGO activities in the field of environmental protection and sustainable development. With an initial endowment of ¥1 billion and a ¥500 million grant for fiscal 1993 operations, the fund supported forty-seven Japanese NGOs working on domestic environmental issues, three overseas NGOs, and fifty-four Japanese NGOs working on environmental protection in developing countries.[21] The MoFA also established a "Grassroots Grant Assistance" fund to provide assistance on the order of hundreds of thousands of yen to ten million yen to NGOs conducting field projects in developing countries.[22]

A big change occurred in March 1998 when the Japanese Diet unanimously passed a bill making it easier for groups to obtain non-profit status. The bill was sponsored by a group of Japanese legislators who recognized the important role that citizens' groups had played in the wake of the Hanshin Earthquake that devastated the Kobe region in 1995. The Non-Profit Organization (NPO) Law aims to strengthen Japan's civil society.[23] Once given legal status as a non-profit organization, it is easier for groups to rent offices, set up telephone lines, and open bank accounts. In the past, groups that had operated without non-profit status were liable to inheritance taxes if the person under whose name the group was registered died. The new NPO law makes it easier for groups to obtain non-profit status although it still fails to provide any tax incentives to strengthen their financial base.[24] Based on an April 1997 survey, the Economic Planning Agency estimated that over 10,000 citizens' groups hope to obtain status as non-profit organizations.[25]

It is also significant that in 1999 a Public Information Disclosure Law, similar to the US Freedom of Information Act, was passed. The law took

---

[20] Japan Council for Sustainable Development, *Japan Report for Rio + 5 Process*.
[21] Japan Environment Corporation, "Chikyû Kankyô Kikin Tayori," 1994.
[22] Japan Council for Sustainable Development, *Japan Report for Rio + 5 Process*. See also Menju and Aoki "The Evolution of Japanese NGOs in the Asia Pacific Context," pp. 150–2.
[23] Pekkanen, "Japan's New Politics," 111–48.   [24] *Japan Times*, March 20, 1998, p. 1.
[25] *Japan Times*, March 4, 1998, p. 14.

effect April 1, 2001. This law has the potential to alter significantly the relationship between citizens and bureaucrats because it will give citizens the right to access information regarding the governmental decision-making process that in the past was normally kept from them.

Environmental NGOs and the Green Party in Germany

The rise of the Green Party was discussed at some length earlier in this book. Here attention will be focused instead on several new environmental groups and think tanks that were formed in response to the emergence of global environmental issues. For the first time in post-war German history, the Green Party also entered a coalition government in 1998 providing the party with new possibilities and challenges. This development and its implications for environmental activism is also considered.

As has been the case in both Japan and the US, environmental groups that were initially established to deal with domestic environmental problems have found it increasingly important to address not only national, but also international and global environmental issues. German NGOs were slow initially to respond to concern about stratospheric ozone depletion and global climate change, but by the 1990s had become active players in a wide range of international environmental matters.[26]

The UNCED process resulted in the formation of several new environmental groups in Germany. Examples include Forum Umwelt und Entwicklung (Forum Environment and Development) and GERMAN-WATCH. The Forum Environment and Development was established as an umbrella organization to give German NGOs a stronger voice in environmental policy making. The Forum focuses on issues like Agenda 21 and the promotion of sustainable development and North–South concerns. Because of an absence of large philanthropists in Germany, the Forum, like other NGOs, relies heavily on government support. Approximately 80 percent of the Forum's money between 1993 and 1999 came from the government. The Forum Environment and Development also has church groups involved in its activities, and the churches, which are relatively wealthy, have helped to support some of the group's activities. Jürgen Maier, who is with the Forum Environment and Development, suggested that while having a Green Party in the government may help environmental interests, the party also has made compromises that put it at odds with the interests of some environmental groups. He stressed that environmental groups although often overshadowed by the Green Party continue to play an important role. They educate the public, conduct policy studies, and launch campaigns.

---

[26] Beuermann and Jäger, "Climate Change Politics in Germany," p. 212.

He lamented, however, the difficulty groups are facing in mobilizing people into action at a time when all they are concerned about is "jobs, jobs, jobs."[27] GERMANWATCH was established to police the activities of industries and the government in their progress towards achieving sustainable development. It also has become a monitor of trade activities for their environmental implications.

As was the case in Japan, German NGOs also felt a need to coordinate and exchange information in order better to influence international policy developments on climate change and to facilitate information exchange among groups. Klima Forum was established in October 1994 six months prior to the first COP to the FCCC in Berlin. It was sponsored by Grüne Liga Berlin, a local environmental NGO and DNR. The network's presence helped to give a more unified voice to NGO calls for action on climate change. Klima Forum took on the role of informing the public regarding the climate change negotiations through the production of the Klima Forum Bulletin and provided logistical support to NGOs who came to follow the negotiations.[28] In addition, many groups, including Greenpeace Germany, the German branch of WWF, and the BUND, actively campaigned domestically for action on climate change and sustainable development. They produced reports that indicate how Germany can best meet its commitments, campaigned internationally to heighten international awareness of climate change, and formed international networks to pressure governments to take action. There has been considerable dialogue between these groups and the Environment Ministry.[29]

The NGO community is also working to push Germany further in the direction of ecological modernization. In an effort to show that it not only preached non-nuclear, green energy, but also practiced it, Greenpeace headquarters in Hamburg became a user of "green electricity" derived from solar panels, co-generation, and wind turbines.[30]

The BUND, one of the largest of Germany's environmental groups, and MISEREOR, a large development NGO tied to the German Catholic bishops, commissioned the Wuppertal Institute for Environment, Climate, and Energy (established in 1991) to produce a study on sustainable development. The report stirred considerable discussion and eventually helped to push the German Environment Agency and the

[27] Discussion panel with Jürgen Maier and Markus Kurdziel, Bonn, Germany, June 9, 1999.
[28] Discussions with Sascha Muller-Kraenner.
[29] Discussion with Franz-Josef Schafhausen (Bundesministerium für Umwelt, Naturschurtz und Reaktorsicherhieit), Bonn, Germany, June 9, 1999.
[30] Discussion with Sven Teske and Roland Hipp, Hamburg, June 11, 1999. See also Greenpeace, "Aktion Stromwechsel, Saubere Stromversorgung: klimaschonend und ohne Atomstrom, Ein Konzept für den ökologischen Energiedienstleister der Zukunft" (Hamburg: Greenpeace e.V., August, 1998).

parliament to produce their own reports on sustainable development. The 466-page study by the institute took as its basis the ideas of environmental space, ecology, and equity. It assumes that countries in the developing world look to the advanced industrialized countries as their own models of development. The South seeks the wealth of the North. Yet, the study suggests that if the countries of the developing world all strive to live the same resource-intense life styles as Germany, and by implication other advanced industrialized countries, do now, then the planet will be overburdened. The study then asks what must Germany do to reduce its "environmental space" to a level that would be sustainable at a global level. The report examines the concept of "environmental space" by looking at material and energy consumption, water use, land use, and emissions. It then considers the reduction in consumption that would have to take place in Germany if equality of "environmental space" is to be achieved for all individuals in the world. The study found, for example, that Germany must reduce its CO_2 emissions by 80 percent by 2050 to achieve this per person equitable level. This figure goes substantially beyond the 50 to 60 percent global reduction in CO_2 emissions called for by the Enquete Commission "Protection of the Atmosphere." The report went on to argue that the reduction in CO_2 emissions must be done without reliance on nuclear energy because of its high risks, but also suggested that simply increasing use of alternative energies was not feasible nor completely desirable since renewables also require resources. Thus, they argued for a mix of more alternative energy use (increasing 3–5 percent per year) and major improvements in energy efficiency. Similar kinds of proposals were made for other issues.[31]

Pushed by the huge popular success of the Wuppertal report, in 1995, the Bundestag appointed the Enquete Commission on Protection of Humanity and the Environment. It was given the mandate to develop objectives for Germany to move towards a sustainable society. The Enquete Commission's report issued in January 1997 focused on how to apply sustainability to land use and construction.[32] A half-a-year later, the Environment Agency came out with its own report: *Nachhaltiges Deutschland* (Sustainable Germany). The report analyses resource use

[31] Wuppertal Instituts für Klima, Umwelt, Energie, *Zukunftsfähiges Deutschland: Ein Beitrag zu einer global nachhaltigen Entwicklung* (Basel: Birkhäuser Verlag, 5th edition, 1997), pp. 56–66.

[32] See Zwischenbericht der Enquete-Kommission, Schutz des Menschen und der Umwelt, des 13 Deutschen Bundestages, *Konzept Nachhaltigkeit: Funamente für die Gesellschaft von morgen* (Bonn: Deutscher Bundestag, 1997); and Christianne Beuermann, "Germany: Regulations and the Precautionary Principle," in Lafferty and Meadowcroft (eds.), *Implementing Sustainable Development*, pp. 85–111.

in the areas of energy, transportation, food, product life cycles, and consumption and has mitigation of climate change as a central goal. The report then provides different scenarios for Germany to consider in working towards sustainable development. The first scenario shows the level of destruction that will ensue with a continuation of the status quo. Another assumes improvements in technologies. A third focuses on changes that are conceivable with large structural and consciousness changes in the socio-economic system. Like the Wuppertal Report, the UBA's report is premised on the notion that sustainable development involves intergenerational equity, elimination of poverty in the developing world, and transition in the industrialized economies to lifestyles that are in tune with nature. It argues that Germany is currently not in conformity with the principle of sustainable development. While there have been successes in reducing emissions, technology efficiency improvements, and a growth in recycling of materials, there are still many problems with the energy and material consumption patterns in Germany. On the controversial issue of nuclear energy, the report stated that it is not the best way to achieve sustainable development and that it is not sustainable in the long term.[33] The dissemination of these reports did much to boost Germany's image as a leader in environmental thinking internationally.

The BUND was also instrumental in promoting NGO–industry dialogue on the use of economic instruments for environmental protection. In 1993, the BUND together with the Federal Association of Young Entrepreneurs produced a report calling for an ecological tax reform. The two groups showed that there need not be a contradiction between the goals of environmental and economic groups.[34]

Industry has had mixed reactions to the greening of government in the 1990s. On the one hand, industry has chosen to take a very different tack on climate change and other environmental issues from the GCC in the US, which has been openly hostile to international efforts to develop a climate protection treaty. German industry must deal with a much greener public than exists in the US. Perhaps as a result, German industry has also taken some initiatives of its own. In March 1995, German industrial and trade groups announced the Declaration of German Industry and Trade on Global Warming Prevention in which they pledged to reduce industrial CO_2 emissions by 20 percent of 1990 levels by 2005. The independent research institute, Rheinische-Westfälisches Institut für

---

[33] Umweltbundesamt, *Nachhaltiges Deutschland: Wege zu einer dauerhaft umweltgerechten Entwicklung* (Berlin: Erich Schmidt Verlag, 1997).
[34] Cited in Beuermann and Jäger, "Climate Change Politics in Germany," pp. 212–13.

Wirtschaftsforschung is monitoring their progress.[35] Yet like American industry, German industry prefers to avoid new regulations and taxes. German industries began pursuing voluntary environmental agreements to address climate change as pressures for environmental taxes began to build within Germany and at the EU level.

German NGOs, the Green Party, and the SPD–Green Party coalition
The formation of new environmental NGOs and networks and environmental think tanks was an important aspect of the transformation of the environmental policy community in Germany. Better known is the Red–Green Coalition that formed in 1998 between the SPD and Green Party/Alliance 90. In the 1998 election, Gerhard Schröder portrayed himself as a technological modernizer in the areas of transportation and the automobile. He also championed a gradual withdrawal from nuclear energy and focused attention on Kohl's policy failures, particularly in the area of unemployment.[36] The Green Party pushed Schroeder's SPD to go farther down the path of greening the German socio-economic landscape than would probably have happened otherwise.

The SPD–Green coalition came in with a plan to put Germany on a new environmentally informed socio-economic trajectory. The approach required finding a way to address the unemployment problem while at the same time pushing forward green politics. Although the Green Party's strength actually dropped somewhat in the election, falling from 7.3 percent to 6.7 percent and from forty-nine to forty-seven seats, it was given three Cabinet posts: foreign affairs, environment, and health. Indeed, it is quite fascinating that the foreign ministers of Germany and Japan at the time of this writing – Joschka Fisher and Yoriko Kawaguchi – are perhaps the most environmentally minded foreign ministers of the advanced industrialized nations.

The major elements of the coalition's October 1998 programmatic agenda included plans for a green tax reform, a new emphasis on the promotion of renewable energies and energy-efficient technologies, and the phase out of nuclear energy. The premise behind the platform of the new coalition was that it was possible to focus on the economy and creating new jobs, while at the same time pushing the economy in a more environmentally benign direction. The green tax reform was introduced as an idea that was to play two primary roles. First, was to help finance a substantial reduction in social welfare taxes, which had skyrocketed because of the high unemployment levels after unification and the aging

[35] http://www.bmu.de/UNBericht/parta3.htm.
[36] *Der Spiegel*, vol. 40, September 28, 1998, pp. 70–8.

of society. Social welfare taxes are to be reduced from 42.3 percent to 40 percent of gross income. Second, was to push the economy in a new direction that would make Germany less dependent on polluting energies. This was to help pull in approximately DM 11 billion.[37] The assumption of the coalition was that by creating new environmental jobs and industries the environmental industry would become one of Germany's top five employers by 2050.[38]

Phase one of the ecological tax reform came into effect as of April 1999. In phase one new taxes were levied on gasoline and diesel, heating oil, electricity, and natural gas. Then for the second stage, which was approved by the Bundestag in November 1999 and covers the period from 2000 to 2003, the tax charge on electricity was increased. Electricity produced from exclusively renewable resources and from highly efficient resources was exempted from the tax. Interestingly, coal was also not targeted for taxation even though coal pollutes heavily. The reason for this was that the coal industry traditionally has supported the SPD and successfully blocked efforts by some members of the SPD and the Greens to tax them. Also, because of plans to harmonize energy taxes within the EU in the future, temporary exemptions were made for energy-intensive industries, such as steel, aluminum, and construction. There was considerable politicking involved in determining which industries classified as energy intensive. In the first phase of the ecological tax reform, the new taxes hit households, the transportation sector, and less-polluting industries the hardest. The biggest greenhouse gas emitters were not the first to be burdened with the new taxes. Thus, while there has been a substantial greening of German politics, it is important to recognize that there are some big exceptions as well.

The SPD–Green coalition policies have had a mixed reception. The eco tax reform did not go as far as some within the Green Party and the environmentalist community would have liked to see. The NGO community demanded that the tax on gasoline, for example, be raised by 30 pfennig per year over the next ten years. Chancellor Gerhard Schröder, who had served on Volkswagen's supervisory board, opposed this. The end result was a 6-pfennig tax on gasoline and diesel. The minister-president of Schleswig-Holstein, a noted environmentalist within the SPD, criticized the eco tax as not going far enough.[39]

[37] Miranda A. Schreurs, "New Directions in German Energy and Environmental Policies," in *Germany After the 1998 Federal Elections* (Washington, DC: American Institute for Contemporary German Studies, December 1998), pp. 17–20.
[38] Federal Ministry for the Environment, Nature Conservation, and Nuclear Safety, "Common Ground," January 1999, p. 6.
[39] *Süddeutsche Zeitung*, November 23, 1998, p. 1.

The chairman of IG Metall, Klaus Zwickel, argued that the eco tax reforms would result in a loss of jobs for workers in energy-intensive industries. Other industries have expressed their fears that they will have to pay higher energy costs, hurting their competitiveness. Some industries, however, see a net benefit in the combined reduction of social welfare taxes and the rise in energy taxes. The German auto industry, for example, decided that it could save as much as 10 million DM under the new tax program because saving from reduced social welfare taxes would more than offset higher payments in the form of eco taxes.[40]

The most controversial element and the internationally best known of the SPD–Green coalition's programmatic agreement was their plan to phase out nuclear energy. Germany has nineteen nuclear power stations in operation. They provide about 30 percent of electricity needs, which amounts to about 10 percent of primary energy use. Since the Chernobyl nuclear accident, the SPD has sided with the Greens in opposing nuclear energy. The SPD–Green coalition's position on nuclear energy is that it has unacceptable risks associated with it. Thus, despite the argument that nuclear energy does not produce greenhouse gases, the coalition has pushed through its plans to phase out nuclear energy. The coalition has also argued that as long as nuclear energy remains a part of Germany's energy mix, incentives for research and development of alternative forms of energy would suffer. Greenpeace produced a study showing that federal and state government subsidies to different technologies have overwhelmingly favored nuclear fission and nuclear fusion technologies. In the period from 1956 (in the case of nuclear fission) and 1974 (in the case of all other technologies) to 1995, nuclear fission and nuclear fusion have received 82 percent of expenditures for research and subsidies. Renewable energies and technologies for saving energy, in contrast, received only 9 percent of research expenditures and subsidies over the same time period.[41]

As a start, the SPD–Green coalition revised the Atomic Act, tightening safety regulations and eliminating subsidies for nuclear energy. Phase out plans, however, were more problematic and required over a year of consensus talks that brought together actors with different interests in the nuclear energy question to find a workable plan of action. The consensus talks were held between the Ministry of Economics, the Ministry for Environment, the chancellor, and the utility companies (RWE,

[40] *Der Spiegel*, November 16, 1998, p. 80.
[41] Volker U. Hoffmann, George Hille, Helmut Dienhart, Ole Langiniss, Jachi Nisch, and Sven Teske, "Employment in Solar Energy in 2010: New Jobs through New Sources of Energy (Executive Summary)" (Hamburg: Greenpeace, April 1997).

Veba, Viag, and Energie Baden-Württemberg) operating nuclear power plants.

There were many points of disagreement. There was disagreement within the coalition. Environment Minister Trittin favored a much more rapid phase out than Chancellor Schröder, who felt it necessary to compromise with the nuclear industry on this question. On more than one occasion differences between the two men strained the coalition and threatened its stability. The minister of the environment backed by the Green Party convention called for a twenty-five-year phase out. The utility companies were pushing for a thirty-five-year target.[42] While there was relatively little opposition to the idea of closing down older plants that were reaching the end of their technological life span, there has been considerable controversy regarding how long to let newer reactors operate. The nuclear industry did not like the phase out plan, but at a maximum wanted as long a period as possible for continued operations and at a minimum, the expected lifetime of a plant. Nuclear power plants in Germany were granted operating licenses without time limit; technical operating time is typically about twenty to forty years. Many of the power plants would have to be shut down in the coming years anyhow because of age factors. No new nuclear power plant orders were made after 1975. Still, there were many legal questions that had to be resolved such as the authority of the government to impose time limits for operating licenses when originally licenses were granted with no time limitation. Also at question was the authority of the government to prohibit reprocessing of waste as the coalition government favored.

Strongly desiring a favorable outcome for ideological and electoral reasons, the Green Party agreed in February 2000 to a thirty-year phase out date. The decision led to ideological splits within the Green Party between those who favored phase out even if later than desired and those who felt that the party had given in almost completely to the demands of the nuclear industry. In the end, a plan was announced on June 15, capping electricity production from nuclear sources at a capacity of 2623.3 billion kWh, which is equivalent to a thirty-two-year phase out life at high utilization. Within this total budgeted allocation, industries have the flexibility of transferring operation among reactors, thus, most new plants would be able to still run for twenty to twenty-five years although some plants could conceivably operate for longer. In addition, reprocessing is to be allowed through 2005 and final storage sites at Gorleben and Konrad are to be pursued. A major public issue has been the transport of spent fuels for reprocessing because of concerns of a transport disaster. In

[42] *Der Tagesspiegel*, July 6, 1999, p. 1; June 20, 1999, pp. 1 and 6.

the meantime, temporary waste storage facilities are to be built close to the existing power plants. This solution was attractive to the nuclear industry, which has faced strong public opposition to the transport of waste via rail.[43]

The phase out is considered feasible given the excess electricity capacity in Europe, plans for enhancing production of energy from renewables, the development of new technologies, such as fuel cells, and the use of more combined heat and power electricity generation. Excess capacity on the European liberalized market is estimated at approximately 40,000 MW. It will, however, be a challenge for Germany to phase out nuclear energy at the same time that it strives to fulfill its greenhouse gas emissions reduction goal. There is also some question as to whether Germany will be phasing out its own nuclear energy sources, but then relying on neighboring France for electricity where most electricity is produced by nuclear power.[44]

Another big question is whether or not a CDU government would try to reverse the policy. The CDU's energy spokesman, Kurt-Dieter Grill, called the agreement "an error, plain and simple." His argument is that the close down will result in the loss of about 190,000 jobs, will result in a loss in technological know-how in a critical field, and will result in other environmental problems because of the need to replace nuclear energy with other fuel sources, among them coal.[45]

The Green Party was split on the compromise. While many in the party were happy to have some kind of phase out plan agreed upon, co-leader of the Greens, Antje Radcke, a *fundi*, sees the plan as unacceptable. Also opposed to the compromise was the head of the Green Party faction of Lower Saxony, Rebecca Harms.[46] Opponents of the plan argued that by making such a substantial compromise with the nuclear industry, the party was setting aside its principles. In the end, however, the party voted by a comfortable majority at its party Congress to accept the plan.

As part of the phase out plan, the government also passed the Renewable Energy Sources Act of April 2000 with the goal of doubling renewable energy production by 2010. The production of renewable energy in Germany has risen sharply since the introduction in 1991 of legislation favoring renewables. The process began during the Kohl era. The 1991 Electricity Feed Law, which obliges the electricity companies

---

[43] Lutz Mez and Annette Piening, "Phasing-Out Nuclear Power Generation in Germany: Policies, Actors, Issues and Non-Issues," paper presented at conference, New Directions in National and International Energy and Climate Change Policies: Germany, Japan, US Energy Experts Annual Network Meeting, Berlin, Germany, June 17–20, 2000.
[44] *Frankfurter Allgemeine* (English edition), June 16, 2000, p. 3.
[45] *International Herald Tribune*, June 16, 2000, p. 4.
[46] *Financial Times* (Deutschland), June 16–17, 2000, p. 1.

in Germany to purchase at least 5 percent of electricity from renewable energy sources at a set minimum price, was introduced as a measure to address climate change. The renewable energy feed-in tariffs were linked to the average electricity rates for all electricity consumers in Germany (90 percent for wind and solar, 80 percent for biomass and small hydro, 60 percent for hydro up to 5 MW). This has given small renewable energy producers assurance that they would be given a high enough price for their electricity to make the installation of wind or solar power a reasonable investment.[47] The act was renewed for an additional nine-year period in April 2000. According to the German Association for Promotion of Wind Energy, wind power capacity in Germany in 1993 stood at 337 mW. By 1998 the figure had risen to 2,875 mW.[48] While still a minute fraction of total energy production in Germany, the rapid rise of this renewable energy source is impressive.

The changes brought on by the SPD–Green coalition have not all been received warmly. The Greens, in particular, have fared poorly since the coalition first took office. In their lifetime, the Greens have done much to green politics and to alter Germany's approach to environmental protection. Becoming a coalition partner with the SPD was a remarkable achievement for the party. The compromises they have had to make since becoming a coalition partner, however, raise some questions about the future of the party. The party had to move far from its original platform of non-violence (a principle that some within the party feel was compromised when the Green Party agreed to Germany's participation in the Kosovo peace-keeping operations and subsequently in Afghanistan), environmentalism, grass roots democracy, and anti-nuclear energy. Younger voters do not have the same attraction to the party. Some have dubbed it a one-generation party.[49]

In the September 5, 1999 regional elections in the Saarland and in Brandenburg, the Greens were removed from the Landtag in Saarland and received only about 2 percent of the vote in Brandenburg. The Greens have lost all political power in the new Länder. They may be struggling for political survival in the old Länder as well. The problems that the Greens face is that their role is no longer clear now that they are in government. Internal party divisions between the *fundis* and the *realos* have made it difficult for the Greens to be effective and for the leaders of the party to

---

[47] Andreas Wagner, "Prospects for Wind Energy in Europe: The Challenge of Politics and Administration," *Renewable Energy World* (January 1999), 39–40.
[48] Andreas Wagner, "The Growth of Wind Energy in Europe: An Example of Successful Regulatory and Financial Incentives," German Wind Energy Promotion Association, June 1999.
[49] *De Volkskrant*, June 24, 2000, p. 4.

maintain party backing for their actions. Ironically, the party's success may be its own undoing.

The United States

Over the course of the 1990s, the environmental NGO community worked hard to try to influence the US government position on climate change, biodiversity, sustainable development, and many other issues, but with mixed success. Relatively loose restrictions on campaign financing have worked in the favor of industry. The effectiveness of the US environmental community in the 1970s appears to have led to a backlash against the community that began in the 1980s and has persisted during the 1990s. Despite public opinion polls that show that a sizeable portion of the US public is concerned about the environment and the fact that the US has the largest environmental NGO community in the world, the US government has shown great resistance to participating in numerous international environmental agreements, ranging from the Biodiversity Convention to the Kyoto Protocol.

One of the primary strategies of the professionalized NGO community that is based in Washington, DC, has been to lobby government and run environmental campaigns. But opponents of the environmental community have learned that they can employ similar strategies. Industrial opponents have far more money than do the advocates of environmental policy change. In the 2000 presidential elections, oil and gas companies gave $10 million in political contributions to the Republicans, compared with $4 million to Democrats.[50] Electric utilities and their employees gave $18.4 million to candidates. $12.4 million of this went to the Republican candidates. Industrial opponents of climate change regulations have formed their own networks and coalitions and found powerful images to link their concerns to, such as concerns about energy security, employment, and national sovereignty. They have portrayed NGOs as the enemy of energy stability and economic growth.[51]

Still, the NGO community has struggled to make a difference. NRDC has been among the more active groups dealing with climate change. The NRDC's global warming campaign in 1999 and 2000 included efforts to persuade the administration to take action to reduce emissions from electric power plants and motor vehicles. They also were involved in public education efforts that focused on building public support for action. In April 2001, NRDC President John H. Adams wrote to President Bush

[50] *New York Times*, The Week in Review, March 25, 2001, p. 3.
[51] *Washington Post*, March 25, 2001, p. A5.

urging him to reconsider the White House position on the Kyoto Protocol. NRDC Climate Center Director David Hawkins testified before the Senate Committee on Commerce, Science, and Transportation in the summer of 2001 regarding climate change technology and policy options, arguing that possibilities for emissions reductions exist and urging the Congress to take action.[52]

WWF, which at the time of this writing chairs the CAN, has been very active on the international front. Jennifer Morgan, the director of WWF's Climate Change Campaign has been a regular attendee of the international climate change negotiations and has lobbied hard domestically and abroad to influence climate change and energy policies. Reflecting on the US pull out of Kyoto, Morgan noted "The protocol includes many of the concepts and approaches that the United States has advocated both nationally and internationally for years, including market mechanisms. Having spent time and having worked in Germany, I can tell you the Germans weren't very keen on these mechanisms before Kyoto." She went on to argue that if the US stays out of Kyoto, American companies will be at an economic disadvantage.[53]

EDF has also been active. Their staff, which includes seventy-five full-time scientists, economists, and attorneys, helped pioneer the cap-and-trade system employed in the 1990 Clean Air Act amendments to address sulfur oxide emissions. They also actively lobbied the Clinton and Bush administrations to adopt an emissions trading system to deal with greenhouse gas emissions. Despite the active efforts of these and many other environmental NGOs, however, the Senate showed strong resistance to the Kyoto Protocol and the Bush administration rejected it all together. Unable to influence US government policy, these groups are developing new strategies.

WRI committed to reducing its own CO_2 emissions to zero by 2005. They are also working on greenhouse gas mitigation projects in developing countries and have partnered with industry in a Green Power Market Development Group to help companies reduce their dependence on non-sustainable forms of energy. WRI has also championed the idea of reverse auctions, where government would ask different sectors for investments to reduce CO_2 emissions, and then pay for the cheapest of those reductions.[54]

Locally based NGOs are trying to make a difference as well, and at times are making quite a splash with their efforts. One of the most

---

[52] http://www.nrdc.org/globalWarming/tdh0701.asp.
[53] Interview, August 22, 2001.
[54] Sustainable Energy Institute, "The Sustainable Energy Top Ten Awards," Washington, DC: Sustainable Energy Institute, 2002.

exciting legislative developments related to climate change mitigation efforts in the US was initiated by a San Francisco-based environmental advocacy group, the Bluewater Network. The Bluewater Network helped to craft legislation to reduce greenhouse gas emissions from vehicles. On July 22, 2002 California Governor Gray Davis, a Democrat, signed the law, which grants the California Air Resources Board power to establish "maximum" but "economically feasible" emission standards by 2005. Vehicle manufacturers will then have until 2009 to implement the new standards.[55]

Bluewater Network recognized that it would be possible to affect national policy by pushing for changes at the state level. Indeed, on a number of occasions, California has led the nation by requiring the use of catalytic converters, unleaded gasoline, and hybrid vehicles. For historical reasons, California is the only state in the US that has the right to establish vehicle emissions standards that exceed those set nationally. Once California introduces new legislation other states may then also do the same. More importantly, because California represents 10 percent of the automobile market in the US, legislative change in California will essentially force vehicle manufacturers to develop new, more environmentally friendly vehicles for the entire US market[56]

Another response of US NGOs has been to turn to groups outside of the US in an effort to apply international pressure on the administration and Congress. When the Bush administration pulled out of the Kyoto Protocol, EDF turned its efforts overseas. The organization notes: "With the United States on the sidelines, prospects for the treaty appeared bleak. But Environmental Defense stepped in, working behind the scenes with Japan, Russia, and the European Union... Our executive director Fred Krupp provided key strategic advice to Japanese negotiators." [57] WWF's Jennifer Morgan did the same.

There are also many efforts to crack industrial opposition to the Protocol. Carol Welch of FOE noted the need for US environmental groups to work to find allies if they were to have a hope of influencing the US position leading into the 2002 Johannesburg World Summit on Sustainable Development (which comes a decade after the UNCED). She complained that the US is averse to discussions about multilateral environmental agreements and argued that because "engaging our government on issues of importance will be extremely difficult. As an alternative, we are working in coalition with environmental, human rights, and

---

[55] *Washington Post*, July 22, 2002, p. A1.   [56] *New York Times*, July 22, 2002, p. A1.
[57] http://www.environmentaldefense.org.

labor organizations to pursue corporate accountability measures through legislative processes."[58]

NGOs are doing their best to find coalition partners in industry. EDF has established a Partnership for Climate Change. The idea behind the partnership is to build support among industries for market-based approaches to dealing with emissions. Companies in the partnership report their greenhouse gas emissions publicly and voluntarily set firm targets for emissions reductions. Members include firms like Entergy Corporation, Alcan, BP, DuPont, Ontario Power Generation, Pechiney, Shell International, and Suncor Energy. Some corporate leaders fear that US non-participation in the Kyoto treaty will harm American competitiveness.[59]

Eileen Claussen, director of the Pew Center on Global Climate Change, has organized a Business Environmental Leadership Council bringing together companies that agree that climate change science is sound and argue that businesses must take action to mitigate greenhouse gas emissions. The growing list of companies that have joined this initiative include United Technologies, IBM, Entergy, Weyerhauser, Boeing, and DuPont among others.

The NGO community is also looking for sympathetic ears in Congress and there are some to be found. Congressman Sherwood Boehlert, Republican from New York, for example, has actively supported raising fuel efficiency standards for sports utility vehicles and light trucks, investing in renewable energies, and cutting emissions of air pollutants. Senator Barbara Boxer, Democrat of California, actively opposed drilling in the Arctic National Wildlife Refuge. Several US Congressmen are also actively involved in GLOBE. Congressman James Greenwood serves as president of GLOBE International and Congressman Mark Udall is a vice president. Senator Jeffrey Bingaman, Congressman Sherwood Boehlert, Senator James Jeffords, and Senator John McCain have actively supported measures to curb greenhouse gas emissions.[60] Many of these politicians communicate regularly with NGO activists and are eager as well to see bi-partisan cooperation on environmental legislation.

Yet, it is clear that the environmental community is fighting a difficult battle. Prior to the September 11 terrorist attacks, the environmental community was having some success at portraying the Bush administration as anti-environmental. They focused their campaigns against his

[58] Carol Welch, "US NGOs Face Steep Road to Johannesburg," http://www.foei.org/LINK/LINK 98/2502.html.
[59] http://www.environmentaldefense.org.
[60] Sustainable Energy Institute, "The Sustainable Energy Top Ten Awards."

support of oil drilling in the Arctic National Wildlife Refuge, efforts to rescind numerous environmental executive orders that Clinton passed in his last days in office, and rejection of the Kyoto Protocol. After the attacks, at least for a time, the environmental community backed off. They are now in a process of regrouping and assessing how best to win public support for their cause and to influence the nation's environmental policies.

Conclusion

The comparison of the Japanese, German, and US environmental NGO communities in this chapter suggests that the internationalization of environmental protection has resulted in substantial changes for all of them in terms of priorities, goals, organizational strategies, and their relationship to other societial actors. There are clear differences among them, however, in how they have been affected. For the weak Japanese NGO community, the internationalization of environmental protection has provided many new opportunities and resulted in substantial institutional changes. The community is still weak, but its influence is slowly growing and its relationship to other policy actors is improving. The German NGO community has also benefited to some extent from greater public concern for global environmental issues and the Green Party has used its position in a coalition government to push for substantial green structural change. The future of the Green Party, however, is uncertain. A major challenge for the Green Party will be to redefine its image in the public's mind and to continue to convince the public that its role is still important. The US environmental NGO community has also altered its strategies as a result of the internationalization of environmental policy making. Many groups are beginning to push for non-regulatory approaches to environmental protection and to find industrial coalition partners to strengthen their policy and practical impact. The nature of the US political system where interest groups thrive, however, has meant that they have had to compete for the ear of politicians with other groups, many of which do not share their vision of the world. A major challenge for the environmental NGO community in the US will be to find new ways both to motivate the public and to influence policy makers to act to protect the environment.

9 Domestic politics and the global environment: Japan, Germany, and the US compared

Despite the general shift that is evident in the world's three largest economies towards thinking of environmental issues in more comprehensive, ecological, and global terms, Japan, Germany, and the US continue to have markedly different approaches to dealing with environmental concerns.

Germany is following what could be called the green social welfare state's approach to environmental protection. This approach tries to mitigate between social welfare needs, high unemployment rates, and environmental protection prerogatives through the use of regulations, environmental taxes, and voluntary agreements. The precautionary principle that calls for environmental protection measures to be taken in cases of scientific uncertainty when the cost of inaction could be serious or irreparable damage is increasingly guiding government policy. This is particularly noteworthy considering the very high unemployment rates that plagued Germany during the 1990s.

In sharp contrast the US leaned increasingly away from the use of environmental regulations towards the use of market-based mechanisms (but not taxes) to control pollution and cost-benefit analysis to determine when environmental protection should take precedence over economic activities. Politicians in the US typically avoid discussion of environmental taxes because they fear the electoral consequences of doing so. A polluter pays principle is accepted, but increasingly cost considerations to industry are being weighed. The precautionary principle does not have firm roots in the US and the US is less inclined towards multilateral approaches to environmental protection than Germany.

Japan, caught in a decade-long recession, found itself between Germany and the US. Because of the legacy of the severe pollution incidents in Japan in the 1960s, a polluter pays philosophy is strongly embedded in Japan. Cost-benefit analysis and risk assessment do not have a strong tradition in government planning. The precautionary principle has gained somewhat greater acceptance than in the US, especially during the 1990s. Japan remains less embracing of market-based approaches to pollution control than is the case in the US although this is changing. The Japanese government prefers voluntary approaches to industrial pollution control and when necessary the use of regulations and incentives to guide industrial change. There appears, however, to be a somewhat higher level of support for market-based mechanisms (other than environmental taxes) in Japan than has been the case in Germany although Germany may be warming to the idea of some market-based approaches as well.

These differences were clearly reflected in the international climate change negotiations. Japan sought to play the role of mediator between the positions of the EU and the US, with only limited success. Still, it is noteworthy that in the end Japan championed the position of the US in the negotiations under the Clinton administration – that is the use of flexible mechanisms and market-based approaches to addressing climate change – in a final desperate effort to get the US to return to the fold of the Kyoto Protocol, but sided with Germany and the EU in moving forward on the Kyoto Protocol even without US participation. This solution has been rejected by the Bush administration which argues that an international emissions trading system is untested, and, thus, dangerous. The Bush administration instead has called for long-term technology-based solutions to climate change. The EU views this as the US shirking its responsibility to act now on a pressing global environmental matter. Japan, while concerned about isolating the US, chose to join the EU in working to ratify the Kyoto Protocol even without the US.

The introductory chapter began with three sets of questions regarding the structure and influence of environmental policy communities. This chapter will return to those questions in an effort to understand why Japan, Germany, and the US are approaching global environmental policy problems in rather different ways.

The institutionalization of environmental policy communities

The first question that was raised is why the environmental communities of Japan, Germany, and the US look so different even though Japan and Germany entered the era of national environmental policy making at roughly similar periods of time and both were strongly influenced by US example?

The analysis first showed how very different the environmental policy communities in the three countries really are. In the US, there are large and highly professionalized environmental NGOs and well-financed environmental research institutes but they must compete with other groups in society to win the attention of policy makers on Capitol Hill and in the White House. In Japan, the environmental NGO community is weak and, thus, the Environment Ministry has had to do its best to promote environmental policy change on its own, gaining support where it can from the international community, domestic groups, and at times from environmentally minded politicians. In Germany, the growth of environmental groups was followed by the birth of a Green Party and its election to parliament. This has instilled a direct voice for environmental interests into the political system.

The environmental policy communities in these states also have noticeably different relationships to government and business. Although in all three societies initially the relationships could be characterized as highly polarized and conflictual, over time as environmental policy making became institutionalized in different ways in the three countries, rather different policy-making processes evolved. Germany has developed the most consultative approach among the environmental community, scientists, businesses, and government in part because of the presence of the Green Party in parliament. In Japan there is much use of administrative guidance linking the bureaucracy to industry, but there has been little involvement of environmental NGOs in this informal decision-making process. In the US decision making is highly pluralistic and often quite confrontational. The relationships among government, business, and environmental NGOs are complex, but on the whole appear more confrontational than is found in Japan or Germany, in part because of the higher propensity to rely on the courts in the US.

Institutional factors are very important to understanding which groups in society have power and influence. Institutions channel protest in particular directions and can limit or provide access to governmental decision makers. One set of institutional explanations that can be looked at is the electoral and party systems of the three countries. The parliamentary system and use of proportional representation in elections certainly aided the formation of a Green Party in Germany. As discussed in Chapter 3, half of the seats to the German Bundestag are determined based on proportional representation. Each voter has two votes, one for a candidate and one for a party. Parties that can obtain 5 percent of the vote have a right to send representatives from a party list to the Bundestag. Testing the waters first at the local level, environmental groups made use of the proportional representation system to win representation at the federal level. In Japan's parliamentary system, proportional representation was only introduced in 1994. The complicated medium-sized multi-member constituency system that was in place prior to this time favored candidates over parties. This system may have inhibited new single-issue parties from emerging. The new electoral system in Japan that was first used in 1996 may be more favorable to the formation of new parties, and not just splinter parties, even though the system is still weighted in favor of candidate-oriented voting. The new system uses proportional voting for 200 of 500 electoral seats (the remainder being chosen in single member districts). A party must win 3 percent of the total number of votes to be represented in the Diet. Whether or not this new electoral institution will eventually lead to the birth of a viable Green Party remains to be seen. In the US case, the electoral system is not supportive of third parties at the federal level. While third parties have made a splash in presidential elections, such as Ross Perot's Reform Party and Ralph Nader's Green Party, they tend not to survive beyond one or two election cycles. Moreover, in the US case, because of the campaign finance system, interest groups with money can have disproportionate influence with Congress. This gives industry an advantage. These differences in the electoral systems certainly influenced the strategies of environmental activists and the organizational forms they took.

Also very important were the institutional opportunities and barriers presented to environmental activists. Initially, the development of environmental movements appears to have been greatly influenced by how the state initially responded to grass roots activism. In Japan's case the government was initially slow to respond to citizen demands, but then once it did pass legislation, it was relatively effective in implementation efforts. This was done through a combination of sticks and carrots. Legislation was introduced requiring companies to pay into a pool for the pollution they emitted. This is a strong case of a polluter pays principle being implemented. The money was used to pay for the health damages to pollution victims. Industries were also given subsidies and tax incentives to promote the introduction of pollution control and energy efficient technologies. To reduce dependence on imported oil a nuclear program that provided subsidies to communities that accepted the construction of a plant was initiated. MITI also shifted the country away from the use of high sulfur content oil and promoted measures to enhance energy efficiency in industry and in products.

But also important were the efforts on the part of the state to eradicate extra-parliamentary opposition by channeling protest in new directions. The state maintained and erected substantial institutional barriers to the formation of a more vibrant environmental civil society. Laws governing the non-profit sector made it extremely difficult for groups to obtain non-profit status. Moreover, there are no major private foundations to provide resources to environmental groups and think tanks. The need to get ministerial approval to incorporate as a legal entity meant that many potential non-profit groups feared being coopted by the government. The Japanese government was remarkably successful in taming the citizens' movements, quieting the courts, and taking environmental policy matters back into its own hands. As a result, throughout much of the 1970s and 1980s, environmental policy making was primarily conducted by the bureaucracy with only minimal input from politicians, citizens, and think tanks.

Germany provides a radically different example of the development of an environmental policy community from that of Japan. An important factor appears to be the different response of the German state to early environmental and anti-nuclear activism. In the early 1970s, locally organized citizens' movements began to reorganize and form national umbrella organizations and environmental groups. They were greatly aided in doing this by financial support from the state. The umbrella organization, BBU, for example, received 45 percent of its funding from government subsidies in the early 1980s.[1] German groups could relatively easily incorporate as not-for-profit organizations and obtain financial support for their activities from the state and the churches. Thus, unlike their Japanese counterparts, they were not almost exclusively dependent on members for support.

Unlike the citizens' groups in Japan, they also began to link environmental concerns with their opposition to nuclear energy and militarism, their support for women's equality, and their desire to see a more social welfare-oriented political system. When the state failed either to implement effectively many of the environmental laws passed in the 1970s (in part an issue of federalism, in part a shift in the priorities of the SPD after the oil crisis) or to respond to the demands of the massive anti-nuclear and peace protests of the late 1970s, the activists chose another route. They began to form green lists in local elections and then eventually a Green Party at the federal level.

The electoral success of the party had profound implications on environmental policy making in Germany. Environmental interests gained a direct voice in parliamentary debates and by the end of the decade Germany was emerging as a global environmental leader on a number of policy fronts.

In the US case, the courts and later Congress provided environmental groups with important new rights. Environmental groups in the US were aided by the amendments to the US tax laws which made it relatively easy for groups to incorporate as not-for-profit organizations even while

---

[1] Kriesi, "The Organizational Structure of New Social Movements in a Political Context," p. 178.

engaging in some lobbying activities. This provided them with important benefits, like the possibility of receiving contributions that are tax deductible for the donor and favorable postage rates for reaching out to the public. Environmental groups could turn both to members and to large private financial institutions for donations; they were also eligible to receive governmental grants and contracts. US groups also won important rights of standing in court to sue on behalf of environmental interests. Using these new rights, over the 1970s and 1980s environmental groups became increasingly professionalized and diversified. Some groups, like NRDC, focused their strategies on legal action against government and corporations that were believed to be harming the environment. Others like EDF focused on economic expertise and influencing the legislative process. Yet others like NWF and the Sierra Club focused on expanding their membership while campaigning, educating, and lobbying Congress.

The success of the environmental movement in the US was in part a result of government support for non-profit activities and the access of NGOs to the courts at a time of high public concern for the environment. Membership numbers declined in the late 1970s but the movement regained momentum when it mobilized to counter efforts by the Reagan administration to roll back environmental regulations, reduce the size of the EPA, and reduce some of the tax benefits accorded environmental groups. This was part of a larger push towards deregulation and reduction of the size of government in the US.

The success of the environmental community also increased their competition from industrial groups that formed counter-lobbies in the form of large corporate associations and coalitions, the largest of which is the GCC (which appears to have disbanded in the beginning of 2002 because it achieved its goal of keeping the US out of Kyoto and because some key industrial supporters quit the coalition). While US environmental groups are very wealthy compared to the groups in Germany and Japan, their wealth cannot match that of large industrial coalitions and associations. There also is division within the US environmental NGO community regarding the extent to which regulatory or market-based approaches to environmental protection should be advocated.

In sum, we see that several important institutional factors influenced movement development in these three countries. Both formal and informal institutional structures can facilitate or impede the formation of environmental and other special interests. The electoral and party systems in a country can influence the potential for social movements to reorganize as single-issue parties. Tax laws, laws governing the formation of non-profit entities, and financial resources provided by the state also can strongly influence a movement's potential to transform itself from informally organized citizens' groups to professionally organized interest groups. Less formal institutional structures can also make a difference. The Japanese propensity to use administrative guidance, for example, links governmental ministries closely with economic interests. The close networks that exist between government and industry further strengthen such ties. NGOs are kept out of this informal decision-making arena.

Environmental policy communities and the policy approaches of states

A second question that was raised in the introductory chapter was whether differences in the organizational form and strength of the environmental communities in Japan, Germany, and the US help explain environmental policy outcome? The answer is mixed. Despite the many differences in the structures, capacity, and goals of their environmental movements, all three countries have pursued generally similar changes in their environmental programs within a few years of each other. They all were addressing acid rain by the early 1990s. All three signed the Montreal Protocol in 1987. They all signed the FCCC in 1992. This lends support to theories that point to the importance of diffusion mechanisms and learning processes that can cut across political and societal boundaries regardless of political system type and the strength of environmental movements.

Moreover, the comparison suggests that environmental movements are not always the driving forces behind environmental policy change. There were a number of cases examined in this book, such as the stratospheric ozone depletion case in Japan and Germany, the introduction of the environmental program of Germany in the 1970s, and the introduction of a global climate mitigation program in Japan in 1990 where environmental groups played little role in policy change. Also of considerable note is that the country with the biggest and richest NGOs in the world – the US – has taken less domestic action on climate change than the country with the smallest NGO community of the advanced industrialized states – Japan. Thus, the strength of environmental movements is not sufficient to help us understand specific environmental policy outcomes.

Yet, there are also many reasons to believe that the relative power of an environmental community and its access to decision makers does matter. This book has focused on these differences. The strength, organizational form, and access to governmental decision-making forum can influence greatly the broad policy orientations of a state as well as, in some cases, specific policy outcomes.

Germany

The German approach to environmental protection reflects both the dominance of a social market philosophy and the strength of environmental groups and the Green Party. Underpinning the social market philosophy is the belief that governments have a responsibility to intervene in the market to redistribute wealth and to protect citizens from market externalities. The belief is that markets will not address all social needs and thus, the government must intervene to help promote a greater degree of equality in society. In 1986, the SPD in a comprehensive review of its policy program insisted that economic growth should be linked to "quality of life" and called for a new compromise between state intervention and market forces in order to address environmental damage, the monopolization of the economy, social problems, and unemployment.[2]

Two years after the UNCED, under a CDU government, the notion of governmental responsibility for environmental protection was incorporated by amendment into the Basic Law. The revised Article 20 reads: "The State, aware of its responsibility for present and future generations, shall protect the natural sources of life within the framework of the constitutional order through [the] legislature and in accordance with the law and principles of justice, the executive and the judiciary."[3]

This shift in thinking and change in institutions in Germany has been gradual; it has not been marked by a "punctuation" in an otherwise static set of institutions. Rather there has been a slow accumulation of policy and institutional changes that have helped green German society.

In the 1970s, Germany followed the leads set by the US and Japan and introduced comprehensive environmental legislation. Yet, as a result of the oil shocks of 1973 and 1979, priority remained with economic development rather than pollution control. When scientists first warned that acid rain was a problem in Europe, Germany paid little attention. When scientists warned that acid rain was causing widespread forest damage within Germany, they started to care. Acid rain emerged in Germany at the same time that the Green Party was gaining political ground at the federal level. The combined impact was to create a great public swell in concern for environmental issues. The Chernobyl nuclear accident of 1985, the discovery of the "hole" in the ozone layer also in 1985, and scientific warnings about the climate change "catastrophe," combined to create a growing sense of concern about the destruction humans were

---

[2] Elim Papadakis, "Green Issues and Other Parties: Themenklau or New Flexibility," in Eva Kolinsky, ed., *The Greens in West Germany: Organisation and Policy Making* (Oxford: BERG, 1989), p. 69.

[3] http://www.bmu.de/UNBericht/parta3.htm.

causing to the planet. This provided considerable fodder for the Green Party and has helped make the public and government more receptive to the idea that Germany must work to reduce the size of its ecological footprint.

Beginning in the early 1980s there was a marked shift in German attitudes towards environmental protection more generally and the Green Party capitalized on this. Thus, from 1983 onward, Germany began to play a more progressive environmental role within the EC and after the Chernobyl nuclear accident, also globally. After the discovery of the "hole" in the ozone layer, Germany began to be more forceful within the EC in negotiations on the use and production of ozone depleting chemicals. When global climate change became a political issue in the late 1980s, Germany was among the first nations to commit to domestic greenhouse gas emissions reduction measures. It has been a leading voice in international climate change negotiations calling on the industrialized north to take substantial steps to reduce greenhouse gas emissions domestically. It has also introduced domestic policies to promote the develoment of a more sustainable socio-economic system.

Critical to this process was the "greening" of the established political parties. In fact, many of the policy changes for which Germany is best known, such as introduction of the Large Combustion Plant Directive of 1983, waste reduction and recycling programs, and plans to reduce domestic greenhouse gas emissions announced in 1990, occurred under the conservative CDU government of Helmut Kohl. The mere existence of the small Green Party and an environmentally conscious public was sufficient to make both the CDU and the SPD more aware of environmental issues. Although the CDU remained steadfast in its support of nuclear energy and its environmental programs did not go as far as some in the country would have wanted, Germany emerged a leader on numerous environmental matters within Europe. The contrast with the approach of the Reagan administration to environmentalists in the US is dramatic.

Also important was the input of scientific information and programatic ideas into the policy process by Germany's many environmental NGOs, think tanks, and scientific groups. Here a big difference can be seen with the case of Japan in the 1980s and early 1990s. Japan had to borrow scientific information and policy ideas from abroad when stratospheric ozone depletion and global climate change were first being discussed. There was almost no domestic capacity within the bureaucracy or the environmental community to address these issues. Initially, Germany's environmental NGOs also were focused primarily on domestic environmental issues, but by the mid- to late 1980s, they rapidly shifted focus to include international and global environmental issues. They had more capacity to make this kind of transition than did their much smaller Japanese NGO counterparts.

The establishment in Germany of special Enquete Commissions to bring together politicians from all political parties with scientists, economists, and other experts to discuss the science, politics, and economics of stratospheric ozone depletion and global climate change was another important development. These commissions were given broad authority to develop a general political understanding of the seriousness of these issues and to formulate policy proposals. They also helped to build consensus across the political parties on the need for policy action. In the process, Germany came out with a far more ambitious climate action plan than other large industrial powers.

Germany has also shown an ability to stand up to the US in international environmental negotiations in a way that still proves difficult for Japan to do. In many ways, Germany has shown considerably more foreign policy adeptness than Japan. Even though the two countries do not differ that much from each other in terms of policy performance, Germany has carved for itself an image as a global environmental leader. Japan is struggling to do the same, but has been less successful in its efforts. This is in large part because whereas Germany has been willing to make bold policy proposals, Japan has a tendency to remain ambiguous and to wait until the final moment to present its policy stance. This reflects Japan's strong ties to the US, its reluctance to upset the US, domestic political fragmentation, and a general political belief within the bureaucracy that goals once stated need to be met. Germany, moreover, has found it easier to build domestic consensus on environmental issues than is true in either Japan or the US. This certainly has much to do with the disproportionately large influence that the relatively small Green Party has.

Nevertheless, despite the substantial greening of German policies suggested by these examples, there are still many clear signs of a conservative politics in operation. Germany failed to introduce speed limits on its autobahns despite environmental and safety concerns. Germany's nature conservation and soil protection policies also remained weak because of the strength of agricultural, industrial, and transportation interests. There are also a number of cases where economic revitalization was given precedence over environmental protection, such as with the development planning simplification law and the law on investment facilitation and residential property of 1993.[4] There have also been several instances where the European Court of Justice found that German environmental law

[4] Heinrich Pehle, "Germany: Domestic Obstacles to an International Forerunner," in Mikael Skou Andersen and Duncan Lieferink (eds.), *European Environmental Policy: The Pioneers* (Manchester: Manchester University Press, 1997), p. 182.

was not in compliance with European Community environmental law. This was particularly true in relation to environmental protection in agricultural areas.[5] Thus, Germany has made the most substantial changes of the three countries in its policy direction, but interests protecting the status quo are still very powerful.

Japan

Over the course of the late 1980s and 1990s, Japan went from being an international environmental policy laggard among the industrialized countries to being one of the primary financiers of overseas environmental programs and a more active player in international environmental negotiations. In the late 1980s, Japan's international environmental record was being harshly criticized in both journalistic and more academic reports. Japan was singled out as the world's largest importer of tropical hardwoods. It was attacked for its drift net fishing practices, whaling, and trade in endangered wildlife products. It was criticized for exporting polluting industries to Southeast Asia.[6]

Now Japan is receiving some recognition for its "greener" politics, most recently in the 2002 OECD Environmental Performance Review of Japan which suggested that Japan had done much to deal with air pollution, energy efficiency, and recycling.[7] Richard Forrest, an environmental activist and specialist on Japanese international environmental policies who was always very critical of Japanese ODA, now concedes that Japan is making some strides in this area although he still terms this "'omiyage' diplomacy – gift offerings of aid and initiatives at international meetings to please international opinion."[8] Helmut Weidner suggests that while there are problems with Japan's approach to the environment – as can be seen by its importation of tropical timbers, its relatively high emissions of CO_2, and its neglect of pollution control technology in overseas investments in the 1980s – in the 1990s the Japanese government has shown that it wants to address these problems in cooperation with industry. He concludes, however, that in comparison the EC still appears more

---

[5] Molly E. Hall, "European Integration vs. State Sovereignty: The European Court of Justice and Harmonization of Germany's Environmental Law," in Gale Mattox, Geoffrey D. Oliver, and Jonathan B. Tucker, *Germany in Transition: A Unified Nation's Search for Identity* (Boulder: Westview Press, 1999), pp. 39–52.

[6] See, for example, Richard A. Forrest, "Japanese Economic Assistance and the Environment: The Need for Reform," National Wildlife Federation, November 1989; *Time*, July 10, 1989, pp. 50–2, and October 23, 1989, pp. 58–60; *New Scientist*, September 16, 1989, p. 24; and *New York Times*, July 31, 1992, p. A7.

[7] OECD, *Environmental Performance Review: Japan* (Paris: OECD, 2002).

[8] Richard A. Forrest, "Japan and Sustainable Development: The Long Road from Rio," in James Feinerman and Richard A. Forrest, *Japan and the Global Environment*, Woodrow Wilson Center Asia Program Occasional Paper, no. 50, February 25, 1993, p. 9.

proactive than Japan. Japan's global environmental politics, he suggests, may still be in a phase of "symbolic politics."[9] The Japan Council for Sustainable Development formed in 1996 assessed progress that Japan has made in achieving sustainable development. They found that many new efforts have been initiated by a variety of actors to promote sustainable development, but that progress remains limited. Current socio-economic conditions continue to pose problems.[10]

Japan's environmental policy community in the 1980s was largely centered in the bureaucracy and was focused primarily on domestic matters. Japan excelled in the implementation of environmental policies that could be made to fit with the interests of the business community. It was weaker in areas like environmental impact assessments, where support from industrial interests and the economic ministries was not forthcoming. There has been much destructive development in the country in order to boost the leisure industry, for example, and this has harmed rivers and coastal areas and threatened biological diversity. The construction industry in Japan remains immensely powerful and environmental protection has not been a major concern of this industry.[11]

Still, it is quite fascinating that in Japan's case, changes to the country's environmental policy orientation in the late 1980s were largely in response to the "greening" of traditionally "brown" thinkers in the Japanese government. The formation of the Montreal Protocol was a turning point. This transition in the perception of environmental policy on the part of some conservative politicians, industry, and the bureaucracy was not of the same hue as that embraced by the Green Party in Germany. It was not really a call for the development of an ecologically sustainable society, but rather the acceptance of environmental protection as a good area for foreign policy activity and possibly for business as well. Japan's political leaders and bureaucrats found a way to link global environmental matters to the country's search for ways to play a larger global role and to use past success with air pollution control and energy efficiency gains to develop new markets and industries in global environmental protection. There are also severe resource and space constraints in Japan that make a more sustainable socio-economic system a goal that Japan has but little choice in moving towards.

Numerous new domestic environmental laws were passed in the 1990s. These include a new recycling promotion law, a law to reduce NO_x

---

[9] Helmut Weidner, "Globale Umweltherausforderungen," in Hanns W. Maull (ed.), *Japan und Europa: Getrennte Welten?* (Frankfurt: Campus Verlag, 1993), pp. 434–55. See also Weidner, *Basiselemente einer erfolgreichen Umweltpolitik.*

[10] Japan Council for Sustainable Development, *Japan Report for Rio +5 Process.*

[11] Brian Woodall, *Japan under Construction: Corruption, Politics, and Public Works* (Berkeley: University of California Press, 1996).

emissions from transportation, a law regulating the import and export of hazardous wastes, a law for the conservation of endangered species, a law for the rational use of energy, and another for the promotion of the development and introduction of alternative energy. An important change was the formulation of the new Basic Environment Law in 1994 and the subsequent development of an Environment Basic Plan that aim at developing a more sustainable socio-economic system. In 1997 an environmental impact assessment law was formulated and after the Kyoto Conference, a Law Concerning the Promotion of Measures to Cope with Global Warming was passed in the fall of 1998. The law requires central and local governments to come up with plans to reduce their own greenhouse gas emissions and local governments and businesses to formulate plans for how they will limit greenhouse emissions and develop carbon sinks in their spheres of activity.

There is now greater involvement by Japan in efforts to address acid rain in Asia. It has, for example, initiated research into acid rain deposition in East Asia. It also funds energy efficiency improvement and pollution control projects in China and Southeast Asia through METI's Green Aid Plan and through regular ODA channels.

There is still considerable skepticism about whether the changes in Japanese environmental laws and institutions are really all that extensive or deep. My view is that the changes are real and that they are leading to important institutional and normative changes. Institutional change, however, is difficult. Old routines die hard. Thus, while many new norms, philosophies, and organizations have been created that are heightening global environmental awareness in Japan, and strengthening the possibilities for environmentally sound policy choices, there are still many obstacles to overcome.

Japan now plays an important and far more visible role in global environmental protection than it did in the 1980s. It is also becoming somewhat bolder in international environmental negotiations as witnessed by its decision not to join the US in opposing the Kyoto Protocol. Yet, until Japan's environmental NGO community matures and more environmental think tanks form, Japan is unlikely to become a leader in the development of new environmental policy ideas. Instead, today, we see the Japanese environmental community increasingly looking towards Europe both for policy ideas and how best to strengthen the position of environmental voices in domestic decision-making institutions.

The United States

The US is commonly recognized as having been an environmental innovator in the 1970s. US environmental laws and institutions became models for consideration by Japan, Germany, and many other countries. The development of a strong environmental NGO community in the 1970s and capacity building in environmental research helped the US to stay at the forefront of new environmental policy development and environmental research into the 1980s. Yet, at the same time, the US was not always a leader in implementation, a reflection both of its federal structure and the widespread use of litigation as a means to block enforcement of regulations. As noted above, Japan did better than the US in reducing air pollution in the 1970s and in improving energy efficiency.

Furthermore, there was a backlash in the US in the 1980s against the regulatory successes of the environmental community. Industry began to complain about the huge number of environmental regulations governing them, the complexity of regulatory requirements, and the high costs and inflexibility of many of the regulations that often delayed or prevented them from pursuing economic activities. Anti-regulatory forces began to organize to counter the successes of the environmental community. This anti-regulatory stance gained the support of the Reagan administration, which tried to weaken the Environmental Protection Agency and undo many environmental regulations.

Although the George H. W. Bush administration tried to distance itself from the Reagan administration's approach to environmental management by enacting the 1990 Clean Air Act amendments to control sulfur dioxide emissions, his administration was cool towards efforts to bring the US into several international environmental agreements. Bush decided only at the very last minute that he would attend the UNCED and then only on the condition that any agreement to come out of the meeting would not set greenhouse gas emissions reduction standards. The administration remained opposed to the Biodiversity Convention on the grounds that it would harm the pharmaceutical industry.

The Republican-dominated Congress in the mid-1990s also questioned the necessity of extensive use of regulations to control industry for environmental reasons. They tried to roll back environmental programs and policies and to limit US involvement in international environmental agreements. Throughout much of the 1990s policy gridlock ensued between the Clinton administration, which was more sympathetic to the use of environmental taxes and regulations, and a Congress that saw these as problematic. Thus, although the US has perhaps the strongest environmental NGO community in the world, continues to lead the world in environmental research, and is the largest exporter of pollution control equipment, it entered the 1990s with an uneven environmental record.

In the area of acid rain abatement, the US trailed behind Japan and Germany. Although the US played an important role in scientific understanding of the long-range transport of acidic compounds, there was no political action on acid rain in the 1980s. Policy gridlock prevented action despite the active campaigning by environmental groups and scientists on this issue. The mid-west states that depended on coal for power production were pitted against the New England states and Canadian provinces, which perceived themselves as the victims of midwest pollution. The issue was debated for years within Congress, but there were strong coalitions on both sides of this issue and no action ensued during the 1980s.

Protection of the stratospheric ozone layer was also jeopardized by the changes in the US approach to environmental protection under the first of Reagan's two terms. In this case, the US, which was a major producer of ozone depleting substances and which had played an important role in pushing internationally for the formation of an international agreement that would control the production and consumption of ozone depleting substances in the 1970s, lost its enthusiasm for the issue in the early 1980s. This was both because of scientific uncertainty at the time about the seriousness of ozone depletion and the markedly different policy orientation of the Reagan administration towards environmental issues compared with earlier administrations. Reagan's first appointee as Environment Agency director showed no interest in the issue.

The US position became more proactive once a new Environment Agency director more supportive of US involvement in international environmental protection had been appointed in response to strong public discontent with Reagan's appointees to the EPA and the Interior Department, the emergence of new scientific evidence, industrial concern about unilateral policy action, and industrial willingness to find substitute chemicals to CFCs. In the period between 1985 and 1987, the US campaigned hard internationally for the formation of the Montreal Protocol.

In the US case, there is a distinct difference between the leadership role that the US played in the case of the Montreal Protocol and withdrawal from the Kyoto Protocol. What explains this difference? It is not the different level of interest that environmental groups showed on these two issues. If anything, there has been much more environmental NGO activity on climate change than was the case with stratospheric ozone depletion, although it may be the case that NGOs have been less willing in the climate change case to target individual consumers as the root cause of the problem. In the ozone layer case, NGOs targeted CFC consumption behavior more aggressively than they have targeted the individual consumer's reliance on energy.

Perhaps, the most important difference between these two cases has been the position of industry. In the case of stratospheric ozone depletion, when the largest CFC producer, DuPont, acknowledged the need to control ozone depleting chemicals (in part a reflection of its ability to produce substitutes), other industries felt compelled to follow suit. The climate change case involves many more industries making a search for substitutes (such as renewable energy) far more complicated.

Despite Vice President Albert Gore's personal expertise and concern with climate change, the Clinton White House followed a cautious approach in the international negotiations largely because of opposition to the Kyoto Protocol in the Senate. In the hopes of eventually gaining Senate support which is necessary for a treaty to be ratified, the US negotiating team pushed for the right to rely heavily on a system that would permit emissions trading and the use of joint implementation to meet domestic emissions reduction goals. Under these systems, the US would essentially gain credit towards its own emissions reduction targets by cleaning up emissions in developing countries. The Senate, however, was not swayed. Opposition to the agreement remained strong, and under a Bush White House the US abandoned the treaty. The Bush administration further attacked the Kyoto Protocol mechanisms (especially a cap and trade permit system) questioning whether such a system could work. Instead, the administration is proposing that industry be given incentives to develop a new generation of technologies in the long run, ten or twenty years down the road, rather than investing those dollars in end-of-the-pipe type mitigation efforts.

What this suggests is that in the pluralist US political system where a strong liberal market philosophy also holds sway, it has been difficult for environmentalists to get their issues on to the agenda unless industry can find win-win solutions. Thus, when environmental activists can find industrial coalition partners, there is potential for policy change. Alternatively, there has to be very strong public support backing environmentalists in order to get politicians to listen to their concerns.

Domestic institutions and actors and global environmental ideas

The third question raised in Chapter 1 is how participation in global environmental decision making is influencing the goals, strategies, and positions of domestic environmental policy actors. Ideas, actors, and institutions are not static; they are dynamic. When major new ideas about global environmental problems were introduced to the public and policy makers in the late 1980s, new actors were pulled into the policy-making process in all three countries. New actors and coalitions of actors, in turn, have tried to influence how environmental matters are framed and the kinds of policy solutions that are pursued. In some cases, they have even pushed for a change to existing institutional arrangements in order to open further the policy-making process or to alter existing policy routines.

Germany

In Germany in the 1990s there was some continuation of the shift towards more globally oriented environmental thinking that had started to take root in the previous decade. Environmental groups launched climate change campaigns and began to address sustainable development issues. New environmental think tanks were established to deal with global environmental issues. The government established Enquete Commissions to deal with issues related to the implementation of climate change policies. The most sweeping structural changes were associated with the Red–Green coalition's introduction of ecological taxes that are meant to help lead German society in the direction of ecological modernization.

The effects of global environmental policy ideas on German environmental programs were checked to some extent, however, by the social and economic costs of unification. Unification was an event of huge political significance. Great efforts have been put into reunifying a nation long divided by ideological differences, economic disparity, and military tensions. The financial and psychological costs of this effort have proved far bigger than anyone initially predicted. They cost Kohl his position as chancellor in 1998.

The electoral loss of the CDU in 1998 provided the SPD and the Green Party with a window of opportunity to shift policy direction in Germany in a more environmental direction. Kohl's plans to reduce greenhouse gas emissions relied heavily on voluntary agreements with industry and programs to promote the introduction of renewable energies. The SPD/Green Party added new elements to this plan. They reached agreement with industry on plans to phase out nuclear energy and introduced a multiyear phase in of new eco taxes that will make polluters pay for the emissions they put into the atmosphere. They are also expanding programs to promote the use of renewable energies by industries and households. While these changes are still limited in their real impact, they are an important step in moving the German economic structure in a greener direction.

One of the biggest challenges for the German Green Party in the future will be to figure out how, and whether, it can continue as a single-issue non-traditional party based on a philosophy of democracy and equality. Compromises made by the Green Party leadership in its position as a coalition partner have angered some *fundis* who believe the party has strayed too far from the original goals of the party's founders. Voters also appear somewhat disillusioned with the party.

Japan

By taking on global environmental matters in the early 1990s, Japan's political leaders ushered in a period of policy change and institution building that they had probably not anticipated. Environmental policy making has become increasingly pluralist.

In order effectively to negotiate at the international level, Japan's bureaucracy had rapidly to expand its capacities to address global scale environmental issues. This has included the injection of money and human resources into global environmental protection offices, the reorganization of existing research facilities, and the creation of new ones to address regional and global environmental problems. Japanese businesses also have felt pressured to become more sensitive towards environmental matters. Many have sought environmental certification under the ISO 14,001 environment management series and have submitted voluntary action plans to reduce energy and resource inputs.

The government, out of concerns for its foreign relations, chose in the early 1990s to pursue global environmental matters. An unintended consequence of this decision was that the state placed pressure upon itself to undo the institutional barriers that it had created to the formation of a vibrant civil society. An advanced industrialized society like Japan that wants to be recognized internationally as an environmental leader needs an environmental NGO community. Initially, the state's interest in NGOs appeared to be superficial. North American and European countries had many NGOs accompanying formal delegations to international conferences; thus, the Japanese government too would have to encourage NGOs to participate to at least some extent in international environmental policy making. Over time, the state has started to recognize that NGOs can actually provide them with valuable resources, such as information about societal perceptions, insights into developments among environmental communities in other parts of the world, policy alternatives, and implementation capacity.

Pressures from the international community and from the small activist community also helped force the Japanese government to take some steps to improve the condition of environmental groups, making it easier for them to obtain non-profit status. There is now considerably more dialogue among government, industry, and NGOs on environmental matters than was true in the past. This is a radical break with the past. This development speaks to Baumgartner and Jones's idea that participant expansion as the result of changing understandings of issues can result in larger changes to institutional structures.[12]

While there is growing support in Japan across all actor groups for playing a more proactive role in global environmental protection, divisions within the bureaucracy remain. The Environment Ministry and the small, but growing environmental NGO community has fairly consistently espoused positions similar to that found in Germany on matters ranging from climate change to the promotion of non-nuclear renewable energies. They also found some sympathy in MoT. MoFA too has been eager for Japan to play a more active role. At times, these ministries found support for their positions among environmental *zoku* members in the LDP, such as when Japan became host of the Kyoto Conference. METI and many industries, which initially were resistant to the idea of hosting the Kyoto Conference, have gone beyond the US in implementing domestic measures to address climate change, but side with the US on many issues as well. METI is concerned that the denuclearization movement that has been so successful in Germany will find its way to Japan. METI does not believe that Japan's economy can function without nuclear energy because of its lack of domestic energy sources. METI is also concerned that because of high energy efficiency levels, cutting back on greenhouse gas emissions to the levels targeted at Kyoto will be too expensive for the country's flailing economy.

Japan's position has fluctuated between that of Germany and the US depending on the strength of the domestic coalitions that formed around the Environment Ministry or METI. When the Environment Ministry could find allies in other ministries and in the LDP it could influence the direction of Japan's environmental programs. Without such support, the Environment Agency and the still weak NGO community have proved too weak to overcome METI's more conservative stance. A case in point was the failure to push through a carbon tax. Yet, a perceived crisis, like the Bush administration's decision to pull out of Kyoto, for a time, at least, pulled the entire community together in calling upon the US to reconsider.

The United States

The US has traditionally been the pacesetter on environmental policy making internationally. In general, the US has shown less interest or

---

[12] Baumgartner and Jones, *Agendas and Instability in American Politics.*

willingness to "learn" from other societies or to be influenced by developments overseas.[13] The resistance in some powerful quarters in the government to active US involvement in international environmental agreements stems in part from an unwillingness to weaken US sovereignty or to bend to the demands of other countries. There is also the perception that the US should lead and that what the US does the rest of the world should accept. As a large country, both politically and economically, the US is better able to act independently and to resist efforts to be drawn into multilateral agreements that it does not champion.

Yet, even the US can be influenced by international developments. Environmental NGOs reorganized in the 1990s creating new global environmental offices in order to be better able to deal with international environmental issues like climate change, biodiversity loss, and tropical deforestation. They also formed international networks to strengthen their ability to influence international developments as well as domestic politics. They are now struggling with the question of how to improve their domestic political effectiveness.

The decision of the EU and Japan to move forward on the Kyoto Protocol without the US has placed tremendous pressure on the US to reconsider its policy position. In an effort to shift the US administration's position, some industries have formed coalitions in support of domestic efforts to reduce greenhouse gas emissions and to pressure the administration to reconsider its position on the Kyoto Protocol. Moreover, although the US sat on the sidelines at Marrakech, some domestic initiatives to address carbon dioxide emissions were launched at the local level. Mayor Daley, for example, announced that Chicago and Mexico City would work together in the design of the Chicago Climate Exchange (CCX). The CCX will be a voluntary market for trading emissions of greenhouse gases and is to be funded through $1.1 million in grants from the Chicago-based Joyce Foundation.[14] Chicago, home to the Chicago Board of Trade, sees a potential big industry in a carbon emissions trading system.

On July 22, 2002 the California legislature enacted a new law that will require vehicle manufacturers to reduce greenhouse gas emissions coming from tailpipes. California is the largest automobile market in the US so the impact of this legislation will reverberate throughout the country.

[13] Richard N. L. Andrews also makes this point in "The United States," in Jänicke and Weidner (eds.), *National Environmental Policies*, pp. 25–43.
[14] *Ascribe Newswire*, November 1, 2001.

In sum, we see that even in the US the globalization of environmental protection is having important impacts on domestic policies and institutional structures although the impact is less dramatic than in Germany or, especially, Japan.

Conclusion

In conclusion, I argue that greater attention needs to be paid to how domestic institutions influence the larger environmental policy approaches of states since this, in turn, heavily influences the possibilities for international environmental cooperation. More research is necessary to understand what the implications of differing national approaches to environmental policy management mean for the environment domestically and internationally. Research is also needed on the effects of the different environmental management models employed in the developed states on the choices made by developing countries as they are faced by increasingly serious environmental problems of their own.

Bibliography

ARTICLES, BOOKS, GOVERNMENT AND NGO DOCUMENTS

Ackerman, Susan Rose, *Controlling Environmental Policy: The Limits of Public Law in Germany and the United States* (New Haven: Yale University Press, 1995).

Agrawala, Shardul and Steinar Andresen, "The United States in the Climate Treaty Negotiations," *Global Governance* 5 (1999), 457–82.

Andrews, Richard N. L., "The United States," in Martin Jänicke and Helmut Weidner (eds.), *National Environmental Policies: A Comparative Study of Capacity-Building* (Berlin: Springer Verlag, 1997), pp. 25–43.

Antunes, Jorge, "Regime Effectiveness, Joint Implementation and Climate Change Policy," in Paul G. Harris (ed.), *Climate Change and American Foreign Policy* (New York: St. Martin's Press, 2000), pp. 183–6.

Assembly of Mathematical and Physical Sciences, National Research Council, *Halocarbons: Environmental Effects of Chlorofluoromethane Release* (Washington, DC: National Academy of Sciences, 1976).

Barnes, Douglas, "Established Parties and the Environment in the Federal Republic of Germany: The Politics of Responding to a New Issue," paper presented at the American Political Science Association Annual Meeting, Palmer House Hilton, September 3–6, 1992.

Barrett, Brendan F. D. and Riki Therivel, "EIA in Japan: Environmental Protection v. Economic Growth," *Land Use Policy* (July 1989), 217–31.

Environmental Policy and Impact Assessment in Japan (London: Routledge, 1991).

Baumgartner, Frank R. and Jones, Brian D., *Agendas and Instability in American Politics* (Chicago: University of Chicago Press, 1993).

Benedick, Richard, *Ozone Diplomacy: New Directions in Safeguarding the Planet* (Cambridge: Harvard University Press, 1991).

Berger, Thomas, *Cultures of Antimilitarism: National Security in Germany and Japan* (Baltimore: Johns Hopkins University Press, 1998).

Beuermann, Christiane, "Germany: Regulations and the Precautionary Principle," in William Lafferty and James Meadowcraft (eds.), *Implementing Sustainable Development: Strategies and Initiatives in High Consumption Societies* (Oxford: Oxford University Press, 2000), pp. 85–111.

Beuermann, Christiane and Jill Jäger, "Climate Change Politics in Germany: How Long Will Any Double-Dividend Last?" in Tim O'Riordan and Jill

Jäger (eds.), *Politics of Climate Change* (New York: Routledge, 1996), pp. 186–227.

Bodansky, Daniel, "Prologue to the Climate Change Convention," in Irving M. Mintzer and J. A. Leonard (eds.), *Negotiating Climate Change* (Cambridge: Cambridge University Press, 1994), pp. 45–76.

Boehmer-Christiansen, Sonja and Jim Skea, *Acid Politics: Environmental and Energy Policies in Britain and Germany* (London: Bolhaven Press, 1991).

Borione, Delphine and Jean Ripert, "Exercising Common but Differentiated Responsibility," in Irving M. Mintzer and J. A. Leonard (eds.), *Negotiating Climate Change* (Cambridge: Cambridge University Press, 1994), pp. 77–96.

Bramwell, Anna, *Ecology in the 20th Century: A History* (New Haven: Yale University Press, 1989).

Brandt, Willy, *Erinnerungen* (Zurich: Propyläen Verlag, 1989).

My Life in Politics (New York: Penguin Press, 1992).

Breitmeier, Helmut, *Wie entstehen globale Umweltregime? Der Konfliktaustrag zum Schutz der Ozonschict und des globalen Klimas* (Opladen: Leske & Budrich, 1996).

Broadbent, Jeffrey, *Environmental Politics in Japan: Networks of Power and Protest* (Cambridge: Cambridge University Press, 1998).

Brooks, Stephen and Alain-G. Gagnon, *The Political Influence of Ideas: Policy Communities and the Social Sciences* (New York: Praeger, 1994).

Bryner, Gary C., *Blue Skies, Green Politics* (Washington, DC: Congressional Quarterly Press, 1995).

"Congress and the Politics of Climate Change," in Paul G. Harris (ed.), *Climate Change and American Foreign Policy* (New York: St. Martin's Press, 2000), pp. 111–30.

"The United States – 'Sorry – Not Our Problem,'" in William M. Lafferty and James Meadowcroft (eds.), *Implementing Sustainable Development: Strategies and Initiatives in High Consumption Societies* (Oxford: Oxford University Press, 2000), pp. 273–302.

Der Bundesminister für Umwelt, Naturschutz und Reaktorsicherheit, Bericht der Bundesregierung an den Deutschen Bundestag über Maßnahmen zum Schutz der Ozonschicht, 11/8166, October 22, 1990.

Bundesministerium für Umwelt, Naturschutz und Reaktorsicherheit, "Bericht des Bundesministers für Umwelt, Naturschutz und Reaktorsicherheit zur Reduzierung der CO_2-Emissionen in der Bundesrepublik Deutschland zum Jahr 2005: Erster Bericht auf der Grundlage des Beschlusses der Bundesregierung zu Zielvorstellungen für eine erreichbare Reduktion der CO_2-Emissionen 13 Juni 1990" (Bonn, June 13, 1990).

Burns, Rob and Wilfried van der Will, *Protest and Democracy in West Germany: Extra-Parliamentary Opposition and the Democratic Agenda* (New York: St. Martin's Press, 1988).

Caldwell, Lynton K., *Between Two Worlds: Science, the Environmental Movement and Policy Choice* (Cambridge: Cambridge University Press, 1990).

International Environmental Policy: Emergence and Dimension, second edition (Durham: Duke University Press, 1990).

Campbell, John C., "Bureaucratic Primacy: Japanese Policy Communities in American Perspective," *Governance: An International Journal of Policy and Administration* 2 (1989), 5–22.

How Policies Change: The Japanese Government and the Aging Society (Princeton: Princeton University Press, 1992).

Campbell, John C. with Mark A. Baskin, Frank R. Baumgartner, and Nina P. Halpern, "Afterward on Policy Communities: A Framework for Comparative Research," *Governance: An International Journal of Policy and Administration* 2 (1989), 86–94.

Carson, Rachel, *Silent Spring* (New York: Fawcett Crest, 1964).

CASA, pamphlet.

Cavender-Bares, Jeannine and Jill Jäger with Renate Ell, "Developing a Precautionary Approach: Global Environmental Risk Management in Germany," in William C. Clark, Jill Jäger, Josee van Eijindhoven, and Nancy M. Dickson (eds.), *Learning to Manage Global Environmental Risks*, vol. I: *A Comparative History of Social Responses to Climate Change, Ozone Depletion and Acid Rain* (Cambridge: MIT Press, 2001), pp. 61–92.

Central Council for Environmental Pollution Control and the Nature Conservation Council, "Establishing a Basic Law on the Environment," October 20, 1992.

Chlorofluorocarbon Manufacturers' Associations Fluorocarbon Panel, "Searching the Stratosphere," 1990 pamphlet.

Chûbachi, Shigeru, "A Special Ozone Observation at Syowa Station, Antarctica from February 1982 to January 1983," in C. S. Zerefos and A. Ghazi (eds.), for the Commission of the European Communities, *Atmospheric Ozone: Proceeding of the Quadrennial Ozone Symposium held in Halkidiki, Greece, 3–7 September 1984* (Dordrecht: D. Reidel Publishing Co., 1985), pp. 285–9.

"Watashi ga Ozon Hôru o Hakkenshita Koro," *Nihon Butsuri Gakkaishi* 48 (1993), 815–18.

Clark, William C. and Nancy M. Dickson, "Civil Science: America's Encounter with Global Environmental Risks," in William C. Clark, Jill Jäger, Josee van Eijndhoven, and Nancy M. Dickson (eds.), *Learning to Manage Global Environmental Risks*, vol. I: *A Comparative History of Social Responses to Climate Change, Ozone Depletion, and Acid Rain* (Cambridge: MIT Press, 2001), pp. 263–5.

Clark, William C. and Nancy M. Dickson (eds.), *The Press and Global Environmental Change: An International Comparison of Elite Newspaper Reporting on the Acid Rain Issue from 1972 to 1992*, Environment and Natural Resources Program Working Paper No. E-95-06, Harvard University, John F. Kennedy School of Government, Center for Science and International Affairs, 1995.

Clark, William C., Jill Jäger, Josee van Eijndhoven, and Nancy M. Dickson (eds.), Social Learning Group, *Learning to Manage Global Environmental Risks*, vol. I: *A Comparative History of Social Responses to Climate Change, Ozone Depletion, and Acid Rain*, and vol. II: *A Functional Analysis of Social Responses to Climate Change, Ozone Depletion, and Acid Rain* (Cambridge: MIT Press, 2001).

Commission of the European Community, "Euro-barometre, Public Opinion of the European Community," June–July 1975.

Commoner, Barry, *The Closing Circle* (New York: Alfred A. Knopf, 1971).

Conca, Ken and Ronnie Lipschutz (eds.), *The State and Social Power in Global Environmental Politics* (New York: Columbia University Press, 1993).

Dalton, Russell J., "The Environmental Movements in Western Europe," in Sheldon Kamieniecki (ed.), *Environmental Politics in the International Arena* (Albany: State University of New York Press, 1993), pp. 41–68.

The Green Rainbow: Environmental Groups in Western Europe (New Haven: Yale University Press, 1994).

Davies, III, J. Clarence and Barbara S. Davies, *The Politics of Pollution* (Indianapolis: Pegasus, 1977).

Denson, Edward and William Chung, "Economic Growth and Its Sources," in Hugh Patrick and Henry Rosovsky (eds.), *Asia's New Giant: How the Japanese Economy Works* (Washington, DC: Brookings Institution, 1976), pp. 63–152.

DeSombre, Elizabeth, *Domestic Sources of International Environmental Policy* (Cambridge: MIT Press, 2000).

Dominick, Raymond H., *The Environmental Movement in Germany: Prophets and Pioneers, 1871–1971* (Bloomington: Indiana University Press, 1992).

Dotto, Lydia and Harold Schiff, *The Ozone War* (New York: Doubleday, 1978).

Downs, Anthony, "Up and Down with Ecology: The Issue Attention Cycle," *Public Interest* 28 (1972), 38–50.

"Economic Report of the President," Washington, DC: United States Government Printing Office, 2002.

Ehrlich, Paul, *The Population Bomb* (New York: Ballantine Books, 1968).

Enerugii to Kankyô, Shukan Enerugii to Kankyô, 1125 (1990); 1126 (1990); 1127 (1990).

Environment Agency of Japan, *Quality of the Environment in Japan* (Tokyo: Environment Agency of Japan, 1972–2000).

"Seisôken Ozonsô Hogo ni Kansuru Kentôkai Chûkan Hôkoku," May 1987.

Japanese Performance of Energy Conservation and Air Pollution Control: How Japanese Performance Has Resulted in its Relatively Low Emissions of Greenhouse Gases among Industrialized Countries, October 1990.

"Summary of the Asian–Pacific Seminar on Climate Change," January 23–6, 1991.

"EU/UN Climate Change: MEPS Press Commission to Present Concrete Proposals," *European Report,* no. 2616, September 8, 2001.

Evans, Peter, Harold Jacobson, and Robert Putnam (eds.), *Double Edged Diplomacy: International Bargaining and Domestic Politics* (Berkeley: University of California Press, 1993).

Federal Ministry for the Environment, Nature Conservation, and Nuclear Safety, "Common Ground," January 1999.

Feinerman, James V. and Kôichirô Fujikura, "Japan: Consensus-Based Compliance," in Edith Brown Weiss and Harold K. Jacobson (eds.), *Engaging Countries: Strengthening Compliance with International Environmental Agreements* (Cambridge: MIT Press, 1998), pp. 253–90.

Fichter, Klaus, "Competitive Advantages through Voluntary Environmental Reporting," Institut für ökologische Wirtschaftsforschung GmbH.

Flippen, J. Brooks, *Nixon and the Environment* (Albuquerque: University of New Mexico Press, 2000).

Fogt, Helmut, "The Greens and the New Left: Influences of Left-Extremism on Green Party Organisation and Policies," in Eva Kolinsky (ed.), *The Greens in West Germany* (Oxford: GERG, 1989).

Foljanty-Jost, Gesine, "Kankyô Seisaku no Seikô Jôken," *Leviathan* 27 (2000), 35–48.

Foljanty-Jost, Gesine (ed.), *Ökologische Strategien Deutschland/Japan: Umweltverträgliches Wirtschaften im Vergleich* (Opladen: Leske und Budrich, 1996).

Forrest, Richard A., "Japanese Economic Assistance and the Environment: The Need for Reform," National Wildlife Federation, November 1989.

"Japan and Sustainable Development: The Long Road from Rio," in James Feinerman and Richard A. Forrest, *Japan and the Global Environment*, Woodrow Wilson Center Asia Program Occasional Paper, no. 50, February 25, 1993.

Fox, Jonathan A. and L. David Brown (eds.), *The Struggle for Accountability: The World Bank, NGOs, and Grassroots Movements* (Cambridge: MIT Press, 1998).

Fukui, Haruhiko, Peter H. Merkl, and Hubertus Müller-Groeling (eds.), *The Politics of Economic Change in Postwar Japan and West Germany*, vol. I: *Macroeconomic Conditions and Policy Responses* (New York: St. Martin's Press, 1993).

GAO Statement, August 6, 2001.

Gehring, Thomas, *Dynamic International Regimes: Institutions for International Environmental Governance* (Frankfurt am Main: Peter Lang GmbH, 1994).

German Bundestag (ed.), *Protecting the Earth's Atmosphere: An International Challenge*, Interim Report of the Study Commission of the 11th German Bundestag, *Preventive Measures to Protect the Earth's Atmosphere*, vol. I (Bonn: Deutscher Bundestag, 1989).

Protecting the Earth: A Status Report with Recommendations for a New Energy Policy, Third Report of the Enquete Commission of the 11th German Bundestag, *Preventive Measures to Protect the Earth's Atmosphere*, vol. II (Bonn: Deutscher Bundestag, 1991).

GLOBE, "Sekai Sôkai Tôkyô Kaigi Hôkokusho," Tokyo, Japan, July 1–3, 1991.

Goldstein, Judith and Robert O. Keohane, "Ideas and Foreign Policy: An Analytic Framework," in Judith Goldstein and Robert O. Keohane (eds.), *Ideas and Foreign Policy: Beliefs, Institutions, and Political Change* (Ithaca: Cornell University Press, 1993), pp. 3–30.

Gore, Al, *Earth in the Balance* (New York: Plume, 1993).

Government of Japan, "Japan's Response to Global Warming," August 1993.

"Proposals on the Elements to be Included in the Draft Protocol to the United Nations Framework Convention on Climate Change."

Greenpeace, "Furon Repôto: Nihon ni Okeru Omona Ozonsô Hakaibusshitsu no Seisan, Shôhi Dôkô," May 1991.

"Aktion Stromwechsel, Saubere Stromversorgung: klimaschonend und ohne Atomstrom, Ein Konzept für den ökologischen Energiedienstleister der Zukunft" (Hamburg: Greenpeace e.V., August, 1998).

Greenpeace Japan, "Guriin Furiizu no Jidai ga Kita" (pamphlet).

Gresser, Julian, Kôichirô Fujikura, and Akio Morishima, *Environmental Law in Japan* (Cambridge, MA: MIT Press, 1981).

Grubb, Michael with Christian Vrolijk and Duncan Brack, *The Kyoto Protocol: A Guide and Assessment* (London: Royal Institute of International Affairs, Earthscan, 1999).

Haas, Peter, *Saving the Mediterranean: The Politics of International Environmental Cooperation* (New York: Columbia University Press, 1990).

"Banning Chlorofluorocarbons: Efforts to Protect Stratospheric Ozone," in Peter Haas (ed.), *Knowledge, Power, and International Coordination*, special edition, *International Organization* 46 (1992), pp. 187–224.

Haas, Peter (ed.), *Knowledge, Power and International Coordination*, special edition, *International Organization* 46 (1992).

Haas, Peter and David McCabe, "Amplifiers or Dampers: International Institutions in the Management of Global Environmental Risks," in William C. Clark, Jill Jäger, Josee van Eijndhoven, and Nancy M. Dickson (eds.), *Learning to Manage Global Environmental Risks*, vol. II: *A Comparative History of Social Responses to Climate Change, Ozone Depletion and Acid Rain* (Cambridge: MIT Press, 2001), pp. 323–48.

Hager, Carol, *Technological Democracy: Bureaucracy and Citizenry in the German Energy Debate* (Ann Arbor: University of Michigan Press, 1995).

Hahn, Robert W. and Robert N. Stavins, "Trading in Greenhouse Permits," in Henry Lee (ed.), *Shaping National Responses to Climate Change* (Washington, DC: Island Press, 1995), pp. 177–217.

Haley, John, *Antitrust in Germany and Japan: The First Fifty Years, 1947–1998* (Seattle: University of Washington Press, 2001).

Hall, Molly E., "European Integration vs. State Sovereignty: The European Court of Justice and Harmonization of Germany's Environmental Law," in Gale Mattox, Geoffrey D. Oliver, and Jonathan B. Tucker, *Germany in Transition: A Unified Nation's Search for Identity* (Boulder: Westview Press, 1999), pp. 39–52.

Hall, Peter, *Governing the Economy: The Politics of State Intervention in Britain and France* (New York: Oxford University Press, 1986).

"Policy Paradigms, Social Learning and the State: The Case of Economic Policymaking in Britain," *Comparative Politics* 25 (1993), 275–96.

Hara, Bunbei, "Statement to the Session of a Special Character of the Governing Council of the United Nations Environment Programme," Nairobi, May 11, 1982.

Hardach, Karl, *The Political Economy of Germany in the Twentieth Century* (Berkeley: University of California Press, 1980).

Harris, Paul G. (ed.), *Climate Change and American Foreign Policy* (New York: St. Martin's Press, 2000).

Harrison, Neil E., "From the Inside Out: Domestic Influences on Global Environmental Policy," in Paul G. Harrison (ed.), *Climate Change and American Foreign Policy* (New York: St. Martin's Press, 2000), pp. 89–110.

Hashimoto, Michio, "History of Air Pollution Control in Japan," in Hajime Nishimura (ed.), *How to Conquer Air Pollution* (Amsterdam: Elsevier, 1989), pp. 1–94.

"The Pollution-Related Health Damage Compensation Law," in Hajime Nishimura (ed.), *How to Conquer Air Pollution* (Amsterdam: Elsevier, 1989), pp. 239–98.

Hatakeyama, Hirobumi and Toshimitsu Shinkawa, "Kankyô Gyôsei ni Miru Gendai Nihon Seiji ," in Hideo Ôtake (ed.), *Nihon Seiji no Sôten: Jirei Kenkyû ni yoru Seiji Taisei no Bunseki* (Tokyo: San'ichi Shobô, 1984), pp. 230–80.

Hatsushika, Masayuki, "Environmental Protection and TEPCO," Environmental Protection Department, Plant Siting and Environmental Protection Administration, Tokyo Electric Power, September 1990.

Hayase, Takeshi, "Taiki Osen," in Kiyoaki Tsuji (ed.), *Gyôseigaku Kôza*, vol. IV: *Gyôsei to Soshiki* (Tokyo: Tôkyô Daigaku Shuppankai, 1976), pp. 175–201.

Hayes, Peter and Lyuba Zarsky, "Environmental Issues and Regimes in Northeast Asia," *International Environmental Affairs* 6 (1994), 283–319.

Heclo, Hugh, *Modern Social Politics in Britain and Sweden* (New Haven: Yale University Press, 1974).

"Issue Networks and the Executive Establishment," in Anthony King (ed.), *The New American Political System* (Washington, DC: American Enterprise Institute, 1978), pp. 87–124.

Héritier, Adrienne, Christoph Knill, Susanne Mingers, and Martina Beckka, *Die Veränderung von Staatlichkeit in Europa* (Opladen: Leske and Budrich, 1994).

Hoffmann, Volker U., George Hille, Helmut Dienhart, Ole Langiniss, Jachi Nisch, and Sven Teske, "Employment in Solar Energy in 2010: New Jobs through New Sources of Energy (Executive Summary)" (Hamburg: Greenpeace, April 1997).

Hopgood, Stephen, *American Foreign Policy and the Power of the State* (Oxford: Oxford University Press, 1998).

Houghton, J. T., G. J. Jenkins, and J. J. Ephraums (eds.), IPCC, *Climate Change: The IPCC Scientific Assessment* (Cambridge: Cambridge University Press, 1990).

Hucke, Jochen, "Environmental Policy: The Development of a New Policy Area," in Manfred Schmidt and Klaus von Beyme (eds.), *Policy and Politics in the Federal Republic of Germany* (New York: St. Martin's Press, 1985).

Huddle, Norie and Michael Reich with Nahum Stiskin, *Island of Dreams: Environmental Crisis in Japan* (New York: Autumn Press, 1975).

IFIAS, ISSC, UNU, "Report of the Tokyo International Symposium on the Human Response to Global Change," Tokyo, Japan, September 19–22, 1988.

Ikenberry, John, *Reasons of State: Oil Politics and the Capacities of American Government* (Ithaca: Cornell University Press, 1988).

Imamura, Tsunao, "Soshiki no Bunka to Kôzô," in Kiyoaki Tsuji (ed.), *Gyôseigaku Kôza*, vol. IV: *Gyôsei to Soshiki* (Tokyo: Tôkyô Daigaku Shuppankai, 1976), pp. 37–82.

"Environmental Responsibilities at the National Level: The Environment Agency," in Shigeto Tsuru and Helmut Weidner (eds.), *Environmental Policy in Japan* (Berlin: Sigma, 1989), pp. 43–53.

Imura, Hidefumi and Hikaru Kobayashi, "Kagakuteki Fukakujitsusei no moto ni Okeru Ishi Kettei," *Kankyô Kenkyû* 68 (1988), 26.

Inoguchi, Takashi, "The Nature and Functioning of Japanese Politics," *Government and Opposition* 26 (1991), 185–98.

Inoguchi, Takashi and Tomoaki Iwai, *"Zoku giin" no Kenkyû* (Tokyo: Nihon Keizai Shimbunsha, 1987).

Institute for Global Environmental Strategies, *Business and Environmental Governance*, March 1999.

Interim Report of the Study Commission of the 11th German Bundestag, *Preventive Measures to Protect the Earth's Atmosphere* (Bonn: Deutscher Bundestag, 1989).

IPCC, *Climate Change 1995: The Science of Climate Change* (Cambridge: Cambridge University Press, 1996).

IPCC Third Assessment Report: Climate Change 2001: The Scientific Basis (vol. I) *Impacts Adaptations, and Vulnerability* (vol. II); and *Mitigation* (vol. III) (Cambridge: Cambridge University Press, 2001).

Jachtenfuchs, Markus, "The European Community and the Protection of the Ozone Layer," *Journal of Common Market Studies*, 28, no. 3 (March 1990), 263–75.

JANIC, *Kokusai Kyôryoku NGO Dairekutorii* (Tokyo: JANIC, 1992, 1996, 2000).

NGO Dairekutori, 1994 (Tokyo: JANIC, 1994).

Jänicke, Martin and Helmut Weidner (eds.), *National Environmental Policies: A Comparative Study of Capacity-Building* (Berlin: Springer Verlag, 1997).

Japan Automobile Manufacturers' Association, Inc., "Basic Position on Global Warming and Related Issues," June 1990.

Japan Council for Sustainable Development, *Japan Report for Rio + 5 Process*, March 1997.

Japan Environment Corporation, "Chikyû Kankyô Kikin Tayori," 1994.

Japan Industrial Conference for Ozone Layer Protection, *JICOP Guide*, 1992.

Jasanoff, Sheila, *Risk Management and Political Culture: A Comparative Study of Science in the Policy Context* (New York: Russell Sage Foundation, 1986).

Jenkins, Craig, "Social Movements, Political Representation, and the State: An Agenda and Comparative Framework," in J. Craig Jenkins and Bert Klandermans (eds.), *The Politics of Social Protest: Comparative Perspectives on States and Social Movements* (Minneapolis: University of Minnesota Press, 1995), pp. 14–38.

Kamieniecki, Sheldon (ed.), *Environmental Politics in the International Arena* (Albany: State University of New York Press, 1993).

Kankyôchô, *Ichiji Sanseiu Taisaku Chôsa Kekka ni Tsuite* (Tokyo: Kankyôchô, 1989).

Dai Ni Sanseiu Taisaku Chôsa no Chûkan Torimatome ni Tsuite (Tokyo: Kankyôchô, 1992).

Kankyôchô 20 Shûnen Kinen Jigyô Jikkô Iinkai, *Kankyôchô 20 Nenshi* (Tokyo: Gyôsei, 1991).

Kankyôchô Chikyû Ondanka Mondai ni Kansuru Kentôkai, *Chikyû Ondanka Mondai ni Kansuru Kentôkai, Dai Ikkai Chûkan Hôkoku*, November 1988.

Kankyôchô Chikyûteki Kibo no Kankyô Mondai ni Kansuru Kondankai, *Chikyûteki Kibo no Kankyô Mondai he no Kokusaiteki Torikumi ni Tsuite: Kokuren Ningen Kankyô Kaigi 10 Shûnen ni Atatte*, 1982.

Kankyôchô Kankyô Hokenbu Hoken Chôsa Shitsu, "Furon Gasu Mondai ni Tsuite," September 1980.

Kankyôchô Kikaku Chôsei Kyoku, *Kankyôchô Kihonhô no Kaisetsu* (Tokyo: Gyôsei, 1994).

Kankyôchô Ozonsô Hogo Kentôkai (ed.), *Ozonsô o Mamoru* (Tokyo: NHK Books, 1990).

Kasuga, Hitoshi, "Health Effects of Air Pollution," in Hajime Nishimura (ed.), *How to Conquer Air Pollution* (Amsterdam: Elsevier, 1989), pp. 95–114.

Katô, Ichirô, Tarô Kaneko, Keiichi Kihara, and Michio Hashimoto, "Kankyô Gyôsei 10 Nen no Ayumi," *Juristo* 749 (1981), 17–62.

Katô, Saburô, "System for Regulation," in Hajime Nishimura, *How to Conquer Air Pollution* (Amsterdam: Elsevier, 1989), pp. 197–238.

Katzenstein, Peter J., *Policy and Politics in West Germany: The Growth of a Semi-Sovereign State* (Philadelphia: Temple University Press, 1987).

"Coping with Terrorism: Norms and Internal Security in Germany and Japan," in Judith Goldstein and Robert O. Keohane (eds.), *Ideas and Foreign Policy: Beliefs, Institutions, and Political Change* (Ithaca: Cornell University Press, 1993), pp. 265–95.

Kauffman, Joanne, "Domestic and International Linkages in Global Environmental Politics: A Case-Study of the Montreal Protocol," in Miranda A. Schreurs and Elizabeth Economy (eds.), *The Internationalization of Environmental Protection* (Cambridge: Cambridge University Press, 1997), pp. 74–96.

Kawahira, Kôji and Yukio Makino, *Ozon Shôshitsu* (Tokyo: Yomiuri Kagaku Sensho, 1989).

Kawashima, Yasuko, "Japan's Decision-Making about Climate Change Problems: Comparative Study of Decisions in 1990 and 1997," *Environmental Economics and Policy Studies* 3 (2000), 29–57.

Kay, David and Harold Jacobson (eds.), *Environmental Protection: The International Dimension* (Totowa, NJ: Allanheld, Osmun, & Co., 1983).

Keck, Margaret and Kathryn Sikkink, *Activists Beyond Borders* (Ithaca: Cornell University Press, 1998).

Keizai Dantai Rengôkai, *Keidanren Kankyô Jishu Kôdô Keikaku*, June 17, 1997.

Keizai Hôkoku Sentaa, Sangyô to Kankyô no kai, *Sangyô to Kankyô no Henyô*, August 1989.

Keohane, Robert and Helen V. Milner, *Internationalization and Domestic Politics* (Cambridge: Cambridge University Press, 1996).

Kerr, Suzi, "Introduction: Trading Toward a Stable Climate," in Suzi Kerr (ed.), *Global Emissions Trading: Key Issues for Industrialized Countries* (Cheltenham, UK: Edward Elgar, 2000), pp. 1–24.

Kingdon, John, *Agendas, Alternatives, and Public Policies* (Boston: Little, Brown, and Company, 1984).

Kitschelt, Herbert S., "Political Opportunity Structures and Political Protest: Anti-Nuclear Movements in Four Democracies," *British Journal of Political Science* 16 (1986), 57–85.

The Logic of Party Formation: Structure and Strategy of Belgian and West German Ecology Parties (Ithaca: Cornell University Press, 1989).

Knödgen, Gabriele, "The STEAG Coal-Fired Power Plant at Voerde or Changing German Clean Air Policy," paper from the International Institute for Environment and Society of the Science Center Berlin, November 1981.

Knoepfel, Peter and Helmut Weidner, *Luftreinhaltepolitik in internationalen Vergleich* (Berlin: Sigma, 1995).

Komiya, Yoshinori, "Furon Kisei Mondai to Nihon no Taiô," *Kôgai to Taisaku* 24 (1988), 46–53.

Krasner, Stephen, "Approaches to the State: Alternative Conceptions and Historical Dynamics," *Comparative Politics* 16 (1984), 223–46.

Krauss, Ellis S. and Bradford Simcock, "Citizens' Movements: The Growth and Impact of Environmental Protest in Japan," in Kurt Steiner, Ellis Krauss, and Scott C. Flanagan (eds.), *Political Opposition and Local Politics in Japan* (Princeton: Princeton University Press, 1980), pp. 187–227.

Kriesi, Hanspeter, "The Organizational Structure of New Social Movements in a Political Context," in Doug McAdam, John D. McCarthy, and Mayer N. Zald (eds.), *Comparative Perspectives on Social Movements: Political Opportunities, Mobilizing Structures, and Cultural Frames* (Cambridge: Cambridge University Press, 1986), pp. 185–204.

"The Political Opportunity Structure of New Social Movements: Its Impact on their Mobilization," in J. Craig Jenkins and Bert Klandermans (eds.), *The Politics of Social Protest: Comparative Perspectives on States and Social Movement* (Minneapolis: University of Minnesota Press, 1995), pp. 167–98.

Kübler, Knut, "Die Energiepolitik zum Schutz der Erdatmosphäre," *Energiewirtschaftliche Tagesfragen* 41 (1991), 899–903.

Kudô, Shin'ichi, "Ozonsô Hogohô o Furikaette," *Kankyô* 14, 44–8.

Kuhn, Thomas S., *The Structure of Scientific Revolutions* (Chicago: University of Chicago Press, 1962).

Kurki, Anja, Miranda Schreurs, Yutaka Tsujinaka, and Fumiaki Kubo, "Beikoku ni okeru Kikô Hendô Seisaku: Beikoku Oyobi Nikkan no Chikyû Kankyô Seisaku Netto Waaku Chôsa kara no Dôsatsu," *Leviathan* 27 (2000), 49–72.

Lacey, Michael J. (ed.), *Government and Environmental Politics: Essays on Historical Developments since World War II* (Washington, DC: Woodrow Wilson Center, 1991).

Lafferty, William M. and James Meadowcroft (eds.), *Implementing Sustainable Development: Strategies and Initiatives in High Consumption Societies* (Oxford: Oxford University Press, 2000).

Leane, Geoffrey W. G., "Environmental Contracts: A Lesson in Democracy from the Japanese," *U.B.C. Law Review* (1991), 361–85.

Lesbirel, Hayden, "Implementing Nuclear Energy Policy in Japan: Top-Down and Bottom-Up Perspectives," *Energy Policy* (April 1990), 267–82.

NIMBY Politics in Japan: Energy Siting and the Management of Environmental Conflict (Ithaca: Cornell University Press, 1998).

Levy, Marc A., "European Acid Rain: The Power of Tote-Board Diplomacy," in Peter M. Haas, Robert O. Keohane, and Marc A. Levy (eds.), *Institutions for the Earth: Sources of Effective International Environmental Protection* (Cambridge: MIT Press, 1993), pp. 75–132.

Lindblom, Charles, "The Science of Muddling Through," *Public Administration Review* 19 (1959), 79–88.

Lipschutz, Ronnie, *Global Civil Society and Global Environmental Governance: The Politics of Nature from Place to Planet* (Albany: SUNY Press, 1996).

Litfin, Karen, *Ozone Discourses: Science and Politics in Global Environmental Cooperation* (New York: Columbia University Press, 1994).

London, Nancy, *Japanese Corporate Philanthropy* (Oxford: Oxford University Press, 1991).

Loske, Reinhard, *Klimapolitik: Im Spannungsfeld von Kurzzeitinteressen und Langzeiterfordernissen* (Marburg: Metropolis Verlag, 1997).

McAdam, Doug, John D. McCarthy, and Mayer N. Zald (eds.), *Comparative Perspectives on Social Movements: Political Opportunities, Mobilizing Structures, and Cultural Frames* (Cambridge: Cambridge University Press, 1986).

McCarthy, John D. and Mayer N. Zald, "Resource Mobilization and Social Movements: A Partial Theory," *American Journal of Sociology* 82 (1977), 1212–41.

McKean, Margaret, "Pollution and Policymaking," in T. J. Pempel (ed.), *Policymaking in Contemporary Japan* (Ithaca: Cornell University Press, 1977), pp. 201–39.

Environmental Protest and Citizen Politics in Japan (Berkeley: University of California Press, 1981).

McSpadden, Lettie, "Environmental Policy in the Courts," in Norman Vig and Michael E. Kraft (eds.), *Environmental Policy in the 1990s: Reform or Reaction* (Washington, DC: Congressional Quarterly Press, 1997), pp. 168–86.

Marland, G., Boden, T. A., and Andres, R. J., "Global, Regional, and National Fossil Fuel CO_2 Emissions," in *Trends: A Compendium of Data on Global Change*, Carbon Dioxide Information Analysis Center, Oak Ridge National Laboratory, US Department of Energy, Oak Ridge, Tenn., USA, 2001.

Markovitz, Andrei S. and Philip S. Gorski, *The German Left: Red, Green and Beyond* (New York: Oxford University Press, 1993).

Marsh, David and R. A. W. Rhodes, *Policy Networks in British Government* (Oxford: Oxford University Press, 1992).

Masumi, Junnosuke (translated by Lonny E. Carlile), *Contemporary Politics in Japan* (Berkeley: University of California Press, 1995).

Matsubara, Akira, "NGOs in Japan: Problems of Legal Framework and Management Issues," Research Institution of Civil Systems paper.

Matsumura, Makoto, "Challenging Acid Rain," *Journal of Japanese Trade and Industry* 2 (1991), 15–16.

Mattox, Gale, Geoffrey D. Oliver, and Jonathan B. Tucker, *Germany in Transition: A Unified Nation's Search for Identity* (Boulder: Westview Press, 1999).

Mayer, Margit and John Ely (eds.), *The German Greens: Paradox between Movement and Party* (Philadelphia: Temple University Press, 1998).

Mayntz, Renate, "Intergovernmental Implementation of Environmental Policy," in Kenneth Hanf and Fritz Scharpf (eds.), *Interorganizational Policy Making: Limits to Coordination and Central Control* (Beverley Hills, CA: Sage Publications, 1978).

Meadows, Donnella H., Dennis L. Meadows, Jorgen Randers, and William W. Behrens, III, *The Limits to Growth* (New York: Universe Books, 1972).

Menju, Toshirô and Takako Aoki, "The Evolution of Japanese NGOs in the Asia Pacific Context," in Tadashi Yamamoto (ed.), *Emerging Civil Society in the Asia Pacific Community* (Tokyo: Japan Center for International Exchange, 1995).

Mewes, Horst, "History of the German Green Party," in Margit Mayer and John Ely (eds.), *The German Greens: Paradox between Movement and Party* (Philadelphia: Temple University Press, 1998), pp. 29–48.

Mez, Lutz, "Von den Bügerinitiativen zu den GRÜNEN: Zur Entstehungsgeschicte der 'Wahlalternativen' in der Bundesrepublik Deutschland," in Roland Roth and Dieter Rucht (eds.), *Neue soziale Bewegungen in der Bundesrepublik Deutschland* (Frankfurt: Campus Verlag, 1987), pp. 263–76.

Mez, Lutz and Piening, Annette, "Phasing-Out Nuclear Power Generation in Germany: Policies, Actors, Issues and Non-Issues," paper presented at conference, New Directions in National and International Energy and Climate Change Policies: Germany, Japan, US Energy Experts Annual Network Meeting, Berlin, Germany, June 17–20, 2000.

Milbrath, Lester, *Envisioning a Sustainable Society: Learning Our Way Out* (Albany: SUNY Press, 1984).

"The World is Relearning Its Story," in Sheldon Kamieniecki (ed.), *Environmental Politics in the International Arena* (New York: SUNY Press, 1993), pp. 21–39.

Miller, Alan and Curtis Moore, *Green Gold: Japan, Germany, the United States, and the Race for Environmental Technology* (Boston: Beacon Press, 1994).

Mintz, Joel A., *Enforcement at the EPA: High Stakes and Hard Choices* (Austin: University of Texas Press, 1995).

Mintzer, Irving M. and J. A. Leonard (eds.), *Negotiating Climate Change* (Cambridge: Cambridge University Press, 1994).

Mitchell, Robert Cameron, "From Conservation to Environmental Movement," in Michael J. Lacey (ed.), *Government and Environmental Politics* (Washington, DC: Woodrow Wilson Center, 1991), pp. 81–114.

MITI, "New Earth 21: Action Program for the 21st Century," 1990.

Miyamoto, Ken'ichi, *Nihon no Kankyô Seisaku* (Tokyo: Ohtsuki Shoten, 1987).

MoFA, *Japan's Environmental Endeavors*, April 1992.

Molina, Mario J. and F. Sherwood Rowland, "Stratospheric Sink for Chlorofluoromethanes: Chlorine Atomic Catalysed Destruction of Ozone," *Nature* 249 (1984), 810–12.

Mori, Kazuaki, "Ozonsô Hogo Mondai no Kagakuteki Chiken ni Kansuru Nichibei Senmonka Kaigô ni Tsuite," *Kankyô Kenkyû* 65 (1987), 53–8.

Müller, Edda, *Innenwelt der Umweltpolitik: Sozial-liberale Unweltpolitik (ohn)macht durch Organisation?* (Opladen: Westdeutscher Verlag, 1986).

Muramatsu, Michio and Ellis Krauss, "The Conservative Policy Line and the Development of Patterned Pluralism," in Kozo Yamamura and Yasukichi Yasuba (eds.), *The Political Economy of Japan*, vol. I: *The Domestic Transformation* (Stanford, CA: Stanford University Press, 1987), pp. 516–54.

Murdo, Pat, "Japan's Environmental Policies: The International Dimension," *Japan Economic Institute Report*, March 9, 1990.

"Naikaku ni Chikyû Kankyô Tantô," *Asahi Shimbun*, July 8, 1989.

Naikaku Sôri Daijin, "Chikyû Ondanka Bôshi Kôdô Keikaku," February 10, 1990.

Newell, Peter and Matthew Paterson, "From Geneva to Kyoto: The Second Conference of the Parties to the UN Framework Convention on Climate Change," *Environmental Politics* 5:4 (1997), 729–35.

Nihon Furongasu Kyôkai (ed.), *Tokutei Furon Shiyô Sakugen Manyuaru* (Tokyo: Nihon Furongasu Kyôkai, 1990).

Nihon Kankyô NGO Sôran (Tokyo: Nihon Kankyô Kyôkai, 1995).

Nishimura, Hajime (ed.), *How to Conquer Air Pollution* (Amsterdam: Elsevier, 1989).

Nitze, William A., "A Failure of Presidential Leadership," in Irving M. Mintzer and J. A. Leonard (eds.), *Negotiating Climate Change* (Cambridge: Cambridge University Press, 1994), pp. 187–200.

Oberthür, Sebastian and Hermann Ott, *The Kyoto Protocol* (Berlin: Springer Verlag, 1999).

Oberthür, Sebastian and Stephan Singer, "Die internationale Klimapolitik am Scheideweg: Ein Bericht über den Stand der Klima-diplomatie am Vorabend des entscheidenden Kyoto-Gipfels in Dezember 1997" (Frankfurt: WWF, November 1997).

Oda, Hiroshi, "The Role of Criminal Law in Pollution Control," in Shigeto Tsuru and Helmut Weidner (eds.), *Environmental Policy in Japan* (Berlin: Sigma, 1989), pp. 183–95.

Odén, Svante, "The Acidification of Air and Precipitation and its Consequences in the Natural Environment," *Ecology Committee Bulletin*, no. 1 (Stockholm: Swedish National Science Research Council, 1968).

OECD, *Major Air Pollution Problems: The Japanese Experience* (Paris: OECD, 1974).

Case History from Germany on the Use of Criteria Documents in Setting Standards for the Control of Sulfur Oxides (Paris: OECD, 1975).

Environmental Politics in Japan (Paris: OECD, 1977).

Energy Policies of IEA Countries: 1991 Review (Paris: OECD, 1991).

"The OECD Environment Industry: Situation, Prospects and Government Policy," Paris: OECD, 1992. OECD/GD (92) 1.

Environmental Performance Review: Germany (Paris: OECD, 1993).

Environmental Performance Review: Japan (Paris: OECD, 1994).

Environmental Performance Review: Germany (Paris: OECD, 2001).

Environmental Performance Review: Achievements in OECD Countries (Paris: OECD, 2001).

Environmental Performance Review: Japan (Paris: OECD, 2002).

OECD Environment Directorate, "Ad Hoc Meeting on Acidity and Concentration of Sulphate in Rain," May 1969 (Paris: OECD, 1971).

"The OECD Programme on Long Range Transport of Air Pollutants, Summary Report" (Paris: OECD, 1977).

O'Neill, Kate, *Waste Trading among Rich Nations: Building a New Theory of Environmental Regulation* (Cambridge: MIT Press, 2000).

O'Riordan, Tim and Jäger, Jill (eds.), *Politics of Climate Change: A European Perspective* (New York: Routledge, 1996).

O'Riordan, Tim and Elizabeth J. Rowbotham, "Struggling for Credibility: The UK," in Tim O'Riordan and Jill Jäger (eds.), *Politics of Climate Change: A European Perspective* (London: Routledge, 1996), pp. 228–67.

Ôshima, Takashi, "Furongasu," *Kankyô Kenkyû* 33 (1981), 128–9.

Papadakis, Elim, *The Green Movement in West Germany* (London: Croom Helm, 1984).

"Green Issues and Other Parties: Themenklau or New Flexibility," in Eva Kolinsky, ed., *The Greens in West Germany: Organisation and Policy Making* (Oxford: BERG, 1989).

Parker, Larry B. and John E. Blodgett, "RL30155: Global Climate Change Policy: Domestic Early Action Credits, Congressional Research Service Report," July 23, 1999 (Washington, DC: Committee for the National Institute for the Environment, 1999).

Paterson, Matthew, *Global Warning and Global Politics* (New York: Routledge, 1996).

Paterson, William E., "Environmental Politics," in Gordon Smith, William E. Paterson, and Peter H. Merkl (eds.), *Developments in West German Politics* (London: Macmillan Education Ltd., 1989).

Pehle, Heinrich, "Germany: Domestic Obstacles to an International Forerunner," in Mikael Skou Andersen and Duncan Lieferink (eds.), *European Environmental Policy: The Pioneers* (Manchester: Manchester University Press, 1997).

Pekkanen, Robert, "Japan's New Politics: The Case of the NPO Law," *Journal of Japanese Studies* 26 (2000), 111–48.

Pempel, T. J., *Policy and Politics in Japan: Creative Conservatism* (Philadelphia: Temple University Press, 1982).

Regime Shift: Comparative Dynamics of the Japanese Political Economy (Ithaca: Cornell University Press, 1998).

Pharr, Susan and Joseph Badaracco, Jr., "Coping with Crisis: Environmental Regulation," in Thomas K. McCraw (ed.), *America versus Japan* (Boston: Harvard Business School Press, 1986), pp. 229–59.

Piening, Annette, "Nuclear Energy in Germany," in Manfred Binder, Martin Jänicke, and Ulrich Petschow (eds.), *Green Industrial Restructuring: International Case Studies and Theoretical Considerations* (Berlin: Springer Verlag, 2001), pp. 403–34.

Potter, David, "Assessing Japan's Environmental Aid Policy," *Pacific Affairs* 67 (1994), 200–15.

Prezorski, Adam and Henry Teune, *The Logic of Comparative Social Inquiry* (Malabar, FL: R. F. Krieger, 1970).

Princen, Thomas and Matthias Finger, *Environmental NGOs in World Politics: Linking the Local and the Global* (New York: Routledge, 1994).

Proceedings of the Thirteenth and Fourteenth Annual Conferences of the Japan Society of Air Pollution.

Putnam, Robert, "Diplomacy and Domestic Politics: The Logic of Two-Level Games," *International Organization* 42 (1988), 427–60.

Der Rat von Sachverständigen für Umweltfragen, *Umweltgutachten* (Stuttgart: Verlag Metzler-Poeschel, 1996).

Raustiala, Kal, "The Domestic Politics of Global Biodiversity Protection in the United Kingdom and the United States," in Miranda A. Schreurs and Elizabeth Economy (eds.), *The Internationalization of Environmental Protection* (Cambridge: Cambridge University Press, 1997), pp. 42–73.

Record of the 108th Diet, House of Councilor's Foreign Affairs Committee meeting, March 26, 1987.

Record of the 108th Diet, House of Representative's Environmental Committee meeting, May 15, 1987.

Reed, Steven R., *Japanese Prefectures and Policymaking* (Pittsburgh: University of Pittsburgh Press, 1986).

Register of International Treaties and Agreements in the Field of the Environment, UNEP/GC.15/Inf.2, Nairobi, May 1989.

Reich, Michael, "Crisis and Routine: Pollution Reporting by the Japanese Press," in George DeVos (ed.), *Institutions for Change in Japanese Society* (Berkeley: Institute of East Asian Studies, University of California,1984), pp. 114–47.

Toxic Politics: Responding to Chemical Disasters (Ithaca: Cornell University Press, 1991).

Reimann, Kim D., "Building Networks from the Outside In: International Movements, Japanese NGOs and the Kyoto Climate Change Conference," paper presented at the 1999 Annual Meeting of the Northeastern Political Science Association (NPSA) and International Studies Association-Northeast, Philadelphia Crown Plaza Hotel, November 10–14, 1999.

Research Institute of Innovative Technology for the Earth, pamphlet.

Risse-Kappan, Thomas (ed.), *Bringing Transnational Relations Back In: Non-State Actors, Domestic Structures, and International Institutions* (New York: Cambridge University Press, 1995).

Rosenau, James N., *Turbulence in World Politics* (Princeton: Princeton University Press, 1990).

Rosenbaum, Walter, *Environmental Politics and Policy* (Washington, DC: Congressional Quarterly Press, 1998).

Roth, Roland and Rucht, Dieter (eds.), *Neue soziale Bewegungen in der Bundesrepublik Deutschland* (Frankfurt: Campus Verlag, 1987).

Rowlands, Ian, "EU Policy for Ozone Layer Protection," in Jonathan Golub (ed.), *Global Competition and EU Environmental Policy* (New York: Routledge, 1998).

Rucht, Dieter. "The Impact of National Contexts on Social Movement Structures: A Cross-Movement and Cross-National Comparison," in Doug McAdam, John D. McCarthy, and Mayer N. Zald (eds.), *Comparative Perspectives on Social Movements: Political Opportunities, Mobilizing Structures, and Cultural Frames* (Cambridge: Cambridge University Press, 1986), pp. 185–204.

"Von der Bewegun zur Institution? Organisationsstrukturen der Ökologiebewegung," in Roland Roth and Dieter Rucht (eds.), *Neue soziale Bewegungen in der Bundesrepublik Deutschland* (Frankfurt: Campus Verlag, 1987).

Modernisierung und neue soziale Bewegungen: Deutschland, Frankreich und USA in Vergleich (Frankfurt: Campus Verlag, 1994).

Sabatier, Paul A., "Policy Change Over a Decade or More," in Paul A. Sabatier and H. C. Jenkins-Smith, *Policy Change and Learning: An Advocacy Coalition Approach* (Boulder: Westview Press, 1993), pp. 13–40.

Salamon, Lester M. and Helmut K. Anheier (eds.), *The Emerging Sector: An Overview* (New York: Manchester University Press, 1996).

Sarkar, Saral, *Green-Alternative Politics in West Germany* (Tokyo: United Nations University Press, 1993).

Scharf, Thomas, *The German Greens* (Oxford: BERG, 1994).

"The Scientific Consensus: Villach (Austria) Conference," in Dean Edwin Abrahamson, *The Challenge of Global Warning* (Washington, DC: Island Press, 1989), pp. 63–70.

Schreurs, Miranda A., "Nihon ni Okeru Kankyô Seisaku no Kettei Katei," *Journal of Pacific Asia* 2 (1994), 3–38.

"Conservation, Development and State Sovereignty: Japan and the Tropical Timbers of Southeast Asia," in Sohail Hashmi (ed.), *State Sovereignty* (University Park: Pennsylvania State University Press, 1997), pp. 181–204.

"Domestic Institutions and International Environmental Agendas in Japan and Germany," in Miranda A. Schreurs and Elizabeth Economy (eds.), *The Internationalization of Environmental Protection* (Cambridge: Cambridge University Press, 1997), pp. 134–61.

"The Future of Environmental Cooperation in Northeast Asia," in Miranda A. Schreurs and Dennis Pirages (eds.), *Ecological Security in Northeast Asia* (Seoul: Yonsei University Press, 1998), pp. 195–219.

"New Directions in German Energy and Environmental Policies," in *Germany After the 1998 Federal Elections* (Washington, DC: American Institute for Contemporary German Studies, December 1998), pp. 17–20.

"Japan: Law, Technology, and Aid," in William M. Lafferty and James Meadowcroft (eds.), *Implementing Sustainable Development in High Consumption Societies* (Oxford: Oxford University Press, 2000), pp. 112–41.

"Competing Agendas and the Climate Change Negotiations: The United States, the European Union, and Japan," *Environmental Law Reporter*, 31, 10 (2001), 11218–24.

"Shifting Priorities and the Internationalization of Environmental Risk Management in Japan," in William C. Clark, Jill Jäger, Josee van Eijndhoven, and Nancy M. Dickson (eds.), *Learning to Manage Global Environmental Risks*, vol. I: *A Comparative History of Social Responses to Climate Change, Ozone Depletion and Acid Rain* (Cambridge: MIT Press, 2001), pp. 191–212.

Schreurs, Miranda A. and Elizabeth Economy (eds.), *The Internationalization of Environmental Protection* (Cambridge: Cambridge University Press, 1997).

Schreurs, Miranda A. and Dennis Pirages (eds.), *Ecological Security in Northeast Asia* (Seoul: Yonsei University Press, 1998).

Schreurs, Miranda A., Patricia Welch, and Akiko Kôda, "Devil in the Sky," in William C. Clark and Nancy M. Dickson (eds.), *The Press and Global Environmental Change: An International Comparison of Elite Newspaper Reporting on the Acid Rain Issue from 1972 to 1992*, Environment and Natural Resources Program Working Paper No. E-95-06, Harvard University, John F. Kennedy School of Government, Center for Science and International Affairs, 1995, pp. G1–36.

Schull, Tad, *Redefining Red and Green: Ideology and Strategy in European Political Ecology* (Albany: SUNY Press, 1999).

Schwann, Kerstin, "How Will Germany Cope with Phaseout of Nuclear Power," *Frankfurter Allgemeine* (English edition), June 16, 2000, p. 3.

Sendai Kita Hôjinkai Shônen Bukai, *Eco-page: Zenkoku Kankyô Hozen Dantai Yôran 1994* (Sendai: Sendai Kita Hôjinkai Shônen Bukai, 1994).

Shaiko, Ronald G., *Voices and Echoes for the Environment: Public Interest Representation in the 1990s and Beyond* (New York: Columbia University Press, 2000).

Shibata, Tokue, "Pollution Control Agreements: The Case of Tokyo and Other Local Authorities," in Shigeto Tsuru and Helmut Weidner (eds.), *Environmental Policy in Japan* (Berlin: Sigma, 1989), pp. 246–51.

Shiga, Setsu, "Norutoveiku Kaigi no Kotonado," in Kankyôchô 20 Shûnen Kinen Jigyô Jikkô Iinkai, *Kankyôchô 20 Nenshi* (Tokyo: Gyôsei, 1991), pp. 426–8.

Shimin Forum 2001 Chikyû Ondanka Kenkyûkai, *Ima, chikyû ondanka mondai ha hataraiteiru!!* March 15, 1996.

Shôsetsu: Chikyû Ondanka (Tokyo: Shimin Forum 2001, 1998).

Siegmann, Heinrich, *The Conflicts between Labor and Environmentalism in the Federal Republic of Germany and the United States* (New York: St. Martin's Press, 1985).

Simonis, U. E., "The German Experience," paper presented at the International Conference on Ecology and Environment in the 90s, Aula des Jeunes-Rives, University of Neuchâtel, August 26–7, 1991.

Smith, Michael, "Advertising the Atom," in Michael J. Lacey (ed.), *Government and Environmental Politics: Essays on Historical Developments since World War II* (Washington, DC: Woodrow Wilson Center, 1991), pp. 233–62.

Soltan, Karol, Eric M. Uslaner, and Virginia Haufler (eds.), *Institutions and Social Order* (Ann Arbor: Michigan University Press, 1998).

Sôrifu Naikaku Sôridaijin Kanbô Kôhôshitsu, "Kôgai ni Kansuru Yoron Chôsa," *Yoron Chôsa Nenpô, Chôsa 11.*

Kôgai Mondai ni Kansuru Yoron Chôsa, Chôsa 19, October 1973; *Chôsa 20*, March 1979.

"Kankyô Mondai ni Kansuru Yoron Chôsa," *Yoron Chôsa Nenpô*, January 1988.

Sôrifu Naikaku Sôridaijin Kanbô Kôhôshitsu (ed.), "Kankyô Hozen Katsudô ni Kansuru Yoron Chôsa," *Yoron Chôsa Nenkan* (March 1990).

Sprinz, Detlef, "Why Countries Support International Environmental Agreements: The Regulation of Acid Rain in Europe," Ph.D. Dissertation, University of Michigan, 1992.

Sprinz, Detlef and Tapani Vaahtoranta, "The Interest-Based Explanation of International Environmental Policy," in A. Underdal (ed.), *The Politics of International Environmental Management* (Dordrecht: Kluwer Academic Publishers, 1997), pp. 13–44.

Stoel, Jr., Thomas B., "Fluorocarbons: Mobilizing Concern and Action," in David Kay and Harold Jacobson (eds.), *Environmental Protection: The International Dimension* (Totowa, NJ: Allanheld, Osmun & Co., 1983).

Stoel, Jr., Thomas B., Alan S. Miller, Breck Milroy, *Fluorocarbon Regulation* (Lexington, MA: Heath, 1980).

Streek, Wolfgang and Kozo Yamamura (eds.), *Origins of Non-Liberal Capitalism: Germany and Japan in Comparison* (Ithaca: Cornell University Press, 2002).

Sustainable Energy Institute, "The Sustainable Energy Top Ten Awards," Washington, DC: Sustainable Energy Institute, 2002.

Tanabe, Toshiaki, *Chikyū Ondanka to Kankyō Gaikō: Kyōto Kaigi no Kōbō to Sonogo no Tenkai* (Tokyo: DaiNippon Insatsu, 1999).

Tarrow, Sidney, *Power in Movement: Social Movements, Collective Action and Mass Politics in the Modern State* (Cambridge: Cambridge University Press, 1994).

Thelen, Kathleen and Ikuo Kume, 1999, "The Rise of Nonmarket Trading Regimes: Germany and Japan Compared," *Journal of Japanese Studies* 25 (1999), 33–64.

Thelen, Kathleen and Sven Steinmo, "Historical Institutionalism in Comparative Politics," in Sven Steinmo, Kathleen Thelen, and Frank Longstreth (eds.), *Structuring Politics: Historical Institutionalism in Comparative Politics* (New York: Cambridge University Press, 1992), pp. 1–32.

Tomino, Kiichirō, "Wildlife and Environment: Citizens' Movement and the Environment: A Mayor's Experiments and Achievements," transcript of a speech presented at the Japan Society, November 4, 1991.

Tonooka, Yutaka, "A Short History of Global Warming Policy in Japan," unpublished paper.

Töpfer, Klaus, "Statement" at the Ministerial Conference on Atmospheric Pollution and Climate Change, *Noordwijk Conference Report, Vol. 1*, November 6 and 7, 1989.

Tsuru, Shigeto and Helmut Weidner (eds.), *Environmental Policy in Japan* (Berlin: Sigma, 1989).

Tsuushōsangyōshō Kisosangyōkyoku Ozonsō Hogo Taisakushitsu, *Ozonsō Hogo Handobukku* (Tokyo: Kagaku Kōgyō Nippōsha, 1994).

Ui, Jun, *Kōgai Genron*, vols. I–III (Tokyo: Aki Shobo, 1990).

"Die Umwelt in Rucksack," *Der Spiegel* 40 (1998), 70–8.

Umweltbundesamt, *Nachhaltiges Deutschland: Wege zu einer dauerhaft umweltgerechten Entwicklung* (Berlin: Erich Schmidt Verlag, 1997).

Umweltbundesamt, *Internationale Konferenz über Flurochlorkohlenwasserstoffe*, Conference Proceedings, December 6–8, 1978, Munich.

United Nations, United Nations Framework Convention on Climate Change.

United States State Department, Bureau of Oceans and International Environmental and Scientific Affairs, "The Kyoto Protocol on Climate Change," January 15, 1998.

Upham, Frank, *Law and Social Change in Postwar Japan* (Cambridge: Harvard University Press, 1987).

Victor, David, *The Collapse of the Kyoto Protocol* (Princeton: Princeton University Press, 2001).

Vig, Norman, J., "Presidential Leadership and the Environment: From Reagan to Clinton," in Norman J. Vig and Michael E. Kraft (eds.), *Environmental Policies in the 1990s: Reform or Reaction* (Washington, DC: Congressional Quarterly Press, 1997), pp. 95–118.

Vig, Norman J. and Michael E. Kraft (eds.), *Environmental Policies in the 1990s: Reform or Reaction* (Washington, DC: Congressional Quarterly Press, 1997).

Vogel, David, *National Styles of Regulation: Environmental Policy in Great Britain and the United States* (Ithaca, NY: Cornell University Press, 1986).

"Environmental Policy in Japan and West Germany," paper prepared for presentation at the annual meeting of the Western Political Science Association, Newport Beach, CA, March 1990.

"Environmental Policy in the European Community," in Sheldon Kamieniecki (ed.), *Environmental Politics in the International Arena* (Albany: State University of New York Press, 1993), pp. 191–6.

Wagner, Andreas, "Prospects for Wind Energy in Europe: The Challenge of Politics and Administration," *Renewable Energy World* (January 1999), 39–40.

"The Growth of Wind Energy in Europe: An Example of Successful Regulatory and Financial Incentives," German Wind Energy Promotion Association, June 1999.

Walker, Jack L., "Setting the Agenda in the U.S. Senate: A Theory of Problem Selection," *British Journal of Political Science* 7 (1977), 423–45.

"The Diffusion of Innovations among the American States," *American Political Science Review* 63 (1979), 880–99.

Mobilizing Interest Groups in America: Patrons, Professions, and Social Movements (Ann Arbor: University of Michigan Press, 1991).

Wallach, H. G. Peter and Ronald A. Fancisco, *United Germany: The Past, Politics, Prospects* (Westport: Praeger, 1992).

Wapner, Paul, *Environmental Activism and World Civic Politics* (Albany: SUNY Press, 1996).

WCED, *Our Common Future* (Oxford: Oxford University Press, 1987).

Weale, Albert, *The New Politics of Pollution* (Manchester: Manchester University Press, 1992).

"The Politics of Ecological Modernization," in John S. Dryzek and David Schlosberg (eds.), *Debating the Earth: The Environmental Politics Reader* (Oxford: Oxford University Press, 1998), pp. 301–18.

Weale, Albert et al., *Environmental Governance in Europe: An Ever Closer Ecological Union?* (Oxford: Oxford University Press, 2000).

Weaver, R. Kent and Bert A. Rockman (eds.), *Do Institutions Matter? Government Capabilities in the United States and Abroad* (Washington, DC: Brookings Institution, 1993).

Weidner, Helmut, *Air Pollution Control Strategies and Policies in the Federal Republic of Germany: Laws, Regulations, Implementation, and Shortcomings* (Berlin: Edition Sigma Bohn, 1986).

"The Capability of the Capitalist State to 'Solve' Environmental Problems – The Examples of Germany and Japan," paper presented at the XVth World Congress of the International Political Science Association, Buenos Aires, July 21–5, 1991.

"Globale Umweltherausforderungen," in Hanns W. Maull (ed.), *Japan und Europa: Gentrennte Welten?* (Frankfurt: Campus Verlag, 1993), pp. 434–55.

Basiselemente einer erfolgreichen Umweltpolitik: Eine Analyse und Evaluation der Instrumente der japanischen Umweltpolitik (Berlin: Edition Sigma, 1996).

Weidner, Helmut and Martin Jänicke, "Vom Aufstieg und Niedergang eines Vorreiters, Eine umweltpolitische Bilanz der Ära Kohl," in Göttrik Wewer (ed.), *Bilanz der Ära Kohl, Christlich-liberale Politik in Deutschland 1982–1998*, special edition of *Gegenwartskunde* (Opladen: Leske and Budrich, 1998), pp. 201–13.

Welch, Eric, Midori Aoyagi-Usui, and Sukehiro Gotoh, "Greening Activity of Japanese Companies: An Application of Organization Theory," manuscript.

Wetstone, Gregory and Armin Rosencranz, *Acid Rain in Europe and North America: National Responses to an International Problem* (Arlington, VA: Environmental Law Bookcrafter, 1983).

Wey, Klaus-Georg, *Umweltpolitik in Deutschland: Kurze Geschicte des Umweltschutzes in Deutschland seit 1900* (Opladen: Westdeutscher Verlag, 1982).

The White House, "Report of the National Energy Policy Development Group, National Energy Policy," May 2001.

Wilkening, Kenneth, "Culture and Japanese Citizen Influence on the Transboundary Air Pollution Issue in Northeast Asia," *Political Psychology* 20 (1999), 701–23.

Woodall, Brian, *Japan under Construction: Corruption, Politics, and Public Works* (Berkeley: University of California Press, 1996).

Wuppertal Instituts für Klima, Umwelt, Energie, *Zukunftsfähiges Deutschland: Ein Beitrag zu einer global nachhaltigen Entwicklung* (Basel: Birkhäuser Verlag, 5th edition, 1997).

Yamamoto, Giichi, "Taiki Osen to Kikô Hendô," *Taiki Osen Gakkaishi* 10 (1975), 1–3.

Yamamoto, Tadashi (ed.), *Deciding the Public Good: Governance and Civil Society in Japan* (Tokyo: Japan Center for International Exchange, 1999).

Yamamura, Tsunetoshi, *Kankyô NGO* (Tokyo: Shinyama Shuppan, 1998).

Yamanouchi, Kazuo and Kiyoharu Ôtsubo, "Agreements on Pollution Prevention: Overview and One Example," in Shigeto Tsuru and Helmut Weidner (eds.), *Environmental Policy in Japan* (Berlin: Sigma, 1989), pp. 221–45.

Yanagawa, Yoshirô, "The Greening of Corporate Japan," *Journal of Japanese Trade and Industry* 5 (1992), 14–16.

Yoon, Esook and Hong Pyo Lee, "Environmental Cooperation in Northeast Asia: Issues and Prospects," in Miranda A. Schreurs and Dennis Pirages (eds.), *Ecological Security in Northeast Asia* (Seoul: Yonsei University Press, 1998), pp. 67–88.

Zwischenbericht der Enquete-Kommission, Schutz des Menschen und der Umwelt, des 13 Deutschen Bundestages, *Konzept Nachhaltigkeit: Fundamente für die Gesellschaft von morgen* (Bonn: Deutscher Bundestag, 1997).

MEDIA

Agence France Presse
Asahi Shimbun
Ascribe Newswire
Associated Press
Associated Press State and Local Wire
Christian Science Monitor

Daily Telegraph (London)
Daily Yomiuri
Deutsche Presse-Agentur
EFE News Service
Ekonomisuto
Environment Daily
Europe Energy
Financial Times
Financial Times (Deutschland)
Frankfurter Allgemeine Zeitung
International Herald Tribune
Japan Environment Monitor
Japan Times
Los Angeles Times
Mainichi Shimbun
New Scientist
New York Times
Nihon Keizai Shimbun
Reuters News Service
Süddeutsche Zeitung
Tagesspiegel
Time
United Press International
USA Today
Volkskrant
Washington Post
Washington Times
Yomiuri Shimbun

Index

acid rain
  and Canada, 104
  and China, 13, 107–9
  comparing national positions and
    policies, 13–14, 30, 92, 112–15,
    247
  emergence as an international issue,
    92–5
  Europe, 93, 95, 100–1
  Germany, 92–101, 112–14, 248
  Japan, 107–12, 114, 253
  and Korea, 109
  long-range transport, 92–5, 107–9
  North America, 95
  science of, 92–3
  US, 102–7, 114–15, 254–5
  see also influence
actors, 16, 18–19, 23, 24, 27, 256–7
Adams, John H., 236
Adenauer, Konrad, chancellor, Germany,
    37
administrative guidance of industry (*gyôsei
    shidô*), 11, 24, 72, 76, 114, 122
Agenda 21, 224
Aichi, Kazuo, 169, 170, 196, 221
air pollution, 30
  comparing national positions and
    policies, 16, 58–9
  Germany, 13, 48–53, 58–9, 80–2, 94,
    97–100, 112–14, 132
  Japan, 39–42, 44, 47, 73–5, 110, 114,
    252
  US, 33–5, 103–7, 114–15
  see also acid rain, Clean Air Act (USA),
    cooperation, Federal Emissions
    Control Act (Germany), global
    climate change, ozone depletion,
    Yokkaichi asthma
Asia, 3, 36, 221, 253

Basic Environment Law, 1993 (Japan),
    170–2

Basic Law (Germany), 56–7
Basic Law for Environmental Pollution
    Control, 1967 (Japan), 43–4, 170
  revision of, 45, 170–2
Baum, Gerhard, 97
Baumgartner, Frank, 28, 88, 259
Benedick, Richard, 137, 142
Berlin Mandate, 179–80
Bluewater Network, 237–8
Boehmer-Christiansen, Sonya, 95
Brandt, Willy, chancellor, Germany, 51,
    53–4
Bund für Naturschutz Deutschland
    (BUND), 6, 213, 227–9
Bundestag, 100
  Home Affairs Committee, 123
Bundesverband Bürgerinitiativen Umwelt
    (BBU), 6, 83
Burford, Anne Gorsuch, 103, 127–8
Burns, Robert, 82
Bush, George W., administration, 9, 10,
    13, 196–208, 242
Bush, George H. W., administration, 105,
    115, 141, 150, 152, 153, 163, 254
  and advisors, 152
Byrd, Robert, 184–6

Carson, Rachel, 32
Central Council for Environmental
    Pollution Control, 46
Cheney, Richard, vice president (US), and
    energy policy, 12, 199–200
Chernobyl, 131, 156, 232, 248–9
chlorofluorocarbons (CFCs), 116, 117–22
  partially halogenated
    chlorofluorocarbons (HCFCs), 116
  proposals to ban, 128–9, 132–4,
    139–42
  world production and/or consumption,
    126–7
Christian Democratic Union (CDU), 6,
    36–7, 67–8, 96–8, 156, 257–8

283